I0897040

Technology Optimization and Change Management for Successful Digital Supply Chains

Ehap Sabri
KPMG LLP, USA & University of Texas at Dallas, USA

A volume in the Advances in Logistics, Operations, and Management Science (ALOMS) Book Series

IGI Global
DISSEMINATOR OF KNOWLEDGE

Published in the United States of America by
IGI Global
Business Science Reference (an imprint of IGI Global)
701 E. Chocolate Avenue
Hershey PA, USA 17033
Tel: 717-533-8845
Fax: 717-533-8661
E-mail: cust@igi-global.com
Web site: http://www.igi-global.com

Copyright © 2019 by IGI Global. All rights reserved. No part of this publication may be reproduced, stored or distributed in any form or by any means, electronic or mechanical, including photocopying, without written permission from the publisher. Product or company names used in this set are for identification purposes only. Inclusion of the names of the products or companies does not indicate a claim of ownership by IGI Global of the trademark or registered trademark.

Library of Congress Cataloging-in-Publication Data

Names: Sabri, Ehap H., 1967- editor.
Title: Technology optimization and change management for successful digital supply chains / Ehap Sabri, editor.
Description: Hershey, PA : Business Science Reference, [2019]
Identifiers: LCCN 2018036426| ISBN 9781522577003 (hardcover) | ISBN 9781522577010 (ebook)
Subjects: LCSH: Business logistics--Technological innovations. | Production control--Technological innovations.
Classification: LCC HD38.5 .T435 2019 | DDC 658.7--dc23 LC record available at https://lccn.loc.gov/2018036426

This book is published in the IGI Global book series Advances in Logistics, Operations, and Management Science (ALOMS) (ISSN: 2327-350X; eISSN: 2327-3518)

British Cataloguing in Publication Data
A Cataloguing in Publication record for this book is available from the British Library.

All work contributed to this book is new, previously-unpublished material. The views expressed in this book are those of the authors, but not necessarily of the publisher.

For electronic access to this publication, please contact: eresources@igi-global.com.

Advances in Logistics, Operations, and Management Science (ALOMS) Book Series

John Wang
Montclair State University, USA

ISSN:2327-350X
EISSN:2327-3518

Mission

Operations research and management science continue to influence business processes, administration, and management information systems, particularly in covering the application methods for decision-making processes. New case studies and applications on management science, operations management, social sciences, and other behavioral sciences have been incorporated into business and organizations real-world objectives.

The **Advances in Logistics, Operations, and Management Science** (ALOMS) Book Series provides a collection of reference publications on the current trends, applications, theories, and practices in the management science field. Providing relevant and current research, this series and its individual publications would be useful for academics, researchers, scholars, and practitioners interested in improving decision making models and business functions.

Coverage

- Decision analysis and decision support
- Marketing engineering
- Finance
- Networks
- Operations Management
- Production management
- Risk Management
- Organizational Behavior
- Information Management
- Computing and information technologies

IGI Global is currently accepting manuscripts for publication within this series. To submit a proposal for a volume in this series, please contact our Acquisition Editors at Acquisitions@igi-global.com or visit: http://www.igi-global.com/publish/.

The Advances in Logistics, Operations, and Management Science (ALOMS) Book Series (ISSN 2327-350X) is published by IGI Global, 701 E. Chocolate Avenue, Hershey, PA 17033-1240, USA, www.igi-global.com. This series is composed of titles available for purchase individually; each title is edited to be contextually exclusive from any other title within the series. For pricing and ordering information please visit http://www.igi-global.com/book-series/advances-logistics-operations-management-science/37170. Postmaster: Send all address changes to above address. Copyright © 2019 IGI Global. All rights, including translation in other languages reserved by the publisher. No part of this series may be reproduced or used in any form or by any means – graphics, electronic, or mechanical, including photocopying, recording, taping, or information and retrieval systems – without written permission from the publisher, except for non commercial, educational use, including classroom teaching purposes. The views expressed in this series are those of the authors, but not necessarily of IGI Global.

Titles in this Series

For a list of additional titles in this series, please visit: www.igi-global.com/book-series

Advanced Macroergonomics and Sociotechnical Approaches for Optimal Organizational Performance
Arturo Realyvásquez (Instituto Tecnológico de Tijuana, Mexico) Aide Aracely Maldonado-Macías (Autonomous University of Ciudad Juarez, Mexico) and Karina Cecilia Arredondo (Universidad Autónoma de Baja California, Mexico)
Business Science Reference • copyright 2019 • 328pp • H/C (ISBN: 9781522571926) • US $225.00 (our price)

Handbook of Research on Contemporary Approaches in Management and Organizational Strategy
Çağlar Doğru (Ufuk University, Turkey)
Business Science Reference • copyright 2019 • 645pp • H/C (ISBN: 9781522563013) • US $295.00 (our price)

Organizational Transformation and Managing Innovation in the Fourth Industrial Revolution
Alicia Guerra Guerra (University of Extremadura, Spain)
Business Science Reference • copyright 2019 • 374pp • H/C (ISBN: 9781522570745) • US $215.00 (our price)

Global Supply Chains in the Pharmaceutical Industry
Hamed Nozari (Islamic Azad University, Iran) and Agnieszka Szmelter (University of Gdańsk, Poland)
Business Science Reference • copyright 2019 • 373pp • H/C (ISBN: 9781522559214) • US $215.00 (our price)

Contemporary Multicultural Orientations and Practices for Global Leadership
Sulaiman Olusegun Atiku (University of KwaZulu-Natal, South Africa)
Business Science Reference • copyright 2019 • 323pp • H/C (ISBN: 9781522562863) • US $210.00 (our price)

Servant Leadership Styles and Strategic Decision Making
Yasir Hayat Mughal (Qurtuba University, Pakistan) and Shahid Kamal (Gomal University, Pakistan)
Business Science Reference • copyright 2019 • 305pp • H/C (ISBN: 9781522549963) • US $195.00 (our price)

Diverse Applications and Transferability of Maturity Models
Shadrack Katuu (University of South Africa, South Africa)
Business Science Reference • copyright 2019 • 390pp • H/C (ISBN: 9781522570806) • US $215.00 (our price)

Personal Values as Drivers of Managerial Innovation Emerging Research and Opportunities
Zlatko Nedelko (University of Maribor, Slovenia) and Vojko Potocan (University of Maribor, Slovenia)
Business Science Reference • copyright 2019 • 314pp • H/C (ISBN: 9781522532507) • US $185.00 (our price)

IGI Global
DISSEMINATOR OF KNOWLEDGE

701 East Chocolate Avenue, Hershey, PA 17033, USA
Tel: 717-533-8845 x100 • Fax: 717-533-8661
E-Mail: cust@igi-global.com • www.igi-global.com

Editorial Advisory Board

Rachel Gibbons, *KPMG LLP, USA*
Amit Gupta, *KPMG LLP, USA*
Varun Gupta, *Pennsylvania State University – Erie, USA*
Matthias Lederer, *ISM International School of Management, Germany*
Mark Levy, *KPMG LLP, USA*
Arif Mohammed, *JDA Software, USA*
Anna Quitt, *ISM International School of Management, Germany*
Salim Shaikh, *JDA Software, USA*
Michael Sony, *Namibia University of Science and Technology, Namibia*
Likhit Verma, *Ericsson, USA*
Andreas Werner, *KPMG LLP, USA*
Chad Wiseman, *KPMG LLP, USA*

Table of Contents

Detailed Table of Contents

This chapter covers the importance of the program management office (PMO) in a digital supply chain transformation. The objective of this chapter is to discuss the key issues in digital supply chain transformations in terms of managing the PMO, followed by a discussion of the solutions and best practices for mitigating these issues and ensuring the PMO is a value-added function and key enabler of a digital supply chain transformation. The reader should have a good understanding of the activities that the PMO should perform, the skills required for PMO resources, and the process of building the business case and using it to track the benefits to prove the transformation was effective.

The authors describe how organizations can leverage the maturity model approach in conjunction with foundational concepts of perspective-based performance evaluation models like the balanced scorecard (BSC) to define a comprehensive performance measurement framework. A maturity model by design provides a road-map to the next level of performance. In this chapter, the authors propose using maturity models as a structured way of identifying current capability or maturity level of any supply chain. The authors provide guidance on selecting the right "causal linkages" between supply chain objectives and performance measures. They then define a mechanism for specifying even more granular definitions of measures linked to strategic objectives, as the level of maturity progresses. In this chapter, the authors survey widely used supply chain/business process maturity models and current practices related to measuring operational metric. And then present a tiered framework for operational metric alignment and KPI governance based on perspective-based modeling design principles.

Supply chains of the 21st century are becoming exponentially more complex due to increased mergers and acquisitions, the omni-channel conflict, direct-to-consumer, rapid proliferation of product configurations, same-day delivery, the recall management problem, shrinking product lifecycles, and market volatility. Moreover, today's consumers are increasingly demanding a personalized, consistent, and seamless experience across retail, online, and mobile. To be able to serve this diverse spectrum of customers, products, markets, and channels and at the same time do so in a win-win profitable manner, organizations need a cognitive integrated business planning process, which has the ability to act with speed, agility, responsiveness, and flexibility, leveraging machine learning and artificial intelligence for predictive and prescriptive analytics, thereby enabling organizations to realign their plans quickly through an always-on, self-learning, and autonomous integrated business planning process.

The discipline of category management has always played an important role within retailers as well as their CPG manufacturer suppliers. While the eight steps within the category management process (category definition, category role, category assessment, category scorecard, category strategies, category tactics, category implementation, and category review) have remained the same, with digitalization the discipline is undergoing a massive transformation, and the approach to the process is getting disrupted through the availability of huge volumes of transactional data, customer loyalty data; advancement in hardware technology through better scanners, image recognition devices, sensors and IoT devices and machine learning, and artificial intelligence. In this chapter, the authors take a closer look at the eight-step category management process, the traditional approach, the enabler for disruption, the new approach, and its benefits and what the future may hold.

This chapter provides an overview of select inventory optimization (IO) techniques for single and multi-echelon optimization. The main goal is to familiarize the reader with various IO models by providing a clearly structured approach, improving the reader's understanding of the mathematical concepts, and by providing an ample number of examples. Furthermore, the guaranteed service model for a three stage serial supply chain is introduced to show the effects of keeping inventory at different echelons in the supply chain in regards to total cost. Lastly an inventory planning maturity model is presented to show actionable next steps to the practitioner.

This chapter answers the following questions: 1) What is the capacity planning process? 2) Why do companies need to perform capacity planning? 3) What are current challenges in the capacity planning process? 4) What are different levels in the capacity planning? 5) What are planning zones? 6) How does capacity planning implementation journey look like? In the chapter, the author touches some of the basics of the capacity planning and then goes into advance level in the capacity planning. The chapter expects readers to have a basic knowledge of the capacity planning.

Modern day organizations have begun to implement the green supply chain management (GSCM) practices in response to demand from various stakeholders which includes customers to create products

Preface

Supply chain management today is a series of largely discrete, siloed steps taken through marketing, product development, production, distribution, and finally fulfilling customers' needs. Digitization removes barriers across siloed processes, and enables the supply chain to become a completely integrated ecosystem that is fully transparent to all stakeholders from the suppliers of raw materials to the manufacturers of finished goods, to the customers.

The digital supply chain includes integrated planning, intelligent logistics visibility, smart warehousing, digital procurement, and prescriptive advanced analytics. The result enables companies to anticipate and proactively address disruptions in the supply chain by fully modeling the end-to-end supply chain, creating 'what-if' scenarios, and adjusting the supply chain in real time as conditions change. This offers a high degree of lean and agility allowing companies to achieve a competitive advantage by providing customers with the most efficient and transparent service delivery. In a nutshell, digital supply chain can advance a business's performance by removing friction in processes and improving decision making.

In a recent KPMG survey and report, Retailers and Manufacturers were asked to identify their main reasons for investing in digital supply chain. Over half of the respondents identified the need for real-time product visibility as a leading driver. Retailers expressed the need for end-to-end visibility (53%) and the ability to manage new fulfilment nodes (50%), whilst Manufacturers were driven by the need to innovate faster (40%) with lower cost-to-serve (33%) through improved planning (KPMG, 2018a).

Also, 58% of all companies have stated they are rethinking their current business model as a result of or to take advantage of the changing digital landscape. Furthermore, 68% of high-growth companies have stated that industry disruption gives them a competitive edge and 70% of them have mentioned that accelerated digital transformation is a strategic focus (KPMG, 2018b).

Digital supply chain will be based on full implementation of several digital technologies: the cloud, big data, the Internet of Things (IoT), Machine Learning (ML), social networks, "what-if" scenario planning, "trace-and-track," and others. Together, they are enabling new business models and strategies, the digitization of products and services, and the digitization and integration of every link in a company's supply chain.

But if companies are to implement the digital supply chain ecosystem, they can't just gather technologies and build technical capabilities (i.e. technology is not the silver bullet). They must have the right digital strategy, proven implementation methodology, an effective performance measurement system, people with the right skills, and the management needed to shift to a culture that is willing to carry out the change. In other words, they must transform their entire business.

The digital strategy should include key characteristics to improve the execution: 1) Flexible strategy as changes occur in the global marketplace in addition to being prioritized and actionable, 2) A three-to-five year roadmap that guides the transformation of supply-and-demand capabilities and takes planning processes to the next level, 3) Clear linkage to one or more corporate goals such as growth or customer service levels, 4) Both large opportunities for improvement that deliver significant ROI over time and "quick win" operations improvements with a fast payback, and 5) Elimination to outdated roles and responsibilities, unnecessary activities, and performance metrics that no longer reflect current realities.

Once the digital strategy is determined, companies must drive changes and develop new capabilities in several areas including the following:

1. **Processes:** Establish the new end-to-end supply chain processes connecting suppliers and customers that digitization makes possible and eliminate non-values activities at the touch points of functions and processes
2. **Technology:** Create a deployment road map for the technologies that will support the digital supply chain, including the information integration layer, database and analytics capabilities, security, and the cloud.
3. **Governance:** Establish a new governance for the new processes which enables the new business models. The new governance should include the following:
   a. **Organization Structure and Culture:** Generate an end-to-end understanding of the mechanics of the supply chain followed by an organizational realignment. This means switching from a firefighter mentality (solving each problem as it pops up) to becoming proactive and acting as a supply chain "orchestrator" (sensing, predicting, and taking prescriptive decisions). It also requires a shift to an open, fast-learning digital culture that promotes communication across different media and stakeholders.
   b. **Talent and Skills:** Develop the talent and acquire new expertise and skills needed to enable the new technology and carry out the new business models. It is rare to find a company with the required in-house digital capability from the beginning. Building strong expertise into an organization relies on the cultivation of long-term partnerships and ecosystems that can provide access to the required capabilities.
   c. **Performance Management:** Develop a set of key performance indicators (KPIs) to maintain the momentum and involvement of people and be able to measure progress. These KPIs should be comprehensive and drive the right behavior.
   d. **Partnering Policies:** Establish new polices to partner closely with other companies. The fully integrated end-to-end supply chain cannot be built without collaborating with a wide variety of suppliers, distributors, and technology providers.

Supply chains are extremely complex networks, and no company has succeeded yet in building one that is truly digital. While it is true that several successful digital use cases have been witnessed, the industry is still waiting for successful digital end-to-end supply chain transformation program. Also, many of the digital applications required are not yet widely used. But this will change radically over the next five years, with different industries implementing digital supply chain at varying speeds.

To add to the above challenge, 70% of all technology-driven transformation initiatives fail. They fail firstly because of lack of preparation and knowledge of the supply chain transformation life cycle, secondly because of a lack of a well-defined supply chain optimization strategy, and thirdly because of poor addressing or altogether neglecting the "people-related" aspects in transformation (Maurer, 2010; Sabri, 2015). Therefore, improvement initiatives have been short lived or incomplete and expected business benefits are not achieved or materialized. It's important to note that these statistics are based on technology that is 5 to 10 years old and not the digital technology that is less mature.

In addition, although there is a lot of hype surrounding digital supply chain and multiple opportunities to apply it across an organization. Often (especially when ROI is unproven) the task of creating and implementing an effective digital strategy can seem overwhelming. 60% of digital laggards mentioned that digital transformations was held back by ROI uncertainty (KPMG, 2018b). One thing is certain, if businesses look to the fanciest new tech to save the day but ignore their overall performance goal, then their strategies are already set to fail.

Therefore, many companies are trying to understand the best practices and master the recipe for success of transformation programs. They are connecting with universities, research centers, and consulting companies. Therefore, the editor decided to write this book to help industry professionals improve their success rate in digital supply chain use cases and their transformation programs.

To address the above challenges in areas such as supply chain optimization, leveraging digital technologies, business transformation, performance measurement, and change management, there is a need for an edited collection of chapters. These chapters would help analyze situation in better way and provide important lesson learned and best practices.

This comprehensive and timely publication aims to be an essential reference source, synergizing with available literature in the field of digital supply chain and business transformation, and providing proven tactics from the industry.

The target audience of this book includes professionals and researchers working in the field of supply chain optimization and business transformation. This book provides:

- Insight and support to executives concerned with achieving value as an output of digital supply chain transformation programs
- Supply chain and IT managers with suggested process, technology, and governance best practices
- Academicians, researchers, and advanced-level students with an excellent reference on digital supply chain and transformations, business challenges, change management, performance measurement, digital supply chain strategy development, case studies, and opportunities to extend the research in this field.

The chapters stand alone in covering their individual topics, but also form a cohesive overview of library-related professional development as it stands now along with future trends in the field. The chapters in this book can be categorized in four broad sections of digital supply chain business transformation: digital supply chain strategy (Chapters 1-3), success factors for digital transformation (Chapters 4-7), recipe for success for optimizing certain supply chain processes in digital world (Chapters 8-12), and key supply chain enablers for digital supply chain transformation (Chapters 13-15).

The first chapter explains how a strategic approach to supply chain management needs to consider wider corporate strategic objectives and initiatives and contribute to the achievement of these goals. It also differentiates between strategic supply chain management (when the supply chain function provides unique competitive advantage) and supply chain strategy (when the supply chain function takes on a supporting role to corporate strategy). Finally, chapter 1 develops a case for strategic supply chain management based on edge computing applications through IoT sensors such as GPS or RFID. This illustrates that supply chain practitioners need to fundamentally rethink the way current supply chain systems process data and information and that the approach to collaboration between supply chain partners needs to change drastically.

Chapter 2 offers best practice strategies for procurement in the context of digital supply chains. It also provides a framework for executing these digital procurement strategies. In addition, the chapter consists of case studies from different industries such as manufacturing (Apple, Beta products, IBM), fast food (Chipotle), and logistics/pharmaceutical (DHL).

Chapter 3, which is final chapter in this section, provides a proposition for digital transformation of a global group into an efficient enterprise. At the heart of the proposition is a transformational practice aimed at creating a customer-focused strategy and data-driven global culture. It argues that the digital age has added a level of complexity to the way we acquire and serve customers. Performing well in the traditional channels is not enough anymore. Online is increasingly becoming the channel of choice with two main customer-interaction paradigms: sell and service. Building a great customer experience is probably the most essential factor of success for both functions.

The next three chapters focus on digital supply chain transformation and related success factors. Specifically, Chapter 4 provides a literature review on supply chain segmentation as a key success factor for digital supply chain transformation, and offers a practical supply chain segmentation framework for companies who are about to take the segmentation transformation journey. A case study from Dell is also presented to illustrate the framework.

Chapter 5 highlights the fact that several organizations are still facing numerous challenges to transform and perform. Perhaps the most common misunderstanding is that digital transformation is all about the implementation and use of cutting-edge technologies. This chapter dives deep to understand the major challenges to digital supply chain transformations, identify the key drivers and enablers of digital opportunity and provide change management framework for digital supply chain transformation. It builds the case that mastering change management is the most important success factor for transformation and offers several best practices and a roadmap for a smooth journey.

Chapter 6 explains the importance of the Program Management Office (PMO) in a digital supply chain transformation. It discusses the key issues in digital supply chain transformations in terms of managing the PMO, followed by a discussion of the solutions and best practices for mitigating these issues and ensuring the PMO is a value-added function and key enabler of a digital supply chain transformation.

Chapter 7 explains the final success factors for transformation: effective supply chain performance measurement and organizational alignment. This chapter describes how organizations can leverage the maturity model approach in conjunction with the foundational concepts of perspective-based performance evaluation models to define a comprehensive performance measurement framework. It also provides guidance on selecting the right 'causal linkages' between supply chain objectives and performance measures.

Next, the book drills down on the optimization of certain supply chain processes. Chapter 8 provides insights for companies that are seeking to enhance their Sales and Operations Planning (S&OP) process to the highest level of maturity which is Cognitive Integrated Business Planning. It addresses the questions amongst supply chain executives from "why do we need to improve at this time?" to "how do we do it?"

This chapter argues that to serve this diverse spectrum of customers, products, markets, and channels, and do so in a win-win profitable manner, organizations need a Cognitive Integrated Business Planning process. This process must have the ability to act with speed, agility, responsiveness, and flexibility. It must also leverage machine learning and artificial intelligence for predictive and prescriptive analytics, enabling organizations to realign their plans quickly through an always-on, self-learning, and autonomous process.

Chapter 9 addresses the discipline of Category Management which has always played an important role within retailers as well as their CPG manufacturer suppliers. It argues that digitalization is undergoing a massive transformation and the approach to the process is getting disrupted through the availability of huge volumes of transactional data, customer loyalty data, and advancement in hardware technology through better scanners, image recognition devices, sensors, IoT devices, and machine learning and artificial intelligence. This chapter takes a closer look at the eight step Category Management process (the traditional approach) and the digital enabler (the new approach) along with its benefits and what the future may hold.

The main value proposition of Chapter 10 is providing the reader an overview of the Inventory Optimization (IO) basics including the multi-echelon optimization concept which enables them to understand important details for a digital transformation journey. It also provides an inventory planning maturity model.

Chapter 11 answers the following questions: 1) What is the capacity planning process? 2) Why do companies need to perform capacity planning? 3) What are the challenges in the capacity planning process? 4) What are the different levels in the capacity planning? 5) What are planning zones? 6) What does a capacity planning implementation journey look like in a digital world?

Chapter 12 explains how contemporary organizations have begun to implement the green supply chain management (GSCM) practices in response to demand from various stakeholders to create products and services which are environmentally sustainable. The digital technology has been a boon in erstwhile supply chain management practices. However, the impact of digital technology on various dimensions of GSCM practices has not been studied yet. This chapter explores the impact of digital technology on Green Supply Chain Management practices. A qualitative study is conducted on managers working in organizations using GSCM. The impact of digital technology is analyzed on the five dimensions of GSCM practices and future research opportunities are identified.

The final three chapters concluding the book cover specific enablers for digital supply chain transformation. In Chapter 13 readers learn how 5G technology is an enabler for digital technologies (namely Artificial Intelligence, Machine Learning, Augmented reality, Internet of Things, Virtual reality, Big Data) where extensive data sharing and analysis is required. This will only be possible if there is a robust telecom network. 5G with its features of low latency, high bandwidth, higher speeds, and low power requirements is expected to unleash the full potential of digital technologies and expedite the digital supply chain transformation.

Chapter 14 provides a scientific classification and practical model to digitalize supply chain processes. One of the essential prerequisites for digitization of supply chains is the ability to model underlying processes. This means that events, work steps, control flows, and resources are described roughly or even specified in full detail. This is especially true for supply chain workflows because modeling (understood as specifying activities, data, resources and control flows) is usually the first step in selecting and implementing digital approaches such as smart factories. It discusses the benefits of specific notations for classical as well as modern challenges of SCM to help in the selection of notations. The resulting specifications serve as basis for the holistic digitization of supply chains.

Lastly, Chapter 15 explores the role of supply chain analytics in managing digital supply chain, as well as the practical implementation approaches of supply chain analytics. The chapter first discusses a typical day in the life of supply chain analysts. It then discusses the categorization of supply chain analytics and some practical recommendations for the implementation. Finally, the chapter provides a case study illustrating some important considerations in supply chain design.

The authors of each chapter followed the adage of "write what you know," having been personally involved in every topic they covered. After writing what they knew, they went beyond their experience to focus on future trends, assessment, and applicability to digital supply chain optimization and transformation. The result is a book that provides useful guidance to supply chain practitioners and researchers in a digital business world.

Thanks are given to the authors of these book chapters. Professionals from the industry and academia contributed excellent write-ups of their work in a timely and professional manner. In addition, many thanks are owed to the Editorial Advisory Board of this book. These experts reviewed proposals, and peer-reviewed the finished chapters quickly and thoroughly. This book would not have been possible without the Board's assistance.

This book illustrates to the reader the best practices in optimizing and transforming supply chain management in contemporary organizations, and presents several ideas for change that provide a roadmap for a smooth transformation journey. Let this book help you deal with the changes and keep current with the profession.

REFERENCES

KPMG. (2018a, May). *JDA, KPMG Supply Chain Survey Reveals Contrasting Digital Transformation Strategies for Retailers and Manufacturers*. Retrieved from https://home.kpmg.com/us/en/home/media/press-releases/2018/05/jda-kpmg-supply-chain-survey-reveals-contrasting-digital-transformation-strategies-for-retailers-and-manufacturers.html

KPMG. (2018b, June). *No normal is the new normal*. Retrieved from https://assets.kpmg.com/content/dam/kpmg/xx/pdf/2018/06/no-normal-is-the-new-normal.pdf

Maurer, R. (2010). *Why 70% of changes fail*. Retrieved from http://www.reply-mc.com/2010/09/19/why-70-of-changes-fail-by-rick-maurer/

Sabri, E. (2015). *Optimization of Supply Chain Management in Contemporary Organizations: Mastering Change Management for Successful Supply Chain Transformation*. Hershey, PA: IGI Global.

Acknowledgment

The editor would like to acknowledge the help of all the people involved in this project and, more specifically, to the authors and reviewers that took part in the review process. Without their support, this book would not have become a reality.

First, the editor would like to thank each one of the authors for their contributions. Our sincere gratitude goes to the chapter's authors who contributed their time and expertise to this book.

Second, the editor wishes to acknowledge the valuable contributions of the reviewers regarding the improvement of quality, coherence, and content presentation of chapters. Several authors also served as referees; we highly appreciate their double task.

Ehap Sabri
KPMG LLP, USA & University of Texas at Dallas, USA

Section 1
Digital Supply Chain Strategy

Chapter 1
Strategic Perspectives of the Digital Supply Chain

Hanns-Christian L. Hanebeck
University of North Texas, USA

ABSTRACT

Supply chain management is one of the oldest aspects of human commerce. It has been around for as long as we can look back in history, and yet, we still have a very limited understanding of what strategic supply chain management entails or constitutes. A strategic approach to supply chain management necessarily needs to consider wider corporate strategic objectives and initiatives, while it has to contribute to the achievement of these goals as all other managerial functions do. We further differentiate between strategic supply chain management, when the supply chain function provides unique competitive advantage and supply chain strategy, when it takes on a supporting role to corporate strategy. The authors develop a case for strategic supply chain management based on edge computing applications through IoT sensors such as GPS or RFID to illustrate that supply chain practitioners need to fundamentally rethink the way current supply chain systems process data and information and also that the approach to collaboration between supply chain partners changes drastically.

INTRODUCTION

Supply chains are as old as commerce itself, they have been enablers for geopolitical shifts and have played a major role in the outcome of virtually every military conflict throughout history. The earliest known supply chains date as far back as human writing itself and we understand today that some of the earliest human records were inventories and trade documents. Yet, supply chain management itself is a fairly new academic field and one that is still evolving rapidly in places. In its simplest form, supply chain management is the movement of material from one point to another and all that it entails. Obviously, this is a very simplistic view in light of our reality today. Large global corporations are moving billions of dollars in material value at any given point in time. These "material chains" are immensely complex, they can be subject to the laws and regulations in more than 200 countries and territories while they are heavily influenced by many different factors ranging from freight consolidation to timing of

DOI: 10.4018/978-1-5225-7700-3.ch001

Copyright © 2019, IGI Global. Copying or distributing in print or electronic forms without written permission of IGI Global is prohibited.

hundreds of concurrent shipments along with their delivery requirements and third-party transportation schedules to name just a few.

For our purpose, we broadly refer to supply chain management as the *business processes related to the planning and fulfillment of market demand*. Implicitly included in this definition is the procurement of materials, transport and storage of spare parts and movement of materials into manufacturing to create products and services. These include a range of core activities such as demand planning, procurement, warehouse and inventory management as well as transportation and distribution. Supply chain strategy is a central element of these core activities as we will show later in this chapter. Adjacent to supply chain management, manufacturing, design, packaging and marketing all have strong influences on the execution supply chain processes. Obviously, so do supporting activities such as business process, performance management and technology capabilities. Figure 1 below illustrates this set of adjacent, core and supporting activities.

The inclusion of supply chain strategy above is not yet common in literature or practice. In fact, it was virtually unheard of just a decade ago and one would have been hard pressed to find a dedicated textbook on the subject at the time. Yet, every managerial activity requires strategic planning and supply chain executives across all industries are hardly an exception to this rule. Before we define supply chain strategy, it is necessary to discuss the concept of strategic management and its foundations in detail.

CORPORATE STRATEGY

The concept of strategic management or corporate strategy has fallen out of favor in recent years. Many executives today claim that the world and certainly their industries are changing too fast for long-term

Figure 1. Core supply chain activities

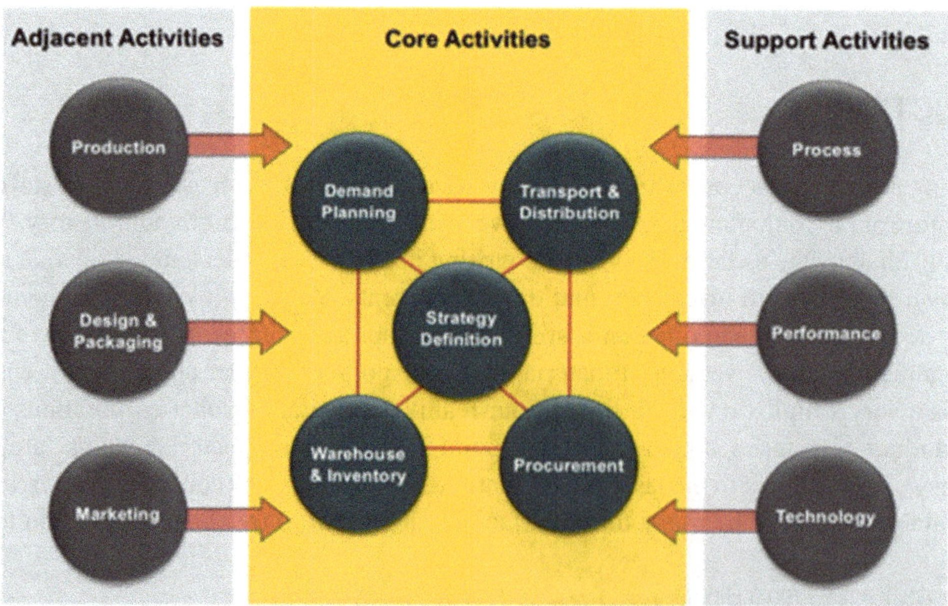

planning. Most notably, Meg Whitman, then CEO of eBay, once proclaimed to a journalist that "my Monday morning meeting is my strategy." Ironically, Whitman previously served as VP of Strategy at Disney where it was her job to do much more than hold a weekly meeting. Yet, we have to ask ourselves whether there is merit in the assertion that strategy is obsolete. Oftentimes managers confuse the fast pace of technological innovation and changes in operational capabilities with the long-term competitive positioning of the organization. As we will see a little further down in this chapter, changes in efficiency are not sufficient to establish a unique and defensible position in an industry. This misunderstanding can be a costly mistake as many high-flying companies found out during the dot-com bubble.

Broadly speaking, strategy refers to the competitive positioning of a company or product in a given market by either adopting to existing industry structures (read: rules) or by changing them in one's favor. Many traditional firms such as General Motors or PepsiCo are examples of the former approach since they have vast resources at their disposal and can thus afford to simply play the same game better than many competitors do. Yet, we are increasingly witnessing the emergence of initially small players who come to dominate an industry through genuine innovation, thus changing the rules of the game. These latter enterprises are often driven by new technologies such as Amazon, which has very successfully and lastingly changed the nature of retail or Uber, which is rethinking the way personal transportation works. In its most basic form, strategy is simply concerned with how to best win the game.

Along these same lines and according to the foremost thinker on the topic, Michael E. Porter[1], the essence of strategy lies in the activities a company performs. Successful organizations either choose to perform the same activities differently from competitors or choose to perform different activities than their rivals altogether. Activities in this context are the business processes of a company. This insight makes intuitive sense because, if there were only one way to serve a given market, there would be no need for strategy. The execution of processes thus either leads a company to be successful or to fail. Successful companies will eventually occupy a position that is unique and defensible because of how they deliver a service or design, manufacture or distribute a product or service. Once the organization gets to the point of being somewhat unique, it can begin to outperform its competitors.

A good example is Southwest Airlines, which entered the industry as a very small player and had to find ways in which to compete against a set of much bigger, financially successful and established industry players. The executives at Southwest managed to build one of the best airlines in the business by deliberately choosing not to perform a number of activities or processes that other competitors were staunchly accustomed to. For example, the company only chose one type of aircraft to minimize maintenance cost, lower the need for parts inventory and to eliminate the need for mechanics as well as flight crews trained on different planes. They also decided to limit the service that passengers receive such as not assigning seats in order to speed up gate departures. Their gate crews are better trained and more efficient than competitors which enables the company to turn planes faster, which provides the ability to better utilize gates to reduce fixed cost. All of these decisions point to the same end result: to keep ticket prices low for consumers. Southwest's performance has clearly shown that it has worked so far.

One important consideration is that successful strategy and operational efficiency are not one and the same. While strategy means that a company chooses a specific set of business processes, efficiency alone does not allow the company to gain an advantage. In fact, quite the opposite is true in that when a more efficient process such as a new technology becomes available to all competitors in an industry, eventually every player will use it and nobody has gained a sustainable advantage. We call this phenomenon the *Table Stakes Effect* because as one competitor raises the stakes in an industry, all others have to follow suit in order to retain their seat at the table.

The degree to which a competitive position is defensible depends on what Porter calls trade-offs: the choice to perform a specific activity often prevents other activities from being available as well as the example of Southwest illustrates e.g. the airline cannot offer individualized service to travelers while keeping the cost of tickets low at the same time. In addition, there are synergies that can tie the activities of a company to one another to create a network for value creation, which is harder to imitate than single activities would be. In this sense, it is the synergy between activities that ultimately ensures success. This view of strategy closely ties into the approach of strategic capabilities[2], often referred to as core competencies, and also into the more recent approach of the resource-based view[3].

In addition to these considerations, strategy and strategic management are always deeply embedded in the culture of an organization. Our fundamental beliefs, values and behavioral norms shape our thoughts and guide our behavior. For example, the way executives conduct themselves will be mirrored on all lower levels of an organization. Culture thus has far reaching consequences to how we view other industry players, how well we perceive threats and opportunities in a given situation or how much integrity we display when we compete.

Equally important, a core strategy requires both a vision and mission to be effective. The vision of an organization describes how it views the world at a point in the future. Famous examples include Microsoft's early vision: "a PC on every desk and in every home" or Googles "to provide access to the world's information in one click." Vision statements usually address objectives that are larger than the organization itself and thus provide a guiding light for all employees. More actionable, the mission of an organization explicitly defines its purpose to create a sense of ownership and provide a shared understanding of what it is the organization actually does. The American National Weather Service, for example, includes "… for the protection of life and property and the enhancement of the National economy …" in its mission statement.

Lastly, every core strategy necessarily has to rely on a thorough assessment of the organization itself, its capabilities and weaknesses, as well as of its competitive environment including opportunities and threats. Often termed SWOT analysis (strength, weakness, opportunity and threat), it is a well-established

Figure 2. Elements of the Core Strategy

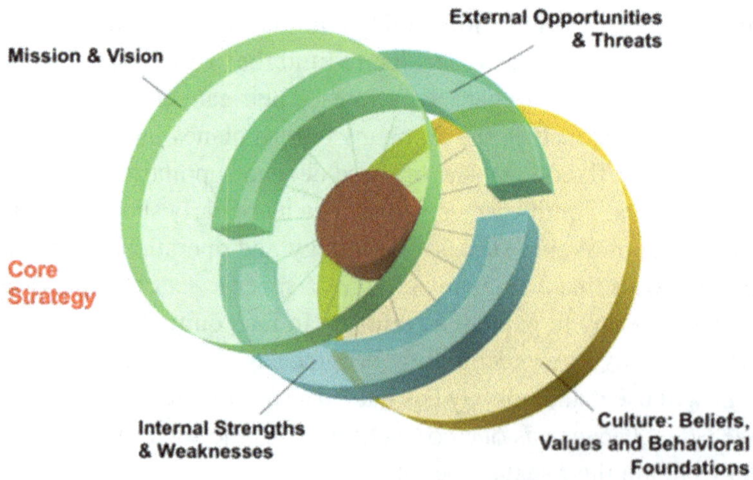

tool and has been covered vastly in research and publications. Figure 2 above illustrates all of the elements surrounding the core strategy of an organization.

Before we venture into the definition of supply chain strategy, it is important to clarify the relationship between strategy and activities further. In its simplest form, a strategy document contains the definition of a desired future state of the company, business unit or product. As stated above, activities are de facto the same as business processes. In this sense, strategy drives the definition of processes while processes in turn rely on technologies as much as on other resources for their execution. The explicit dependencies between strategy, process and technology are illustrated by the framework as shown in Figure 3.

The strategy framework highlights several key points. Most important, without a solid strategy, there is no point in executing processes well or possessing the best available technology. A highly efficient organization that has chosen the wrong strategy will simply fail faster than an inefficient one. Conversely, technology in and by itself is never valuable. Its merit only stems from how it is used. The best technology in unskilled hands is just as useless as having none at all.

One of the first approaches to define the organization itself as chains of activities through which materials flow to create value for stakeholders also came from Harvard's Michael E. Porter[4], who defined the concept of activity selection described above. In his approach, Porter was one of the first authors to truly describe a supply chain from inbound materials to finished product and maintenance. The concept, shown in figure 4 below, became known as the value chain and is still widely used to date. Porter convincingly argued, here as well, that firms cannot be best at everything and thus need to pick and choose those activities that allow for a differentiation in the market.

In many ways, our understanding of supply chain management today originates from the concept of the value chain.

I. Supply Chain Strategy

Figure 3. Strategy Framework

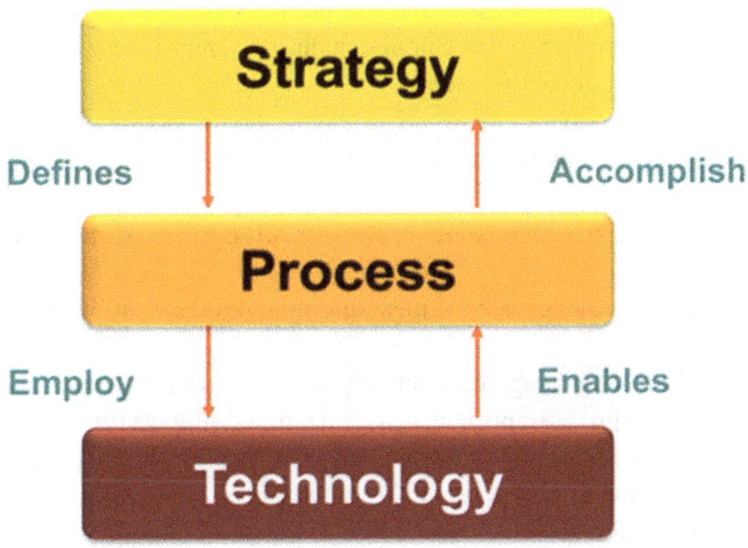

Figure 4. Porter's Value Chain

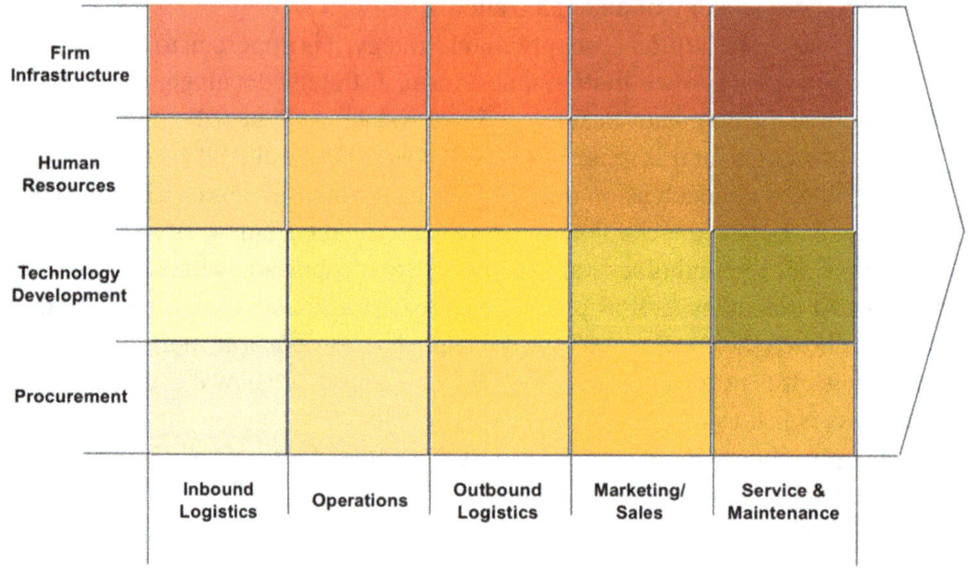

Having established the key concepts to understand strategic management and corporate strategy, we can now define supply chain strategy. If corporate strategy is the selection and execution of specific activities in a given firm, then supply chain strategy necessarily is the selection and performance of unique activities within the fulfillment of customer demand to ultimately achieve higher corporate goals. However, it is important to differentiate between organizations that derive their unique and defensible competitive position through supply chain management activities (strategic supply chain) and those where the supply chain is primarily an enabling function (supply chain strategy).

In its support role, supply chain management translates corporate strategy into strategic supply chain objectives. These strategic objectives then drive the definition of processes through the choice of activities. These processes, in turn, are supported by supply chain technologies as we had seen in figure 3. As a result, supply chain strategies, processes and technologies subsequently are a directly dependent function of a higher organizational strategy. Supply chain managers in this situation have to perform three tasks to drive their own strategic objectives:

1. Definition of supply chain activities in close alignment to the essence and intent of the organizational strategy.
2. Creation (as opposed to depletion) of synergy between all supply chain activities as well as towards all other activities of the firm.
3. Continuous monitoring of strategy achievement throughout the execution of supply chain activities.

Seen in this light supply chain management actively contributes to the accomplishment of organizational strategy objectives and is just as important an organizational support function as marketing, finance or human resources. This view of supply chain as a support function has gained in relevance over the past few years and will continue to do so. Examples of supporting organizational strategy include the configuration of the supply chain network based on cost, time and quality considerations, selection of fulfillment and distribution centers based on customer experience goals and overall customer satisfaction as well as handling of returns and management of warranty claims in accordance with marketing and sales objectives.

In its strategic role, supply chain management drives the definition of the organizational strategy and translates its own strategic requirements into business processes and technologies. Supply chain management in a strategic role takes on a life of its own in that the dominant elements of corporate strategy are ultimately supply chain activities. The core competency of an organization is oftentimes based on supply chain management. The relation between supply chain strategy, processes and technologies is much more immediate as well, yet the general relationships remain the same as in the support function.

As initially stated supply chains are rarely, if ever confined to the operation of a single organization. Activities are typically performed by several legal entities, which requires a much higher degree of collaboration and coordination as well as trust. Contrary to other corporate functions such as marketing or finance where the organization largely controls processes and thus work performed, supply chain activities have to rely on each node doing what they are supposed to. This can pose a unique and quite complex set of challenges. Supply chain managers are often confined to spent vast amounts of time monitoring and reconciling exceptions that occur when their own organization Is not in control of the process. To establish how organizations can support the organizational strategy or drive true innovation in supply chain management, we will need to take a closer look at the technology layer of the framework illustrated in figure 3.

II. Digital Supply Chain Capabilities

Digital supply chain capabilities can greatly enhance the ability of an organization to innovate beyond mere efficiency gains. However, as mentioned above, the vast majority of digital supply chain applications fall into the category of supporting measures rather than allowing organizations to create unique and defensible competitive positions.

Along with the logistical challenges of moving physical goods by many different hands, there is a vast and often underestimated challenge of how to collect, share and reconcile information throughout the execution of supply chain processes. Virtually every organization today uses some form of enterprise resource planning (ERP) system such as SAP or Oracle. Most also have their own supply chain planning and execution systems including different demand planning(DPS), transportation management (TMS) warehouse management systems (WMS) to name a few. Data that originates in one system is often not easily shared with the others. In practice, there still is a high degree of redundant manual data input, which is error prone and expensive. Even in situations where the sharing of data has been automated, problems typically arise to understand and use the shared data widely within the receiving organizations.

To understand why there are so many complexities, we have to look back in time. Many of the enterprise-class systems in use today were initially developed in the 70s to early 90s, at a time when they were never intended to enable the rapid sharing of information across enterprise boundaries and beyond the walls of a single organization. To be fair, a lot has changed since then and virtually all software providers offer application programming interfaces (API) and connectivity as well as data sharing applications today. However, it is still rare to see organizations that consistently share their data with all supply chain partners and even rarer for organization to share data about transactions that may not have been executed all that well.

More and more software providers today turn to electronic marketplace functionality as well as event management platforms to alleviate these issues. These are certainly steps in the right direction and we may well witness more progress through the application of technologies such as Blockchain and smart contracts. In this scenario, data exists in the cloud and can be accessed by a variety of permissioned systems that participate in supply chain transactions. It just requires an immutable ledger which is kept either publicly or by a trusted third-party such as a large neutral organization. There already are several technology providers who have established these kinds of platforms or supply chain application backbones and we are certain that many more are to follow.

With a reliable supply chain application backbone in place, data sharing becomes easy as all participants just need to follow a single protocol and agree on standards for admission and retention of all participants. Some of the most interesting applications will include those that allow for sharing of sensor and actuator data that is generated by wireless devices, electronic chips or assets such as containers, vehicles and vessels themselves to name a few examples. Based on our definition of supply chain strategy as the selection and performance of supply chain activities, the execution of processes then constitutes an integral part of leveraging the underlying technology layer within the strategy framework illustrated in figure 3.

The integration of Internet of Things (IoT) sensor data into existing system is also an instructive example of how organizations can move from the supporting to a strategic role in their supply chains. Over the past two decades, we have witnessed the emergence of GPS-based technologies that allow the tracking of large assets such as vehicles or containers and of small, sensor-based technologies such as RFID to tag and identify small items such as a product, package or carton. These technologies greatly enhance the capabilities of digital supply chains as they add a tremendous amount of highly granular data to all systems that are connected.

For example, some time ago a senior executive at a large consumer electronics company shared an anecdote that is very indicative of today's highly integrated yet still insensitive supply chain systems. His company had shipped a new generation of game stations from Asian plants to retail locations across the US. The containers cleared customs in Los Angeles and were transported by truck while consumers were lining up at the stores to be among the first to purchase the new product. The truck serving North Texas drove through the night and was expected at the first retail store just before 6 AM. With customers gathered outside, the truck did not arrive in time for the opening of the store. It took several hours to establish what had gone wrong. The company finally found that the vehicle had broken down in a remote area of New Mexico which left the driver without the ability to communicate his predicament.

Needless to say, consumers where furious while staff and management were highly frustrated. The situation could have been avoided with a simple GPS unit mounted to the truck. It is obvious that this exception led to lost revenues and inefficiency across the entire supply chain e.g. play stations from other stores had to allocated to the unsupplied one, inventories needed to be shifted around and new orders placed, etc. The time and money spend on phone calls, conversations and investigations easily reached into the thousands of dollars as well, all because a simple piece of information was not available: that the truck had broken down.

The most important aspect of this anecdote is the fact that information needs to be shared and acted upon. Without the ability to do something about an exception, even the most timely and reliable data is useless. In other words, merely collecting data is not a sufficient measure by itself. A new breed of information systems exclusively focused on event management has emerged over the past few years.

These systems filter and sort through hundreds, sometimes thousands of events concurrently to identify those that are truly important and that threaten to bring processes to a halt.

A second important aspect is that event management rarely stops at a single company or node in the supply chain. As the game station example illustrates, many different actors from a variety of organizations needed to know what was happening in near real-time. Obviously, event management systems need to allow for fast and efficient sharing of information among supply chain partners. These types of applications are just now emerging in wider deployments supplied by large integrated vendors many of whom offer all of the required services, software and hardware from a single source.

Naturally, wide-spread information sharing leads to the ability to make well-founded decisions at all points throughout the supply chain, which unlocks competitive advantage for those companies that implement all of these underlying technologies. Figure 5 below illustrates this concept as a series of steps, from left to right, that organizations have to undertake in order to create the ability to react fast and efficiently to unforeseen events.

III. Data Management at the Edge

The decision-making framework shown in figure 5 obviously requires the collection of data in places that are far removed from central ERP and SCM systems outlined earlier. This in turn necessitates that many decisions are made at the point of data collection, which poses a serious problem, namely that this has never been done before in supply chain applications. Older systems, simply cannot comply easily, which requires the implementation of a new breed of systems.

Conversely, organizations that build data and material management competencies at the edge of the enterprise pull ahead of their competition through strategic advantages that touch virtually every business process in their respective organization and their greater environment. This is a key difference between older enterprise solutions and edge technologies. CRM is an example of the former in that it allows companies to build a deeply integrated database about customers, prospects and targets. By doing so CRM supports a single process of sales and customer retention. In contrast, edge technologies

Figure 5. Framework for Real-Time Decision-Making

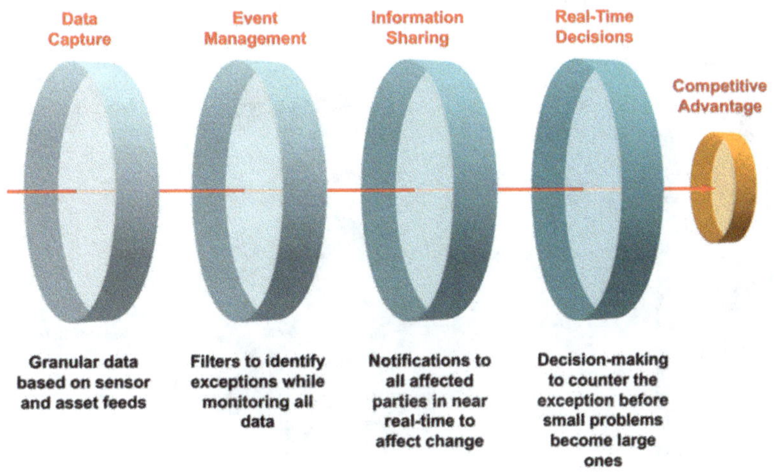

deepen the entire operation from understanding customers to creating substantial time, cost and quality advantages for administrative, manufacturing and distribution processes.

Edge technologies tie suppliers and customers closer to the value creation process and they enable near real-time information sharing between all participants in a supply chain. More importantly, edge technologies are highly synergistic in that they allow companies to gain many detailed insights about a specific application area which are then equally applicable to many others. For example, an organization might begin with a simple project to track products all the way through retail while the retailer now has the ability to show how and when these products are sold and by whom they were bought, if this data is shared between the two parties. We are still in the early stages of seeing information sharing such as this, but these types of projects are gaining acceptance and naturally lead to larger, more strategic initiatives down the road. In this light, IoT and sensor integration as part of edge computing can become an inflection point for lasting, rich innovation across an entire organization. To illustrate this point, it is instructive to look at how IoT data itself is used today and how the approach to data management changes within a given organization.

Take an RFID tag, for example, where the data that is stored on a tag itself. It is a plain string of numbers that only acquires meaning when it is decoded into a company prefix, an item reference and finally a unique product ID number. Eventhough some tags and tag data standards specify more information, the fact that an RFID tag does not give us all of the needed information remains. Not even the process of decoding RFID tags is enough to provide contextual information that a highly sophisticated ERP system can utilize. On the contrary, these integrated and very large systems require edge data to be transformed into edge information and ultimately into edge knowledge.

Figure 6 illustrates this concept through a hierarchy from edge data to information and finally knowledge. As we begin to make sense out of edge data and information, the application of context-specific business rules allows the creation of edge knowledge that then, and in many cases only then, is passed on to an enterprise resource planning system.

An instructive example is a typical shipping transaction. In today's environment, without electronic tags or sensor inputs, we prepare a number of pallets along with reference documents such as a manifest, airway bill or bill of lading for transport. As pallets are loaded, a dock worker or supervisor ideally observes them as they move onto the truck to establish the correctness of the shipment right there on the

Figure 6. Edge Computing Framework

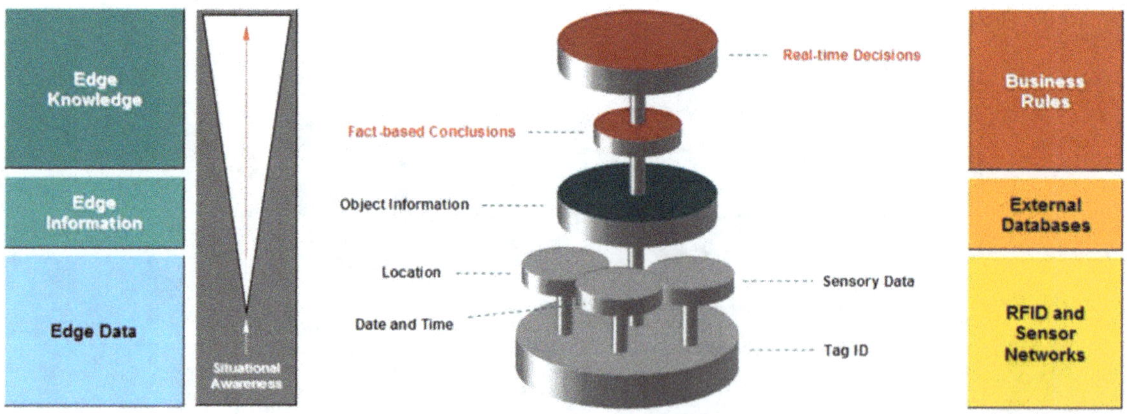

spot. However, oftentimes errors and mistakes are not found until much later in the supply chain when it is costly and cumbersome to reverse them. In this scenario, a number of expensive reconciliatory steps have to take place until the transaction finally closes. Not surprisingly, the general process is more or less the same when we employ electronic label technology. However, there are a number of important cost and time savings when we apply our new and highly sophisticated edge process.

Figure 7 shows the shipping process after it has been automated through RFID technology. For the purposes of this example, we can take a consumer goods company that ships products out of a manufacturing facility. When the truck arrives at the point of pickup an RFID door portal is able to read an RFID tag on the back of the truck to uniquely identify the vehicle. We can now also display information about the truck's destination and the shipment itself. In this way, it is easy to avoid moving the wrong materials onto a parked truck.

The shipping process begins when a warehouse worker loads the first pallet onto the trailer thereby setting off a motion sensor at the dock door. The sensor sends an alert to the edge computing system, which turns on the RFID antennae and readers at the dock door to begin the shipping process. The underlying edge computing system then receives a first tag ID or a set of tag IDs when carton tags are used as well as the dock door location with date and time. All of this information is processed in the edge computing system and will be retained for the duration of the transaction. The edge computing system now triggers a lookup for a document of reference in a warehouse management or enterprise resource planning system. This document contains all needed electronic tag codes for the transaction and it immediately alerts the warehouse worker in case a pallet is not intended to be loaded onto the respective truck. While the warehouse worker proceeds to load remaining pallets onto the truck, the underlying edge computing system automatically matches each tag ID to the reference document and alerts the warehouse worker when something is missing or when another pallet does not belong on the truck. In cases where exceptions occur, the edge computing system executes predefined business rules that notify users of problems and provide guidance to solving the issues on hand. Problems can now be solved while they arise rather than much later down the line.

Figure 7. Example of a Shipping Transaction

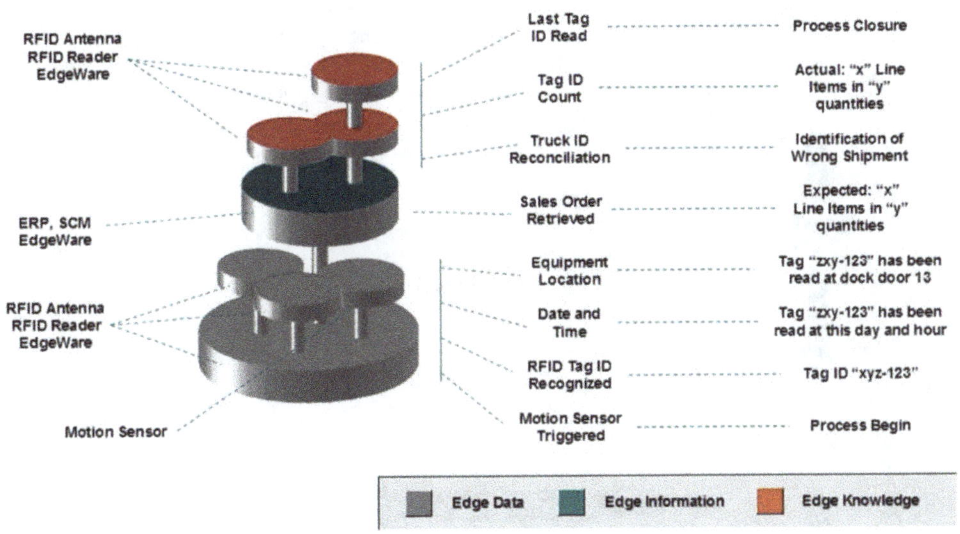

In this simple example IoT technology has drastically reduced the risk of wrong shipments and eliminated the need for later reconciliation when errors occur at the point of shipping. At the same time, IoT-based shipments reduce the time it takes to transact and allow for more efficient allocation of warehouse personnel. In many cases employee morale increases substantially as a result of the reduction in human error sources. The process further reduces the need for oversight so that supply chain managers can focus on the resolution of true exceptions rather than preoccupy themselves with monitoring all transactions. This exemplary process has been vastly simplified and it does not address issues of picking the right items as well as preparing them for shipment. However, prior and following business processes, too, will be drastically improved through edge technologies.

The example also brings to light that decision-making at the edge can happen in real-time and that typical disconnects between information about an item and the item itself have been eliminated through the application of electronic tags. Most important, edge technology has substantially shortened decision-making processes and has increased the value of information used in the process. Figure 8 above illustrates these outcomes by comparing the decision time of traditional processes to those at the edge. Traditional systems are much more latent and typically cannot react in near real-time. The value that edge technologies provide to companies across all industries lies in the speed of decisions at the edge where errors can be corrected without inconveniencing business partners or clients later on.

To summarize, the *edge* is where things happen: a supplier warehouse, a loading dock, a truck-trailer combination, a retail shelf or a customer site. Decisions are moved from large central systems to small, nimble and decentralized ones. The velocity of data and information increases greatly as we move towards the edge. It is important to note that these capabilities are often enabled through wireless communication. As mentioned earlier under strategic considerations, it is easy to lose track of what matters most: not the technology but the underlying rationale for applying it in the right way. Without strategic objectives to greatly improve the performance of business processes, there is little use for any of what

Figure 8. Value of Near Real-Time Information

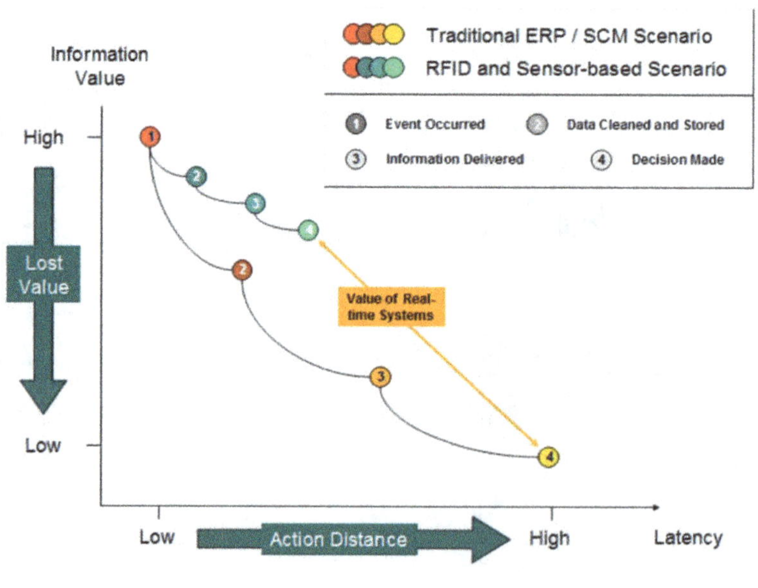

we have discussed above and old processes run the danger of simply become expensive old processes through improvements.

IV. Implementing Supply Chain Strategy

We have established that supply chain strategy falls into one of two categories: either the supply chain function in an organization translates larger strategic objectives into actionable ones (support role) that it will execute or it leads strategic initiatives as a source of competitive advantage (strategic role). In both scenarios, the strategic direction of an organization needs to be implemented for the supply chain function. We have also shown, through the example of near real-time technologies and edge computing systems, that strategic supply chain initiatives require entirely new approaches to the way we handle data and information. Implementing these strategic changes can be daunting and requires a structured approach such as the one we discuss below.

The ability of any given innovation to change the competitive landscape in an industry merits further consideration through the lens of strategic capabilities to determine how and where new business processes play into core strengths of an organization in novel and useful ways. This determination requires a structured approach to technology evaluation before its adoption. Management ultimately has to embed technology choices into an organization's overall strategy. In this discussion, we focus on how to integrate the continuous assessment of supply chain innovation into the process of strategy definition for the organization.

To reiterate, supply chain innovation generally allows companies to differentiate through both: defining new activities or performing activities differently from rivals. An example, albeit not a traditional supply chain case, are sports teams which use electronic RFID labels on their season tickets. The initial aim was to deter counterfeits and to create process efficiencies for fans (this is their supply chain aspect) by allowing them easy access to venues, to pay for concessions quickly and also access to VIP areas without the hassle of being held up. In the US, the Seattle Seahawks deployed an RFID-based payment system to find that concession sales increased by 18% based on the ability to process payments substantially faster at stands. In cases like this, consumers are able to experience innovative process capabilities as unique and pleasant. From a strategic perspective, it is important to keep in mind that these sports teams face a wide range of unlikely rivals. With very few exceptions, they do not compete with other teams in the same sport. Rather, competition for hockey teams, for example, comes in the form of local basketball, baseball or hockey teams as well as, of course, other types of entertainment, such as theater, concerts and even TV. In essence any differentiation that is perceived as valuable by consumers is a strategic capability which makes it easier to draw new consumers into the arena while retaining existing ones by performing the same activities differently.

An example of performing different activities to obtain a competitive advantage would be to use the same tickets in a raffle where a random scan of a ticket leads to winning a prize. Likewise, sports teams can use kiosks and terminals to provide customized information by reading these tickets when the consumers are in front of a monitor. Sports teams could offer the ability to sell seats for part of a game when season ticket holders want to leave early for example. In these cases, the underlying technology can have a viable impact on an organizations strategy as well as foster process efficiencies in terms of cost, time, quality and flexibility. Ultimately the determination of how innovative capabilities influence the overall strategy needs to be based on an in-depth assessment of the technology and processes within the context of every specific organization.

Generally, before embarking on any endeavor to create competitive advantage, it is necessary to assess the overall strategy along with supply chain capabilities. Below are five steps that can serve as a guide.

1. **Organizational Strategy:** In the first step, management takes a look at the current market position, key competitors and the organizations' competencies at a minimum to establish where competitive differentiation is desirable and how much given capabilities influence customer perception or the competitive position. In today's fast changing business environment, this is typically a continuous endeavor and not all aspects of a company's strategy necessarily need to be documented in writing. An effective way to accelerate a strategy assessment, which is often used by consultants, is to ask executives about how they envision the organization in two or three years from present. One approach, which is particularly helpful and usually leads to diverse results when working with an entire management team, is newspaper article writing: asking each executive to headline and write a one-page article that looks back on the organization from a future date.
2. **Fit between Supply Chain Capabilities and Strategy:** The technological capabilities in the supply chain management field are changing rapidly and we still see new and exciting applications emerge regularly. Better processes, better hardware and increasingly sophisticated software continually allow for a growing number of applications. The cost of technology is an important consideration in that more affordable technology enables a larger number of business cases yet it is usually available to a broad number of competitors. The assessment of supply chain capabilities can occur within the explicit context of the strategy (top-down), but it is equally feasible to look at a technology itself to determine which of its features might allow for a specific competitive differentiation (bottom-up). This type of assessment is also very interesting when it is conducted for major competitors. A useful approach in this context is scenario planning: determining how supply chain technology might evolve over time and defining which strategic capabilities a given technology scenario enables for the organization and /or its competitors.
3. **Prioritize Ideas and Opportunities:** Once it is clear how supply chain innovation influences an organization's capabilities, it is possible to define a list of strategic and tactical opportunities. For a retailer, for example, these may include several applications in logistics, in-store and backroom inventory management solutions as well as innovative ways to interact with consumers. In our experience the list should contain 25 to 35 opportunities although not all need to be implemented. Naturally these will vary by industry and company. The criteria to evaluate each opportunity includes how the opportunity influences the organizations' competitiveness and industry position as well as how economically feasible it is at the present point in time. Technology maturity is also important since there may well be opportunities which need to be implemented later. In detail, the evaluation begins with the mapping of as-is and to-be processes, includes a high-level assessment of the required project investment and also a first return on investment (ROI) or net present value (NPV) calculation. In addition, the use of scoring models is a great way to uncover intangible benefits and to aggregate management feedback across the entire team.
4. **Create an Implementation Roadmap:** The list of prioritized opportunities serves as the main input for a roadmap by placing all opportunities that have been selected for implementation on a timeline. The roadmap defines when projects should begin, which resources will be needed and what the expected outcomes for each project are. If there are synergies between projects, e.g. later implementations leveraging the infrastructure created by previous ones, this should also be noted. The explicit inclusion of tangible and possibly intangible project goals is an important component

of the roadmap since it ensures accountability later on. Naturally, roadmaps are only valuable when they are executed. In this sense, an executive sponsor should own and drive the evolution of the roadmap. One important aspect is that it may very well make sense to combine several different or even all relevant information technologies on a company-wide roadmap. There certainly is no reason why supply chain innovation should not be fully integrated the company's technology vision.

5. **Continuously Assess and Revise the Roadmap:** When new supply chain capabilities are not mature enough, when the business case is not immediately attainable or when the implementation is not possible for other reasons, implementation candidates typically go on a reassessment list. As the competitive environment changes or as new supply chain capabilities become available, the roadmap is then revisited to reflect these developments. The roadmap requires organizations to stay on top of developments in supply chain and related innovation fields to continuously reevaluate their own position in regard to competitive capabilities.

V. Summary

Digital supply chains are a fact of life today and they will keep evolving very quickly over the next few years. It is obviously easier to view these developments from the perspective of a spectator, rather than from that on an innovator. Yet, as we have shown in our discussion of strategy, only organizations that act on innovation opportunities will gain a better competitive position than those who choose to follow. It is necessary for executives and management to continually assess innovation, technology and business process capabilities within the industry and also in other industries. Supply chain management is no exception and has great potential to drive the organization strategy well into the future.

KEY TERMS AND DEFINITIONS

Activities: Are single tasks or chains of tasks that form business processes and that allow a firm to differentiate itself in the market place.

Bullwhip Effect: A situation in which ineffective network effects occur because each successive node in the supply chain orders more supplies than the previous one based on wrong assumptions, a lack of communication and flawed planning processes.

Strategic (Supply Chain) Role: A situation in which supply chain management is the most important corporate function and thus dominates the definition of corporate strategy.

Strategy: Is the competitive positioning of a company or product in a given market. In its essence strategy means choosing to perform the same activities differently or different activities from rival firms.

Strategy Framework: Strategy drives the definition of processes, which in turn rely on technologies for their flawless execution.

Supply Chain Management: Is all activities that are related to the planning and fulfillment of demand.

Supply Chain Strategy: Is the choice and performance of unique activities within supply and demand management to ultimately achieve corporate strategy.

Supporting (Supply Chain) Role: Is a situation in which supply chain management is driven by other, more important corporate functions and subsequently translates corporate strategy into specific requirements for supply chain management.

ENDNOTES

1 Porter, Michael E.: What is Strategy, in: Harvard Business Review, November – December 1996.

2 Stalk, G.; Evans, P; Shulman, Lawrence E.: Competing on Capabilities: The New Rules of Corporate Strategy, in: Harvard Business Review, March – April 1992, pp. 57 – 68. Hamel, G.; Prahalad, C.: Core Competencies of the Corporation, in: Harvard Business Review, 1990, pp. 79 – 91.

3 Collis, David J.; Montgomery, Cynthia A.: Competing on Resources: Strategy in the 1990s, in: Harvard Business Review, July – August 1995, pp. 118 – 128. Kaplan, Sarah; Schenkel, Andrew; von Krogh, Georg; Weber, Charles: Knowledge-based Theories of the Firm in Strategic Management: A Review and Extension, Submission to the Academy of Management Review, 2001.

4 Porter, M.E.: Competitive Advantage: Creating and Sustaining Superior Performance, Simon & Schuster, 1985.

Chapter 2
Procurement Strategies for Digital Supply Chains:
Concepts and Best Practices

Varun Gupta
https://orcid.org/0000-0002-0714-0298
Pennsylvania State University – Erie, USA

ABSTRACT

The purpose of this chapter is to provide the basic concepts and the best practices for procurement in the context of digital supply chains. This chapter consists of three sections. In the first two sections, a review of digital supply chain procurement literature and theories is presented, followed by a detailed discussion of the best practices in procurement strategies comprising of the six-step framework for procurement strategies digitalization. Finally, the chapter concludes with future trends in procurement strategies. The chapter consists of case studies from different industries such as manufacturing (Apple, Beta products, IBM), fast food (Chipotle), and logistics/pharmaceutical (DHL). EVA (economic value added) model is discussed in the chapter, which is useful to evaluate the value of digitalization. This chapter is intended for all practitioners and academics who are interested in learning about the current best practices and the challenges associated with procurement for digital goods.

INTRODUCTION

'Procurement is the process of finding, agreeing on terms and acquiring goods, services or works from an external source, often via a tendering or competitive bidding process. The process is used to ensure the buyer receives goods, services or works at the best possible price, when aspects such as quality, quantity, time, and location are compared' –Van Weele (2010). The purpose of this chapter is to provide a background, then introduce and describe the most important factors for the procurement strategies for digital supply chains. We do this by first reviewing the history and evolution of procurement processes, next we review the relevant literature on the digitalization of procurement processes. Subsequently, we develop a 6-step framework for procurement strategies in digitalized supply chains. We build the framework using

DOI: 10.4018/978-1-5225-7700-3.ch002

Copyright © 2019, IGI Global. Copying or distributing in print or electronic forms without written permission of IGI Global is prohibited.

specific case studies such as Nath et al. (2008), and Mabert and Schoenherr (2001, and literature such as Thompson et al. (2000), Neef (2001), Forbes (2012), Glas and Kleeman (2016), and Brich (2018). Thus, the chapter provides a practical framework and reference for procurement managers who are looking to get an in-depth understanding of the digital transformation for their procurement processes.

Procurement is a more comprehensive area than purchasing in the context of supply chain management (SCM), as purchasing focuses more on tactical aspects of acquiring the goods, services or work from an external source, whereas procurement encompasses development of business strategies that align with an organization's mission and goals. Strategic procurement enables companies to develop and/or enhance their advantage over its competitors –both by cost advantage or differentiation advantage.

Emerging digital and advanced analytics tools promise new levels of procurement performance. To deliver that promise, CPOs must discover which of them are best suited to the needs of their company.
– McKinsey & Co. (2017)

Digitalization of supply chains has helped companies with both cost reduction as well as creating a difference in values based on the digital transformation products used for procurement (*cf.* Farahani et al., 2017, Büyüközkan, G. and Göçer, 2018, and Ivanov et al., 2018). The first instance of a digital technology developed for procurement was the *Replenishment Management System and Method (RMSS)* by IBM in 2000. IBM used the technology to solve the complex procurement process for their laptop producing plant in Mexico (Guadalupe, 2011) and the plant production grew from USD 1.6 billion (annually) to USD 3.6 billion after three years of its implementation. This is arguably one of the first success stories of digitalization of the procurement process. Through digitalization, businesses are able to better adopt, design, and deliver new smart and connected products that change the way they compete in the markets (Porter and Heppelmann, 2014).

Modern-day procurement processes have become increasingly complex due to globalization, volatile and uncertain global tariffs, complex supply chain networks ("VUCA" world), digitalization including online shopping and e-commerce, changes in customer demands, shorter product life cycles, and a rapid increase in the number of SKUs (stock keeping units). This complexity is further aggravated by budgetary constraints on businesses and mass customization (hyper-personalization[1]) for customers, which requires businesses to use procurement processes as a key strategic tool to deliver profits at the least operational and sourcing costs. Consequently, it is increasingly important for procurement managers and supply chain managers to learn how to best use digitalized procurement strategies to remain relevant in the industry.

The chapter discusses the concept of procurement for digital supply chains by first presenting the background that includes a detailed analysis of state of the art literature in the area, importance of it, and the key theories. Next, a discussion of best practices in procurement strategies comprising of different industries via specific case studies is presented. Next, a discussion of the practical and proven managerial procurement strategies for digital supply chains is presented. This is followed by a brief discussion on future developments and other developing areas in the procurement of relevance but beyond the scope of the detailed presentation in the chapter. Finally, the chapter concludes with some of the limitations of the information presented as well as the scope for future research.

BACKGROUND

Definition for Procurement for Digital Supply Chains

Despite the wide use and inception of digital technologies in procurement processes since the dawn of the 21st century, surprisingly, there are not many academic definitions of procurement for digital supply chains. One of the definitions used in practice by Accenture (Accenture), a leading consulting company is stated as follows:

'Digital procurement (or digital supply chains) automates repeatable tasks to boost efficiency and reduce costs; it equips stakeholders across the business with real-time insights and analytics through artificial intelligence (AI) and easy-to-use online tools; it deploys new and smarter ways to infuse data models to enrich day-to-day operations and decision making. Furthermore, it transforms buyer interactions with suppliers and other third parties by serving as a platform for new levels of collaboration.'

From the above definition of digital procurement, it is easy to note the role of digitalization (introduction of digital technologies) in revolutionizing the traditional procurement process. In traditional procurement processes, there were inefficiencies due to repeated processes, manual verification of processes, and collaboration was lacking due to lack of transparency and collaboration between different supply chain partners. Jordan (2017) discuss the need for curiosity, creativity, and collaboration across digitally integrated supply chains, industry organizations that can enable them to reduce operational costs, making them more reliable and competitive. Use of modern digital technology solutions that include ERP (enterprises resources planning) systems, data mining, AI, blockchain, etc., have truly changed the traditional landscape of procurement and taken it to the next level. Procurement is an essential function of any organization and can represent up to 80% of an organization's costs. It is worth noting at this point that digitalizing the procurement process may seem a novel idea with a huge emphasis on AI and data analytics, surprisingly, this is not a new idea. This revolution began with electronic procurement or e-procurement in the early 2000s and its background is detailed in the following section.

Digitalizing Procurement Process Is Not New: E-Procurement

The use of digital technologies for reshaping the procurement process is not new and started with the IT revolution. IBM was one of the first developers and users of digital procurement solutions when they built RMSS in 2000 and used in their production operations in Mexico. Even before IBM's RMSS, starting 1980s, retailers used EDI (electronic data interchange) systems to exchange information with their suppliers and send purchase orders electronically. This followed by the use of (simple) IT software by retailers and suppliers that helped in faster exchange of more information. Therefore, the use of electronic software tools or information and communications technology (ICT) is not new and is commonly referred to as **e-procurement**.

Ageshin (2001) conducted a case study on e-procurement solutions used at the General Motors (GM). In this case study, he first describes the e-procurement process, its advantages as well as its disadvantages for business. They summarize four important advantages of using e-procurement as:

1. Low barrier to entry into the market for a business,
2. Transparency in prices across supply chain members,
3. Better buyer-seller relationship due to transparency and visibility, creating a better balance in their power relationship, and
4. Higher opportunities to avoid issues with buying and use *preferred* supplier networks.

The key disadvantages of e-procurement discussed in their study include mismatches in expectations between the buyer and the seller, high-risk of compromising any sensitive data, high training costs for employees, and restructuring of existing processes to align with newer e-procurement processes. It is fascinating to note that all these factors still highly applicable to the use of modern-day digital solutions. GM was interested in implementing e-procurement in 1999, when their technology partners i2 Technologies and Commerce One, created a B2B (business-to-business) trading community called TradeXchange. However, in early 2000, GM, Ford and DaimlerChrysler AG jointly started to build a single internet-based procurement network, in collaboration with Oracle. This alliance was designed to have better bargaining power with their suppliers as well as to achieve economies of scale (and scope). For GM, the e-procurement system would enable them to reduce time and costs and help with better forecasts and information sharing throughout the supply chain. Further benefits also entailed supply chain optimization and a favorable R&D environment using the supplier database. He also points out some of the disadvantages for GM such as tailoring existing logistics and supply chain for higher responsiveness that will result in the elimination of some workers and supply chain members. In conclusion, this early case study gives a good insight into e-procurement, its advantages, and disadvantages, and apply these concepts to study the implementation of e-procurement system at GM.

Presutti (2003) studied the impact of e-procurement on the value creation in SCM processes for businesses. He indicates that businesses will increasingly focus on SCM as they continue to adopt e-procurement solutions and argue that procurement and supply managers need to carefully understand the impact of technologies to make the best use of e-procurement solutions. The study first provides an overview of the traditional procurement process as shown in Figure 1. Traditionally, the procurement process begins with a buyer listing her requirements, which are based on the product requirements and the time of delivery. In the next stage, the buyer invites request for proposals (RFPs) from different suppliers that may meet the requirements and then design the contracts with a selected supplier. This stage is followed by placing an order and receiving the order with the supplier including payments. Finally, the buyer reevaluates the supplier performance for potential future procurements. Besides describing the advantages and disadvantages of e-procurement, Presutti (2003) also study its impact on the revenues, costs, and the assets of the business using the economic value added model (EVA model). EVA can be calculated as:

$$EVA = operating\ profit\ after\ taxes - cost\ of\ capital$$

It is important for procurement managers to understand EVA as a key financial measure to understand the impact of using digital technologies and for making a business case of technology adoption and usage. He points out that for businesses adopting e-procurement the material cost reductions can range from 5–20%, whereas the transaction costs can be reduced to as high as 65%. E-procurement also reduces the time-to-market cycles by about 10–15%. In conclusion, the study provides a useful approach, i.e., the EVA model for procurement managers to evaluate the impact on revenues, costs, and assets through e-procurement.

Angeles and Nath (2007) surveyed 185 businesses to understand their current B2B e-procurement practices and described the key success factors and the important challenges to technology implementation. They conducted factor analysis on the survey data and found three key success factors as:

1. Supplier and contract management,
2. End-user behavior and e-procurement business process, and
3. Information and e-procurement infrastructure.

The challenges identified in their study include:

1. lack of system integration with existing processes and issues with standardization,
2. lack of maturity in e-procurement-based market services and resistance to technology adoption from the end-user, and
3. incoherent buying practices and difficulty in integrating e-commerce with other systems.

For current and future procurement managers who are tasked with the adoption and/or the use of e-procurement systems in their businesses, this study sheds light on some of the best practices (success factors) and the challenges that are expected in implementation. We refer the reader to Turban et al. (2018) to learn more about how order fulfillment and procurement in e-commerce have evolved and the corresponding best practices for managers.

The Chartered Institute of Purchasing and Supply (CIPS) define e-procurement as – "The combined use of electronic information and communications technology (ICT) in order to enhance the links between customer and supplier, and with other value chain partners, and thereby to improve external and internal processes. E-Procurement is a key component of e-business and e-commerce."

Next, a framework for procurement in digital supply chains is developed, which is based on four pillars of an organization that affects its procurement strategy in the context of digital supply chains. Modern and future procurement is highly strategic in comparison to traditional and e-procurement practices. Because of this strategic importance, it is important to capture and highlight the key difference in interactions between the customer, the product, company's supply chain, and the procurement functional unit.

Figure 1. Traditional procurement process
(adapted from Presutti, 2003 and Van Weele, 2010)

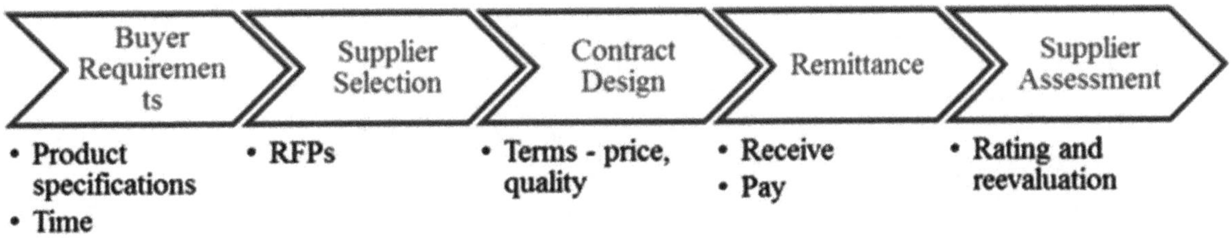

Four Dimensions of an Organization in Digital Supply Chains

To fully understand the role of procurement for an organization refer to Figure 2, which presents the four pillars of an organization that affects a company's strategy in the context of digital supply chains. These first three dimensions include market trends that identify the current needs of customers, this drives the product design, development, and production, and finally, we have the supply chain to produce and deliver the product. Traditionally, businesses compete with others on the first three dimensions. However, with the introduction of digital technologies, we increasingly see strategic procurement practices by businesses where they compete with each other by establishing strategic supply partnerships, low-cost and low-risk supply base, and also use technology (such as machine learning, data mining, and AI) to automate procurement processes and optimizing it. It is important to note that because of these strategic implications, we observe the impact of supply-side procurement processes affecting the supply chains (partnerships, information sharing, and collaborations, etc.), as well as how fast products are delivered to the market affecting the life cycle of a product. Now we discuss a case study conducted by Nath et al. (2008) on Apple Computers Inc. that explore issues with its supply chain and how the company reshaped its digital content delivery. The case study is a basis for the proposed framework in Figure 2.

Apple: Transforming Digital Content Delivery for Supply Chains in the Early 2000s

Nath et al. (2008) conducted a detailed case study on Apple Computers Inc. to explore issues with its supply chain and how the company reshaped its digital content delivery (for music, movies, etc.) using digital technology solutions. Apple reinvented itself as a major player in the music and entertainment industry for both hardware products (such as iPod) as well as content delivery (using iTunes for music and movies). Before this happened, in the early 1990s and to counter the demand uncertainty Apple relocated its production facilities to Southeast Asia, as the cost of procurement was considerably lower in Asia as compared to the US. However, due to the large transportation distance between Asia and the US, the risk of unfulfilled demand increased for them. A couple of years after iPod's introduction (2001)

Figure 2. Role of procurement in digital supply chains

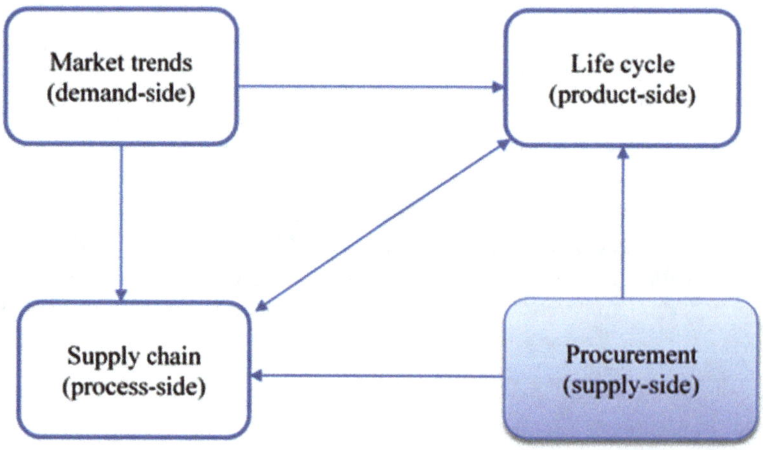

Apple launched its own digital technology store iTunes after they secured contracts with four major record labels, EMI, Sony BMG, Universal and Warner Bros. These contracts were not easy to obtain and Apple utilized their strong leadership to set up these deals. With the digitalization of music and movies (online streaming and downloading) there was no need for a physical supply chain and Apple's investments in digital technology to strategically procure content (from the major record labels), along with a streamlined digital delivery has created an efficient and smoothly functioning supply chain for Apple's digital content.

Framework for Designing Procurement Strategies for Digital Supply Chains

The key success factors for companies to effectively utilizing the digital technologies for procurement is to fully understand the position of the procurement process within an organization and with an organization's external stakeholders. The successful design of procurement process strategy entails incorporating all the four dimensions of an organization as shown in Figure 2. These four dimensions consist of all the customers, the product (and services), the entire supply chain, and all the procurement operations or processes. It is important for the management to have a framework that can be used by procurement managers or technology implements; that helps them to harness the full potential of their digital supply chains. This framework is depicted and summarized in Figure 3 as a continuous six-step process.

Three key success factors are emphasized in Figure 3 to ensure the effectiveness of procurement strategies for digitalization. These success factors make sure that the procurement process is well-aligned with customer needs, product, and the needs of the supply chain members, as well as makes sure that digitalization preserves or improves the alignment of the other three dimensions of the digital supply chain based organization.

The above success factors and the six-steps are detailed out in the section below which describes the best practices for procurement strategies in the world of digital supply chains.

The 6-Step Procurement Strategy Framework for Digital Supply Chains

Step 1: Define Corporate Goals for Digital Supply Chain

The first step in procurement strategy is to develop and define the vision, objectives or the goal of their business. It also includes brainstorming and generating various ways a business plans to utilize the digitalization in short-term, medium-term, and long-term. An example is a steel manufacturing company who develops the goal of producing USD100 million steel annually in 4 years and grow at a rate of 5% annually. The steel company wishes to implement an ERP system that will be implemented for all of their supply chain operations such as purchasing, supply management, and interactions with customers. Their short-term goal is to grow at a steady rate of 5%, and the medium-term goal is to be among the top 10 leading steel supplier in the United States. In the long-term, they want to sell a USD 1 billion worth of steel annually across the globe.

The key success to factor in this step is to clearly define the goals for the business while thinking about how digitalizing the supply chain can aid in realizing the specific goal. The business needs to find a balance between short-term goals and long-term goals to see when and how they would want to utilize

Figure 3. Framework for designing procurement strategies for digital supply chains

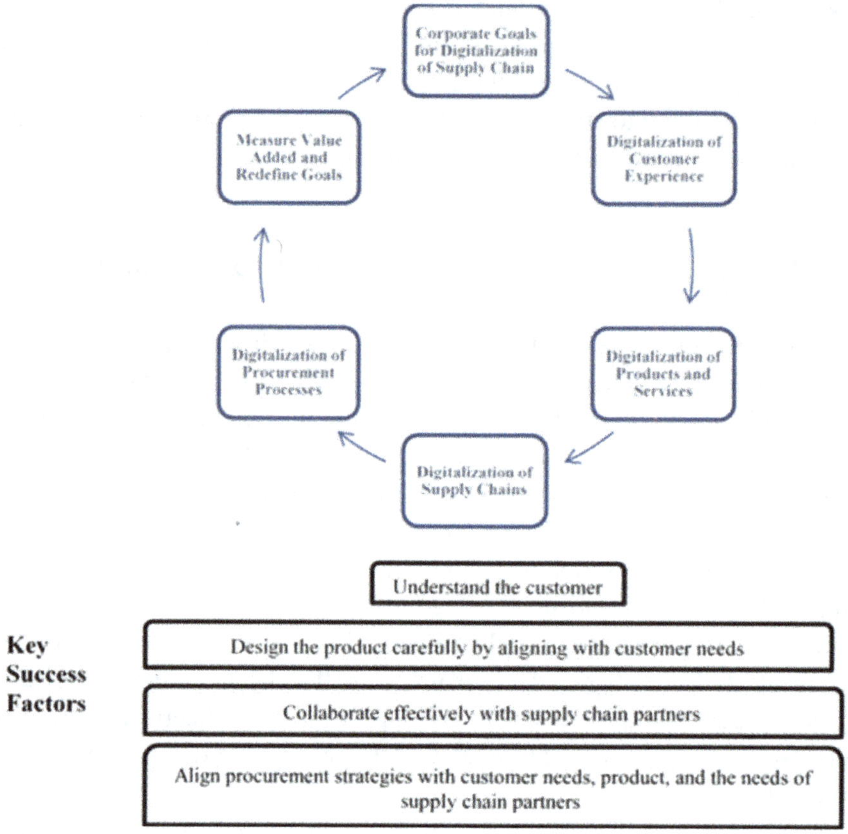

the efficiencies and the information realized by implementing digitalization in procurement processes as well as other parts in their supply chains.

After clearly laying out the goals, it is important to have all the stakeholders and the top-level management across all functional areas of the business. It is less costly to resolve any issues or conflicts across stakeholder and functional units before investing in digitalization, compared to post-digitalization.

Step 2: Digitalization of Customer Experience[2]

You are in the Customer Experience Business, Whether You Know it or Not – Forbes (2012)

In this step, the business needs to develop a plan to digitalize the customer experience including digitalizing some or all of the interactions between the business and the (external) customer, the final recipient of the product and services. Traditional procurement strategies consider customers as passive actors and the business as the key influencer, whereas, in digital supply chains, customers are the key influencers for the business and communication between the customer and the business is two-way (Rogers, 2016). It is important to adapt to the changing trend where customers are highly dynamic and influence all aspects of business processes. A business must also consider the internal customer who supports the procurement processes. This includes cross-functional teams that work directly with procurement as part of the business operations, such as finance may work directly with procurement on the financial budgeting associated with purchasing from suppliers, while accounting can help them measure and provide them with the key performance indicators (KPIs) for the suppliers.

In today's volatile markets, it is difficult to forecast customer demand and their needs accurately, and implementing the right digital technology to meet the demand and the needs is always challenging. Due to uncertain demand, risk-averse management typically invests more than optimal, and often report losses or failures in implementing the technology in the long-term. Businesses can utilize the EVA model to simulate the impact of digitalization of customer experience on their revenues, costs, and assets to ensure profitability and effective use of digitalization.

The current trend of hyper-personalizing the customer experience using big-data analytics[3] has enhanced the value of digitalization for businesses. However, this personalization has made the process of implementing digitalization more pronounced. Implementing a highly customized experience for all kinds/segments of customers using data in real-time uses advanced and complex tools such as data-mining, machine learning, and faster than ever cloud-based-computing. Brinch et al. (2018) conducted a sequential-mixed method study to determine the value of big data for improved decision making in supply chains. They found that big data is currently more about data collection instead of management and utilization. They also indicate that in its current form, bid data is more applicable in logistics and service instead of sourcing, manufacturing, and returns. As a result, it is important for procurement managers to note this as they thinking about utilizing big data in their procurement.

Businesses should determine the level and extent of digitalizing the customer experience based on the characteristics of internal and external customers. A few characteristics that should be evaluated for digitalization of the internal and external customers are mentioned in Table 1.

After evaluating the above-mentioned characteristics (Table 1, details left from the chapter) of the internal and external customers, the business needs to align the digital technology with the requirements of internal customers as well as the external customers to the best extent possible. The business should also make sure that this alignment contributes towards realizing the corporate goals defined in the first step. Executives and managers can also use the scorecard approach to rank the above characteristics in increasing importance to internal and external customers and assigning weights for resource consumption vs. the benefits of investment in digitalization. This can help the business to prioritize important customer characteristics with a higher ROI (return on investment). A case study is presented next discussing the

Table 1. Characteristics of Internal vs. External Customers

	Internal customer	External customer
a.	Size (small, medium, or large)	Sales channel (web-based, mobile, physical, etc.)
b.	Location (centralized or decentralized)	Volume and variability of demand
c.	Existing digital technologies	Profit margin
d.	Current channels (such as warehouses, retail stores, online, mobile, etc.)	Size of individual customers – small vs. large
e.	Product variety	Buying behavior (online, in-store, seasonal, etc.)
f.	-	Lead time
g.	-	Buying power and strategic importance
h.	-	Contracts or SLAs (service-level agreements)

best practices at *Beta* Products – a global manufacturer of engineered products for the transportation industry with an annual purchasing budget over $3 billion (Mabert and Schoenherr, 2001).

Online RFQ System: A Case Study of Internal Customer Experience

In late 1998, Beta Products (Mabert and Schoenherr, 2001) decided to enhance its supply chain processes by using online tools. The purchasing team (PPS team) and engineering teams worked together to improve purchasing materials from vendors. The goal was to become more efficient by using electronic tolls such as e-mail and Internet for purchasing by: a) using an extensive vendor database, b) global price information, c) increasing responsiveness, and d) consolidating company's product informational into a centralized knowledge database. This tool was designed to improve the experience of internal customers – engineering and procurement teams, making their procurement processes faster and more effective. The PPS team was empowered to make their own arrangements and the entire digitalization was done with their inputs. It was challenging as the company was always a customer to their supplier but now they had to learn to be a supplier to their internal customer. This change in roles required a different mindset and new communication skills. The company did two things to overcome this challenge – retrained the existing workforce and recruited new people with these new skills. Some of the examples of training that were conducted were based on communication skills such as influencing, persuading, and presentation. In addition to these skills, people were also trained in cross-functional skills such as IT, finance, and marketing. Most people who were recruited were those who had a mindset around customer experience and who understood the importance of delighting the customers instead of the traditional silo-approach for functional units. As a result, a lot of people who were in senior roles were redeployed or laid off as they were unable to adopt the changes in technology or the culture. It is an important lesson for all young and senior procurement professionals, that those, who are unable to keep pace with the evolving technology or changes in the culture, will be ultimately redeployed or laid-off.

Step 3: Digitalization of Products and Services

When both internal and external customer processes have been digitalized (or customer needs have been assessed), the next step is to digitalize the products and services. Thompson et al. (2000) and Neef (2001) define and distinguish between the *direct* and *indirect* products (importance) for a business in the e-procurement setting. Direct goods and services contribute to the company's sales, either through production or resale, whereas, indirect goods support the primary operations of a business and are viewed as enablers. As an example for a steel manufacturing company, direct goods are the raw materials for producing steel such as iron, coal, etc., as well as the finished goods including different forms of steel they procure from their suppliers. On the other hand, indirect goods for the steel company are the machinery and capital assets including office supplies. Although businesses often want to digitalize both the direct and indirect products and services, prioritizing indirect goods over direct goods is a more commonly used strategy, especially when the resources for digitalization are scarce. This is because the investments required for digitalizing indirect products is usually lower as compared to the investments for digitalizing the direct products because of their size and strategic importance to a business. This also protects the business from any misgivings due to digitalization. In conclusion, this strategy enables the business to reap the benefits of digitalization much more easily and with a lesser risk.

Other commonly used distinctions for products are based on standardized vs. personalized (personalization), low-value vs. high-value (valuation), and readily vs. scarcely available (availability). Therefore, we have four key characteristics for any product as summarized below:

1. Importance – direct or indirect,
2. Personalization – standardized or personalized,
3. Valuation – low valuation or high valuation,
4. Availability – easy vs. complex or readily vs. scarce.

Once, products (and services) are evaluated on the above four characteristics, they should be evaluated for digitalization as follows:

- Importance for the business – The cost and strategic importance of indirect products are lower than the direct products. Indirect products should be prioritized for digitalization.
- Level of personalization required – A standardized product by nature is much easier to purchase, maintain and delivered to the customers as compared to personalized products. Therefore, their digitalization is easier.
- Value of the product – Lower valued products are usually easier to digitalize due to their lower costs. This also reduces the risk of failures associated with digitalization.
- Product availability – A product that is relatively easier to access and has a larger supplier base is much easily digitalized as compared to the product that is scarce. Easy access can also help to bring competitive prices and economies of scale from the supplier base.

The above discussion is summarized in Table 2 and must be followed after digitalizing the customer experience.

Typically, the management must follow the priority order presented in Table 2, however, if the customer experience and their needs (or corporate goals) require a departure from the above product strategies, the digitalization strategy needs to be revised accordingly. For instance, if the largest customer of a company requires the business to digitalize their process as a requirement, the business must prioritize that as a strategy instead of their indirect products.

Step 4: Digitalization of Supply Chain

Digitalization of supply chains in the next step in the overall procurement process strategy framework presented in the chapter. Digitalizing supply chain integration is becoming increasingly dynamic and has evolved from using simple EDI systems to smart and complex networks using AI, machine learning, robotics, and big-data analytics. These technologies will help to alleviate supply chain issues such as forecasting, a collaboration between supply chain members, responsiveness or lack of agility. According to PwC (2016), supply chain professionals expect the impact of digitization to both the bottom and top lines of businesses, i.e., it can help a business to gain efficiency by about 4.1 percent annually, as well as an increase in the revenues by about 2.9 percent a year.

Even though there is little argument about the benefits of digitalization of the supply chain, a survey conducted by DHL (DHL, 2018) indicates that 95% of businesses do not observe the full benefits of (supply chain) digitalization. The two primary reasons indicated in the study are: i) rapid evolution of

Table 2. Product characteristics and priority for digitalization based on cost and risk minimization

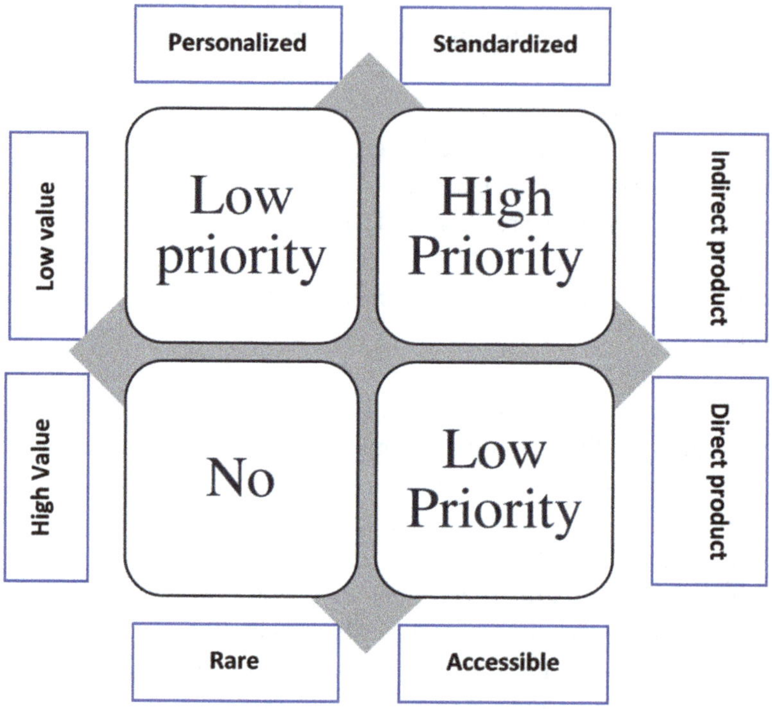

the technology makes it difficult to adapt to; as new technologies keep replacing the existing ones, and ii) organization challenges such as cross-functional collaboration prevents the full benefits of digitalization. According to José F. Nava, Chief Development Officer, DHL (DHL, 2018) said – "This is a transformative juncture for the supply chain industry. The traditional model is facing unprecedented levels of disruption from new hardware technologies combined with information and analytics solutions. Technology offers considerable opportunity to reduce cost and improve profitability but it also means businesses that fail to adapt risk being left behind. Our customers are increasingly looking to us to lead the way during this transition."

The adoption benefits of digital technologies are realized differently over short-term vs. long-term. ATKearney (2015) conducted a study along with WHU-Otto Beisheim School of Management on the future role of digitalization in supply chains. The study indicated that most companies expect traditional benefits such as IT integration, use of big-data analytics to reduce outbound inventory costs, and reduction in paper-based processes over the next three years, whereas, over a longer period benefits such as 3D printing, robotics, and AI. Another important impact of the digitalization trend in supply chains is a reduction in traditional jobs such as operational logistics while increasing (slightly) the employment opportunities in the area of tactical and strategic supply chain planning utilizing the technology.

Figure 4 depicts the interactions between different supply chain entities in the digital supply chain setting. This shows that due to digitalization, communication is possible among all the entities resulting in an agile, transparent, collaborative environment. In addition, there is a centralized supply chain coordinator, which has the ability to monitor, regulate, and control all these communication channels in alignment with the goals in step 1. As these communications can happen real-time, it is important to implement the technology such that the supply chains are highly responsive as well as flexible to the ever-changing needs of both internal and external customers. The most important implication of digitalization is an increase in transparency and faster communication across the supply chain. Next, a discussion on the track-and-trace technology based on blockchain is presented using business cases on Chipotle and DHL.

Track-and-Trace Technologies in the Supply Chain Using Blockchain: Chipotle And DHL

Digitalization increases visibility and transparency across the supply chain and helps businesses to accurately track and trace the movement of goods and services in the supply chain. New technologies in logistics such as the use of radio-frequency identification (RFID) and Bluetooth are used in inventory management to track them in the warehouses, trucks, and on the shelves. In conjunction with mobile, wireless networks, and satellite communications these technologies can be used in global supply chains. The absence of supply chain visibility makes it difficult for businesses to identify the root-cause for defects in the product and can lead to quality issues in end products.

A recent example is with Chipotle in late 2015 (Forbes, 2016). Multiple people in Simi Valley California came down with norovirus, followed by, more people sickened by Salmonella-tainted tomatoes. Finally, in November 2015, more than 100 students in Boston picked up E. Coli. All these incidents were traced back to Chipotle restaurants, which resulted in the revenue decrease of 6.8% for Chipotle. Subsequently, the same store sales declined by 14%, net income decreased by 44%, and the stock price plummeted 39%. The brand value of Chipotle has not revived fully and consumers are still skeptical about the quality of food at Chipotle. This issue was a result of supplier issues which was difficult to trace back to the actual suppliers in absence of any track-and-trace systems. Track-and-trace systems based on blockchain technology is the answer to Chipotle's problems and the problem in general of maintaining supply chain visibility (see for e.g.; Casey and Wong, 2017).

Another example of track-and-trace technology is DHL's partnership with Accenture to prevent counterfeiting of drugs using blockchain technology (DHL, 2018). It is estimated that counterfeit drugs result in the death of about 1 million people every year. In this partnership, DHL will incorporate blockchain into pharmaceutical supply chain via a track-and-trace serialization system. This would enable DHL to securely capture the unique identifier of each unit of a pharmaceutical shipment as it moves through the supply chain, thereby securing the supply chain from any counterfeits. José F. Nava, Chief Development Officer, DHL Supply Chain, said on this – "The technology is nascent, yet promising, and we are excited about the opportunities it could bring to our customers in the future."

Overall, the degree of supply chain digitalization depends on the previous steps, especially the corporate goals (short-term and long-term), customer needs and the type of industry (or product) of the business. More interestingly, there are well-known benefits of digitalization yet there is still some time for businesses to realize the full potential of the implementation. Additionally, it is important for both academics and business to be aware of the changes in employment trends due to supply chain digitalization leading to a reduction in the traditional logistics and operations jobs, and an increase in more tactical and strategic opportunities.

Figure 4. Digitalized supply chain interactions

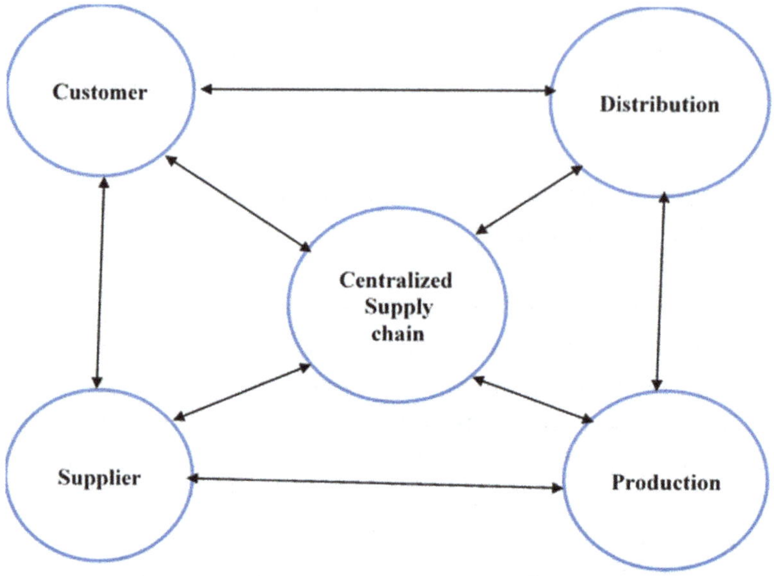

Step 5: Digitalization of Procurement Process Based on Customer, Product, and Supply Chain

It is important to fully understand the process and impacts of digitalization of customer experience, product, and the supply chain before moving forward with planning and implementing the procurement process digitalization. As mentioned previously, procurement digitalization is not a novel concept and started in the early 1980s with the implementation of EDI systems and more recently at the dawn of the 20th century with IBM's implementation of RMSS. Compared with traditional passive procurement strategies, digital procurement strategies are more responsive and requires collaboration from end-to-end in the supply chain including customers and the product. As shown in Figure 4, there is communication between all supply chain entities and for procurement (supply-side) to be effective and value-adding to the business the procurement strategies must align with the corporate goals, customer needs, product strategies, and other supply chain strategies. The digitalization and its effective use in procurement is **Procurement 4.0** (see for e.g.; Glas and Kleeman, 2016; Nicoletti, 2018), discussed in detail in the following by first providing a description followed by its advantages and the best practices.

Procurement 4.0

Industry 4.0 is referred to as the fourth industrial revolution, which is a direct result of rapidly evolving digital technologies such as machine learning, AI, big-data analytics, robotics, etc. that are transforming and changing customer needs (*cf.* Tjahjono et al. 2017). The impact and implementation of the industry 4.0 technologies in procurement is Procurement 4.0. This evolution is shown in Figure 5, which shows the evolution of procurement systems from MRP (material requirements planning) systems in the early 19th century to ERP (enterprise resource planning) systems in the 1990s, followed by eProcurement (e.g.; Davila et al., 2003) and most recently as Procurement 4.0. This change has seen an increase in the breadth of supply chain integration of technology as well as an increase in automation of processes which were manual and required human intervention. At the same point, the survey study by Glas and Kleeman (2016) indicates that the implementation of Procurement 4.0 must assure the dynamic cooperation of the supply chain members or organizations which benefits all collaborators. This must be done while ensuring that the risk exposure for the business is not increased due to issues with digitalization such as data leaks or misuse of information by supply chain members. In a more recent study, Bienhaus and Haddud (2018) indicated that Procurement 4.0 can result in benefits such as: supporting daily business and administrative tasks, and complex decision-making processes, more focus on strategic decisions and activities, organizational efficiency, effectiveness, and profitability, and supporting the creation of new business models, products, and services. Bär et al. (2018) discuss the implementation of Industry 4.0 and develop a new 5-step framework for small and medium-sized enterprises (SMEs), providing a manual for Industry 4.0 implementation. This framework can help the practitioners and SMEs on developing a competitive advantage for their companies based on a unique customer experience (see Figure 4) which is critical to Industry 4.0 (and Procurement 4.0) implementation.

Step 6: Measure Value Added by Digitalization and Redefine Goals, Repeat Steps 1-6

Once the roadmap for digitalization is prepared and implemented, the next step is to measure the impact of digitalization on the business. Once the impact is measured, it needs to be compared with the corporate goals set in the first step of the six-step framework. In case, there is any gap between the realized impact of digitalization vis-à-vis the projections made in step 1, the goals need to be refined and/or redefined to leverage the benefits of digitalization. This is needed to ensure a continuous improvement culture across the business units and across the supply chain members. At this stage, it may be necessary to collaborate with other supply chain members and also obtain customer feedback to improve the implementation of digital technologies in the business aligning them with the redesigned corporate goals.

Figure 5. Evolution of Procurement Systems from MRP (material requirements planning) to Procurement 4.0 with an increase in automation and breadth of supply chain integration

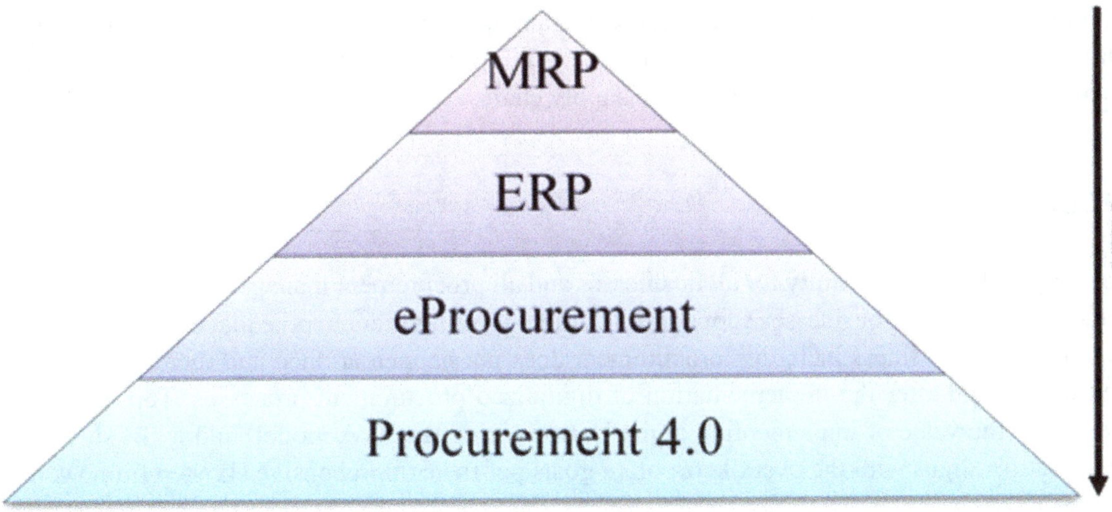

Digitalization is not an overnight success and does not stop after implementation; it is a continuous improvement process that needs to be analyzed, measured, redefined, and improved from time-to-time. This cycle can be monthly, quarterly, annual or it can even extend to once every 2-5 years based on the lifecycle of the technology or the rapid evolution of customer needs. Some of the best practices associated with this continuous improvement culture in a business are:

1. Executive commitment and culture of support,
2. Effective collaboration and communication between functional units and supply chain members, and
3. Effective and comprehensive measurements or KPIs for evaluating digitalization.

Most digitalization measures fail because of lack of commitment from the top management who are not willing to invest time and resources in digitalizing or are not willing to give the technology enough time to become effective. Sometimes the top management fails to see the rapidly evolving industry trends in digitalization such as the importance of cybersecurity, the importance of transparency and visibility, etc. At the same time, it is important for the company to maintain a culture of support that entails effective support and communication between all the business units as well across the company hierarchy. Effective communication helps to identify the issues with digitalization and provides opportunities for the company to use digitalization tools in a more comprehensive way that benefits all business units and supply chain members. Finally, it is important to have comprehensive measures that capture the impact of digitalization from end-to-end in the supply chain and on the business. This must include all the relevant business processes such as forecasting (demand predictions), inventory accuracy and management, the total cost of goods sold, order cycle times, lead-times from order to delivery, etc. With digitalization, it is easier to record and access such data across the supply chain, it is also important to digitalize those aspects of operations, which can enable effective measuring of KPIs such as tracking inventory or products across the supply chain.

After measuring and analyzing all the KPIs, and accordingly redefining the goals, the business must again implement steps 1 to 6 as presented in Figure 3. Digitalization is a cyclical process that ensures continuous improvements and value-add with newer uses of technology that can help businesses to gain a competitive advantage by reducing costs, increasing revenues, in addition to realizing process efficiencies through automation and robotics. The six-step framework presented in this section can be used by procurement managers and business leaders in implementing and evaluating the efficacy of digitalization of procurement processes as well as the entire supply chains.

CONCLUSION

Digital supply chains are a reality for all businesses and all procurement managers must be aware of the best practices when their businesses adopt digitalization. It is important to note that digitalization across all domains of the business including procurement does not happen at once and there will be lessons learned during and after the implementation of digitalized procurement processes. Top management must evaluate the value of implementing digitalization (using the EVA model) and make sure that the implementation aligns with the overall corporate goals per the comprehensive six-step framework laid out in the chapter.

Procurement strategies for digital supply chains are grounded in theory with roots in the demand-side, supply-side and the product-side of the business. It is important to fully understand the needs of the customers (both internal and external), characterize the product, evaluate the impact on the supply chain and then align the procurement process strategy with them. The digitalization of procurement processes does not end with implementation; its impact should be measured and evaluated to enhance the synergies across the entire supply chain as when as within all the functional units of the business.

Digital supply chains including the digitalization of procurement processes are not just a trend; it's a fundamental change in how businesses carry out their transactions and have significantly changed the landscape between the buyers and the suppliers. Digitalization, if used effectively can improve collaboration and be a win-win for all the parties, it is therefore critical to have all the parties on board with their full support to make digitalization of procurement successful.

FUTURE TRENDS IN PROCUREMENT STRATEGIES FOR DIGITAL SUPPLY CHAINS

Digital supply chains are the future and present many opportunities for all businesses to tap efficiencies and add value to their products and customer experience. Procurement is an important as well as a strategic component of all supply chains and with digital supply chains, its role is increasingly strategic and critical to the business. Procurement 4.0 will help businesses gain competitive advantage, reduce costs and increase revenues as well as with efficiency gains in operations by cutting down manual operations, make processes automated and highly responsive with increasing flexibility. This will be a must-have in the VUCA world with the advent of disruptive technologies and volatile global markets.

In the next few years, more companies will start to implement procurement digitalization strategies based on the following principles/ technologies (in alphabetical order):

1. **3D printing:** Procurement strategies which usually requires supplier selection, contract management, etc. will become dated once 3D printing is widely adopted by manufacturing companies. With 3D printing, components can be easily produced in a shorter duration of time in existing facilities without heavy dependence on suppliers or labor for production and then sourcing. Procurement strategies within the gambit of 3D printing will help companies with material cost savings as well as shorter production lead times.
2. **Blockchain:** Implementation of blockchain technology in procurement processes will result in an increased transparency and visibility of buyer-supplier transactions in the supply chains. For instance, DHL is currently collaborating with Accenture to prevent counterfeiting drugs in the pharmaceutical supply chain using trace-and-track technology, which has its backbone in the blockchain technology. Procurement strategies in future will make use of blockchain technology to secure the supply and maintain transparency in the entire process.
3. **Cyber Security:** Procurement professionals work with sensitive business information that may include customer and supplier financials, contracts, and pricing information. Traditional procurement operations such as invoicing, purchasing, tenders, etc. may result in a data breach resulting in the loss of sensitive information. Digitalization, if not implemented securely, makes it easier for breach and can result in heavy losses to the business including a loss of their competitive advantage.

4. **Nearshoring:** Nearshoring is the latest supply chain trend in which developed countries such as the United States (US) and countries in Western Europe are increasingly sourcing from nearby countries as the labor costs in developing countries such as China are increasing. According to a survey study by Alix Partners (2017), more than two-thirds of respondent companies were considering nearshoring as a possible alternative to meet the demands of the US and western Europe. This enables businesses to be more responsive due to shorter lead times. Nearshoring can also be driven by businesses looking to protect their intellectual property, reduce their shipping costs and is also beneficial for businesses looking for equitable labor regulations such as laws regarding the use of child labor in manufacturing.
5. **Corporate Social Responsibility (CSR) and Sustainability:** Another trend in digital procurement is the increasing need for businesses to invest their resources in CSR and other sustainability practices such as the use of renewable and recyclable resources in their operations. Sustainability based procurement is driven by two important factors – evolving consumer preferences for brands that emphasize sustainability and increasing government regulations to protect the environment such as reduction in carbon footprints and carbon trading laws.
6. **Talent Management:** Increasing digitalization in procurement has led to a decrease in traditional jobs such as logistics and purchasing. Procurement processes have become tactical and strategic, resulting in a different skill-set required for current and future employment in procurement based jobs. Finding the right talent and managing it will be critical as we observe increasing digitalization and use of newer technologies in procurement. A 2015 report by Deloitte emphasizes the importance of talent hunting and management in procurement and provides a roadmap for top management to do this effectively. For instance, the report highlights that leading procurement functional units are aggressively recruiting strong leadership candidates from the best universities, often offering highly attractive compensation. For example, in the consumer packaged goods industry, sell-side category managers are often future business leaders and CEOs. On the other hand, buy-side category managers essentially run their own mega-category, which is similar to running an entire services business. In conclusion, the future of procurement lies in effectively cultivating, mentoring, and managing talented and knowledgeable individuals who have the potential to be future business leaders.

To summarize, the overall trends in procurement strategies for digital supply chains, in the coming years, more and more companies will focus on technologies such as 3D printing and blockchain, business practices such as sustainability and nearshoring. None of this is possible without talented individuals, who know how to use these tools and best practices to effectively leveraging their business. On one hand, digitalization will lead to a reduction in traditional employment areas such as invoicing, logistics, and purchasing. On the other hand, there will be an increase in employment of talented individuals, who fully understand the digitalized supply chains and are able to harness them effectively.

LIMITATIONS AND SCOPE FOR FUTURE RESEARCH

This book chapter gives an overview of the introduction and the background for procurement strategies for digital supply chains with several case studies and tips for academics and practitioners. The contents in the book chapter are written with an organization and managerial view where procurement is the core or the organization or the focal process. Procurement processes, in practice, are also affected by the size of the organization and its supply chain partners, country, legal regulations, etc. which are not discussed in the current book chapter. In addition, as indicated in the section on future trends in procurement strategies, the procurement processes are undergoing radical changes and in the near future, some of the steps and processes which are highlighted in the book chapter may not be relevant anymore. Detailed future research must be carried out to observe and predict the changes in procurement strategies due to the implementation of Procurement 4.0 as part of Industry 4.0. It will also be interesting to see the detailed impact of the use of social media and social networks on Procurement 4.0. In a recent book chapter, Zincir et al. (2018) conducted a case study research on the procurement and supply chain professionals' online social network. Their study focused more on entrepreneurship and is an excellent reading for all those who are interested in the area of entrepreneurship. It will be interesting to see a more detailed study on online social networks with a focus of digitalization of the procurement processes. In conclusion, the area of procurement strategies for digital supply chains is still evolving rapidly and more studies are required in future to assess the overall impact of the process changes and to build useful case studies for academics and practitioners.

REFERENCES

Accenture. (n.d.). Retrieved from https://www.accenture.com/us-en/insight-digital-procurement-process

Ageshin, E. A. (2001). E-procurement at work: A case study. *Production and Inventory Management Journal*, *42*(1), 48–53.

Alix Partners. (2017). *Homeward bound: nearshoring continues, labor becomes a limiting factor, and automation takes root*. Retrieved from https://emarketing.alixpartners.com/rs/emsimages/2017/pubs/EI/AP_Strategic_Manufacturing_Sourcing_Homeward_Bound_Jan_2017.pdf

Angeles, R., & Nath, R. (2007). Business-to-business e-procurement: Success factors and challenges to implementation. *Supply Chain Management*, *12*(2), 104–115. doi:10.1108/13598540710737299

ATKearney. (2015). Retrieved from https://www.atkearney.com/operations-performance-transformation/article?/a/digital-supply-chains-increasingly-critical-for-competitive-edge

Bär, K., Herbert-Hansen, Z. N. L., & Khalid, W. (2018). Considering Industry 4.0 aspects in the supply chain for an SME. *Production Engineering*, 1–12.

Bienhaus, F., & Haddud, A. (2018). Procurement 4.0: Factors influencing the digitisation of procurement and supply chains. *Business Process Management Journal*, *24*(4), 965–984. doi:10.1108/BPMJ-06-2017-0139

Brinch, M., Stentoft, J., Jensen, J. K., & Rajkumar, C. (2018). Practitioners understanding of big data and its applications in supply chain management. *International Journal of Logistics Management*. (accepted for publication)

Büyüközkan, G., & Göçer, F. (2018). Digital Supply Chain: Literature review and a proposed framework for future research. *Computers in Industry*, *97*, 157–177. doi:10.1016/j.compind.2018.02.010

Casey, M., & Wong, P. (2017). Global supply chains are about to get better, thanks to blockchain. *Harvard Business Review*, 13.

Davila, A., Gupta, M., & Palmer, R. (2003). Moving procurement systems to the internet: The adoption and use of e-procurement technology models. *European Management Journal, 21*(1), 11–23. doi:10.1016/S0263-2373(02)00155-X

Deloitte. (2015). *Procurement talent management: Exceptional outcomes require exceptional people.* Retrieved from https://www2.deloitte.com/us/en/pages/operations/articles/procurement-talent-human-capital-management.html

DHL. (2018). Retrieved from https://www.dpdhl.com/en/media-relations/press-releases/2018/95-percent-of-companies-yet-to-realize-full-benefits-of-digitalization-technologies-for-supply-chains.html

Farahani, P., Meier, C., & Wilke, J. (2017). Digital supply chain management agenda for the automotive supplier industry. In *Shaping the digital enterprise* (pp. 157–172). Cham: Springer. doi:10.1007/978-3-319-40967-2_8

Forbes. (2012). *You Are In The Customer Experience Business, Whether You Know It Or Not.* Retrieved from https://www.forbes.com/sites/forrester/2012/08/28/you-are-in-the-customer-experience-business-whether-you-know-it-or-not/#7839e4025df8

Forbes. (2016). *Chipotle Lessons: Supply Chain Visibility and Higher Prices.* Retrieved from https://www.forbes.com/sites/kevinomarah/2015/12/16/chipotle-lessons-supply-chain-visibility-and-higher-prices/#24e6a5f2332b

Glas, A. H., & Kleemann, F. C. (2016). The impact of industry 4.0 on procurement and supply management: A conceptual and qualitative analysis. *International Journal of Business and Management Invention, 5*(6), 55–66.

Guadalupe, R. T. (2011). Compras Inteligentes. *Expansion Magazine.* Retrieved from https://expansion.mx/expansion/2011/09/14/compras-inteligentes

Ivanov, D., Tsipoulanidis, A., & Schönberger, J. (2018). Digital Supply Chain, Smart Operations and Industry 4.0. In Global Supply Chain and Operations Management (pp. 481-526). Springer.

Jordan, C. (2017). Curiosity, creativity and collaboration–creating a digitally integrated supply chain. *APPEA Journal, 57*(2), 477–480.

Mabert, V. A., & Schoenherr, T. (2001). An online RFQ system: A case study. *Practix, 4*(2), 1–6.

McKinsey & Co. (2017). Retrieved from https://www.mckinsey.com/industries/consumer-packaged-goods/our-insights/driving-superior-value-through-digital-procurement

Nath, A. K., Saha, P., & Salehi-Sangari, E. (2008). Transforming Supply Chains in Digital Content Delivery: A Case Study in Apple. In *Research and Practical Issues of Enterprise Information Systems II* (pp. 1079–1089). Boston, MA: Springer. doi:10.1007/978-0-387-76312-5_32

Neef, D. (2001). *E-Procurement: From strategy to implementation.* FT Press.

Nicoletti, B. (2018). The Future: Procurement 4.0. In *Agile Procurement* (pp. 189–230). Cham: Palgrave Macmillan. doi:10.1007/978-3-319-61085-6_8

Porter, M. E., & Heppelmann, J. E. (2014). How smart, connected products are transforming competition. *Harvard Business Review*, *92*(11), 64–88.

Presutti, W. D. Jr. (2003). Supply management and e-procurement: Creating value added in the supply chain. *Industrial Marketing Management*, *32*(3), 219–226. doi:10.1016/S0019-8501(02)00265-1

PwC. (2016). *Industry 4.0: How digitization makes the supply chain more efficient, agile, and customer-focused.* Retrieved from https://www.strategyand.pwc.com/media/file/Industry4.0.pdf

Rogers, D. L. (2016). *The digital transformation playbook: Rethink your business for the digital age.* Columbia University Press. doi:10.7312/roge17544

Thompson, M., Jones, G., & Lawson, A. (2000). *E-procurement: Purchasing in the Internet based economy.* Butler Group Report.

Tjahjono, B., Esplugues, C., Ares, E., & Pelaez, G. (2017). What does industry 4.0 mean to supply chain? *Procedia Manufacturing*, *13*, 1175–1182. doi:10.1016/j.promfg.2017.09.191

Turban, E., Outland, J., King, D., Lee, J. K., Liang, T. P., & Turban, D. C. (2018). Order Fulfillment Along the Supply Chain in e-Commerce. In *Electronic Commerce 2018* (pp. 501–534). Cham: Springer. doi:10.1007/978-3-319-58715-8_13

Van Weele, A. J. (2010). *Purchasing & supply chain management: analysis, strategy, planning and practice*. Cengage Learning EMEA.

Zincir, O., Ünal, A., & Erdal, M. (2017). Lean and Digital: A Case Study on Procurement and Supply Chain Professionals' Online Social Network. In Key Challenges and Opportunities in Web Entrepreneurship (pp. 79-102). IGI Global.

KEY TERMS AND DEFINITIONS

3D Printing: Is the process of creating three-dimensional products using computer technology. This process is currently used by businesses for rapid prototyping and additive manufacturing.

Big Data: Are large data sets that are so big and complex that conventional computers are unable to process the data at all or not in real time. Additionally, big data refers to the use of large volumes of data to make business decisions or to predict customer choices in real time using customer data.

Blockchain: Is a digital ledger that is decentralized, distributed and public. Blockchains are used to record transactions across many computers so that the records have the ability to be tracked and traced for any changes.

Digitalization: Is the process of converting information into a digital (bits – 0,1) format (i.e., readable by computers). This allows any information to be stored, processed, and transmitted easily by using a network of computers.

End-to-End Supply Chain: Refers to the philosophy of considering the entire supply chain starting from the customer to the end supplier, to eliminate any wasteful processes or middle steps, to optimize the entire supply chain.

E-Procurement: Is the process of electronic or online (web-based) network for buying and selling goods in a B2B setting or a B2C setting. It is also used by government organizations for procurement. Processes such as RFQ, RFP, etc. are conducted online in an e-Procurement setting.

Machine Learning/AI: Is the statistical process that gives machines the ability to learn and act intelligently (take decisions using information) by using historical data.

MRP: Is the process of production planning, scheduling production runs, and inventory control system used to manage manufacturing operations by eliminating waste and meeting customer demand.

Procurement: Is the process of finding, agreeing on terms and acquiring goods, services or works from an external source, often via a tendering or competitive bidding process. It is used to ensure the buyer receives goods, services or works at the best possible price when aspects such as quality, quantity, time, and location are compared.

Sustainability: Is an approach or the process where the use of non-renewable resources, economic investments, and the orientation or goal of development of business, government, or technology are all in harmony with each other. This ensures that there are enough resources for current and future generations with minimal impact on the environment.

ENDNOTES

[1] Refers to the use of customer information for delivering custom and highly personalized products, services, and content.

[2] Customer experience is how customers perceive their interactions with the business.

[3] Big data analytics examines very large amounts of data (such as consumer purchase behavior data) to discover hidden patterns, correlations, and other insights.

Chapter 3
Corporates in the Digital Age

Hammad Azzam
Independent Researcher, USA

ABSTRACT

A proposition for digital transformation of global groups into efficient enterprises is introduced. At the heart of the proposition is a transformational practice aimed at creating a customer-focused, data-driven global culture in any customer-serving company. The digital age has added a level of complexity to the way we acquire and serve customers. Doing a good job in the traditional channels is not enough anymore. Online is increasingly becoming the channel of choice with the two main customer-interaction paradigms: sell and service. And building a great customer experience is probably the most essential factor of success for both functions.

INTRODUCTION

The digital revolution is far more significant than the invention of writing or even of printing. - Douglas Engelbart

The world is flat. Global enterprises are undergoing disruptive paradigm shifts where thinking outside the box and working with cutting edge technologies will create extraordinary synergies. These synergies will help conglomerates push the envelope and will allow thought leaders to leverage human capital and technological assets to break down new barriers and make a step change in the performance of organizations.

If the above sounds like empty business-techno jargon to you, it's because it is. We will do our best in this chapter to avoid all such generic clichés and focus on pragmatic approaches to solve a monumental problem: "How is digital transformation changing with time?".

It's public knowledge that the single most important driver in any corporate transformation journey is digital transformation. If you don't already know that, then welcome back from your 3 years hibernation. Jump on your nearest WIFI so you can get up to speed with the crazy things that have been happening around the world while you were slumbering (just a teaser, Trump is president, France won the World Cup, and Britain existed the EU). Seriously though, there is no denying that digital is on every agenda. Few stats for you to know:

DOI: 10.4018/978-1-5225-7700-3.ch003

Copyright © 2019, IGI Global. Copying or distributing in print or electronic forms without written permission of IGI Global is prohibited.

- *$1.3 trillion will be spent on digital transformation technologies in 2018 (IDC, 2017)*
- *By 2019, 5% of revenue will come through interaction with a customer's digital assistant (IDC, 2016)*
- *By 2021, one third of CEOs and COOs of Fortune 2000 companies will have spent at least 5 years of their career in a technology leadership role (IDC, 2016)*
- *27% of senior executives consider digital transformation a matter of survival (Coleman, 2017)*
- *The biggest disruptive technologies, as specified by global respondents, are the cloud (58%), mobility and collaboration (54%) and data (52%) (DCO Conclave, 2018)*
- *By the end of 2018, two-thirds of the CEOs of Global 2000 companies will have digital transformation at the center of their corporate strategy (IDC, 2017)*

Self-service is the path forward. Companies are slowly transforming to serve customers by helping them serve themselves, and as companies put their new strategy statements together, digital is being mentioned in every other sentence as the main growth agent.

Growth itself is the most important goal of any corporation. To grow a business you have to constantly acquire new customers and retain them as long as possible. If your attrition rate (opposite of retention) is bigger than your acquiring rate, your business is doomed.

To acquire customers, you have to have a reasonably priced product appealing to a segment of the population.

To retain customers, you have to service your customers well once they are acquired.

Sounds simple and straightforward. It also sounds too obvious to even mention. It's like saying "to swim, you have to be in the vicinity of water" or "to have a successful business you will need to make money."

In reality however, the digital age have added a level of complexity to the way we acquire and serve customers. Doing a good job in the traditional channels is not enough anymore. Online is increasingly becoming the channel of choice with the two main interaction paradigms: sell and service.

It also became very clear even at the early stages of the digital, that the first wave of digital transformation was not very effective. Just exporting existing applications from call centers or retail locations to online does not create a successful digital solution. To truly create a great customer experience we need to enable a casual user like the customer (as opposed to a trained profession like call center reps) to successfully use the digital assets. That was the main driver of the second digital transformation wave which was all about customer experience. In the next four sections, we will explore the four important factors that are crucial to enabling a customer-driver digital transformation in an enterprise.

AVOID THE HYPE AND STAY GROUNDED

First and foremost is tackling the most obvious question: Why are companies struggling with customer experience practices and why dream results like the ones we see in Amazon or Google are so out of reach for so many companies? Executive teams are so obsessed with these companies they have created acronyms for them -- FANG (Facebook, Amazon, Netflix, Google) or FAAMG, etc. To be fair, it's an interesting question and deserves some space in this chapter. The revenue of just four companies, Apple, Amazon, Google and Facebook, is around $600 Billion. That's equivalent to the GDP of the following countries put together:

Gabon, North Korea, Brunei, Mozambique, Iceland, Cambodia, Equatorial Guinea, Papua New Guinea, Georgia, Botswana, Senegal, Zimbabwe, Congo, Republic of the, Jamaica, Namibia, Albania, Chad, Burkina Faso, Mauritius, Mongolia, Mali, Nicaragua, Laos, Macedonia, South Sudan, Armenia, Madagascar, Malta, New Caledonia, Benin, Tajikistan, Haiti, The Bahamas, Niger, Moldova, Rwanda, Kyrgyzstan, Kosovo, Monaco, Guinea, Liechtenstein, Malawi, French Polynesia, Bermuda, Suriname, Mauritania, Timor-Leste, Sierra Leone, Montenegro, Togo, Fiji, Swaziland, Barbados, Eritrea, Cayman Islands, Andorra, Curaçao, Guyana, Maldives, Burundi, Aruba, Greenland, Liberia, Lesotho, Bhutan, Cape Verde, San Marino, Central African Republic, Belize, Djibouti, Seychelles, Saint Lucia, Somalia, Zanzibar, Antigua and Barbuda, Guinea-Bissau, Solomon Islands, Sint Maarten, British Virgin Islands, Grenada, Saint Kitts and Nevis, The Gambia, Samoa, Vanuatu, Turks and Caicos Islands, Saint Vincent and the Grenadines, Comoros, Dominica, Tonga, São Tomé and Príncipe, Federated States of Micronesia, Cook Islands, Anguilla, Palau, Marshall Islands, Nauru, Kiribati, Montserrat and Tuvalu put together!

They must be doing something right!

Looking closely at FANG, you will notice that they never relied on overhyped initiatives. Their most profitable programs are well within-the-box ventures. The differentiator is execution. All hyped efforts are done for pure research and PR.

This is what we will explore in this chapter. The lines between futuristic concepts and practical implementations is not that thin, yet frequently organizations jump that line and dive heads on into science fiction like endeavors that are good for nothing more than a Hollywood effect. We will focus on what makes business sense and what needs to be done to move the digital train forward. We believe in three main paradigms that are prerequisites for digital transformation:

- Impeccable Technology Implementation: Including customer experience, usability and stack stability
- Customer-obsessiveness
- Artificial Intelligence

This chapter will address the first two.

FOCUS ON IMPLEMENTATION

So, why do so many fail to replicate the fantastic user experiences that these elites have mastered? Why can't every company have these capabilities? Why can't everyone have that edge? Well, for starters, if everyone has it, it won't be an edge. If all companies can do these experiences effectively, customer experience will stop being a differentiator. Remember, to mathematically have superbly performing top 1%, you need to have tons of mediocre ones. There is still a lot of room for hard working, persistent, deep-pocketed enterprises to quantum-advance their customer experience, so why are we not seeing that happening often enough? Let me put on the table my theory, most of which are really opinions from experience.

First and foremost, there is a clear misunderstanding of what constitutes customer experience. Executive are convinced of the argument that engineers cannot build anything remotely usable and they need the UI/UX teams to really take the lead and make that significant jump into usability. UI eccentrics would love to tell you it's the sexy, beautiful front end screens that matter. UX teams would swear that it's all about the experience overall (flows, interactions, etc.) not just the look and feel. Engineers would focus on the correctness, stability and scalability of the application. The reality is all three disciplines are important, but engineering takes center stage. We are not discounting the importance of usability and customer experience, but rather than bringing another standalone discipline to the game, you need to equip your engineering organizations with the right usability-focused design/engineering resources. Separation of the two disciplines is the wrong thing to do. The core of the organization needs to be great engineering teams and usability needs to be instilled in the organizations DNA, not sit outside manufacturing exquisite UI and smooth flowing flows.

Every customer facing application consists of two parts:

1. Things You See. That includes the screens you browse, the paths you traverse, the errors you come across, etc. Most of that is built by engineers and UI teams and is governed by UX teams, as it should be.
2. Things You Don't See. That includes everything that goes on under the hood to make the application run well.

Corporate executives think that good experience is about the first, "Things You See". In reality, that is barely the tip of the iceberg. The majority of poorly performing websites and applications suffer from issues related to "Things You Don't See". Sounds very theoretical and abstract, so let's roll up the sleeves and zoom in.

"Things You See" is about designing the screens, the flows and the usability of the interface. It's about creating the web pages or the mobile screens that make sense from a customer perspective. Every screen should have easily understandable language, logically progressing flows and proper exception handling.

"Things You Don't See" is about everything else. It's about the web server, the authentication/authorization engines, the security framework, the logging framework, the session tracking application, the cloud services, the internal APIs, the external APIs, the load balancer, the application servers, the ports, the firewalls, the middleware, the databases, the messaging queues, the workflow manager, the Hadoop framework, the Kafka servers, the core platforms, the mainframes, the hardware, the EMC drives, IDMZ/EDMZ, the fault tolerance platforms, the data center, etc. The points of failures are almost infinite in this complex, technology behemoth.

My contention is that most poorly performing websites and applications get their low marks on the "Things You Don't See" while most executive teams focus on "Things You See". ***It's all about building a correctly functioning, consistent, stable stack.*** There is no argument that aesthetics matter and eye candy enhance digital applications, but that is only a tiny piece of the good experience puzzle. A website UI needs to be good looking, but not necessarily mold-breaking. We are building a business application, not the next generation Hollywood visual effect box office blockbuster. Look at the most successful innovations out there and you will clearly see that beautiful UI is not a differentiator. Google Search is almost UI-less. Amazon is nothing to write home about. In fact, their website UI is borderline mediocre and it feels like something that an 18 year old savvy high school student can put together. Facebook front end is barely ok. Apple might be an exception. They pay extraordinary attention to aesthetics and it seems to be part of the brand. Based on these few data points, correlation between UI and success does not exist. Good UI is good enough. What is more important is to build a flawlessly performing stack.

Let's take closer look at Amazon. Why do we love that company? Is it because of the sexy website? Is it because of the graphics? Is it because of user experience? Is it because of the prices? The answer is "No" to all these questions. There is nothing beautiful about their website and no mind blowing structure in its flows that stands out. And if you want better prices, just go to your nearest Walmart.

We love amazon because of the following very important and very boring features:

1. The website works every time. Every click on every page has a very predictable outcome. I have never ever seen a technical error, a "page cannot be displayed" response, or slow performance/timeout on their site. If I want to know if there is a problem with my WIFI connection, I check Amazon or Google websites. That's how stable their stack is.
2. Their fulfillment process works every time. They give me an estimated day of delivery and almost every time the item arrives on schedule. They have never failed to deliver one single item to my doorstep. And they have rarely failed on quality. I almost always get what I expect.
3. Their customer support is a true customer support. You will almost never hang up unhappy with them.

The anecdotes about the amazing exchanges that people had with Amazon Customer Support are almost endless. Each of us has either experienced it firsthand or heard it from close acquaintances. Sometimes it's about a package that arrived late (to make up for that Amazon refunded the customer, while the customer kept the product.) Another maybe about the product that never arrived, so Amazon sent another one. When both arrived and, being the honest man that you are, you called to inform them, you were told to keep both items as a little gift from Amazon. Granted these practices might be expensive, but they have made great impact on customer base through the best marketing tool of all: word of mouth. Amazon is willing to lose great margins for the sake of keeping the customer happy.

KEEP YOUR EYES ON THE CUSTOMER

Even if you make it idiot-proof someone will make a better idiot to break it

Getting a fully functional, stable, usable stack is not enough. A good digital team needs to also make sure that the application in place is servicing the customer well. The best way to make sure that the customer is happy is to obsessively watch every step he takes, every move he makes, and every word he says.

All tactical and strategic decisions at all levels need to be driven by the customer. In other words, the company needs to be customer-centric, which usually comes in one of two forms:

1. *Customer-centric by name*, where the company touts its focus on the customer in presentations, in meetings, in mission statements, in high level strategic discussions, around the water fountain, in executive off-sites and every other PR venue possible.

2. *Real customer-centric companies*, where every employee is engaged every day, first and foremost with the customer, whether it's directly through the traditional channels, or indirectly through extraction of reports and insights about the customer behavior last week, yesterday, and even an hour ago.

And if you had problem getting my borderline sarcastic message, let me be more explicit. 1 is bad. 2 is good. However, 1 is easy. 2 is very hard. Most companies are somewhere in the middle of these two models with tendency to be closer to 1. Given how anxious all executives teams about building a great customer experience, it's surprising how little energy is spend on that. As a CEO, to get a good sense of how customer centric your company is, ask yourself the following questions:

- **Operations:** How often do I, and everyone in my organization, look at customer feedback. In any good size enterprise, customers leave hundreds, if not thousands, of comments every day on websites, on mobile apps, in branches and in every other channel. If there exists a properly formatted, easy to read data that your management team is looking at every day (won't take more than 10 minutes) to get a feel on what's happening on the ground, then customer-centricity is on your radar screen. If not, then you are leaving the most important part of the company's strategy out of your immediate agenda.
- **Strategy:** Are all your strategic decisions driven by what your customers are telling you, directly or indirectly? Are you driving how you invest in the company through your understanding of what your customers want and need? If yes, then you are customer centric.

Customer centricity is so important that it cannot be left to a specialized department to manage. It has to be sown into the fabric of the company's operations, at every level and in every organization. Fifteen years ago, this was very hard to do. Now, it's do-able, not easily, but do-able!

The journey to really make sense of the humanely-incomprehensible digital footprints that the customers leave behind is very difficult but the prize is well worth it. Some customers leave plenty of feedback behind, but many don't. It's extremely important to digest the feedback, but what's more important is to know the state of mind of those that don't communicate at all. These silent customers that click away on apps and websites are sending, in hidden code, thousands of messages every day telling enterprises what they can do to serve them better. Every requirement, every enhancement and every feature in every project should be derived from what feels like an infinity of unstructured clutter. The fact that the digital wave sweeping enterprises come with disproportionate increase in customer traffic makes the problem even harder. Not only customers are becoming digital, they are coming to our doorsteps 10 times more often than they used to. This tsunami of footprint makes it harder and harder for the enterprises to keep their arms around the customer. As less customers visit the traditional channels and more customers connect digitally, our ability to understand what customers need and want is diminishing and the pursuit to become customer focused is becoming harder. In call centers, stores, or other traditional channels, customers will communicate their intent explicitly and we learn what's on their minds firsthand. Online customers, on the other hand, are rarely verbose and we will increasingly need to do forensic work to really understand what's on their mind. The trick to successfully manage a digital stack is figuring out how to extract simplified insights from the piles of logs. These insights will be part of a continuous feedback loop that will real-time course correct the performance of the channel.

Static Insights

The types of data to be monitored will vary and new reports need to be created continuously to keep the organization informed and up to date. There are however a certain set of static reports that are essential to the performance of the company and need to be in place first and foremost. These reports will focus on four aspects of customer behavior that are critical to successfully serve the customer.

The first batch is transaction reports. These are mostly business reports detailing transactions performance on a daily basis. They reflect the business performance of the organization and need to be circulated daily to the whole organization to keep everyone on the same page.

The second batch is error reports. These reports should have detailed views of all exceptions with indicators to show which ones are spiking on the last day. There are two types of errors to track, acceptable and unacceptable. Acceptable errors are correct and valid responses to failing scenarios. For example, when a customer enters the wrong password on a website, the proper response need to be handled and an error needs to be logged into the system. The unacceptable errors are technical issues or mishandled exceptions that are completely unexpected. Usually the acceptable errors are much more than the unacceptable ones and organizations strive to eliminate the second type. However a spike in any type of error (acceptable or not) needs to be addressed immediately. A "wrong password" error spike is most likely related to a systemic issue, rather than a sudden increase in the erroneous passwords entered by the customer.

The third set is performance reports. That should include response times of backend systems and screen performance and snappiness. Properly optimized applications have a number of benefits for the company and the customer including better customer conversion, reduced hosting costs, and improved Google Search ranking.

Last but not least, customer feedback reports. These reports will show, in a structured way, the feedback customers leave behind.

Every self-respecting executive wants to constantly know what's going with the customer. The problem is that retrieving and digesting that information is just too hard. Important, properly distilled data is very hard to come by and getting that information in easy to sip doses is mission impossible. That is at the core of the concepts we propose. No matter how complex the problem, creating the easy to understand reports is a must. The skill of converting the heaps of data into a form share-able with the world is a must-have skillset for every manager.

Executive management teams need to be the first in line. The reason they don't dive daily into customer data is not because they prefer to spend their time in high level management meetings, off-sites, presentations, etc. The real reason is the lack of worthy reports.

When the full structure is in place, the benefits to the corporation will be immense. With executives watching the company's performance daily, the impact on the team will be great. The organization will be self-correcting. Before issues are spotted by the CEO, or the CIO, the vice president is aware and working the problem. Before the vice president picks up the phone to call the director about the issue, the coder is already fixing the code. He/she knows that everyone up the chain is seeing the problems he sees and his/her phone is about to start ringing. Before the CMO get the chance to ask about the lack of progress on sales after the campaign that launched yesterday, the business analyst is doing the investigation and working on course correction with the rest of the marketing team. This transparency in viewing the data can put everyone on the same page and align the organization behind what's important, the customer and the results.

Dynamic Insights

Obvious is the most dangerous word in Mathematics - E.T. Bell

Sometimes, hidden in the deep folds of obvious statements are false assumptions that lead to disastrous results. Instinctive reactions are helpful and true most of the time, but occasionally they are barely correct, and in some rare cases they are completely off. Take for the example the little trick we show in Figure 1. If you track the logic, you'll find it impenetrable, almost. I mean how could it be all true? It's a shot at the basic fundamentals of mathematics.

If you are the kind of person that always wants to solve the puzzle without help, then stop reading now and go bang your head against the table trying to CSI the problem. For those not in the mood, let me explain the very little and obscure hole in the logic above. The problem is in the second line. When we derived by x, we did not account for the change in the length of the right side. dy/dx is change of y divided by a change of x. As x changes, each entry in the sum changes by dx, but also the length of the series itself changes proportionally, impacting all the individual x increments.

This section of the chapter is about how to see the obscure, and how to systematically construct insights from data without falling into the trap of the obvious. Data is everywhere now. Chief Data Officers are popping up like daisies in the corporate world and they keep making their way upwards, justifiably so. The data compound is large and complex. As new data points get created, the permutations needed to extract truths grow exponentially. And the demand is growing proportionally. Hardly a day goes by without breakthrough articles being published that accentuate the importance of running data driven organizations in every company and at all levels. This borderline-unhealthy obsession with data has sent many corporations chasing dreams that are nonconcrete and, in some cases, imaginary. Worse, many groups and organizations are blindingly pursuing the abstract concept without really understanding what

Figure 1. How to entertain a mathematician!

$$y = \overbrace{x + x + x + \cdots + x}^{\text{x-time}} = x^2$$

$$\frac{dy}{dx} = \overbrace{1 + 1 + 1 + \cdots . +1}^{\text{x-times}} = 2x$$

$$\frac{dy}{dx} = x = 2x$$

$$x = 2x$$

$$1=2$$

bottom line to pursue. The outcome, more often than not, is an organizational structure and a mission statement that do not tie, in any form, to the principal goals of the company.

To be clear, we are not discounting the significance of data. In fact we unreservedly believe that data will have more impact on the digital transformation journey than any other concept. Collecting, distilling and acting on the data is the only way to create the intelligent machinery that can help the organization run effectively and efficiently.

To less abstractly explain the benefits of running a data-driven organization, we will demonstrate the concepts of this section using a scaled down model which is devised purely for illustrative purposes. Our model, Tinymart, is a successful supermarket chain with 10 stores sprinkled on the US map. They sell 10 products called mini1 through mini10 and they are open weekdays from 8 AM to 10 PM and on weekend from noon to 6 PM. Christina Ellen Orlando is the CEO and she feels that running companies came second nature to her since early years of adulthood. Christina relies on her data officer, Douglass Oak, to get accurate details of the performance of the company.

The most basic report will have the number of items sold every day, by store and the revenue associated with every sale. That is a straightforward, easily generate-able view that makes sense. However, it's pretty much useless. It will look like a spreadsheet with product names and number of items sold by store (see Figure 2). It's actually not really completely useless, but it requires serious effort to understand what the numbers mean. Let's for example take the data point Mini1 sales in Store 2. Looking at the number by itself is meaningless. Looking at it in comparison with the rest of the stores is more insightful. The first question that comes to mind: why is Store 2 the lowest selling store for Mini1? Now data is starting to stand out. An obvious answer is maybe because Store2 is a smaller store, or maybe it's the worst location of the bunch. That theory does not hold ground. If that is the case then why are other products performing better in Store2? Store2 Mini1 sales are low because of something else. That last statement is a fantastic find. It's a vector, with magnitude and direction, pointing towards the best places to investigate, fix and improve performance.

Take this one step further. You don't want to scan the table looking for the low numbers. You want the low performing numbers to stand out. So instead of showing the raw data, Figure 4 shows the relative performance of every product in every store. This is accomplished by simply dividing each cell by the average sale for a product per store. For example, on average, Mini1 sold 6.8 units per store. That is the baseline for Mini1. Any store selling more than 6.8 Mini1 units is doing better than the average. Any store selling less than 6.8 Mini1 units is doing worse than average. Store 2 sold one Mini1 unit, which is

Figure 2. Corporate product sales by store and product

	Store1	Store2	Store3	Store4	Store5	Store6	Store7	Store8	Store9	Store10
Mini1	9	1	5	6	8	7	10	10	5	7
Mini2	6	9	6	5	10	7	9	9	8	9
Mini3	5	6	9	10	7	8	10	7	10	8
Mini4	6	10	9	5	5	7	5	6	6	10
Mini5	7	10	10	9	9	6	5	5	8	8
Mini6	9	7	7	5	7	7	6	7	10	9
Mini7	8	5	8	7	5	6	9	10	10	9
Mini8	7	10	10	7	5	5	7	8	8	6
Mini9	5	9	10	10	6	10	7	10	5	7
Mini10	9	7	9	10	5	10	8	8	6	5

15% of the average, clearly underperforming compared to the rest of the stores. Now color code the cells and the bad performers will stand out (in red in Figure 4). The end result is a simple way to effortlessly glance at a report and spot actionable issues.

If what is more relevant is to compare how the products perform compared to each other in the same store, then Figure 5 is more fitting. Essentially, it shows the performance of each product baselined by the average the average number of units sold in the same store. After that, color coding will help you see which product is doing less than the rest in a specific store. An example for clarification, the third column shows the sales, by product, of Store 2. Sales of each product in that store are:

Mini1: 1
Mini2: 9
Mini3: 6
Mini4: 10
Mini5: 10
Mini6: 7
Mini7: 5
Mini8: 10
Mini9: 9
Mini10:7

Figure 3. Corporate product sales by store, with average

	Store1	Store2	Store3	Store4	Store5	Store6	Store7	Store8	Store9	Store10	Average
Mini1	9	1	5	6	8	7	10	10	5	7	6.8
Mini2	6	9	6	5	10	7	9	9	8	9	7.8
Mini3	5	6	9	10	7	8	10	7	10	8	8
Mini4	6	10	9	5	5	7	5	6	6	10	6.9
Mini5	7	10	10	9	9	6	5	5	8	8	7.7
Mini6	9	7	7	5	7	7	6	7	10	9	7.4
Mini7	8	5	8	7	5	6	9	10	10	9	7.7
Mini8	7	10	10	7	5	5	7	8	8	6	7.3
Mini9	5	9	10	10	6	10	7	10	5	7	7.9
Mini10	9	7	9	10	5	10	8	8	6	5	7.7

Figure 4: Corporate product sale by store, with significant drops highlighted

	Store1	Store2	Store3	Store4	Store5	Store6	Store7	Store8	Store9	Store10
Mini1	132%	15%	74%	88%	118%	103%	147%	147%	74%	103%
Mini2	77%	115%	77%	64%	128%	90%	115%	115%	103%	115%
Mini3	63%	75%	113%	125%	88%	100%	125%	88%	125%	100%
Mini4	87%	145%	130%	72%	72%	101%	72%	87%	87%	145%
Mini5	91%	130%	130%	117%	117%	78%	65%	65%	104%	104%
Mini6	122%	95%	95%	68%	95%	95%	81%	95%	135%	122%
Mini7	104%	65%	104%	91%	65%	78%	117%	130%	130%	117%
Mini8	96%	137%	137%	96%	68%	68%	96%	110%	110%	82%
Mini9	63%	114%	127%	127%	76%	127%	89%	127%	63%	89%
Mini10	117%	91%	117%	130%	65%	130%	104%	104%	78%	65%

The average number of units sold per product in Store 2 is 7.4. Dividing each entry for Store 2 by the average you get:

Mini1: 14%
Mini2: 122%
Mini3: 81%
Mini4: 135%
Mini5: 135%
Mini6: 95%
Mini7: 68%
Mini8: 135%
Mini9: 122%
Mini10:95%

Finally, color coding shows the underperforming products, Mini 1 in this case.

Suppose the demographics that each store serves vary widely. Let's take Figure 6 for example. The population that Store 9 service is much larger than that of the rest and the stores. Also Store 2 population is much smaller than the rest. Any comparative views are useless. What will be useful in this case is to normalize the table by the population. Basically divide every entry by the total number of customers serviced by that store. The result is a view that differentiates the performance of a store regardless of the population served.

So, putting data in a spreadsheet and circulating it by email is a useless act. On the other hand, designing and building properly structured, insights-extracting, efficient reports can help you run a company efficiently.

Figure 5. Corporate product sale with store drops highlighted

	Store1	Store2	Store3	Store4	Store5	Store6	Store7	Store8	Store9	Store10
Mini1	9	1	5	6	8	7	10	10	5	7
Mini2	6	9	6	5	10	7	9	9	8	9
Mini3	5	6	9	10	7	8	10	7	10	8
Mini4	6	10	9	5	5	7	5	6	6	10
Mini5	7	10	10	9	9	6	5	5	8	8
Mini6	9	7	7	5	7	7	6	7	10	9
Mini7	8	5	8	7	5	6	9	10	10	9
Mini8	7	10	10	7	5	5	7	8	8	6
Mini9	5	9	10	10	6	10	7	10	5	7
Mini10	9	7	9	10	5	10	8	8	6	5
Average	7.1	7.4	8.3	7.4	6.7	7.3	7.6	8	7.6	7.8

	Store1	Store2	Store3	Store4	Store5	Store6	Store7	Store8	Store9	Store10
Mini1	127%	14%	60%	81%	119%	96%	132%	125%	66%	90%
Mini2	85%	122%	72%	68%	149%	96%	118%	113%	105%	115%
Mini3	70%	81%	108%	135%	104%	110%	132%	88%	132%	103%
Mini4	85%	135%	108%	68%	75%	96%	66%	75%	79%	128%
Mini5	99%	135%	120%	122%	134%	82%	66%	63%	105%	103%
Mini6	127%	95%	84%	68%	104%	96%	79%	88%	132%	115%
Mini7	113%	68%	96%	95%	75%	82%	118%	125%	132%	115%
Mini8	99%	135%	120%	95%	75%	68%	92%	100%	105%	77%
Mini9	70%	122%	120%	135%	90%	137%	92%	125%	66%	90%
Mini10	127%	95%	108%	135%	75%	137%	105%	100%	79%	64%

Figure 6. Corporate product sale normalized by population

	Store1	Store2	Store3	Store4	Store5	Store6	Store7	Store8	Store9	Store10
Mini1	5715	2536	7937	6688	5622	5346	5667	7075	18042	9787
Mini2	6837	3208	8997	5182	9757	9081	6376	8908	12156	8789
Mini3	9973	3346	5864	8716	9960	5003	6303	7147	13765	6423
Mini4	7570	3030	8858	7304	6721	5635	7653	9729	17061	6550
Mini5	8657	3510	6818	6356	7592	9782	7565	7213	10645	6886
Mini6	8431	2067	6879	8813	9375	8206	7658	9632	12540	5527
Mini7	7060	3370	9347	5319	9194	8764	6265	6605	19973	8214
Mini8	8653	2265	8803	6084	9655	6393	9977	8832	17194	6228
Mini9	8217	3355	6271	5413	7378	5672	7694	5640	9396	6598
Mini10	6594	3357	8473	6301	8704	5774	8884	8213	9591	7240
Population	111544	62000	107059	102531	110690	115951	109059	106608	210000	103153

	Store1	Store2	Store3	Store4	Store5	Store6	Store7	Store8	Store9	Store10
Mini1	5	4	7	7	5	5	5	7	9	9
Mini2	6	5	8	5	9	8	6	8	6	9
Mini3	9	5	5	9	9	4	6	7	7	6
Mini4	7	5	8	7	6	5	7	9	8	6
Mini5	8	6	6	6	7	8	7	7	5	7
Mini6	8	3	6	9	8	7	7	9	6	5
Mini7	6	5	9	5	8	8	6	6	10	8
Mini8	8	4	8	6	9	6	9	8	8	6
Mini9	7	5	6	5	7	5	7	5	4	6
Mini10	6	5	8	6	8	5	8	8	5	7
Average	7.1	7.4	8.3	7.4	6.7	7.3	7.6	8	7.6	7.8

	Store1	Store2	Store3	Store4	Store5	Store6	Store7	Store8	Store9	Store10
Mini1	127%	14%	60%	81%	119%	96%	132%	125%	66%	90%
Mini2	85%	122%	72%	68%	149%	96%	118%	113%	105%	115%
Mini3	70%	81%	108%	135%	104%	110%	132%	88%	132%	103%
Mini4	85%	135%	108%	68%	75%	96%	66%	75%	79%	128%
Mini5	99%	135%	120%	122%	134%	82%	66%	63%	105%	103%
Mini6	127%	95%	84%	68%	104%	96%	79%	88%	132%	115%
Mini7	113%	68%	96%	95%	75%	82%	118%	125%	132%	115%
Mini8	99%	135%	120%	95%	75%	68%	92%	100%	105%	77%
Mini9	70%	122%	120%	135%	90%	137%	92%	125%	66%	90%
Mini10	127%	95%	108%	135%	75%	137%	105%	100%	79%	64%

The art of the reporting is also an important enabler. Data has to be shared daily, in emails (not on websites or portals) and has to be straightforward and easy to understand effortlessly. Figure 7 is an example that shows how a 30 second glance at a table will allow anyone to know exactly what is working well and what's not (1 means yesterday's performance was like the average of the past 10 weeks. 1.2 means 20% better than the average. 0.5 means 50% less than the average). Nothing in the report requires explanation. It's blasphemy to use engineering terms. You cannot have a row titled "Transaction 4325", or "ord_fbr_rsd". Instead titles should be in plain terms that a person not familiar with the program can understand, like "New Fiber Residential Orders." Note the use of the word yesterday, instead of a specific date. You basically want to minimize effort when it comes to reading the data. It all has to be self-explanatory and straightforward and all data need to be actionable with no need for deciphering and analysis. This is in line with the theme of the whole chapter. Usability is not about creating beautiful art. Usability is about exerting energy in creating easy-to-understand themes across the company.

LOOK FORWARD: AI

No data-driving digital transformation discussion is complete without a section on Artificial intelligence. No doubt we will need tens if not hundreds of data scientists running forensic jobs across all channels in order to produce new batches of intelligent reports, especially with the impending Internet of Things

Figure 7. Corporate product sale by date with sale drops highlighted

		Yesterday	Yesterday-7	Yesterday-14	Yesterday-21	Yesterday-28	Yesterday-35	Yesterday-42	Yesterday-49	Yesterday-56	Yesterday-63
Mini1	0.523	4343	2812	7559	7660	7437	8539	9214	7598	17161	6790
Mini2	1.038	8407	3714	9330	6402	9759	9835	9103	6836	9406	6629
Mini3	0.785	6557	3876	8324	9520	7886	8078	9838	7193	15153	9437
Mini4	1.135	9421	2560	7237	8767	7578	9735	5637	7362	11321	9962
Mini5	1.136	8934	2217	7300	7140	9855	6712	8609	8876	12442	8307
Mini6	1.067	8254	2663	7791	7167	6877	7640	6670	7856	13605	7576
Mini7	0.859	6257	3496	5113	5854	6543	7024	9475	5075	12706	7906
Mini8	1.142	8780	2748	7918	6644	9429	7710	9954	5181	17062	8509
Mini9	0.839	6915	2565	9330	6084	6073	9904	6805	5123	17790	9608
Mini10	0.991	8103	3479	5022	5328	6639	9998	8588	5145	19846	9831

(IoT) at the gates. IoT is picking up steam and its market is vast and fast growing (we are quickly approaching $1trillion annual revenue.) Close to 30 million devices are plugged into the hive every month. That's like adding the population of the United States to the Internet every year. Cisco estimates that by 2020 there will be more than 3 devices per person on IoT.

With so many devices connected, the amount of data generated by IoT is enormous and borderline unmanageable which will only make data science orders of magnitude more complex. However, there is no escaping this. Enterprises will have to understand their digital customers better and those companies that will mine that data effectively will be the ones that prosper (whether the data comes directly from the customer or from IoT devices serving the customer). To do this right we need to infuse artificial intelligence in most technology initiatives and we need to change the way we view this mountains of data from being a problem to being an opportunity. Machine Learning based systems that can autonomously sift through the heaps of data deposited by the customer will thrive and help propel AI forward. Machine learning is most effective when the parameters needed are not clear. In essence, when you unleash a competent set of algorithms using machine learning on such unstructured data like, you can potentially get answers to questions you haven't even started to ask.

AI is going to be a major enabler in the future and we will need to create intelligent frameworks in every aspect of the enterprise to unlock its potential, but that is a discussion for another chapter.

CONCLUSION

The digital transformation journey has an offspring called Customer Experience. As digital is becoming the norm and migration to digital is coming to completion, most transformed corporations are shifting the focus to perfecting the customer experience. The most successful organizations are the ones less focused on building overhyped futuristic programs and more focused on the mundane task of managing all customer interactions efficiently. Unfortunately, the volume of interactions have grown exponentially since the shift to digital. Those who mastered mining the footprints left behind by these interactions efficiently will excel in the digital age.

REFERENCES

Coleman, K. (2017). *Digital Transformation Strategy: A Matter of Survival.* Retrieved from http://www.projectmanagement.com

CDO Conclave. (2018, March). *10 amazing statistics about digital transformation.* CDO Conclave.

IDC. (2016). *IDC FutureScape: Worldwide Digital Transformation 2017 Predictions*. IDC.

IDC. (2017). *IDC Forecasts Worldwide Spending on Digital Transformation Technologies to Reach $1.3 Trillion in 2018*. IDC.

Section 2

Success Factors for Digital Supply Chain Transformations

Chapter 4
Transformation Framework for Supply Chain Segmentation in Digital Business

Ehap Sabri
KPMG LLP, USA & University of Texas at Dallas, USA

ABSTRACT

The purpose of this chapter is to explore the factors that influence digital supply chain segmentation and provide a best practice transformation approach to ensure a successful journey. The initial research is based on a review of supply chain segmentation literature and the application of relevant transformation steps to specific case studies, comprising of companies from different industries. Digital supply chain segmentation strategy presents huge opportunities that are being tapped by very few companies who achieved significant benefits and gained competitive advantage. The chapter provides a practical and proven digital supply chain segmentation framework for companies who are about to take the segmentation transformation journey.

INTRODUCTION

In response to the dramatic changes in the business landscape over the past few years, companies are assessing whether they have the right supply chains to support their dynamic and digital business, and exploring supply chain segmentation to reduce complexity and increase profit. Today's supply chains have become increasingly complex due to globalization, outsourcing, complicated networks, logistics capacity uncertainty and volatility, and the rapid proliferation of stocking keeping units (SKUs) and product configurations. However, many manufacturers and retailers continue to use an outdated approach to supply chain segmentation which is more of a hindrance than a help towards reducing complexity and improving margin.

It is also critical to deliver the right level of service for each product/customer/channel segment, especially as consumer behavior pushes towards more product customization and better service leading to a more compressed supply cycle.

DOI: 10.4018/978-1-5225-7700-3.ch004

Copyright © 2019, IGI Global. Copying or distributing in print or electronic forms without written permission of IGI Global is prohibited.

Digital technology is transforming supply chain management and driving significant innovation. Machine learning as a concept has been around for some time, but has taken on new meaning as the industry sees massive advancements in computing power and memory. In addition, change is happening faster than ever as technology trends such as IoT, virtual reality, and big data are providing countless opportunities for manufacturers and retailers across the globe.

The tightening of budgetary constraints have driven more companies to explore ways to make the supply chain more agile, customer-focused, and profit-driven (i.e. to do more with less). This is another pressure driver for the increase in supply chain segmentation popularity.

Therefore, taking the journey of supply chain segmentation is no longer optional; it is a strategic mandate in order to stay relevant in the industry. The future belongs to companies who can profitably match their supply chains to the specific needs of their customer segments.

This chapter explains the concept of segmentation, its historical background, its importance for today's business, and challenges to implementation. The chapter also provides an end-to-end supply chain practical segmentation framework. Companies can utilize this to ensure a smooth and successful implementation journey leveraging digital technologies. A number of existing frameworks are relevant but none are adequate or comprehensive by themselves. Several case studies will be discussed to illustrate the "fast track to success" framework.

BACKGROUND

Definition for Supply Chain Segmentation Concept

Sabri (2015) defined Supply Chain segmentation as managing profitably different virtual end-to-end supply chains defined by a combination of channel/customer requirements, product characteristics, business value considerations, and differentiated supply response strategies.IT research and advisory firm Gartner (http://www.gartner.com/it-glossary/supply-chain-segmentation) describes supply chain segmentation as "Designing and operating distinctly different end-to-end value chains (from customers to suppliers) optimized by a combination of unique customer value, product attribute, manufacturing and supply capabilities, and business value considerations. In essence, supply chain segmentation is the dynamic alignment of customer channel demands and supply response capabilities optimized for net profitability across each segment".

The Segmentation Concept Is Not New

The concept of supply chain segmentation is not new in literature research. It started when Fisher (1997) mentioned that the root cause of the problems troubling many supply chains is a mismatch between the type of product and the type of supply chain response. For the past 20 years supply chain literature has introduced several methods for segmentation using different criteria such as product demand volume, product demand variability, product handling, production variability, selling channel type, and end customer behavior. Authors agree that a 'one size-fits-all' supply chain management is an outdated concept, yet, they use very different criteria (dimensions) and profiles for supply chain design selection.

Fisher (1997) used "Product characteristics", in particular the volume of product demand and the variability of that demand, as the criteria for supply chain segmentation and created two profiles to define the product dimension: "functional" products and "innovative" products. "Functional" products, which have stable demand and long lifecycles, are necessitating an efficient supply chain model whilst 'innovative' products, with unpredictable demand and short lifecycles, are necessitating a responsive supply chain model. Fisher drew on examples from a diverse range of consumer products, including food, fashion apparel, and automobiles, to illustrate why different supply chain designs (models) were required depending upon whether products were "functional" or "innovative".

Naylor et al. (1999) compared the lean and agile manufacturing paradigms and argued neither paradigm is better than the other. Rather, they complement one another. In addition, they developed a two-by-two matrix based on the product demand variability and production variability, and assigned lean and agile supply chain models to them. For example, low variability for demand and production requires a lean supply chain model, while high variability requires an agile supply chain model. They also highlighted that the way in which an agile supply chain differentiates its products from the lean supply chain is by concentrating on the service levels at the expense of reducing costs.

Similarly, Mason-Jones et al. (2000) suggested that the best approach is to design and implement a "leagile supply chain''. "Lean" can be achieved by eliminating waste (non-value added time), while "agility" usually requires technology advances. They demonstrated how the "lean'' and ``agile'' paradigms may be combined. They introduced "order winners" as a segmentation criterion, and developed a two-by-two matrix that uses "order winners" criteria to determine the appropriate supply chain model. For example, if "cost" is the order winner then a "lean" supply chain model should be selected. When service level is the order winner then an "agile" solution should be recommended.

Lovell et al. (2005) also explored supply chain segmentation by examining product characteristics but used different criteria and profiles to define it. Two profiles (high value-density products such as microchips, and low value-density products such as packaging) were introduced and assigned two different supply chain models. Products with high value-density should be manufactured in a few centralized, large-scale plants while low value density items require production on a decentralized basis as close to the point of consumption as possible. The authors also mentioned that product handling characteristics should be considered in the supply chain model. Lovell et al. (2005) mentioned that perishable products are very different from fragile products, which are different from hazardous goods. This will influence the type of packaging, the mode of transport, and the type of storage.

Christopher et al. (2006) argued the importance of considering "supply lead time" as another segmentation criterion. This is very relevant to the globalization trend that started at that time. The authors developed a two-by-two matrix where demand variability and supply lead time are the segmentation criteria. The authors came up with four different profiles and assigned four supply chain designs to them:

1. When the profile is unpredictable demand and short supply lead time, an agile supply chain model should be assigned to provide flexibility and responsiveness
2. When demand is predictable and supply lead time is long, a lean supply chain model should be used to reduce supply chain costs
3. When demand is predictable and supply lead time is short, a "continuous replenishment" model should be recommended
4. When demand is unpredictable and supply lead time is long, a "postponement" (leagility) model should be proposed

Christopher et al. (2006) highlighted that global sourcing and offshore manufacturing have dramatically altered the landscape of today's business and added to the importance of agility and responsiveness as competitive success factors. The challenge to today's global business is first to identify the appropriate supply chain models to meet the different needs of the different product/channel characteristics and then to manage virtual multiple supply chains.

Gattorna (2006) was the first to consider consumer behavior as a supply chain segmentation criterion and argued that segmentation criteria should go beyond just product characteristics, demand/supply attributes, and order winners. The author explained that companies should segment their customers along buying behavior lines sharing a specific value proposition and then assign the right supply chain design. The author identified four different profiles for buying behaviors segmentation criterion and recommended a specific supply chain design for each one of them:

1. 'Understand Me' requires a "continuous replenishment" design that handles stable demand perfectly and allows certain degree of collaboration
2. 'Be Consistent' requires a "lean" supply chain design to ensure an efficient response for fairly stable demand
3. 'Respond' is often associated with innovative or new products with typical surge in demand and requires an "agile" supply chain design
4. 'Surprise' is associated with unpredictable products and a "fully flexible" supply chain design

Gattorna (2006) also introduced the "dynamic alignment' concepts which allow the supplier to switch between the four supply chain models as the needs of the customer or consumer behavior change.

Christopher et al. (2009) explored more segmentation criteria and suggested five dimensions: stage of product lifecycle, delivery lead time window, volume based on Pareto classification, product form and variability of demand.

Roscoe and Parker (2013) combined Fisher's (1997) product attributes, Mason-Jones et al.'s (2000) value proposition and order winning criteria, Christopher et al.'s (2006) demand predictability and lead times, and Gattorna's (2006) behavioral segmentation and concept of dynamic alignment. The authors came up with four supply chain models for the sporting goods industry based on the combined criteria tailored for a sporting goods manufacturer:

1. Agile – Customization
2. Agile Quick – Response
3. Lean
4. Continuous Replenishment

In summary, Table 1 shows the links between segmentation criteria (dimensions), profiles, and supply chain models for the previous work done in this area. It is clear that the concept of segmentation is not new in academia (Sabri, 2015).

Table 1 demonstrates how a number of existing segmentation methods may be relevant to a specific company or industry but none are adequate by themselves for every company or across industries. The literature conceptualizes the theory of supply chain segmentation but, when it comes to reality, there are more factors in play. It is possible that pre-defined, scripted supply chain models based on certain segmentation profiles might not even be relevant to the company's customers or products (Sabri, 2015).

Table1. Summary of segmentation dimensions, profiles, and related SC model

Author(s)	Segmentation Dimensions	Profiles	Supply Chain (SC) Models
Fisher (2007)	Product	Innovative Products Functional Products	Efficient SC process Responsive SC process
Naylor, Naim, and Berry (1999)	Product & Production	High variability of products and related production High variability of products and related production	Lean SC Agile SC
Mason-Jones, Naylor, and Towill (2000)	Order Winner	Cost Service Level	Lean SC Agile SC
Lovell, Saw, and Stimson (2005)	Product	High product-value density Low product-value density	Centralized large-scale plants Decentralized close to customer plants
Christopher, Peck, and Towill (2006)	Demand &Lead Time	Unpredictable demand and short lead time Unpredictable demand and long lead time Predictable demand and long lead times Predictable demand and short lead times	Agile SC Leagile (postponement) Lean SC Lean (continuous replenishment)
Gattorna (2006)	Buying behavior	'Understand Me' – collaborative approach 'Be Consistent' – efficient response 'Demanding' – respond approach 'Surprise Me' – innovative solutions	Continuous replenishment Lean SC Agile SC Fully flexible SC
Roscoe and Parker (2013) –Case Study for Sport Goods	Product Demand Channel & Order Winner/ Value Proposition	Innovative, unpredictable & Online Innovative, hi quality, unstable demand & specialist stores Price sensitive, predictable & sports generalist Fit, brand, stable demand & lifestyle generalist	Agile – Customization Agile Quick –Response Lean Continuous Replenishment

As previously stated, the concept of supply chain segmentation is not new. The author observed several manufacturing, fashion and retail companies which have multiple supply chain models, but the majority of them were developed out of necessity (reactive mode) with manual and inconsistent business practices.

Therefore, there is an urgent need for a comprehensive and practical framework for supply chain segmentation. This should not only provide best practices in profiling and identifying different supply chain models, but also provide an end-to-end approach for implementing and sustaining segmentation and successfully leveraging digital technologies.

The Benefits of Supply Chain Segmentation

Addressing Today's Business Challenges

Executives and supply chain leaders face many challenges today in every aspect of their operations and enterprise integration. The following are considered to be the top ten challenges:

- The need to be more customer oriented while managing the supply chain cost (bottom-line) more efficiently. Companies have long known the importance of designing offerings to serve the needs of different markets and consumers, but accomplishing this can be difficult given how quickly customers' behaviors and expectations change. Also, more business to business (B2B) customers are expecting a business to consumer (B2C) experience when interacting with other businesses.
- Information delay or latency, which creates the need for companies to design business processes that realize the information flow between business partners.
- Globalization which intensifies the competition and makes the competitive advantage crucial.
- The increased complexity of supply chains including the need for tighter control, the growing complexity of managing information flows, SKU proliferation, channel complexity, and the increasing trends of 3rd party logistics.
- Long and unpredictable product life cycles. Rapid product innovation forces the product introduction cycle to be faster to react to the market needs and gain competitive advantage.
- The shift from vertical integration to horizontal supply chains which calls for more efficient and effective collaboration with suppliers and customers. The new trend is for companies to buy out competitors in the same business or merge with them instead of buying their suppliers (i.e. to expand vertically instead of horizontally).
- Expensive operating cost structures, especially when companies are facing intensified competition. Related to that is the increase in transportation cost due to outsourcing
- The disruption to the supply chain from demand and supply mainly caused by supply chain uncertainty and variability.
- Supporting the redesigned processes with leading edge technology that is easy to integrate, cheap to maintain, and fast to achieve results.
- Outsourcing and having suppliers across the world. Companies continue to outsource assembly work, information systems management, call centers, and product engineering to contractors. The challenge is to decide what to outsource, and how to make sure that customer satisfaction, delivery service, and quality are not compromised.
- The need to explore insourcing for certain clusters to improve responsiveness rate. More than a decade ago, many companies started moving their production operations to lower-cost countries. The industry is again on the brink of a major global shift. Various of the offshore cost advantages that once existed are beginning to erode. Wage inflation, tariff taxes, rising oil prices — even natural disasters — are among the factors affecting outsourcing supply chain profitability, agility, and risk. Several companies underestimated the offshore impacts of long lead times and high inventory carrying costs. They are discovering that maintaining service levels, in addition to the inventory and logistics buffering costs necessary to support the long-distance supply chain, far outweigh any labor cost advantages. In addition, outsourcing production introduces a latency lag in bringing new products to market and responding to market trends (Johnston, 2012).

In order to address the challenges mentioned above, companies should look for certain key enablers to implement in their operations (Sabri, 2015). Supply chain segmentation is one of these key enablers. Other enablers can be grouped as follows:

1. **Cross organizational collaboration**: Cross organizational collaboration can improve efficiency, reduce quality risk, and streamline processes
2. **Customer-centricity & Agility**: This includes building flexibility into product designs and manufacturing processes to become more "customer-oriented" and to mitigate the challenge of supply and demand uncertainty by providing the ability to change plans quickly. Flexibility in manufacturing is measured based on the ability to shift production load, change production volumes and product mix, and modify products to meet new market needs. It is important to note that cost reduction initiatives usually inversely impact flexibility
3. **Visibility**: Real time visibility reduces uncertainty and enables the reduction of safety stock. This in turn drives down operational costs. Visibility also improves customer satisfaction, which increases revenue by presenting the real picture and providing the ability to proactively address potential problems. Finally, visibility reduces the impact of disruption to the supply chain caused by demand and supply variability and uncertainty.
4. **Process innovation**: This addresses the following questions: How can companies reengineer their processes to increase speed of delivery when introducing new products? What supply chain process improvements and digital technologies should companies invest in to gain competitive advantage? How can companies restructure their supply chains to reduce cost and increase profitability across their total global network? How can companies reduce their supplier base? How can companies leverage best in class technology to enable best practice processes?
5. **Risk Management**: This addresses the risks related to product quality and service delivery that arise from a global supply chain and the rushing of new product introductions.

Impacting the Company's Bottom Line

Any manufacturer or retailer knows, no two customers are the same. Each customer's perception on the value of a product or service and how much they are willing to pay for it is different. This is true for almost every product category available in the market from cars to snack bars.

That said, many retail and manufacturing companies are still using 'one size fits all' supply chain processes; over-serving some channel/product combinations and under-serving others. For example, research of one industry showed that around 50% of a company's customer and product portfolio was unprofitable which would require different supply chain response to reduce cost.

Through in depth understanding of the profit profiles of their customers, channels, and/or products, companies can tailor a more profitable supply chain strategy to each of them and thus increase the overall margin of their portfolios. It can also increase inventory turnover through optimal inventory positioning and aligning fulfillment, logistics, demand planning, manufacturing, and procurement strategies. For example, an apparel retailer can satisfy the demand for their basic products through an efficient (less costly) supply chain model and deliver their fashion products through a highly responsive supply chain model. This creates one model for standard (predictable) products and another for fashion (unpredictable) products. Each model will have different demand planning, stocking, and fulfillment policies.

In addition, supply chain segmentation would improve customer service which would improve sales by increasing the reliability of delivering on promises and improving forecast accuracy.

Companies that successfully deploy a segmentation strategy will improve the reliability of their customer service while increasing profitability across their product portfolio through better alignment of supply chain strategies/policies to customer/product value propositions. These companies will also increase inventory turnover through inventory positioning and aligning supply chain assets to customer value propositions and profitability (Thomas, 2012).

FRAMEWORK FOR SUPPLY CHAIN SEGMENTATION TRANSFORMATION

The recipe for success in managing the journey of supply chain (SC) segmentation transformation is mastering the change transformation cycle, leveraging digital technologies, and ensuring effective change management. Figure 1 introduces a practical and comprehensive SC segmentation transformation framework to help with implementation. This figure shows the 10-step transformation journey which typically lasts two to three years and consists of three phases: "plan" (five blue steps), "implement" (two yellow steps), and "sustain" (three green steps).

Planning starts by defining the vision and objectives and aligning them to corporate goals and needs. This is followed by profiling and clustering. Process analysis and associating clusters to supply chain models is next followed by identifying the changes in process, technology, and people required to support the new supply chain models and the new end state. The final step of the planning phase is building the business case (estimating benefits and costs) and defining the program implementation roadmap.

The "implement" phase starts by configuring the segmented supply chain networks and is followed by conducting training on the new processes and monitoring progress and adoption.

Figure 1. Supply chain segmentation transformation framework

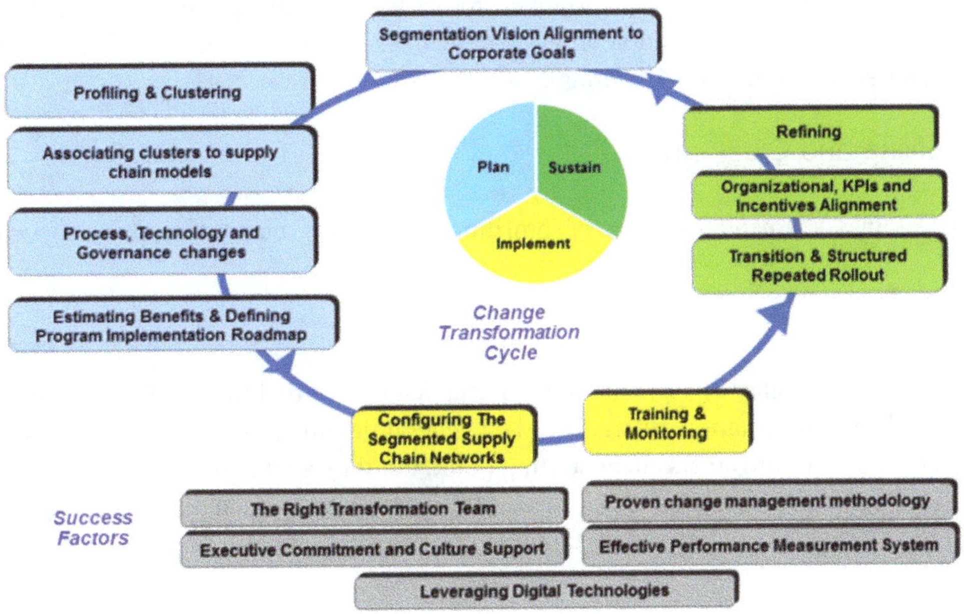

The "sustain" phase consists of three steps starting with transition and structured repeated rollout. This is followed by ensuring organizational, metrics, and incentives alignment and concluded by the "refining" step. The next planned transformation cycle can kick in after months of refining, corrective actions, and incremental improvement of the first cycle. Supply chain segmentation is not a one-time exercise or sprint; it is a journey. Five success factors are also emphasized in this framework to ensure the required support for the segmentation transformation program:

1. The right transformation team
2. Culture support & executive commitment
3. Leveraging digital technologies
4. Proven change management methodology
5. An effective performance measurement system (PMS) which includes data availability, metrics, andKPIs

These success factors, in addition to the discussed 10-steps, will be detailed out in the coming section highlighting several best practices.

The 10-Step Supply Chain Segmentation Framework

Step 1: Segmentation Vision Alignment to Corporate Goals

This step helps in establishing clearly how the supply chain segmentation transformation program is a crucial strategy to achieving corporate goals. It includes developing the vision and objectives of the segmentation transformation initiative

The key to supply chain segmentation is finding the right balance between agility and efficiency (lean) for each product/customer/channel combination. A one-size-fits-all strategy will not allow a company to compete on a global scale in today's business. Segmentation allows companies to get the right product/service with the right value to the right customer while optimizing the supply chain. Once the linkage is established and transformation program objectives are defined, communicating this to upper management and all stakeholders is important.

Step 2: Profiling and Clustering

This step determines segmentation criteria, profiling, identifying customer value propositions, and clustering.

Segmentation Criteria

Companies need to determine the segmentation criteria that will fit their needs. The author would argue against a pre-defined segmentation criteria based on general literature or a specific case study. Existing literature and case studies are an excellent starting point, but they should not be the ultimate reference. Comprehensive segmentation criteria are presented in Figure 2 under each of the segmentation dimensions. Selected criteria were underlined to highlight examples that will be detailed later in this chapter.

- **Product Characteristics**:
  - Product lifecycle stage
  - Shelf life
  - Functional or innovative
  - Handling characteristics
  - Product value density
  - Supply lead lime
  - Product variety
- **Customer Characteristics**:
  - Demand volume
  - Margin
  - Demand variability
  - Large customers vs. small customers
  - Buying behavior (such as seasonal, planned or spontaneous)
  - Customer lead time
  - Strategic importance
  - Service-level agreements (SLAs)
- **Channels**
  - Online (website)
  - Retailers
  - Warehouses
  - End consumers: business-to-consumers(B2C)
  - Business-to-business (B2B)
  - Geography

Profiling

Once the segmentation criteria are determined, the company needs to document a portfolio of products, customers, channels, and related profiles based on detailed analysis. This analysis is typically more extensive than the analysis most companies would have carried out previously because in this step they are trying to predict the market conditions and customer (consumer or B2B customer) behavior that will prevail in the next three to five years, rather than examining how best to compete in the present time. Such forward-looking thinking requires extensive customer research and detailed marketing analysis. The aim is to understand the company's average customer, and get a solid appreciation for each existing and potential customer type. It is not just customer profiling, it is product/customer/channel profiling.

Customer Value Proposition

Companies need to identify the customer value proposition by conducting customer satisfaction surveys, and using business intelligence, market analysis reports, etc. This can also be accomplished by identifying the complexities that are present and identifying whether they are good complexities or bad complexities. Good complexities are those that improve the product or service and, most importantly, customers are willing to pay for. Bad complexities add no value and come at a price lie increased inventory or expediting.

Figure 2. Segmentation criteria and related profiling list

AREA	Profiling
Product Characteristics	❖Product Lifecycle Stage ❖Shelf Life ❖**Functional or innovative** ❖Handling characteristics ❖Product value density ❖Supply Lead Time ❖Product Variety
Customer Characteristics	❖**Demand volume** ❖**Margin** ❖**Demand variability** ❖Large vs. Small ❖buying behavior ❖Customer Lead Time ❖Strategic Importance ❖SLAs
Channels	❖Online ❖Retailers ❖Warehouses ❖**End Consumers (B2C)** ❖**Businesses (B2B)** ❖Geography
Customer Value Proposition	❖Brand name ❖**Lead Time** ❖**Cost** ❖**Availability** ❖**Flexibility** ❖**Delivery Performance (DP)** ❖After-sales service

Figure 2 provides a list of seven typical customer value propositions listed below:

1. Brand name
2. Lead time or speed
3. Cost (price)
4. Availability
5. Flexibility
6. Delivery performance (DP)
7. After-sales service

The company can select from the list based on the previously discussed analysis.

Clustering

The key for most companies who are interested in segmentation is to identify and better align to the natural tradeoffs that exist within their business. A simple but effective way to model this is by identifying the key customer value propositions that the customers apply to the company's business offering. These value propositions have natural trade-offs between them that allow the company to develop a differentiated supply chain response.

For example, university students often prioritize price. However, growing up with Amazon.com has made short lead time (speed) another deciding factor. To get that speed and low price, they are willing to forego other value propositions such as after-sales service. Segmentation allows companies to specialize and compete for all customers on their terms, rather than an average that appeases, but never delights (Mellins-Cohen, 2012).

In this activity, companies need to identify sets of clusters that best represent their business profiles and value propositions. Figure 3 provides a hypothetical example of profiling and clustering. In this example a company selected 'Functional vs Innovative' as a profile parameter for the product characteristics segmentation dimension. 'Demand volume', 'margin', and "demand variability" were selected under the customer characteristics dimension. In addition, B2B and B2C are the selected channels and four customer value propositions (lead time, cost, flexibility, and delivery performance) are considered.

The next activity is to determine the clusters that best represent the selected profile parameters and value propositions. It is recommended to think big when creating this initial version and create clusters for as many profiles as possible that are relevant to the company. However once the profile types are exhausted, it is critical to reduce them to the key few and bear in mind that each cluster probably represents a new supply chain design (model).

In the example in Figure 3, Cluster 1 represents the innovative products and customers with low volume, high margin, and high demand variability (i.e. low forecast accuracy). Furthermore, this cluster represents B2C channel only. The value proposition for this cluster is reduced lead time (fast delivery), high degree of flexibility, and high delivery performance (on time delivery). Cost is not a decision making factor as shown in the figure.

During this activity, it is often recommended to conduct a cost-to-serve analysis. The objective of this exercise is to understand which customer/product/channel combinations are winners and losers, and then to structure the clusters so that some or all of the losers are turned into winners. For example, a large consumer goods company, with a significant portion of business coming from Wal-Mart, would likely have an assigned team and a set of strategies dedicated to that account. The high value of the Wal-Mart

Figure 3. Profiling and clustering approach with an example

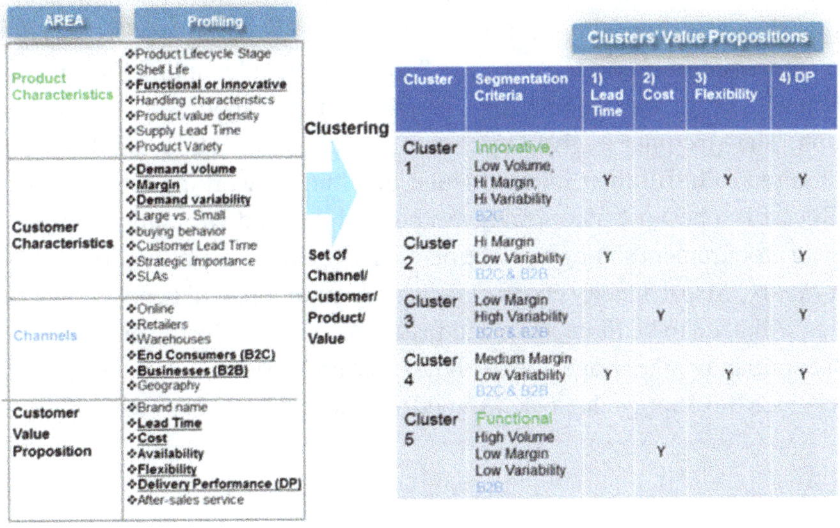

Cluster	Segmentation Criteria	1) Lead Time	2) Cost	3) Flexibility	4) DP
Cluster 1	Innovative, Low Volume, Hi Margin, Hi Variability B2C	Y		Y	Y
Cluster 2	Hi Margin Low Variability B2C & B2B	Y			Y
Cluster 3	Low Margin High Variability B2C & B2B		Y		Y
Cluster 4	Medium Margin Low Variability B2C & B2B	Y		Y	Y
Cluster 5	Functional High Volume Low Margin Low Variability B2B		Y		

business warrants this level of premium service. However, the cost-benefit ratio (cost to serve) would not be positive if the same strategy is applied to every mom-and-pop store that also buys the same products. The company would need a different supply chain design for those customers.

In another example, the cost to serve a customer in the US for a US company will be different than the cost to serve a customer overseas. Estimating the cost to serve across extended supply chains requires visibility into many cost data elements. These can be enabled by the digital technologies which are one of the key success factors for supply chain segmentation that will be discussed. This may require changing the replenishment model and service-level agreements for a specific customer/product combination. The author worked with a tire manufacturer to adjust its replenishment model to store products for customers (similar to cluster 1) in the centralized and factory distribution centers (DCs) instead of storing it closer to customers in regional DCs. This moves the inventory buffer point upstream in the supply chain, reducing overall inventory. The upstream DCs hold a larger pool of inventory, increasing the odds that downstream demand will be filled with the required product.

Step 3: Associating Clusters to Supply Chain Models

When the clusters have been finalized, the next step is to decide what needs to be done to deliver each of them top value. It is time to design the supply chain models and Step 3 is conducting process analysis and associating clusters to supply chain designs (models). The supply chain models will be driven by the unique value propositions of the clusters from the previous step. It is important to remember that the number of supply chain designs (models) should be manageable. Most literature reviews suggest two or four models. The author typically recommends the number to be based on the business requirements and the company's capabilities in managing different supply chain models.

In Figure 4, five supply chain models are selected against five clusters. Column 3 covers the value propositions which put emphasis on lead time (responsiveness), cost, flexibility, and delivery performance (reliability). Let's assume that the key processes for supply chain management are supply planning, demand planning, procurement, and order fulfillment. For every key process, key strategies will be implemented to support certain value propositions.

For example, for Cluster 1, under supply planning, postponement (keeping inventory upstream in factories or central DCs) and flexible capacity strategies are selected since one emphasis (customer value proposition) of this cluster is flexibility. In this highly innovative, product-driven, and highly variable environment with a 'premium' type of customer, a "postponement" manufacturing strategy is required. Under order fulfillment, air is selected as the main transportation mode since the other emphasis is on lead time reduction. The customer is given the benefit of choice and a fast and more flexible-focused supply chain is required to fulfill their requirements. In addition, working closer with customers when generating the forecast is a best practice strategy to control demand variability.

A multi-sourcing procurement strategy will be needed to provide flexibility in case of supply shortages for nonproprietary parts. Also, capacity contracts with key suppliers will need to have flexibility built in and delivery routes will need to be more agile and faster. As a result, the lower volumes of these innovative products will command higher price due to higher cost and differentiated service. This should not be a customer barrier since this supply chain is designed around the customers who are willing to pay for it.

Cluster 5targets purely cost-driven customers. The route to address 'lowest-cost' emphasis is often an efficient supply chain. This supply chain uses 'lean' concepts to streamline and eliminate waste from the process, implements a build to stock manufacturing supply strategy since demand variability is low for this cluster, and positions inventory closer to the customers due to high volume. In addition, advanced planning like forecasting enables high forecast accuracy which allows things to be booked much in advance and for suppliers and logistics companies to plan ahead for optimization. Offshore manufacturing capacity and slower, cheaper routes — such as ocean — can be also used, allowing the company to reduce cost and provide the best price for the customer in this cluster.

By working with various clusters —combinations of customer types, channels, products, and value propositions — to identify their requirements and tailor their supply chain, companies can optimize their capabilities and improve the bottom line.

Step 4: Identifying Process, Technology and Governance Changes

The segmented supply chain strategy requires process, technology, and governance changes to demand planning, supply planning, procurement, and order fulfillment processes. In doing so, even though physical supply chain resources could remain the same, the supply chain response operates differently from one supply chain model to another and from one cluster (segment) to another.

It is important to complete a detailed, future-state process map after supply chain models are approved by key stakeholders. A value stream mapping method can be leveraged to understand the cost drivers and come up with a more granular design of the future state. It is crucial to capture process, technology, and governance (organizational structure, metrics, and policies) changes and capabilities for every supply chain process that enables implementing the proposed strategies for every supply chain model in the previous step.

Figure 4. Associating clusters to supply chain models approach_with an example

			Supply Chain Processes' Key Strategies			
Cluster	**Supply Chain**	**Value Propositions**	**Supply Planning**	**Demand Planning**	**Procurement**	**Order Fulfillment**
Cluster 1	Supply Chain (SC)A	1, 3, 4	• Postponement • Six Sigma to control variability • Flexible Capacity	• Customer Collaboration	• Multi Source	• Air
Cluster 2	Supply Chain B	1, 4	• Build to Stock • Stored in Regional DC	• Demand Shaping	• Buffer stock • VMI	• Cross Docks
Cluster 3	Supply Chain C	2, 4	• Build to Order • Direct Ship	• What if Analysis	• Flexible Contracts	• FTL for B2B
Cluster 4	Supply Chain D	1, 3, 4	• Stored in Centralized Warehouse • Near shore capacity	• POS Forecasting	• Bulk buys • FTL for inbound material	• Expedites
Cluster 5	Supply Chain E	2	• Inventory stored closer to customers • Lean for streamlining • offshore capacity • Build to stock	• Statistical forecasting with exception driven adjustments	• Blanket PO with locked annual QTY	• Ocean & Rail with no expedites

SC A = Responsive & Flexible Supply Chain
SC B = Responsive Supply Chain
SC C = Efficient & Reliable Supply Chain
SC D = Efficient & Flexible Supply Chain
SC E = Efficient Supply Chain

Companies have long struggled to deploy segmented supply chains because underlying decision support (planning) technologies have not been readily available for end-to-end supply chains. This has changed recently which will make it easier for companies to go through the segmentation journey.

To summarize, the segmented supply chain strategy requires process, technology, and governance changes to demand planning, supply planning, procurement, and order fulfillment processes. In doing so, even though physical supply chain resources could remain the same, supply chain response operates differently from one supply chain model to another and from one cluster (segment) to another.

Figure 5 reflects an example from a real manufacturer. These are the changes that were required to support a supply chain design similar to Supply Chain A from Figure 4 (Responsive & Flexible Supply Chain).

Under demand planning, the manufacturer needed to implement a customer collaboration strategy which would require a process change of modifying the forecasting process to include the customer input, a technology change to enable a collaboration workbench leveraging digital technologies, and two people-related changes. The first people-related change was an organizational structure changed which formed a decentralized Demand Planning Group to be closer to the customer and corresponding sales person. The second people-related change was adding customer forecast accuracy to the set of existing metrics to establish accountability to the customer forecast.

The manufacturing company can no longer forecast demand based on past sales history alone. The segmented strategy will require market intelligence on similar products and markets along with close collaboration with marketing and sales personnel to get customers' input. The cluster (product/customer/channel) under this supply chain design (model) would need to be tracked differently to monitor market acceptance and utilize more frequent feedback cycles relative to other clusters in the company's portfolio.

Under the supply planning process, demand prioritization needed to be adjusted to increase the planning priority associated with this cluster since margin was high and supply lead time was a competitive differentiator (customer value proposition). Profiling the expected lead time by customers is important to decide if a replenishment postponement strategy (such as build-to-forecast to a semi-finished stage and assemble-to-order thereafter) could be enabled for this cluster.

Figure 5. Example for identifying process, technology and governance changes

Key Process, Technologies and Governance Changes for Supply Chain A

	Supply Planning	Demand Planning	Procurement	Order Fulfillment
Process	• Profiling Customer Lead Time • Demand prioritization	• Modifying the forecasting process to include the customer input	• Establishing a process and criteria to split the sourcing demand by the vendors	• Establishing a process for allocation
Technology	• Implementing Inventory Optimization Tool	• Enabling a collaboration workbench	• Enhancing the supplier portal to provide real time visibility for in-transit inbound material	• Supporting different modes of transportation • Enabling order promising based on allocation
Governance	• Establishing Center of excellence to supervise 6 Sigma initiatives	• Decentralized Demand Planning Group • Adding customer forecast accuracy to the set of existing metrics	• Adding supplier flexibility metric to the supplier scorecard	• Establishing a long term agreement with UPS and DHL

Under order fulfillment, a substantial emphasis was put on allocation planning and order promising sub processes. As the company strove for margin growth, finished goods supply needed to be allocated more heavily toward this cluster. The company needed to adjust its allocation policies. Additionally, higher service levels for this supply chain model required faster replenishment. This often meant smaller, more frequent shipments which raised transportation costs. Careful planning of shipments associated with this cluster, including load consolidation, mode selection, routing, and carrier selection, could significantly reduce transportation costs while ensuring high service levels. Establishing a long term agreement with carriers was recommended to handle expedited high value products effectively in this cluster.

Finally, under the procurement process, establishing a process and criteria to split the sourcing demand by vendors was necessary to provide flexibility and address the risk of shortage in raw material and components. Investment in technology to provide real time visibility for in-transit inbound material was required to reduce lead time variability and enable the company to react faster to delays.

Segmentation-based supply chain processes have helped this manufacturer balance value to the business against service levels required to support corporate goals for their strategic products (Cluster 1).

Step 5: Estimating Benefits and Defining the Roadmap

Cost-to-Serve Analysis

The first activity of this step is to validate "cost-to-serve" analysis against the new supply chain designs. "Cost to serve" analysis is very similar to Activity Based Costing (ABC). However it must be much more granular because in virtual supply chain there will be shared assets that necessitate allocating costs differently since each virtual supply chain (supply chain design) must be managed differently. Various resources such as power, overheads, equipment, and technology costs, must be allocated differently for each line according to usage. For example, premium freight service is used heavily for the Responsive & Flexible Supply Chain model which requires speed in delivery (short lead time) but not used the Efficient Supply Chain. Therefore, no premium freight cost should be allocated to the Efficient Supply Chain. Currently, many companies assign all these resources to one area labeled as 'overheads,' but to execute the supply chain segmentation strategy effectively, they need to be separated. They also need to be analyzed more granularly in order to accurately estimate cost and price profitability. Based on the author's experience, getting finance involved early on during this step is crucial.

Capturing the Expected Benefits

The next activity is to estimate the benefits for every supply chain model and highlight the impact on key performance indicators' (KPIs) targets. During this phase, there is a need to: 1) identify the critical supply chain KPIs to grow the business and improve profitability, 2) capture an accurate baseline for each of these KPIs, and 3) explain how the new/updated supply chain models will impact the KPIs - positively (green color), negatively (red), or neutral (empty box) as shown in Figure 6. For example, supply chain A will get a hit from supply chain cost perspective due to the use of Air as the main transportation mode, but this strategy will improve other KPIs like order cycle time.

It is important to mention that KPIs should be the same (applicable) for all supply chain designs; it is only the targets that change. Once these KPIs (such as SCM cost, cycle time, etc) are established, average targets across all supply chain designs must also be agreed on. These targets can be internal-based, industry–based, or competition-based. Then KPIs targets are defined for each supply chain design based on strategies that are being implemented with a goal of achieving the average targets across all of the supply chain designs. For example, the target for "Order Cycle Time" for an Efficient & Reliable Supply Chain will be lower than the average target while it is higher in Responsive Supply Chain. On the other hand, Responsive Supply Chain is higher than the average target when it comes to supply chain cost KPI. To re-iterate: positively impacting one KPI might inversely affect others.

Building the Business Case

The next activity is to build the business case and significant ROI (benefits – costs) for executives to secure their buy-in on pursuing the supply chain segmentation journey.

To be able to conduct this activity successfully, the defined KPIs (as in figure 6) should be aligned to corporate goals like increased margin, cost reduction, improvement in customer service, etc.

Building the Roadmap

The final phase of this step is to build the roadmap for the transformation program which should be broken into multiple phases (projects) with definitive outcomes for each to ensure manageable change. The idea here is to 'think big', 'start small', 'act quick', and 'win fast'. No matter what your situation is, the journey to supply chain segmentation success is a radical ongoing overhaul of culture, process, organizational structures, technology, measurement framework, and operating models.

Senior management must approach supply chain segmentation as more than a single project. It must be approached as a transformation program and must become the new way of doing business.

Step 6: Configuring the Segmented Supply Chain Network

This step is the starting point for execution and implementing the supply chain segmentation strategy ('Implement Change' phase). It includes conducting detailed design and new process/technology deployment. As a best practice, it is recommended to use several pilots and implementation waves to "turn

Figure 6. Different supply chain models impact KPI targets differently

	Key Performance Indicators				
Supply Chain	Supply Chain Cost	Order Cycle Time	Demand Forecast Accuracy	Perfect Order	Time to Recovery
Responsive & Flexible Supply Chain	↑	↓	↑	↑	↑
Responsive Supply Chain	↑	↓	↑	↑	
Efficient & Reliable Supply Chain	↓	↑		↑	↓
Efficient & Flexible Supply Chain	↓	↓	↑	↑	↓
Efficient Supply Chain	↓	↑	↑		↓

on" capabilities and strategies piece by piece to reduce risk and allow enough time for stakeholders to adopt the change. Advanced supply chain planning software applications should be in place as a pre-requisite to support different virtual supply chains from a planning perspective. It is important to note that although a technology investment is not necessarily a requirement for supply chain segmentation, inadequate technology frequently surfaces as a concern in the segmentation process. Also, leveraging digital technologies will make segmentation much easier and scalable

While a company's physical supply chain assets — raw materials, factory resources, warehouses, distribution centers, retail centers, and channels — are typically the same across all supply chain designs (models), its processes and governance (organizational structure, metrics, and policies) for predicting customer demand, positioning supply, procurement, and fulfilling orders can be different. In executing these differentiated processes and enforcing governance, supply chain professionals help drive competitive advantage and profitable growth across all clusters.

After configuration is complete, a formal readiness assessment to 'go live' with the new supply segmentation networks should be conducted.

It is important to re-iterate that the transformation program should be broken into multiple stages with definitive outcomes for each to implement manageable change and achieve quick wins (Sabri, 2015). One example would be that a company might decide to enable two supply chain models in the first stage (which might take a year) and leave the last 3 to the second stage. Another example is to stack the stages based on the supply chain processes like implementing the process, technology, and governances for the demand planning process in the first stage, followed by supply planning in the second stage, etc. This depends on the maturity of these processes and the size of changes. A third example would be to divide the process, technology, and governance changes into three groups: 1) 'crawl', 2) 'walk', and 3) 'run' and then stack the stages to implement "crawl" changes first, followed by 'walk' and implement the remaining changes in the third stage. Some of the stages can overlap from a timing perspective and a coordinated timeline that highlights critical stop-gate dependencies can improve the efficiency of managing these initiatives (stages).

Step 7: Training and Monitoring

A structured and comprehensive education plan—starting with the transformation team and end users and ending with engaging key stakeholders and leaders—should be developed early and executed effectively as changes move through the organization. The plan should cover planning, implementing, and sustaining the segmentation transformation. This step is critical to ensure the effectiveness of the execution.

Additionally, the education plan for end users should be tailored based on which segment they work on. For example, enabling "efficient supply chain" model requires strong knowledge in lean principles.

Monitoring is another phase of this step to ensure employee adoption to the new process of the segmented supply chain. It is important to proactively monitor the experience of the employees, suppliers, and customers to identify performance issues and provide additional training when needed to sustain positive behavior by all stakeholders including supply chain leaders, managers, and planners.

Step 8: Transition and Structured Repeated Rollout

This step is the starting point for sustaining the new state of doing business ("Sustain Change" phase). During this step, the transformation team typically transitions to a different team (business team) to take over the transformation initiative. The transformation team is responsible for planning and implementing the process, technology, and governance changes needed to support segmented supply chain strategy. The business teams (demand planning, supply planning, procurement, and order fulfillment teams), with the help of IT customer support, would take over to lead this step and the next two steps of making the changes part of running the business environment.

During this step, a repeated rollout to other business units might occur based on the previously predefined roadmap for the segmentation transformation. Segmentation must be a living thing, with the ability to assign new products easily to existing clusters and eventually to existing supply chain designs (models).

Step 9: Organizational structure, KPIs, and Incentives Alignments

Organizational Realignment

The first activity of this step is to ensure that organizational alignment (part of the governance changes defined earlier) is happening. Human resources department might need to update job descriptions and bonus structure to reflect the changes. This might require creating a pipeline of candidates for hiring with a mix of demand, supply, and product expertise. Also, incentives for the company's talent should be aligned with the skill requirements for the new process.

Incentive Alignment

The second activity is to ensure KPIs and incentives are aligned so each supply chain model can drive the right business decisions and behavior effectively. This requires a clear set of goals (targets for the KPIs) and incentives to be defined earlier during Step 5. Incentives, including bonuses, should always be based on the KPIs; getting the KPIs right allows the incentives to be altered to match, which will in turn stimulate behavioral change where it is required. For example, if sales people are to provide input in the forecasting process, they will need an incentive (such as a 20% percentage of their bonus) to ensure that this is done in a way to which the supply chain organization can respond accordingly (i.e. no overestimating or underestimating). Equally, in terms of supply, the procurement team must be incentivized to work in line with the supply chain strategy like total landed cost rather than simply focusing on lowest-cost scenarios.

Cost and Benefits Data Gathering

During Step 2, cost allocation is determined for every supply chain model. This is needed to break down the shared overhead charges that have traditionally been spread equally across all products. This is important in order to validate the cost to serve analysis and to estimate the cost and saving of a certain supply chain model. During this step (Step 9), the actual costs are captured and should be compare with the previous estimate. Also, the actual benefits would start to be realized and the expected business case (ROI) can be confirmed in this step.

Step 10: Refining

Fine-tuning profiles, clusters, and cost allocations are necessary as products move through their life cycles and demand shifts. Technology can be leveraged to move a product/customer/channel combination automatically from one cluster to another as the underlying attributes change. Revisiting and adjusting KPIs targets is also needed to ensure a continuous improvement culture. A cross-functional governance monthly review cadence should exist such as a monthly meeting like Sales and Operational Planning (S&OP) review. This will also allow the company to continually align with customer value.

The transformation journey is ongoing and not a onetime exercise; it is a multi-year journey which requires multiple cycles. Each cycle might take between two and five years. Refining is the last step in the cycle during which incremental improvements and fine tuning are done. Once the success criteria, expected benefits, and KPIs targets are achieved, a new transformation cycle should be considered. This is when the company goes from Step 10 back to Step 1 to repeat the cycle to achieve additional improvements and benefits. Changes in the business and new opportunities such as an emerging market should also trigger another transformation cycle.

The 5 Success Factors for Supply Chain Segmentation

There are five key success factors required to ensure the successful implementation of supply chain segmentation as shown earlier in Figure 1.

Success Factor # 1: Having the Right Transformation Team

Having the right transformation team is crucial for the supply chain segmentation journey. Special skills should be considered in selecting the transformation team such as process design and automation, lean principles knowledge, Six Sigma expertise, data analytics, systems optimization, program management, organizational influence, and communication.

Success Factor # 2: Executive Commitment and Culture Support

Supply Chain segmentation is not just a business initiative, it is a change to the culture. Executive commitment and visible support are key to the success. For example, executives need to enforce the culture of customer-driven and differentiation, the culture of promising what you can deliver and delivering on every promise, the culture of commitment to continuous improvement as a way of life for the organization, and the culture of praising and promoting the managers who avoid fires (being proactive) versus promoting the fire fighters (being reactive).

Establishing a clear segmentation vision strategy enabled by digital technologies is so fundamental to a firm's future success that the CEO must inspire employees to pursue a vision of the company. However, many CEOs feel that segmentation is somewhat beyond their grasp. The CEO must step up and collaborate with the CMO, COO, and CIO to jointly create a vision that the CEO can sponsor.

Establish "a differentiated supply chain response" culture, collaboration, agility, and digital innovation are second nature to employees in today's businesses. Therefore, its crucial fuel the differentiated response mindset by educating, training, and inspiring employees with roadshows and education programs,

Success Factor # 3: Leveraging Digital Technologies

Technology management teams must play a pivotal role in enabling digital transformation for supply chain segmentation. CIOs must champion a business technology agenda — investments in digital technologies to facilitate financial governance capture KPIs, conduct cost-to-serve analysis, and collaborate with sales leveraging social media and research data to find out the value propositions for customers in order to win, serve, and retain them.

Let's give one use case as an example. Customers' perceptions on the value of a product or service and how much they are willing to pay for it is difficult to predict. On one end of the extreme, you have value-conscious customers who always looking for a deal. On the other end, you have customers that will only buy premium goods and services. The other issue is that customers' behaviors and expectation change. Therefore, many firms struggle to segment their customers and markets intelligently and provide tailored products and services to those segments on an ongoing basis. Using digital technologies like "machine learning" and predictive analytics can be leveraged to analyze customers by collecting data from thousands or even millions of customers. Mining the collected data and combining it with external data like social media will help to keep pace with the analysis required to identify new correlations at all times. This will help in identifying the segmentation criteria and making it dynamic.

Also, machine learning will enable firms to support different supply chain strategies/responses for each segment like higher visibility, simplifications, etc. Machine learning can support creating intelligent customer-product-channel segments and then developing supply chain strategies to deliver differentiated offerings to these segments (all while balancing the cost to serve each segment against the value that segment brings to the business).

Success Factor # 4: Proven Change Management Methodology

Having a structured and proven methodology to show the way in the change transformation journey is a must. Any supply chain transformation program creates uncertainty and resistance. New leaders emerge, job descriptions are changed, and new skills and capabilities need to be developed. Dealing with these change management issues on a reactive, case-by-case basis puts timeline, morale, and results all at risk. A structured plan for managing change—beginning with the transformation team and then engaging key stakeholders and leaders—should be developed early and executed effectively as changes move through the organization. The plan should be comprehensive to cover planning, implementing, and sustaining the transformation changes (Sabri, 2013).

For transformation programs to work, there must be convergence between the new process, new technology capabilities, people readiness with the required new skills, and organization structure alignment changes.

Success Factor # 5: Effective Performance Measurement System (PMS) – Data, Metrics, and KPIs

Comprehensive end-to-end measures of supply chain performance, such as total cost, inventory, forecast accuracy, and perfect order, must be established to show the trade-offs required. Supply chain performance results should be communicated to all layers. Operational and financial data will be needed at both aggregated and granular levels to analyze performance and conduct corrective actions.

The author has not come across many firms that could claim that they have mastered performance measurement across all of their processes and levels. The widespread feeling among supply chain managers is that they measure too much, too little, or measure the wrong metrics. For the supply chain segmentation strategy to work, the culture of measurement should be anchored within the organization while leveraging some best practices such as: 1) focus on a handful of key KPIs and related metrics, 2) sustain KPI tracking, 3) conduct root cause analysis on a regular basis, and 4) align incentives to achieving KPIs targets. Finally, the list of the KPIs should be comprehensive enough to include related KPIs necessary to measure achieving the customer value propositions such as delivery performance and flexibility (Sabri, 2012).

In addition, data availability and accessibility is very important. It is considered a pre-requisite for supply chain segmentation because visibility to data such as customer requirements, demand, cost, materials, forecasts, product life cycle, revenue, and margin is required to drive the right decisions regarding segmentation during planning and implementing phases.

Most supply chain leaders and executives understand the difference between "lean" and "agile" supply chain models. The first one seeks operational efficiency and cutting waste while the other one focuses on responsiveness, flexibility, speed, and targeting higher service levels. The challenge for these leaders is when to apply each supply chain model and how. Here is how Dell and Caterpillar addressed that challenge in the context of the above framework.

CASE STUDY FROM DELL

Dell faced a challenge with its supply chain in 2008 when it realized that the highly responsive 'configure-to-order direct-to consumer' supply chain that had made its online store the world's largest channel for personal computers sales no longer fit the needs of its new physical retail channel, its enterprise sales, or even its high-volume consumer products. Facing increasing pressure from emerging and revitalized competitors, Dell found its supply chain model was no longer right for all aspects of its business, especially the emerging ones. For example, when Dell entered the retail channel, the company tried to use the same supply chain model as its online configure-to-order business. Because competition in conventional retail can be fiercer than its online channel and Dell's supply chain was not designed for lower cost, it was determined that Dell's 2008 supply chain model would not work well at the store level. Most retail orders are large and focused on fewer configurations compared to online orders.

Adding to this challenge, the company faced corporate and public sector customers who were looking for a complete and customized package for their IT needs. This required a different supply chain model than one used for online customers (Simchi-Levi, Clayton, & Raven, 2012).

The company had been in the top five of the Gartner Supply Chain Top 25 every year since it started in 2004, but demand for commoditized products, changes in customer channel preferences, emerging market growth, a more capable supply base and globalization had challenged the one-size-fits-all supply chain model (Davis, 2010). Clearly, Dell needed to segment its supply chain and implement new supply chain models to serve new customers in new channels with new product types.

For the past several years, the company has been transforming its supply chain into a multichannel, segmented model, with different policies for serving consumers, corporate customers, distributors, and retailers. Through this transformation, Dell has moved up to the number two spot on Gartner's "Top

25 Supply Chains" list (Thomas, 2012). Dell's supply chain segmentation journey is summarized in the following section in the context of the segmentation framework explained in the previous section.

Segmentation Vision Alignment to Corporate Goals

Dell decided to create multiple supply chain models, each dedicated to a different segment of the PC industry and configured differently from a demand planning, inventory planning, production planning, and distribution planning perspective. But, they would be designed in such a way that the company could take advantage of synergies to reduce complexity and benefit from economies of scale (i.e. virtual supply chains with one physical supply chain).

Dell embarked on a three-year segmentation journey to achieve two of the corporate goals: improving margin and gaining market share in retail business.

Profiling and Segmentation

Dell started the profiling and segmentation step by determining how different groups of customers derive value from its products and services. The business-to-business (B2B) market demands predictability, speed, customization, services, and precision delivery. While business-to-consumer (B2C) market wants multiple channel options, the ability to personalize for niche products, low-price options, and devices that deliver content. Historically, Dell was organized by products and/or region (Davis, 2010). As part of globalization, Dell aligned organizations to customer value consistently across regions. Dell moved to the following segmentation dimensions to come up with the segmentation criteria: product characteristics, customer characteristics, and channel. Figure 7 shows the profiles that were selected to represent the majority of the business. During this step, customer value propositions were analyzed. Dell used historical customer data from contracts, survey results, and business intelligence (BI) data to begin its exercise. To provide a robust, outside-in perspective, Dell invested in several resources to complete the detailed configuration profitability analysis, targeted surveys, and external marketing insights from multiple industries (Davis, 2010). Three customer value propositions were selected: 1) lead time, 2) cost, and 3) flexibility in configuration. Based on the segmentation criteria, four clusters were selected as shown in Figure 7.

Associating Clusters to Supply Chain Models

With a good understanding of selected clusters and the direction of the market, Dell began to design the new supply chain models by balancing the supply chain extremes of agility and efficiency. Dell used the 'voice of the customer approach to identify the range of strategies it would require in different functions. The combination of these strategies created the unique supply chain models. The company originally defined eighteen potential supply chain models simplified to six supply chain models. This resulted in models based on a mix of configurations predetermined by Dell and products configurable by customers (Davis, 2010).The six supply models were further consolidated into four supply chain models which have been referred to as Build-to-Order, Build-to-Plan, Build-to-Stock, and Build-to-Spec (Simchi-Levi et al., 2012). Since Dell is not using this exact naming convention for the supply chain models, the author refers to them as follows:

Figure 7. Selected profiles and clusters for Dell

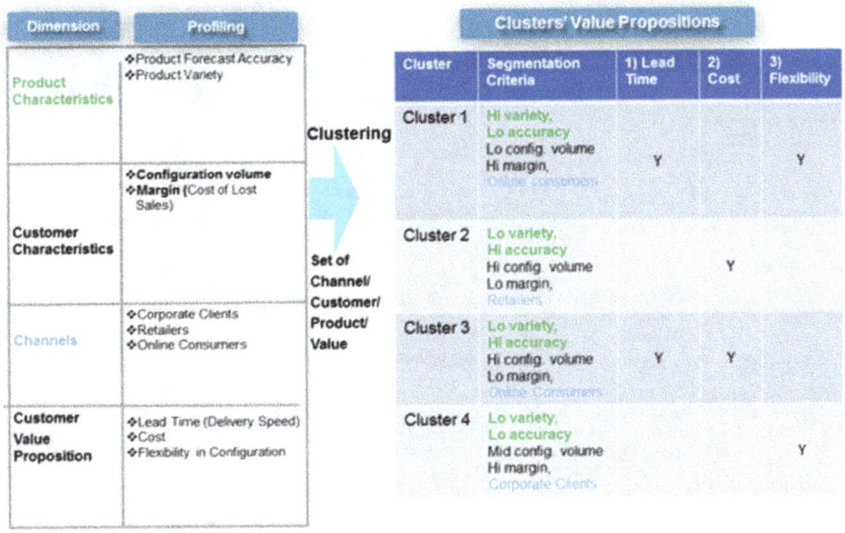

1. Responsive & Flexible Supply Chain
2. Efficient Supply Chain
3. Responsive & Efficient Supply Chain
4. Flexible Supply Chain

In the first cluster shown in Figure 8, the interaction with online consumers and volume by configuration is low. As Dell offers to satisfy customers' value propositions of flexibility in defining the configuration and having short lead time for delivery, the focus of Dell is on higher margins and the cost of a lost sale is high. The supply planning strategy should be based on realized demand (sales order) or a pull strategy. This is the strategy that Dell uses in its traditional business. Dell employs a pull replenishment strategy where component inventory is managed based on forecast while sales order determines the final configuration. So, assembly is driven by the individual customer order and the production batch size is one. Direct ship to consumer and using 'air' as the main transportation mode are needed order fulfillment strategies to achieve a short lead time (high degree of responsiveness).

In 2008, as part of globalization, Dell began to heavily leverage its partner network of suppliers to perform assembly (outsourcing its assembly lines), which put more emphasis on strengthening relationship with suppliers to ensure high level of quality and delivery performance with tracking capability. For this cluster, there is need for assembly suppliers to master the production batch size of one.

The second cluster targets retailers and is associated with higher forecast accuracy, less product variability (configuration), and lower margin, since retailers demand low prices to make money. This makes the traditional push-based replenishment strategy better because managing the supply chain based on long-term forecast lowers cost through economies of scale (high volume) and high forecast accuracy. In this supply chain model, procurement, assembly, and shipment decisions are all based on forecast. Extensive collaboration on the configuration and related forecast is expected between Dell and retailers. Ocean transportation mode is typically used to reduce cost.

Figure 8. Selected supply chain models for Dell

		Supply Chain Processes' Key Strategies			
Cluster	**Supply Chain Model**	**Supply Planning**	**Demand Planning (including Marketing & product Design)**	**Procurement**	**Order Fulfillment**
Cluster 1	Responsive & Flexible SC	• Pull Replenishment • No finished goods inventory	• Configuration is defined by Customers • Statistical Forecasting for components	• Outsourced Assembly • Collaborative relationship with suppliers • Production batch size is 1	• Air • Direct ship to consumer
Cluster 2	Efficient SC	• Push replenishment • Inventory kept at retailers	• Small # of configurations identified for market • Collaborating on the demand plan (forecast)	• Outsourced Assembly • Large production batch size • leveraging volume scale to reduce purchasing costs	• Ocean • Direct ship to Retailers
Cluster 3	Responsive & Efficient SC	• Push replenishment • Inventory including safety stocks stored in centralized locations	• Small # of configurations identified for market • Statistical Forecasting	• Outsourced Assembly • Large production batch	• Ocean
Cluster 4	Flexible SC	• Pull Replenishment • No inventory	• Small # of configurations defined by corporate client • Tight collaboration with sales	• Outsourced Assembly • Large production batch	• Ocean • Direct ship to clients

Cluster 3 is defined for online end consumers who select popular configurations sold online. This cluster has limited configuration options (product variety) which increase forecast accuracy, and call for a push-based replenishment strategy. In this supply chain model, popular product configurations are prepositioned in the supply chain network based on long-term forecasts, to provide a high response time (which is a customer value proposition). In this model, procurement, assembly, and ocean shipping to stocking points are all based on forecast, while shipment to consumers is based on sales orders using air for high response delivery.

Finally, a fourth cluster is defined for enterprise clients (corporates) where forecast accuracy is high and product variety is customized for individual corporations. The menu of available options offered to corporate clients has a longer product lifecycle with more overlap across generations of technology. This enables corporate clients to order the same configuration over a long period of time and lower their total cost of ownership. Because Dell has a close relationship with its corporate clients, forecast accuracy and volume are high (Simchi-Levi et al., 2012). Therefore, Dell uses the flexible supply chain model for this cluster. This model does not keep a finished goods inventory and products are assembled to sales order using components ordered well ahead of time, based on forecast.

In addition to adopting different strategies across different supply chain models, Dell adopted some best practice strategies to be the same across all supply chain models. The idea here is that one physical supply chain should be able to support several virtual supply chains. Some of the key common strategies are:

1. Procurement strategy to reduce purchasing cost by leveraging volume across the various supply chain models
2. Procurement/manufacturing strategy to outsource and consolidate manufacturing infrastructure
3. Product design strategy to standardize the components on the bill of material (BOM) across all supply chain models and reduce product portfolio

4. Order fulfillment strategy to use one physical infrastructure to support all supply chain models

Simchi-Levi et al. (2012) referenced an example where Dell took advantage of synergies in order fulfillment for the North American supply chain by using one infrastructure for all four supply chain models. Dell has U.S. fulfillment nodes in Atlanta, Chicago, Los Angeles, and New York and employs some of them in more than one supply chain model. In the online business, where speed is critical, items are air shipped from manufacturing in Asia to the four locations in the U.S, and from there by parcel to customer locations. Retail is different. Because cost is the customer value proposition, products are shipped by ocean to Los Angeles and Chicago, and from there by truck to the retailers. However, for online consumers interested in popular products, items are shipped by ocean to North America and then trucked to two key locations (Los Angeles and Nashville) for shipping to individual consumers. This results in a simple logistics network that still meets the needs of a complex business.

Process, Technology, and Governance Changes for Dell

It is important to mention that one of the biggest challenges of segmentation is to coordinate the required changes across several supply chain processes to support different virtual supply chains.

Dell created a standard process to introduce new processes, technologies, and governance changes to enable the large range of supply chain strategies that were defined in the previous step. It has a dedicated center of excellence (COE) that collects requirements from sales, marketing, and operations, then evaluates the customer benefit and business strategy, and finally recommends the right changes within product development and supply chain design.

Critical factors to this effort were continuous improvement that utilizes lean methodologies to maintain a focus on customers' value and conducts benchmarking to provide an outside-in perspective (Davis, 2010).

Organizational realignment was a critical governance change to the new supply chain models. Dell went through this realignment in every aspect of their business, including product design, manufacturing, transportation, customer care, warranty, and technical support. Dell also simplified internal interactions by centralizing global operations and aligning to customer verticals.

Dell undertook a comprehensive transformation of the legacy technology that had only supported Dell's configure-to-order strategy. With the implementation of different supply chain models to support different customer segments, there was a need for technology to support large lot sizes and imply the existence of a finished goods inventory, something Dell had never considered before. As a result, the company needed to rethink its IT infrastructure so it could support multiple supply chain models.

Segmentation creates the need to develop a single process to allocate manufacturing capacity to different supply chain models and related clusters. This is sales and operations planning (S&OP) — one process applied across all supply chain clusters to align demand, supply, and inventory, and to allocate production capacity to the various supply chains based on actual and forecast demand.

Another process change benefiting mainly the "efficient & flexible" supply chain model was to simplify its product lines and market the most popular configurations. This simplification reduced costs and improved responsiveness through improved forecast accuracy. It also enabled the company to identify popular products which are good candidates to be produced in advance, prepositioned in the network, and offered online to consumers, thus enabling Dell to respond quickly to consumer demand (Simchi-Levi et al., 2012).

Implementation Roadmap for Dell Segmentation Transformation

Dell recognized that the scope of this transformation change would require a multiyear roadmap. The company set short-term project goals with specific benefits to show traction against the overall plan. Another key component of the implementation approach was to pilot segmentation capabilities manually, while designing the automated, scalable solution in parallel. Both of these strategies allowed quick wins to build momentum and mitigated risk during the transformation (Davis, 2010).

Refining and Evolving Journey

The result of Dell's supply chain segmentation was the creation of end-to-end supply chain models in which multiple capabilities can be arranged in unique designs to satisfy specific customer requirements. These models were rolled out to different regions. There is a need to sustain it and refine it to achieve the expected benefits. The key for Dell is that end-to-end supply chain segmentation is an ongoing, evolving journey. Improvement is never done, but rather continuously realigned to changing customer values.

Key Success Factors for Dell

Dell identified four critical success factors (Davis, 2010):

1. **The Right Transformation Team:** Dell identified 12 key work tracks (teams). Each had a VP sponsor, with small teams coordinating and program-managing the change. Certain skills for certain roles were required. For example, during the first part of the planning phase, the skills required were an outside-in perspective focused on customers, knowledge of market and other industries, end-to-end supply chain design. Then, for the second part of the planning phase, the skills required were process design, lean/Six Sigma expertise, data analytics, systems optimization, and process automation. Now, for the change management work stream, the following skills were required: program management, organizational influence and communication.
2. **Executive Sponsorship:** The supply chain segmentation strategy and potential benefits were shared with the entire executive leadership team to drive cross-functional buy in. Dell's Vice Chairman was the sponsor of the effort throughout the transformation program.
3. **Unified, End-to-End Business Strategy for Culture Support:** The key to this was the ability to clearly articulate and communicate the need for change, the vision, and the role of different organizations in the end state. To support this communication, several leaders started an internal blog to keep people up to date and engaged.
4. **Start With Customer Value:** Historically, customers were segmented by verticals (e.g., consumer, corporate, government, and small business) as well as regions. Dell had to look across an aggregated view of these existing groupings to identify shared values relating to product features and supply chain capabilities. A global view for customer value and KPIs was critical to this process. Dell wanted to balance customer metrics with operational metrics and achieve a Balanced Scorecard with clear accountability. In addition, data was essential. Visibility to customer requirements, demand, cost, materials, forecasts, product road maps, revenue mix, and multiple views to margin were required to drive the right decisions.

Achieved Benefits

Three years after starting the transformation program, Dell started to gain some significant benefits. Product availability has improved 37%, and order-to-delivery times are 33% shorter. Dell now offers significantly fewer configurations resulting in a dramatic improvement in forecast accuracy by a factor of three. The tailored matching of transportation mode with supply model led to a 30% reduction in freight cost for laptops and slashed manufacturing cost by 30% (Simchi-Levi et al., 2012). Dell also realized approximately $1.5 billion in operational cost reductions between 2008 and 2010. This transformation was a critical factor in that reduction (Davis, 2010). Key operational drivers in this improvement were:

- Leveraging supplier capability and scale
- Addressing customers' value propositions,
- Simplified design and reductions in complexity
- Improved internal collaboration through collaboration across product design, supply chain, marketing, sales, and finance
- Improved forecast accuracy due to reduction in complexity and better connection to demand which resulted in a significant increase in forecast accuracy at the product, platform, and configuration levels

To summarize, Dell, which revolutionized both the computer industry and supply chain management with its direct-to-consumer business model in the 1990s, is one of a number of companies that are transforming their supply chains by leveraging supply chain segmentation and achieving significant benefits. Instead of using a one-size-fits-all approach to supply chain processes and policies, segmentation is helping these companies determine specific channels and customers that should be sourced from specific locations within their supply chains — and how these supply chains should be managed to profitably service all of those clusters (Johnston, 2012).

Lessons Learned

Dell's situation is not unique. Many global companies underperform because of a mismatch between business needs and supply chain designs (models). Supply chain segmentation is increasingly necessary to compete in today's business and reverse poor/declining performance.

Supply chain segmentation strategies often result in manufacturers taking different value propositions to market to meet the needs of different customers while supporting corporate objectives. For instance, when pursuing market share growth for certain product-customer-channel combinations, manufacturers may need to adopt one supply chain model: aggressive and dynamic pricing, high-product availability and superior lead times. When looking to retain market share for other product-customer-channel combinations, the supply chain posture may be different: fixed pricing and competitive lead times.

The above case study was previously published in a book chapter under the title of "*Optimization of Supply Chain Management in Contemporary Organizations:* Supply chain segmentation - Concept and best practice transformation framework" in IGI Global, written by Ehap Sabri, pp. 87-116, Copyright 2015

FUTURE TRENDS

More companies are realizing that gaining competitive advantage is no longer feasible by only optimizing their own resources without considering customers' needs and suppliers' capabilities. They need to get involved in the management of all upstream organizations that are responsible for the supply, as well as the downstream network that is responsible for delivery and after sales market. The challenge for companies is synchronizing supply chain processes (from product design and procurement to marketing and customer service management) in order to be more responsive to customer needs. The trend of mergers and acquisitions will continue to rise, and the complexity of supply chains will increase. This will intensify the need for supply chain segmentation to streamline the process of collaboration between different entities and satisfy the value propositions for customers.

The author predicts the explosion of supply chain segmentation strategy implementation in the next few years. As companies redefine supply chain processes that span across suppliers and customers, there will be a need for segmentation that will result in a significant improvement in efficiency and help them achieve competitive advantage. Companies that do not come on board will realize soon that they are losing ground and customers soon.

The widespread use of supply chain segmentation strategy will lead to new options for improving business-to-business and business-to-consumer collaborations, in addition to supply chain performance, monitoring, and controlling. Intelligent performance measurement systems that can capture negative performance trends and select the correct resolutions are expected to come into widespread use in the next few years. This will open new methods of integration between supply chain partners like system-to-system integration using web services (e.g. integrating one firm's inventory control system and another's logistics scheduling environment), the use of wireless devices, and the tight integration of front-end web-site with the back-end systems of supply chain partners.

In the coming years, more and more companies will need to take the supply chain segmentation journey to deliver customer value propositions and gain competitive advantage and market share. Digital technologies will make the journey smoother and more effective. The future belongs to companies who can match their supply chains to the specific customers' needs, and therefore supply chain segmentation remains one of the key interests of supply chain leaders.

Segmentation criteria will be able to use structured and unstructured data (SNEW – social, news, events, and weather) and process large amounts of data. Leveraging ML / AI it would be possible for ML to leveraging self-clustering algorithms and create the segments dynamically in an automated fashion.

Also, where as in the past, companies were limited to a few segments, supply chain designs would be increased beyond 2 or 4 segments. Digital technology would do the heavy lifting ultimately leading to significant number of segments to satisfy customers' expectations and requirements.

CONCLUSION

Segmentation is gaining ground in manufacturing as well as in retail and the questions around it have evolved from "what is it?" to "how can we do it?". Supply chain segmentation is not a one-time exercise; it is a multi-quarter journey, but it does get easier after your first venture through the ten steps discussed as part of the proposed segmentation framework. Also, structured assessment of the five success factors should be executed early on. Segmentation must be living and ongoing, with the ability to repeat the exercise. Segmentation is a continuous journey to keep your supply chain(s) relevant to your customer(s).

The supply chain segmentation is not just a business initiative; it's a change in the organization's culture. Therefore, executive commitment and visible support is mandatory to the success.

Technology is typically needed for the implementation since segmentation often uncovers issues and gaps with current tools. Leveraging digital technology makes the supply chain segmentation journey smoother and more effective. In absence of the right decision-support tools, segmentation strategies will not yield the expected benefits.

Supply chain segmentation strategy presents huge opportunities that are already being tapped by a few companies and supply chains who achieved significant benefits. Implementing supply chain segmentation strategy is key to gain competitive advantage, streamline processes, reduce waste, and eventually achieve business agility which is significantly needed in the new age of globalization and intensive competition.

REFERENCES

Christopher, M., Peck, H., & Towill, D. (2006). A Taxonomy for Selecting Global Supply Chain Strategies. *International Journal of Logistics Management, 17*(2), 277–287. doi:10.1108/09574090610689998

Christopher, M., Towill, D., Aitken, J., & Childerhouse, P. (2009). Value Chain Classification. *Journal of Manufacturing Technology Management, 20*(4), 460–474. doi:10.1108/17410380910953720

Davis, M. (2010). *Case Study for Supply Chain Leaders: Dell's Transformative Journey Through Supply Chain Segmentation*. Retrieved from https://www.gartner.com/doc/1468717/case-study-supply-chain-leaders

Fisher, M. L. (1997, March). What Is the Right Supply Chain for Your Product? *Harvard Business Review*, 105–116.

Gattorna, J. (2006). *Living Supply Chains*. Harlow: Pearson.

Johnston, D. (2012). *The Shift to Reshoring*. Retrieved from http://www.jda.com/realresultsmagazine/view-article.cfm?did=2867

Kartz, J. (2011). *Creating High-Value Supply Chains*. Retrieved from http://www.industryweek.com/companies-amp-executives/creating-high-value-supply-chains

Lovell, A., Saw, R., & Stimson, J. (2005). Product Value-Density: Managing Diversity Through Supply Chain Segmentation. *International Journal of Logistics Management, 16*(1), 142–158. doi:10.1108/09574090510617394

Mason-Jones, R., Naylor, B., & Towill, D. (2000). Engineering the Leagile Supply Chain. *International Journal of Agile Management, 2*(1), 54–61.

Mellins-Cohen, D. (2012). Segmentation: A How- To Guide. *High Beam Research*. Retrieved from http://www.highbeam.com/doc/1G1-289725005.html

Naylor, J., Naim, M., & Berry, D. (1999). Leagility: Integrating the Lean and Agile Manufacturing Paradigms in the Total Supply Chain. *International Journal of Production Economics*, *62*(1–2), 107–118. doi:10.1016/S0925-5273(98)00223-0

Roscoe, S., & Baker, P. (2013). Supply chain segmentation in the sporting goods industry. *International Journal of Logistics Research and Applications*, *17*(2), 136–155. doi:10.1080/13675567.2013.837869

Sabri, E. (2012). *Enduring Transformation: Performance measurement and governance make the difference.* Retrieved from https://www.apics.org/apics-for-individuals/apics-magazine-home/magazine-detail-page/2012/10/04/enduring-transformation

Sabri, E. (2013). *Strategies for Supply Chain Transformation: Supply& Demand Chain Executive Magazine.* Retrieved from http://www.sdcexec.com/article/11122122/companies-struggle-to-decide-when-and-where-to-begin-and-how-to-translate-their-vision-into-goals-goals-into-strategies-and-strategies-into-process-changes-and-projects

Sabri, E. (2015). Supply Chain Segmentation - Concept and Best Practice Transformation Framework. In A. DeMarco (Ed.), *Optimization of Supply Chain Management in Contemporary Organizations* (pp. 87–116). Hershey, PA: IGI Global. doi:10.4018/978-1-4666-8228-3.ch004

Simchi-Levi, D., Clayton, A., & Raven, B. (2012). *When One Size Does Not Fit All.* Retrieved from http://sloanreview.mit.edu/article/when-one-size-does-not-fit-all/

Thomas, K. (2012). Supply chain segmentation: 10 steps to greater profits. *Supply Chain Quarterly.* Retrieved from http://www.supplychainquarterly.com/topics/Strategy/201201segmentation

KEY TERMS AND DEFINITIONS

Clustering: The process of associating and grouping very similar (but not identical) profiles that reveals patterns, trends, requirements, characteristics, relationships, and structures.

End-to-End Supply Chain: The philosophy of considering all value-added processes from supplier to customer and embracing the concept of eliminating middle steps and barriers to optimize the performance of supply chain.

Governance: Encompasses the establishment of organizational structure, metrics, policies, and monitoring of their effectiveness.

Profiling: The process of learning information about behavior patterns, business characteristics, trends, requirements, relationships, and structures.

Supply Chain Segmentation: Is managing profitably different virtual end-to-end supply chains defined by a combination of channel/customer requirements, product characteristics, business value considerations, and differentiated supply response strategies.

Transformation: Is the journey of taking an organization in a new direction and reaching an entirely different level of effectiveness. It is a change to processes, systems, structure, and culture.

Value Proposition: A concise statement to why a customer should buy a product of service or how it will add value. It should be appealing to the customers' decision makers.

Chapter 5
Mastering Change Management for Successful Digital Supply Chain Transformations

Ehap Sabri
KPMG LLP, USA & University of Texas at Dallas, USA

ABSTRACT

In response to the dramatic changes in the business landscape over the last few years, many companies are launching business transformations leveraging digital technologies to drive sweeping changes in their supply chain processes. The digital supply chain transformation can be evident establishing collaborative forecasting processes, optimizing networks and inventories, etc. Digital supply chain transformation is not a new buzz word. It is the application of digital capabilities to processes, products, and assets to improve supply chain efficiency, enhance customer value, manage risk, and achieve competitive advantage. However, organizations are still facing numerous challenges to transform and perform. Perhaps the most common misunderstanding is that digital transformation is all about the implementation and use of cutting-edge technologies. This chapter will dive deep to understand major challenges to digital supply chain transformations, identify the key drivers and enablers of digital opportunity, and provide a change management framework for digital supply chain transformation.

INTRODUCTION

In today's complex and ever-changing business world, firms of all types are rethinking every aspect of their supply chain performance. Firms are exploring new enablers like digital technologies to optimize and manage their supply chains; beginning with demand planning and order management reviewing the entire supply chain up to procurement and transportation.

In today's globalized world, firm's success is not just dependent on its own efforts. However, the success of an organization depends largely on how effectively it can orchestrate a vast, global network of supply chain partners to deliver goods and services that meet the needs of individual consumers. It's all about engaging with customers efficiently through new and improved customer experiences. Early

DOI: 10.4018/978-1-5225-7700-3.ch005

Copyright © 2019, IGI Global. Copying or distributing in print or electronic forms without written permission of IGI Global is prohibited.

adopters of digital disrupters such as Amazon, Uber, Netflix have redefined the traditional business model and demonstrated how it's to be done. They focused on customers and not just provided exceptional, unique customer experience, but also engaged customers that keep coming back for more.

Digital Transformation is not restricted to the supply chain; it's everywhere. It's in the marketing, sales, products, Support, HR, Supply chain etc. It opens new opportunities, challenges traditional methods and changes the way we think and act. One of the key challenge faced in transforming a business is to train workforce new skills necessary to participate in the new way of doing business and to make the changes for digital transformation.

In all kinds of industries from the relatively slow-moving ones such as Utilities and Cement to the rapidly changing businesses of the High-Tech and Retail industries, efficient and agile supply chain processes have become critical in achieving competitive advantage. Companies can no longer view the supply chain as a back office and a transactional focused function. It is becoming extremely prevalent in that companies are not simply looking to drive cost out of their businesses, but also striving to be more agile in securing a supply chain that can quickly adapt to a rapidly changing market.

Taking the initiative to transform supply chain leveraging best practices and the latest digital technologies is no longer an option; it is a strategic mandate in order to stay relevant in the industry. Evidently, it is crucial to act rapidly and launch transformation activities. However, the industry's reality is that 70% of all transformation initiatives (programs) fail. The author has witnessed several firms struggle with implementing the transformation improvement programs and achieving the promised value or "Return on Investment" (ROI).

The low success rates of other transformation programs and the scary statistics make firms who are about to take the transformation journey to reconsider moving forward. These firms typically have doubts and questions about the best practice in integrating new digital technologies into supply chain operations. At times they even postpone their efforts until an expert is able to address their concerns. Firms seek how to:

- Master change management and ensure users' adoption
- Address the need for new skills to support processes that span across suppliers and partners
- Ensure continuous senior management support
- Identify comprehensive metrics and ensure continuous monitoring
- Choose the right digital technology and the right software provider

Based on relevant research and the author's professional experience, the main cause for the low success rates of business transformation initiatives can be grouped into two categories: 1) The lack of preparation and familiarity with the transformation lifecycle, and 2) People-related aspects that are poorly managed or altogether neglected. This chapter provides the top 7 challenges under each respective category and explains how to address these challenges during supply chain transformation programs. This chapter also provides a practical change management framework to ensure a smooth and successful digital supply chain transformation programs. This framework includes 8 steps (phases) needed to implement change in the culture of the organization and 5 success factors for companies to maintain throughout the lifecycle of change. These five factors can be used as a checklist to evaluate the readiness of the organization to change and its chances of a successful digital transformation.

Historic background on change management in the context of digital supply chain transformations is provided in the next section.

BACKGROUND

Direct Correlation Between Change Management and Transformation

The complex, cross-functional nature of supply chains forces executives and managers to be more knowledgeable about the successful implementation of change. Greer and Ford (2009) conducted an extensive study on this topic and provided evidence in support of the differences between implementing non-supply chain management (NSCM) changes and supply chain management (SCM) changes, and a lower level of success was shown to be realized when implementing SCM changes than when implementing NSCM changes due to complexity. Therefore, the majority of supply chain leaders are keen to transform their organizations, but they recognize that their organizations lack the knowledge and readiness to do so successfully.

Nadler and Tushman (1989) mentioned that because broader change programs are often more difficult to implement, the degree of success realized from implementing SCM changes might differ as well. Their article provides a good insight into managing large-scale planned change.

Research shows the success rate of supply chain transformation has a direct correlation to the degree of mastering change management. Ford and Greer (2005) research has indicated relationships between various change management activities and change achievement or success.

In Prosci's 2009 benchmarking study (http://www.change-management.com/tutorial-case-mod3.htm), the top trend identified by study participants was a greater recognition of the need for mastering change management. The same study showed a direct correlation between struggled projects and lack of effective change management as shown in Table 1.

The table shows a clear correlation between effective change management practice and meeting project objectives while staying on budget and according to the schedule. For example, of the participants that had effective change management programs in place, 95% met or exceeded objectives; while only 16% - or about 1 in 6 - of those with poor change management programs met or exceeded objectives. The Prosci's benchmarking studies over the last few years suggest that mastering change management increases the success rate of organizational changes to as high as 95%.

Therefore, mastering change management is very crucial for successful supply chain transformations.

Table 1. Change management impact on meeting project objectives, staying on schedule and budget

Project Criteria for success	Poor Change Management	Effective Change Management
Correlation of excellent change management to **meeting project objectives**	16%	95%
Correlation of excellent change management practice to **staying on schedule**	16%	71%
Correlation of excellent change management practice to **staying on budget**	51%	82%

Source: Prosci's 2009 Change Management Benchmarking Report

Effective Change Management Practices

Effective change management practices embrace both the inner shift in the individual's values, aspirations and behaviors and the outer shift in process, strategy, policies, and systems (Karp 2005). So, effective change management practices target the organizational culture, organizational structure and recruiting, performance measurements, incentive compensations, and alignment with corporate goals and strategies.

Carolyn Aiken and Scott Keller (2009) have identified insights into how human nature gets in the way of successfully by applying the following four conditions required for behavioral change:

Creating a Compelling Story

What motivates senior leaders may not motivate most of the employees. Therefore change leaders need to be able to tell change story that covers what motivates employees the most in their work. In doing so, they can unleash a tremendous amount of drive. Secondly, Leaders should give an opportunity for employees to write their own story. It's detected in human nature that when we choose for ourselves, we are far more committed to the outcome. So, employees should be asked to suggest change rather than directly implementing change. Then this will help drive change that comes through a sense of ownership.

Role Modeling

It is a misconception that if we believe that if the leader is strong and influential then change will be successful irrespective of employees view. Carolyn and Scott (2009) has experienced that working with change program suggest that success depends less on how persuasive a few selected leaders are and more on how receptive the society is to the idea.

Reinforcing Mechanisms

Although it's difficult to establish a clear linkage between the successful change and money to be compensated, token of appreciation for the hard work of employees boost them to be more productive.

Capacity Building

Often change management initiatives require employees to develop the skills and talent needed for the desired change (new state of business). The important thing to understand here is that if employees are expected to play a new role with no proper training, they often feel neglected and lose belief. So, training is crucial and should include elements related to personality types, emotional intelligence, and another new process specific training.

Transformation Programs' Common Mistakes

Ramanan and Anil (2011) from Wipro Consulting Services believe that most of supply chain transformation fails because most companies tend to make common mistakes such as: Falling Into the "Leading Practices" Trap, where companies fails to understand its own supply chain situation in order to make the right choices and try to follow leading practices in market. They believe that companies will be more successful if they rethink their supply chain in a way that is driven by how it supports their business strategy and meets customer requirements. They believe that if supply chain technology is deployed without incorporating critical business requirements and process redesign then it will be simply a collection of an automated system with routine supply chain issues.

Use of technology as an enabler is definitely important for effective supply chain but one needs to understand that technology can't fix the flawed supply chain design. Whenever processes are refined and new technology is implemented, organizational structure must be aligned to support these initiatives.

In the quest for growth, many companies implement change initiatives to create strong, differentiated and better customer experience. Leonard and Coltea (2013) believe that majority of failed transformation change initiatives didn't focus front-line managers on the exact actions they need to take to achieve the company's desired business outcomes.

In many companies, front-line employees receive dozens of high priority messages from managers, executives and change managers daily. These messages become conflicting to front-line managers to know what task or metrics should focus on during a given day to deliver service. So, in this situation, front-line managers are unclear about work to perform which ultimately affects the productivity of the company.

Leonard and Coltea (2013) highlighted also that implementing a successful change management initiative isn't a one-time thing. Creating lasting change requires companies to evolve, and those that evolve successfully can achieve stronger financial performance.

Mastering Change Management Framework

Sabri and Verma (2015) provided a detailed analysis of the most common transformation failures. They also suggested a practical and comprehensive framework to master change management addressing typical challenges and common mistakes in addition to leveraging best practices. This framework will be leveraged and enriched in this book chapter to support digital supply chain transformation.

The next section will explain the top 7 transformation challenges for supply chain transformations based on research, including the above ones, and the authors' experience.

TRANSFORMATION LIFE CYCLE CHALLENGES

"Where" and "When" to Start

When making these kinds of drastic changes, the biggest challenges are often to know when and where to begin in order to translate the vision into goals, goals into strategies and strategies into process changes and projects. Very few companies have a good digital supply chain strategy. Some reasons are: 1) The lack of resources and time, 2) The lack of familiarity with the strategy development process in general, 3) The lack of knowledge of the full opportunities that digital technologies can bring to supply chain processes, and 4) The difficulty of securing a consensus since digital supply chain strategy is an integrated cross-functional strategy and requires investment from resources and money standpoints.

The author has observed some companies try to take the easy route and avoid spending time on rethinking their supply chain in a way that is driven by how it supports their business strategy; meets customer needs, and deploys key enablers like digital technologies.

Environment Is Not Ready

The culture of "playing it safe" is the first challenge. Firms get used to executing low-risk incremental improvements on the same business environment for an extended period of time, and they become resistant for big ideas of significant improvement because they do not know how to handle transformation programs and target big results.

Specific related challenge, which is relevant to digital supply chain transformation, is the need for intensive cooperation and cross-functional collaboration among executive peers. This would force executives to get out of their comfort zones and their respective areas of responsibility and find time out of their busy daily operation schedule to envision an entirely new business.

In a consulting engagement for the author with a semiconductor company, and after conducting a risk analysis workshop with the respective managers and directors, the highest significant and probable risk for the transformation initiative came to be a definite commitment from executives to follow through and provide the needed support. There were 3 previous half-baked and half-hearted transformation initiatives in the past targeting the same supply chain processes, which undermined confidence that the current program will be treated differently (Sabri and Verma, 2015). When a company has a previous record of transformation failure, lack of strong vision, no visible commitment from above, and no clear articulation of why this program is different, then the result would be upsetting.

Also, McKinsey research (2009) showed that organizations that took the transformation journey for defensive reasons (to stem trouble) due to the difficult circumstances had lower success rates than the companies that took the journey for offensive reasons (like boosting growth or increasing market share). Extra care from the top is much needed when a transformation initiative is taken for defensive reasons, and more emphasis on people change management and sufficient resources are crucial.

Lack of Convincing "ROI"

Several companies struggled to find the best way to determine the business case and ROI (return on investment), and identify the right metrics that would capture and display the benefits in addition to defining "success" when it comes to business transformations. Therefore, they couldn't sustain the buy-in from executives.

Also, success and performance measures' targets have to be defined for the intermediate phases of the transformation in addition to the end state to sustain a high level of energy and focus. In one of the industry conferences, the author asked an audience of more than 80 managers to raise their hands if they are "OK" with their own performance measurement governance (metrics identification, measuring, tracking, and controlling), only 3 managers raised their hands! The widespread feeling among managers is that they are measuring too much or too little, or are measuring the wrong metrics. The majority also feel that their performance measurement governance doesn't drive good behavior.

Inability of Selecting "the Right" Software Provider

Selecting a software provider is a hard undertaking and consumes time and internal resources. Companies is not just struggling in identifying the right software provider (partner) for digital technology but they are still struggling with choosing the right supply chain planning technology platform. In addition, executives frequently express their concern about their companies' ability to ensure that the technology is fully utilized once deployed. Supply chain applications especially the planning ones require a steep learning curve for most companies.

New Technology Is the "Silver Bullet" Perception

Some executives perceived the new technology to be the "silver bullet" to all of their business problems and forgot the fact that it is just an enabler for best practice processes and requires effective change management to be adopted.

When the transformation program is driven by a date given by IT instead of a value achieved the milestone, then it is a recipe for disaster. In an attempt to meet the target date (often unrealistic); training, documentation, and change management are often neglected, resulting in something that has a short life span (people stop it after some time) or that does not deliver the full benefit. These transformation programs might be able to "go live" from an IT standpoint but will not be well accepted or embraced by end users.

For transformation programs to work, an amalgamation has to happen between process changes, new technology capabilities, people readiness with the required new skills, and organization structure alignment changes.

No Clear Priorities for Day-to-Day Operations

Typically, the day-to-day operation is already at full capacity when the executives call for a transformation program. Some companies try to add transformation activities to the preexisting calendar of "run the business" meetings, but it doesn't work because short-term operational issues typically come first. People are in most cases occupied more than 100% of their capacity. This affects the productivity of transformation activities since people find it difficult to prioritize their activities. Sometimes due to unavailability of the right person for transformation activity because of their preoccupancy with another day to day jobs, a substitute is chosen who may not be fully aware of the desired transformation activity and hence overall productivity is affected.

Also, when companies are in the process of implementing several incremental improvement projects like six sigma or Kaizen projects, it will be a challenge to add a transformation program to the mix targeting the same functions. Companies that try to stuff too much into the organization will clog it causing employees and managers' capacity to execute to become a choke point unless the programs are prioritized and sequenced correctly.

Lack of Proven Transformation Methodology

Not having a proven, comprehensive and practical methodology to show the way in the transformation journey makes it impossible to address any of the above challenges. To be successful, the transformation team will require having not only knowledge and skills in organizational design and change management, but also a comprehensive methodology for planning, implementing, and sustaining the transformation changes (Sabri and Verma, 2015). There are at least three common methodology mistakes:

1. Some companies put more emphasis on IT activities compared to change management activities. They rush things and focus only on IT activities that they have to accomplish and cannot shorten.

2. The author has also witnessed the other extreme, where companies spent a huge amount of time on the planning phase, little time on implementing the change, and no time on sustaining it.
3. Other companies put significant emphasis on the transformations' soft factors, such as culture, leadership, and motivation while missing out on the hard factors of change management like financial results, commitment level of executives, the resources required to execute the program, and program roadmap and duration.

The following real-life story would provide examples for some of the challenges mentioned in this section. A few years back, the author was asked to play the executive process advisory role for a global high-tech company. Their largest end-to-end supply chain transformation program was underway. The program included process improvement and technology implementation to the following processes: Sales and Operation Planning (S&OP), Demand Management, Supply Planning, Order Planning, Inventory Planning, Order Fulfillment, Logistics, and Channel Management. The author joined 18 months after the program started. In the first phase of his engagement, he spent two weeks on site conducting his own assessment and came to a conclusion that the transformation is at risk and immediate corrective action is desperately needed. Here are a few of the findings:

First, the company is taking the transformation journey for defensive reasons; they were losing market share to competition, their margin was getting smaller and smaller, and they wanted to reverse the trend. Everyone in the company was fearful for his or her job.

Secondly, the author uncovered that the employees did not understand why the business must change and their own role in making it happen, so before providing any specific recommendations, the author wanted to investigate this further to find out why there was a lack of communication and articulation of the need for change to employees. He started by asking for the business case and to his surprise, the sponsor didn't have it handy. During the meeting with the finance representative on the program regarding the business case, the author discovered that the major cost-saving element was "laying off" employees! This was the main reason why the company didn't want to give enough clarity to employees about the program.

Thirdly, all program tracks were working in silos with little coordination. There was no master project plan covering the overall program progress and dependency. The author had to attend the project status meetings for all tracks to have a good picture about the status of the program. It was easy to notice the mistrust that every team had regarding the other teams' ability to deliver on time. In addition, around the same time, the blame game had just started.

Fourthly, the author investigated the transformation program structure, and he found out that 9 different tracks were identified to execute the program; like program management, process, technology, data, testing, suppliers, and change management track. The role for the author was under the process track. The shocker was that appropriate expertise was identified for all tracks except for change management track, it was "TBD"! Basically, a major transformation program was underway for defensive reasons, a layoff is one of the outputs of the program, the culture of the company to work in silos, the company has not done this type/scale of transformation before, and yet no one is assigned for change management!

Fifthly, there was no clear and structured transformation methodology. The transformation team took 18 months to identify the business requirements and socialize it with the IT organization. And since the duration of the first phase of the transformation program was two years; everyone was under pressure to implement, go-live, and transition in the remaining 6 months. Senior management from the business organization decided to take the IT date to "go-live" as the date they would communicate to their executives. They thought that IT will be the bottleneck and assumed that all other activities like designing the new (to-be) process, coming up with new policies, developing training manuals, conducting training sessions, defining roles and responsibilities for the new processes, defining new metrics and reports to support the new processes, and overcoming resistance issues will not be the bottleneck and will fall within the IT timeline!

Finally, there were no supply chain strategies defined. The transformation team came up with all the business requirements without considering the new strategies that they have to adopt to address their challenges and reverse the trend of losing market share.

It took this company several months and several drastic adjustments to clean this mess and start going in the right direction. Unfortunately, several senior managers and executives lost their jobs because they were slow to react.

The challenges of supply chain transformation related to people are explained in the next section.

PEOPLE CHANGE MANAGEMENT CHALLENGES

This section will cover the top 7 people change management challenges based on the authors' experience and relevant research.

Executives Are Slow to Come Aboard

Not having all executives on the same page early on is one of the first challenges that the change agent has to address. It is highly recommended, for this purpose, to schedule a 15-minute one-on-one meeting with all executives in the first week of the engagement. This practice is used by the author and it was very effective in highlighting the disconnect and identifying the root cause behind it, which would make it easier to address it and bring all executives on board to support the transformation program.

Reluctant executives to support the transformation program visibly will disrupt the speed of the company's progress in planning effectively and undermine transformation significantly. Even the best-planned supply chain transformation initiative would fail if top management fails to demonstrate a commitment to creating the sense of urgency necessary to overcome resistance to change. Executives' support is key to set proper expectations for their employees.

Keeping Stakeholders Engaged and Motivated

Stakeholders are the employees and managers who will be impacted by the process changes or will play a role and have an impact on the success of the transformation program. In a nutshell, the stakeholders are the people who will make the transformation happen. Disengaged stakeholders can really slow down progress and can be a reason by itself for transformation failure.

Many firms underestimate this challenge which results in catastrophic implications because no matter how sophisticated and powerful the software applications or digital technologies are and how effective best practices processes may be, in the end, it is the stakeholders who play the most significant role in the success or failure of the program. Supply chain stakeholders represent different organizations and different roles (operators, managers, planners, suppliers, customers, warehouse receivers, carriers, etc.) which add another dimension to the challenge.

Lack of Organizational Structure Alignment

It is necessary to look at the structural support for the change transformation program. If the foundation structure is deemed to be inadequate, restructuring becomes critical. Restructuring changes range in degree from minor adjustments to large-scale organization-wide changes that affect virtually every member of the organization.

One of the author's organizational change management engagements was to help a tire manufacturing company become a global supply chain organization and to streamline and standardize their processes. One of the deliverables was to recommend a structure for the global supply chain organization and the related roles and responsibilities. Assigning an executive vice president reporting to CEO and leading a centralized and global supply chain organization was one of the recommendations. Unfortunately, the sponsor did not have enough political clout with the CEO to make it happen before starting the design phase. This was one of the main reasons that the transformation program ran into serious delays in the program and severe change management and ownership issues.

Gartner research (July 2012) captured several organizational alignment challenges: the top two are: 1) determining the optimal level of centralized leadership, and 2) finding and cultivating capable planning talent.

Inability to Build the Right Transformation Team

Building the right transformation team is the most important change management activity in a business transformation program. In the process of building the team, senior management must be sensitive to the unique needs of the program environment. For example, it requires training and experience for the transformation team members to identify resistance and find its root causes, then, come up with strategies to handle and overcome resistance.

Building the right (effective) team optimizes the efforts of the team and increases the chances of having a successful program. On the other hand, a weak team structure would undercut the efforts of hard-working team members, reduce moral, and impede project success.

Lack of Effective Communication Plan

Most of the time when people resist change it is not because they are unwilling to change, it's just because they don't know why. Effective communications within the transformation team and between the team and other program stakeholders are essential for a smooth and successful journey.

It's a common misconception that if people are talking to each other it means they are communicating; communication needs to have a framework and format to be effective. Another common pitfall is that one communication plan template fits all programs or projects. While all programs or projects share the need for a communication plan, they differ in the type of information needed, frequency, and methods of communication (Sabri, Gupta, and Beitler, 2006).

Inability to Sustain On-Going Learning and Coaching

Supply Chain transformation programs require extensive and on-going training especially when it includes digital technologies and new skills and attitudes for the users of the new or improved processes.

The proper allocation and commitment of resources (time, energy, and money) to conduct training and coaching to help employees in their skills acquisition is critical to the success of implementing and sustaining changes.

Although the "sustain" phase is the most difficult phase in any transformation program, there is relatively little attention by executives concerning sustaining change in organizations. While planning and implementing a change can occur relatively quickly, sustaining change involves a long period of time. Maintaining a sense of urgency and a significant level of interest is difficult over a long period of time. This phase can take months and sometimes a few years. Therefore, the author typically suggests a separate budget for this phase to bring attention to it.

During this phase, the new process must be reinforced by the policies for recruiting, selecting, promoting, compensating, evaluating, and on-going training of employees. Also, acknowledging and rewarding stakeholders for new behaviors are essential to stabilize the new process and anchor the new culture.

Lack of Comprehensive Incentive Program

While the Communication plan addresses the "why" question by providing the "awareness" about the importance of change and the risks of not changing for the company, the incentive plan addresses the "what's in it for me" question and creates the "desire" to change. Only when managers and employees have the "awareness" of the need to change and the "desire" to support the change, then learning "how" to change can start.

Unfortunately, the lack of comprehensive incentive programs is an issue in almost every transformation program that the first author has audited. In some companies, they make the incentive programs limited to managers and executives and don't include the employees. In other companies, incentive programs are in place, but not aligned to support the desired behavior and new process. Very few companies go the extra mile to come up with an incentive program for every member of the transformation team and stakeholders who are responsible to plan and implement change.

The rule of thumb that every stakeholder, which their processes will be impacted by the change or who will have an impact on the transformation, should be part of the incentive program. Also, the objectives of the transformation should be reflected in the stakeholders' scorecards and aligned with their incentives. Therefore, the company's human resources (HR) department should be involved early on.

COMPREHENSIVE FRAMEWORK FOR MASTERING CHANGE MANAGEMENT

Figure 1 provides a comprehensive framework for mastering change management to ensure a smooth and successful digital supply chain transformation programs, and address the above challenges. This framework includes 8 steps (phases) needed to implement change in the culture of the organization and 5 success factors for companies to maintain throughout the lifecycle of change.

What follows are the required steps to be taken during the life cycle of change transformation and success factors for effective change management (as shown in Figure 1). Using these steps as a systematic and comprehensive framework, executives and managers can understand what to expect and how to engage the entire organization in the process.

Figure 1. Digital supply chain change management framework

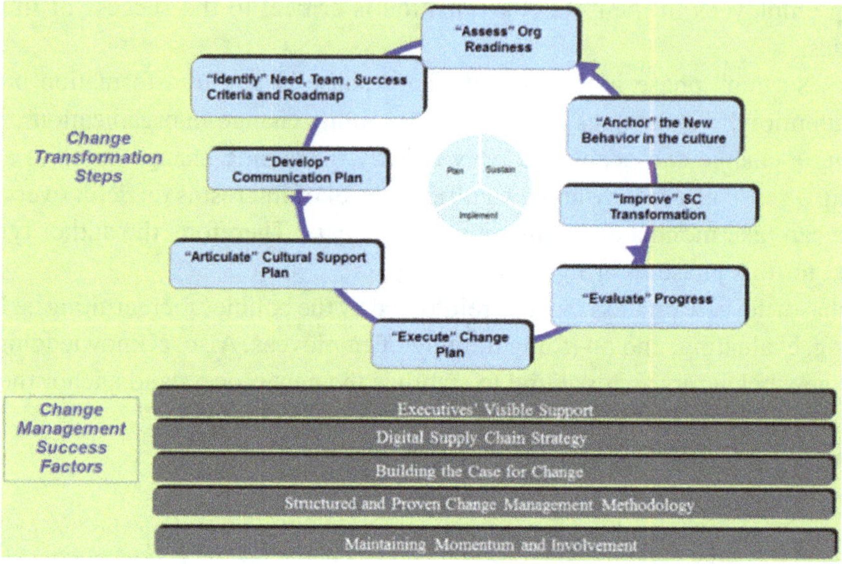

Eight Change Transformation Steps

The proposed framework proposed suggests eight steps to go thru the life cycle of change transformation effectively as shown in Figure 1 which are summarized as follows: 1) Assess, 2) Identify, 3) Develop, 4) Articulate, 5) Execute, 6) Evaluate, 7) Improve, and 8) Anchor. These steps can be also grouped under 3 phases:

- **Plan phase** which includes steps 1 to 4
- **Implement phase** which includes steps 5 & 6
- **Sustain phase** which includes steps 7 & 8

Let's understand about every step in more details:

Step 1: "Assess" Organization Readiness

Organization Readiness for change gives an idea about the current state of the organization with respect to the desired position after the change. So the first activity in assessing organizational readiness is to identify the anticipated and desired change (end state). To clearly define the desired change, start off with program description which an organization is considering for change. This will help assure whether stakeholders have the same vision. Then next activity is to assess the alignment of the proposed change project with the organization's current vision, mission, and strategic plan.

A SWOT Analysis is a beneficial exercise in assessing organizational readiness for implementing a new program. SWOT identifies an organization's strengths and weaknesses and may identify any areas that need a change in order to move forward. It identifies opportunities which can contribute towards success and also identifies threats which may be barriers in the process.

Another major activity for this step is evaluating the existence of the five success factors for mastering change management: 1) executives' engagement and visible support, 2) commitment to developing end-to-end SC strategy, 3) the ability to develop a convincing business case, 4) deciding on change management methodology, and 5) the ability and previous record in maintaining the engagement & involvement of all stakeholders. This evaluation can be accomplished by scheduling one-on-one interviews, group meetings, questionnaire, and reviewing documentations.

Step 2: "Identify" Need, Team, Success Criteria, and Roadmap

Once the problem statement is defined, stakeholders are identified, the scope of supply chain transformation is fixed and aligned with organizational goals then there is a need to articulate clearly the need for change. This activity is crucial to answering the question that everyone in the organization across all levels will have "why we need to change". It provides the "elevator pitch" or the key message that will be communicated to provide awareness. One example of a key message from a Manufacturing company is "we need to transform our supply chain to penetrate new market channels while maintaining low inventory levels and gain a competitive advantage in order to increase market share profitably" (Sabri, 2015). This activity is also important to secure the buy-in from the upper management who typically ask for an explanation of how the change helps in implementing the organization's strategic plan and achieving corporate goals.

Building the right (effective) team optimizes the efforts of the team and increases the chances of having a successful program. One of the biggest challenges of building and developing a transformation team for supply chain improvement programs in today's business is that every transformation program has its own nature and resources requirements. The senior management and sponsor must be sensitive to the unique needs of the program environment. Also, the structure of the organization plays also a big role in selecting and building the transformation team. There is a need to document the required skills for every role (functional consultant, change agent, process consultant, developer, architect, program manager, project manager, etc...) based on the program charter document. This includes also determining the number of resources needed for every role. In addition, establishing a process to evaluate the performance of resources and define an incentive plan to keep them motivated is crucial (Sabri and Shaikh, 2010).

This activity should consider "why we are changing" key message to come up with the success criteria which typically provides some guidance on the expected benefits and how to measure success. A success criteria example for a company trying to improve market share by gaining competitive advantage in customer service would be; 1) improve customer service level by 10%, 2) improve market share by 2% next year, 3) and maintain inventory turnover rate.

This activity is needed to identify the required process, technology and governance (KPIs, policies, roles, and responsibilities. etc.) changes and finalizes the implementation timeline to achieve the expected benefits (success criteria) of the transformation program. This activity includes conducting process analysis for supply chain processes based on the transformation scope. Process analysis determines the extent of process & governance changes and identifies additional software capabilities required to support the "end state" processes. Several industry-proven process analysis methodologies can help in this exercise like six sigma, value stream mapping, benchmarking, etc.

Step 3: "Develop" Communication Plan

Communications should have majorly two focus areas: communications about the program (why and how we are changing), and communications about the end state and solution being delivered. This includes communication with stakeholders, team members, support team members, functional group members and, front-end users (both inside and outside the company).

Communications about the project to stakeholders is very important for the success of supply chain transformation programs. Lack of information about the project progress to stakeholders can be threatening to the program. Regular, targeted communication enables stakeholders to be educated, prepared and confident that the project is supporting their business needs. The mode and interval of communication should be clearly defined and shared with stakeholders. Program communication should be based on facts and figures. Showing progress helps to maintain confidence among stakeholders, instill pride in program members, and continue program energy. Program communication includes setting expectations, creating awareness of the desired solution, organizational changes, concerns, success. This communication should flow across all the stakeholders not only within the organization but also to vendors, suppliers, and customers etc. Many organizations underestimate the value of this part of the communication but awareness of solution to suppliers and customer helps them to prepare and understand their role and if required also help them plan their resources in advance.

Effective communication provides a clear understanding of what is taking place, motivates the team members, avoids any miscommunication between transformation team members, keeps senior executives committed, reduces the risk of conflicts, and more importantly keeps everyone informed on the progress.

The communication plan should be comprehensive enough to satisfy the information needs of all of the stakeholders. It should provide a description of what piece of information is needed, who needs it, why it is needed, when it is needed, how it is communicated, and by whom. In addition, the communication plan identifies meetings, reporting, methods and format of communications that will occur with the transformation team, program sponsor, stakeholders, partners, IT, internal and external organizations.

Step 4: "Articulate" Cultural Support Plan

Once the communication plan is established, it's necessary to articulate a culture support plan which includes the education plan and organization structure realignment activities. Any transformation program requires culture support. Organizational culture by its very nature refuses to accept change, but over time and with education, organization structure realignment, enforcement from executives, culture does change.

Leadership development is essential if some of the individuals who will be responsible for the program who have little or no leadership experience. The education plan should be tailored to help the individuals acquire these skills. Conflict resolution is one example of the soft skills that leaders need to master if the transformation program is to be effectively implemented and sustained.

Training and skills acquisition for end users should be part of the education plan as well. Digital supply chain transformation programs require training, new skills, and attitudes for the end users of the new or improved processes. The proper allocation and commitment of resources (time, energy, and money) to conduct training and help employees in their skills acquisition is critical to the success of changes.

On major activity of this step is to plan for organizational realignment to support the end state. Human resources department might need to update job descriptions and bonus structure to reflect the changes. This might require a pipeline of candidates with a mix of demand, supply and product expertise. Also, incentives for the company's talent should be aligned with the skill requirements for the end state.

Change leaders and agents (part of the transformation team) must anticipate resistance and be prepared to deal with various change adoption rates. It is important to focus on pioneers and early adopters first. These individuals who are a subset of the stakeholders group are the most open to change; they are the first to embrace something new. Therefore, it is recommended to get these stakeholders on board as quickly as possible to help in changing the culture.

Step 5: "Execute" Change Plan

Once the change plan (which includes change implementation roadmap, communication plan, education plan, and organization structure alignment changes) is approved by senior management/executives, then transformation team has the green signal to go ahead and execute the plan.

Supply chain transformation program typically takes two to five years, with several intermediate projects (Go-Lives) that can pay for the rest of the program. Therefore, it is recommended to develop the change plan on the idea of incremental value delivery. It is crucial to have long-term (program) plan for success, but one should not ignore the importance of providing some quick wins (projects). Organizational stakeholders look for short-term results, and transformation team is under pressure to present short-term wins. Short-term wins should be woven into the timetable of the program. Each project delivers a set of capabilities that have a positive impact on process, metrics, and people and addresses a distinct business need and contributes to the success criteria.

Step 6: "Evaluate" Progress

In the transformation program, regular evaluation (health check) helps to understand the current progress status and also helps anticipate the future progress trend. It is critical that the transformation team understand the current progress and take key actions to avoid any unwanted delays. The prompt and proactive actions of the transformation team can save the transformation program from going off-track. If the program is delayed and the team is not able to bring back on track, then most of the time it goes off the radars of high-level executives' dashboard and eventually importance is lost and the program fails. Progress evaluation should be done against the schedule and expected benefits (success criteria). Since the implementation delivery strategy is to accomplish it in incremental steps (projects), the achieved value of the projects need be tracked and checked off with time.

It is acceptable for the program manager and sponsors while tracking the transformation progress toward achieving the expected benefits and reaching the new targets of the KPIs to rethink the goal and even adjust the targets either because of encountering roadblocks or because of some emerging opportunities that didn't exist earlier.

This step requires senior management's best efforts to stay engaged to build momentum for the change. Whenever executives or senior management let up before the job is done, critical momentum can be lost and the change effort can stall.

Step 7: "Improve" Supply Chain Transformation

Although the sustaining phase is the most difficult phase in any transformation, there is relatively little research concerning sustaining change in organizations. While planning and implementing a change can occur relatively quickly, sustaining change requires a significant amount of time. Maintaining a sense of urgency and a significant level of interest is difficult over a long period of time. This phase can take months or years.

Once positive a successful project improvement (short-term win) is accomplished, management must work to make it part of the organizational culture. Step # 7 helps in this aspect by encouraging the culture of continuous improvement and fine-tuning the new solution (combination of new process and technology). Improvement can also be achieved by enforcing the new process through drafting policies, providing additional coaching when needed and recruiting people based on the new required skills. In addition, developing corrective actions for the root causes when performance measure targets are not achieved would achieve incremental improvement.

Step 8: "Anchor" the New Behavior in the Culture

Acknowledging and rewarding stakeholders for new behaviors are essential to stabilize the new process and anchor the new culture. Because using new skills involves risk (the risk of failure), and acknowledging and rewarding those who use the new skills encourages others to do the same.

This step is also responsible for updating performance measures to reflect the process or the new performance baselines, by coming up with new performance measures, modifying existing ones, modifying targets or establishing owners to the performance measures.

Five Change Management Success Factors

Success Factor 1: Executives' Visible Support

Since change is difficult and inherently unsettling, stakeholders will turn to the CEOs and executives for direction and answers. The leaders of the organization must embrace change first and then display their commitment and support. They must speak with one voice and model the desired behaviors especially since supply chain transformations require intensive cooperation and cross-functional collaboration among executive peers. This would force executives to get out of their comfort zones and their respective areas of responsibility and find time out of their busy daily operation schedule to envision an entirely new business.

While there are many reasons for the failure of the transformation initiatives, but lack of executive's commitment is ahead of all the reasons. Interestingly enough, many executives don't know there is a direct correlation between leadership engagement levels and the success of a transformation initiative.

Having a broad picture about change in mind, executives would need dashboards and indicators in order to successfully pilot an organization to the desired destination. Actively executives will build planned benefits/results into their own and the leadership team's performance plans. They will initiate project-relevant communications in direct report meetings on a regular basis, visibly hold the organization's leaders accountable for the change and if required will ask frequently for their direct participation. They also engage in communication events at all levels of the organization, try to resolve resource issues or constraints, understand the implications of the change across the organization's groups and demographic groups, also monitors, identify and address organizational resistance.

Another important aspect regarding the leadership of change is to understand the level of effort required for success. The executive's role and importance continue to increase over the life of the project. At times while leading change the change leaders will have to let go some of their functional responsibility and tasks as their efforts become more critical than the roles of the program team. Towards the end of the change cycle, efforts from transition team are maximum because of sustain phase of change cycle. Everything done up to implementation phase can fall apart if leader's proper attention and commitment are not there in the last phase of the change process.

Success Factor 2: Digital Supply Chain Strategy

Very few companies have a good and documented supply chain strategy. Executives struggle with assessing the current state of the supply chain and envisioning the new state that is required to support the vision and address current challenges, from digital technologies and processes to human resources and governance. They also struggle to decide when and where to begin and how to translate the vision into goals, goals into strategies and strategies into process changes and projects. Serious considerations should be given to following while developing strategy.

There is a growing trend to assign a Chief Digital Office role to responsible for defining and executing the digital use cases. This role would work closely with the head of supply chain on the digital supply chain strategy.

- **Market changes** - Strategies often fail because the market conditions which were intended to be exploited change before the strategy takes hold. Reasons can be shorter product life cycle, competition with new technology, and unexpected change in the financial market etc.
- **Uniqueness of the strategy** - Good strategy is one which can distinguish the company from others in ways that it makes a difference to customers. Michael Porter (1996) has written extensively and persuasively on this topic. So leaders should take three simple steps in developing a distinctive strategy – understand the company's genuine strengths (particularly those that span multiple functions), examine the marketplace to understand what market positions are unoccupied, focus the company's strategies on bringing its variable strengths to bear in capturing those unoccupied strategic positions. Also, the strategy must consider the potential reaction to a strategy by competitive companies. In order to effectively anticipate the reaction of competitors over strategy, a company should have competitive intelligence capability. The study should involve understanding the competitor's market position, their competitive advantages, and disadvantages, future planning, management decision trends etc.
- **Organizational design, capabilities and business models with the strategy** – Sometimes companies' fail to align their digital supply chain strategy with the organizational goal. This is a critical step which is often overlooked. A basic assessment of organizational capabilities and the capability gaps created by a change in strategy is a very direct means of improving alignment. Also, some strategies fail because they are based on the poorly conceived business model. Lack of research of market trend, miss connecting to customers, gap or misunderstanding of how demand would be met in the market can lead to a poor business model.

- **Culture of "playing it Safe"** – Companies get used to executing low-risk incremental improvements on the same business environment for an extended period of time, and they become close-minded for drastic improvements because they do not know how to handle transformation programs and target big results. The scope can be overwhelming.

When companies are in the process of implementing several incremental improvement projects like Six Sigma or Kaizen projects, it will be a challenge to add a large transformation program to the mix especially when it includes new technology like digital technologies. Companies that try to stuff too much into the organization will clog it causing employees and managers' capacity to become a choke point unless the projects are prioritized and sequenced correctly.

Digital Supply Chain Strategy Ideally Includes

1. Flexible strategy as changes occur in the global marketplace,
2. Prioritized, actionable and practical improvement plans,
3. A three-to-five year roadmap that guides the transformation of supply-and-demand capabilities and takes planning processes to the next level,
4. Linkage to one or more corporate goals like growth or customer service levels,
5. Both large opportunities for improvement that deliver significant ROI over time, as well as "quick win" operations improvements with a fast payback,
6. Elimination to outdated roles and responsibilities, unnecessary activities, and performance metrics that no longer reflect current realities, and
7. Metrics across the supply chain to reflect the overarching digital supply chain strategy.

Success Factor 3: Building the Case for Change

The author believes strongly, in coming years, no better core competency will help companies to compete in the market other than the ability to effectively implement transformation change. With increasing pressure both external and internal, organizations will tend to undertake more projects and initiatives to remain competitive in the market. So the ability to achieve profit and benefits will directly be tied to how effectively we manage change by engaging employees. Building the business case for change is crucial to compel leadership to give the go-ahead for the transformation change program.

Developing a good business case for change is very important where every stakeholder's requirement is taken into consideration. Three steps should be followed in developing the case: First, articulate a convincing need for change based on the company's current situation and market opportunities. Here supporting details have to be strong enough to draw the attention of executives. The change case should be directly linked to the organizational goals, as this helps in grabbing the attention of stakeholders.

Second, quantify the expected operational and financial benefits, estimate cost, and calculate the return on investment (ROI). This can be a challenging step sometimes because when the case is in initial stage one has to come up with expected financial benefit and return on investment close to actual. If the exercise is done with detailed consideration then the case becomes very convincing and can grab the attention of executives based on the extent of research that went through developing the case.

Third, explain how to show progress and measure success, which metrics will be improved to achieve the expected benefits, what will be the new performance targets and deadlines, and who will accountable.

If this step is not developed well then whole change process efforts can fail. As a part of developing the case, equal consideration should also be given in developing performance measurement governance to track progress (Sabri, 2015).

As mentioned earlier, when 80-plus member audience were asked to raise their hands if they are "OK" with their own performance measurement governance only three managers raised their hands. The root causes of these challenges can be summarized under four categories:

- The difficulty in identifying the metrics that would yield the most information on success
- Difficulty in identifying root causes when metrics targets are not achieved
- Lack of clear ownership and responsibilities
- Lack of consistently clean data

During business case development if consideration is given on identifying the key performance measures then while executing change program these performance indicators (measures) becomes more refined and can give accurate information on success. These measures should be able also to measure the additional improvement in efficiency and effectiveness of leveraging digital technologies.

Success Factor 4: Structured and Proven Change Management Methodology

Ensuring a structured and proven methodology to show the way in the change transformation journey is a must. Any significant supply chain transformation program creates uncertainty and people resistance. New leaders emerge, job descriptions are changed, new skills and capabilities must be developed for the digital age. Dealing with these change management issues on a reactive, case-by-case basis puts timeline, morale, and results all at risk.

A structured and formal plan for managing change—beginning with the transformation team and then engaging key stakeholders and leaders—should be developed early and executed effectively as changes move through the organization. The plan should be comprehensive to cover planning, implementing, and sustaining the transformation changes. It should also allow enough time for covering the soft factors of change management such as culture, leadership, and motivation because it takes time to change attitudes or relationships which are deeply ingrained in people as well as the organization. It requires time and efforts to change the culture.

In addition, the structured change plan should not miss out on the hard factors of change management like financial results, commitment level of executives, the number of resources and skills required to execute the program successfully, benchmarking and gap analysis, and program roadmap and duration which are vital for the success of the transformation program.

Success Factor 5: Maintaining Energy and Involvement

As transformation programs progress from defining strategy and setting targets to design and implementation, they affect different organizational levels and stakeholders. Disengaged stakeholders can really slow down progress and can cause by itself for transformation failure. Setting right KPIs & tracking, performance measurement and, award & recognition have the most significant impact in sustaining organizational improvement.

- **Right KPIs & tracking:** In order to maintain the momentum and involvement of people in change programs, it's important to develop and measure right performance tracking metrics. For example, as part of change initiatives a company adopts a new pricing strategy to obtain high margins. Measuring volume of sales was chosen to tracking the progress. But if were observe deeply we find that measuring volume encourages discounts, rebates, and warranties, all of which erode margins. So it becomes very important to measure the right things in order to create the right change (Sabri, 2015).
- **Performance measurement and support mechanism**: When an organization is going through change then management's fostering of organizational trust, respect and caring pays off. Mistakes and unwanted things will occur in the change process but at that time benefit of the doubt and continuing support to employees helps build trust. Having a structured performance system also pays off. Communicate goals and performance targets to employees upfront and let them know about the expected behavior and importance of the change with respect to the employee (what's in it for them) and organization is crucial.

It is important to provide resources, key materials, training and enable tools for employees to achieve target performance. This proactive activity helps build positive energy among employees which signifies support of senior management in change implementation phase. Evaluating the performance of employees based on their target whether not achieved or exceeded, and providing feedback is a critical activity. Performance feedback activity should be motivating, encouraging including performance compensation to maximize the target performance. If employees are in sync and excited about the change initiatives they will give their maximum to achieve the target.

- **Award & recognition**: This is closely related to above two and refers how positive attitude and work gets rewarded. It's been observed that reward may not be exact compensation to the amount of effort put by employees but even a small token of appreciation encourages employees to such an extent that they may be able to boost their level of effort. So, highly visible incentives, such as promotion, bonuses, and recognition should be provided as reinforcements to maintain energy and sustain change.

To summarize, stakeholders should understand why change is happening, how their work will change, what is expected of them during and after the transformation program, how they will be measured, and what benefits success will bring to them personally. Transformation team leaders should be addressing all of these questions explicitly and keep stakeholders involved in the process and informed to maintain momentum throughout the organization.

The key driver for this success factor is the transformation team. Building and empowering an effective transformation team is very crucial to maintaining excitement and eventually embracing change. In building the transformation team, executives must be sensitive to the unique needs of the program environment and ensure that the team is having the right skills like identifying resistance root causes and coming up with strategies to overcome resistance. The team should also try to avoid resistance in the first place by being proactive and mitigate the risk ahead of time (Sabri, 2013).

CONCLUSION

Success of digital supply chain transformation depends majorly on mastering the change management throughout the life cycle of the change program. To be successful in the journey, the change leaders have to be more knowledgeable about the change lifecycle since digital supply chain transformations are complex and multifunctional in nature. For an effective supply chain, one must undergo a regular change in order to respond to the ever-changing operating environment.

For effective change management, it is very important to have strong support from executives throughout the transformation cycle. Attacking change management with Digital Supply Chain Strategy and proven change management methodology makes transformation change cycle smooth. In order to sustain change management outcome, it is necessary to maintain energy and assurance of everyone's involvement.

When firms make the decision to implement digital supply chain management transformation programs which typically includes process improvement, software implementation, and organizational realignment across their global operations, there is a strong influence of cultural component to this program. The changes include in the way work gets done every day, in individual roles and responsibilities, and in key performance indicators (KPIs).

A proven and well-defined change management framework for digital supply chain transformation can help companies overcome the culture of "this is the way we've always done it" and get employees at every level on board with the transformation plan — and achieve the expected benefits from improving supply chain performance. It will also help in accelerating the pace of change and achieve the success criteria quicker.

Every digital supply chain transformation program is unique because every firm has its own culture, industry challenges, organizational structure and skills, process maturity, and performance. However, the proposed framework in this chapter is a comprehensive one that addresses all common challenges in implementing digital supply chain transformation programs and a practical one which provides executives and managers a good roadmap on what to expect and how to engage the entire organization in the process. This would ensure a successful and smooth supply chain transformation journey.

FUTURE TRENDS

Mastering change management is critical for the success of Digital SC Transformation. Importance of change management as a separate department within an organization is increasing. Development of structured approach and a formal process is a concern for many industries as the still failure rate of transformation programs is high. Several initiatives around the industry are under progress to develop the effective and efficient methodology on how to adopt a change in the organization. There is a demand to integrate change management throughout all levels of the organizational system. Leaders have to link organizations goals to functional level department goals to personal level individual goals. With the advent of increase in transformation initiatives, there is great demand for integration of project management methodology with change management cycle.

The author predicts more serious attention and enough allocated budget for change management track for transformation programs. This will be translated into higher industry success rate. This will have an impact on academia in two aspects: 1) more research and case studies will be available in this area, and 2) witnessing the introduction of change management as a separate MBA program in the universities.

REFERENCES

Aiken & Keller. (2009). *The irrational side of change Management.* McKinsey & Company.

Cynthia, B., & Keith, L. S. (2011). Organizational Change Management: A Test of the Effectiveness of a Communication Plan. *Communication Research Reports*, *28*(1), 62–73. doi:10.1080/08824096.2011.541364

Ford, M. W., & Greer, B. M. (2005). The Relationship between Management Control System Usage and Planned Change Achievement: An Exploratory Study. *Journal of Change Management*, *5*(1), 29–46. doi:10.1080/14697010500036031

Greer, B., & Ford, M. (2009). Managing Change In Supply Chains: A process Comparison. *Journal of Business Logistics*, *30*(2), 47–63. doi:10.1002/j.2158-1592.2009.tb00111.x

Isern, J., Meaney, M., & Wilson, S. (2009). *Corporate Transformation under Pressure.* McKinsey & Company. Retrieved from http://www.mckinsey.com/insights/organization/corporate_transformation_under_pressure

Karp, T. (2005). Unpacking the Mysteries of Change: Mental Modeling. *Journal of Change Management*, *5*(1), 87–97. doi:10.1080/14697010500057573

Kotter, J. P. (1996). *Leading Change*. Boston Harvard Business School Press.

Leonard & Coltea. (2013). *Most Change Initiatives Fail -- But They Don't Have To.* Retrieved from http://businessjournal.gallup.com

Nadler, D. A., & Tushman, M. (1989). Organizational Frame Bending: Principles for Managing Reorientation. *The Academy of Management Executive*, *3*(3), 194–204.

Porter, M. (1996). What is Strategy. *Harvard Business Review*. PMID:10158475

Ramanan & Anil. (2011). *The Top Three Reasons Supply Chain Transformations Fail.* Wipro Consulting Services.

Sabri, E. (2013). Strategies for Supply Chain Transformation. *Supply & Demand Chain Executive Magazine*. Retrieved from http://www.sdcexec.com/article/11122122/companies-struggle-to-decide-when-and-where-to-begin-and-how-to-translate-their-vision-into-goals-goals-into-strategies-and-strategies-into-process-changes-and-projects

Sabri, E. (2015). *Optimization of Supply Chain Management in Contemporary Organizations: Mastering Change Management for Successful Supply Chain Transformation*. IGI Global.

Sabri, E., Gupta, A., & Beitler, M. (2006). *Purchase Order Management in B2B Environment: Best Practice & Technologies. J.* Ross Publishing.

Sabri, E., & Shaikh, S. (2010). *Lean & Agile Value Chain Management: A Guide to the Next Level of Improvement*. J. Ross Publishing.

Chapter 6
Establishing the Program Management Office:
A Key Enabler for Digital Supply Chain Transformation

Chad Wiseman
KPMG LLP, USA

ABSTRACT

This chapter covers the importance of the program management office (PMO) in a digital supply chain transformation. The objective of this chapter is to discuss the key issues in digital supply chain transformations in terms of managing the PMO, followed by a discussion of the solutions and best practices for mitigating these issues and ensuring the PMO is a value-added function and key enabler of a digital supply chain transformation. The reader should have a good understanding of the activities that the PMO should perform, the skills required for PMO resources, and the process of building the business case and using it to track the benefits to prove the transformation was effective.

INTRODUCTION

PMOs can sometimes be perceived as unnecessary overhead for already expensive supply chain transformations. In reality, the opposite is true, and if they are not constructed, supported or structured properly, the project will fail. The author's intent in this chapter is to describe in detail what the challenges are in managing the PMO and what the best practices are to lead and operate a successful PMO.

BACKGROUND

Supply chain transformations are very complex projects that require coordinated activities in finance, operations, supply chain, procurement, engineering, product development and leadership functions. The Program Management Office (PMO) is responsible for the coordination of activities between

DOI: 10.4018/978-1-5225-7700-3.ch006

Copyright © 2019, IGI Global. Copying or distributing in print or electronic forms without written permission of IGI Global is prohibited.

these groups of people. Its essential objective is to actively support and partner with senior business leaders to ensure the transformation will deliver the expected value while not significantly disrupting the day-to-day operations. It does this by identifying and prioritizing the issues and risks, identifying the complex interdependencies that exist between workstreams, managing the communication process with the stakeholders and making decisions on behalf of the project sponsors. In terms of executing the work, the PMO does not handle that. That responsibility resides with the individual workstreams. For a digital supply chain transformation, examples of workstreams would include Demand Planning, Supply Planning, Inventory Management, Integration, Master Data Management, etc. When designed and set up correctly, the PMO provides a competitive advantage for firms undergoing a transformation. If the PMO is set up sub-optimally, projects tend to fail. In the Project Management Institute's Pulse of the Profession survey from 2018, only 58% of organizations fully understand the value of project management. The organizations that undervalued the PMO for driving change reported an average of 50% or more of their projects failing outright (PMI, 2018). The focus of this chapter is to highlight the specific challenges of the PMO and how the team can solve them.

MAIN FOCUS OF THE CHAPTER

Issues Necessitating PMO Excellence in Supply Chain Transformation

There are several issues that make supply chain transformations challenging. Most of these issues are the result of so many organizational functions being involved at the same time, while tasking them with both transforming their operation and continuing their operation at the same time. The intent of this section is to emphasize and cover in detail the specific issues below.

1. On-going operations can de-prioritize the project and steal resources.
2. Scope creep results in unbudgeted and non-value-added work.
3. Lack of single integrated project plan prevents overall coordination.
4. Competing initiatives or interdependencies within the transformation cause confusion.
5. Lack of dedicated, supported and skilled PMO resources cause overall poor execution.

On-Going Operations Steal Resources and Deprioritize the Project

Executing a digital supply chain transformation is like completely renovating a 1930's era mansion with the latest smart appliances, HVAC, security and energy monitoring, all the while expecting the family to still live in the house and perhaps even expecting year over year improvements in home efficiency and overall enjoyment. Let us suppose that during this operation there was a critical point in the schedule in which the home contractor needed the homeowner to be available to decide on a number of critical set points in the main controller, but the home owner was unavailable for this because he or she had to address a project that was not going as well (e.g., the family car had broken down). As a result, the HVAC would not cool below 80 degrees, the outdoor lighting turned off at the wrong times, and the security system would not function. This caused the homeowner to have the contractor install window A/C units in every window, convert the lighting back to manual controls, and hire a full time security service to monitor the house. Obviously, this has resulted in unnecessary costs and schedule setbacks, and it was the result of a project stakeholder reacting to a competing priority.

In the same fashion as this fictional home renovation example, organizations very often reallocate resources based on operational issues with perceived higher priority because their consequences are immediate. When this occurs, more harm than good can occur. The day-to-day issues may be addressed, but the firm typically continues to use antiquated non-digital ways of performing their supply chain operations. This delays the implementation of any technology implementation, which delays the resulting financial benefits to the firm. In many cases, when resources gravitate away from the transformation and back to the day-to-day operations, it is just simple resistance to change. In the 2018 Digital Supply Chain Executive Survey, 57% of manufacturers cited resistance to change as the top impediment to supply chain initiatives (JDA, 2018). How companies prevent this natural issue is covered in Solutions and Recommendations.

Scope Creep Sets In

Project scope management includes the process required to ensure that the project includes all the work required, and only the work required, to complete the project successfully. These scope management processes include collecting requirements, defining the scope, creating the work breakdown structure (WBS), verifying the scope, and controlling the scope. Essentially, the scope defines what is and what is not part of the transformation. When work is performed outside of the originally agreed upon scope, that is referred to as scope creep. In a 2018 survey from PMI, 52% of the projects completed in the past year experienced scope creep (PMI, 2018), but this figure is conservative in the author's experience. It is important to understand that scope creep is sometimes a welcome challenge, if the new scope is an opportunity that provides significant value to the business.

Changes to projects will always happen. As discussed in the previous section, ongoing operations will create disruption and will also identify supply chain issues that the transformation could or should address. The point is not that PMOs should reject all changes; rather, there must be a process of assessing, authorizing and controlling the changes that do occur. When changes are simply worked on without approval from the PMO, the project team devotes time to the unauthorized changes. The work to incorporate these changes must often be done within the original time and budget estimates, leaving less time for approved parts of the scope. That could mean approved features don't get completed, and the end-product is not what was chartered. Or, it can mean that time and cost overruns to finish the authorized parts of the scope will occur. If cost overruns are not an option, and the budgeted investment is used, the project will have to be closed out, even if that means prematurely ending the project without achieving the benefits.

It is worth detailing the reasons this occurs in supply chain transformations.

Scope Creep Reason 1: Not Clearly Defining the Scope Boundaries

When stakeholders are developing the business case for the supply chain transformation, the scope assumptions made by the business may be different than the PMO's assumptions. It is very important to clearly identify what is in scope and what is out of scope. For example:

- Which business units are in scope? Does it include the subsidiaries, acquisitions or joint ventures?

- Which business functions? Does the transformation also include significant changes to finance, operations, procurement, HR, IT, in addition to supply chain?
- What geographies? Does it include foreign continents as well?
- What business processes? Is it supply chain strategy, planning, execution, manufacturing, logistics, or fulfillment processes? Does it include the S&OP process?

If these elements remain unclear, it will eventually become clear in a couple of inefficient ways. First, the project team will interpret the requirements and build what it thinks is right and helps the business. Secondly, the team will get details from the supply chain practitioners and subject matter experts, which will often times be misaligned with the intention of the project sponsors. As an example, if a business intends to replace its supply chain system of record, but it does not provide clear guidance on the business units, processes and geographies in scope, scope creep is bound to occur. If the project stakeholders are mostly from a single business unit and are all responsible for day-to-day supply chain execution, then the end product will be focused on that business unit's execution, and less on a planning and strategy platform for their enterprise.

Scope Creep Reason 2: Poorly Gathering and Documenting the Business Requirements

In the process of developing the charter for the project, it can be challenging to gather and fully document all the detailed requirements of the supply chain solution. As result, new requirements can be discovered during the design phases or even after go-lives. If the original requirements were not detailed enough, it will be difficult to determine if these are new requirements or were part of the original list, and will likely just be included in the scope going forward. Likewise, if the original requirement is too vague, the developers will have to make a judgment on what was intended and will potentially guess wrong, resulting in costly re-work. Even when requirements are adequately detailed, stakeholders can persuade the solution design to include elements that do not address the original list of requirements. Without the guidance provided by trancing requirements back to business and project objectives, project teams often rely on their own judgment about whether to include individual requirements. The software developers may also add product features that they think are useful, even if they were not part of the requirements. Although this may add value to the customers, it is still scope creep. This can especially happen when the project team is trying harder to satisfy the customer due to other project challenges.

Scope Creep Reason 3: Not Adequately Involving Project Sponsors in Decisions

Supply chain transformation sponsors are typically busy with other initiatives or day-to-day operations. It is often the case that they are not even aware that they are not as involved as they should be in terms of scope decisions. It could be an issue with how the PMO is communicating with the sponsor. If it is not in the preferred type of communication (e.g., email, status meeting, conference call, etc.), he or she may become disengaged. A scheduled PMO status meeting, milestone or other event such as a missed deliverable then tends to bring the project back into focus. A disengaged sponsor is more likely to hand over project decisions to the team. The more disengaged the sponsor becomes, the more likely scope creep becomes because the project team will make decisions in the absence of sponsors making them. These decisions may or may not be the correct ones, but if they bypass the change request process, or the sponsor is simply not involved in the change request process, it will result in work outside the agreed upon scope that is not authorized by the sponsor.

Scope Creep Reason 4: Accepting Too Many Changes Because the Transformation Is So Long

Supply chain transformations typically will typically take longer than a year, and they can take up to 3 years or longer. The longer a transformation is, the longer a sponsor has to change his or her mind, identify other requirements, re-prioritize capital funding, or for the overall business to change. This all causes scope creep to the original project. It simply opens the possibility for more and more product features and functions to be added by simply adding to the time stakeholders are working in it. When additional features are identified, it is imperative that they go through the change control process. Again, with longer projects there is a greater risk that additions can bypass the change control process.

The detailed solutions and recommendations to manage these scope creep issues are laid out in the Solutions and Recommendations section.

Lack of a Single Integrated Project Plan Prevents Coordination

When multiple workstreams and cross-functional groups are working on the same project, as is the case in supply chain transformations, there is a risk of disparate project plans being developed that do not necessarily work together. The individual workstreams will typically create and manage their project plan in MS Project or even MS Excel. Most of the time, teams are constantly making small changes to their plans and updating statuses and progress. It is hard to keep up with such day-to-day fluent changes. Even if the plans are stored on some common drive or web-based location like Sharepoint or a project portal, the plans are not truly connected.

In addition to the lack of single integrated plan, version control of the individual plans becomes an issue because as workstreams make updates to their individual plans, there cannot be real time updates to the overall project plan. This issue of plan proliferation will create all sorts of problems for the PMO. It will take hours of PMO staff time to update and reconcile the plans. Ultimately, there will not be one single source of the truth when it comes to the overall transformation plan. This erodes confidence in the PMO and consumes PMO resources in the administrative tasks for tying them all together.

Interdependencies Between Workstreams Create Coordination Challenges

Supply chain transformations will present many challenges in terms of sequencing activities and managing dependencies. Dependencies are the relationships that the activities or milestones have with each other that dictate their order. For example, in a supply chain transformation, it is necessary to first develop a solution design document before configuring the solution. When the dependency is between two activities that are in two different sub-projects, or workstreams, the relationship is considered to be an interdependency. An example of an interdependency in a supply chain transformation is that the master data workstream must clean and validate the master data before system integration testing for the functional areas (demand, supply, inventory) may begin. Although this interdependency is not difficult to identify, it is not easily managed between multiple workstreams. In this example, the demand, supply and inventory workstreams must recognize this interdependency in their project plans. Their plans must react to any change in the duration or end date of the master data cleaning activity in the master data management workstream. Therefore, the PMO must integrate both sets of plans into a single integrated plan to facilitate the management of this interdependency. Details on this process are discussed in the Solutions and Recommendations section.

Lack of Dedicated, Supported and Skilled PMO Resources Cause Overall Poor Execution

In a 2013 Forrester Research poll, most organizations viewed project management as something additional to everyone's daily job. It was only the most strategic projects with the highest visibility to leadership that were assigned an actual dedicated project manager (Forrester, 2013). Simply layering on PMO responsibilities to the business or operations teams is a mistake. This approach makes two faulty assumptions: that people have time for it and that they are properly skilled for the job. Supply chain transformations deserve their own dedicated PMO. Leadership must support the PMO, hand over decision making authority to it, and then hold the PMO accountable for the expected benefits from the transformation.

SOLUTIONS AND RECOMMENDATIONS

The challenges highlighted in the previous section become exaggerated with supply chain transformation projects given the complex and organizationally broad nature of the endeavors. To prevent and combat these challenges, the authors have focused on three critical areas:

1. Firmly establish the framework for structure, routines, communication, governance and other knowledge areas of the Program Management Office.
2. Ensure a highly skilled leadership team is leading the PMO and is fully supported by the business leadership.
3. Create the business case and "burning platform" for change and then measure the improvements as soon as viable.

Establishing the PMO Framework

It is absolutely critical to create a framework for managing plans, budgets, risks, and reporting. It's important to establish program-level routines that track milestones and objectives, communicate progress and help identify issues early without putting a lot of extra work on the workstreams. The industry standard for establishing this structure is the Project Management Body of Knowledge (PMBOK). The PMBOK provides the best practices that PMOs should follow as the project progresses through its lifecycle of Initiating, Planning, Executing, Monitoring and Closing the project (PMI, 2008). This text will not comprehensively provide the details from the PMBOK, but it will discuss the specifics of each of these project lifecycle phases as they relate to digital supply chain transformations.

Initiating

The Initiating phase consists of the activities necessary to define a new project or a new phase of an existing project by obtaining authorization from the sponsor. The Project Charter is the document that authorizes a project or phase and documents the initial requirements, scope and financial resources.

The best practice is for the sponsor to physically sign the Charter. The charter document should include at a minimum the project proposal or justification, measureable project objectives and related success criteria, high level requirements, high level project description, high level risks, a summary milestone schedule and a summary budget. Historically, PMOs have chosen to use a more comprehensive statement of work (SOW) to serve as the charter, but best practice is to summarize that to the elements described here. The project charter is a critical document that justifies the project and provides authority to the PMO to drive the transformation. It needs to be referenced when the purpose of the project is questioned.

This is also where the PMO determines the full list of stakeholders. The stakeholders include individuals or groups that have an interest, involvement or influence in the project. For a supply chain transformation, this would include a large number of cross-functional roles throughout the organization. It is important to include stakeholders not just from supply chain and operations teams, but from engineering, finance, human resources, procurement and sales as well. Keeping this cross-functional team aligned with the objectives, benefits and resource requirements of the transformation is critical to success. The stakeholder register is a document the PMO should build to list these stakeholders, their function and role in the transformation, and some general summary on how the stakeholder should be managed.

The most important outcome of the Initiating phase is to properly endorse and authorize the PMO. It's crucial to authorize and establish the PMO early as project managers often have accountability but little authority. If the PMO is developed after the Project Charter has been developed for the transformation, it will take time to ramp up their knowledge of the project background. Ultimately, this discredits the PMO, which is a critical mistake that cannot be resolved during the project. The PMO should be composed of key stakeholders that have been part of the development and socialization of the business case up to this point. Once the PMO resources are identified, the business leadership must publicly announce the launch of the project, that the PMO has the authority to run the project, and that all workstreams effectively report to the PMO (PMI, 2008).

Planning

In the Planning Phase, the total scope is detailed out, the objectives are defined and refined, and a detailed course of action is developed to attain these objectives. This takes the high level work in the Initiating phase to a detailed level. A multi-dimensional transformation like a digital supply chain transformation requires repeated feedback loops in which more project information, characteristics or events are understood, triggering a need to change some of the plans. This iterative process of changing the plan or making it more detailed based on new information is called "rolling wave planning." This type of planning goes on throughout the transformation (PMI, 2008).

The project management plan and project documents developed as outputs from the planning phase will explore aspects of the scope, time, costs, quality, communication, change management, risk, and procurements. These documents should be updated as the project progresses and requires changes to achieve the objectives. The list below provides details on these documents, or deliverables, that are necessary in the Planning phase.

1. **List of Requirements –** The List of Requirements is a formal deliverable resulting from the exhaustive process of defining and documenting stakeholders' needs to meet the project objectives. These requirements include the quantified and documented needs and expectations of the sponsor, customer, and other stakeholders. These requirements need to be elicited, analyzed and recorded in

enough detail to be measured once project execution begins. For technology that supports a digital supply chain transformation, these requirements would include information on technical requirements, security requirements, performance requirements, etc. An example of a requirement would be "the future process and system must provide daily updates of customer orders provided in a view that can be aggregated from days to weeks to months to years and from SKU to product family to business unit." The process of acquiring these requirements starts with a thorough assessment of the current state process, identification of the pain points, and a summary of the process or technology requirements that would help address the pain point. This process needs to be facilitated through a series of workshops with the stakeholders. Requirements gathering should be performed only with the project stakeholders that are responsible for the strategy and execution of the supply chain processes. Care should be given when involving manufacturing, finance, engineering or other teams, as it could potentially result in scope creep since the other functions will want to add requirements that solely benefit their function (PMI 2008).

2. **Work Breakdown Structure:** The Work Breakdown Structure (WBS) is the subdivision of project deliverables into smaller, more manageable components until the work and deliverables are defined to a more tangible and actionable level. This involves identifying and analyzing the deliverables and related work, structuring and organizing the WBS, and decomposing the upper levels to the lower levels (PMI, 2008). For a digital supply chain transformation, the authors recommending breaking the WBS into major workstreams such as Demand Planning, Supply Planning, Inventory Management, Change Management Master Data Management and Integration. Underneath that, they are further divided into phases or sub-phases of work. The figure below provides an example WBS.
3. **Integrated Project Plan:** The integrated project plan is the document that organizes the WBS into distinct activities and identifies the owner, schedule, duration and any dependencies. The best practice is to display the project plan in the form of a Gantt chart (PMI, 2008). Due to the com-

Figure 1. Example work breakdown structure for a supply chain transformation
(KPMG, 2017)

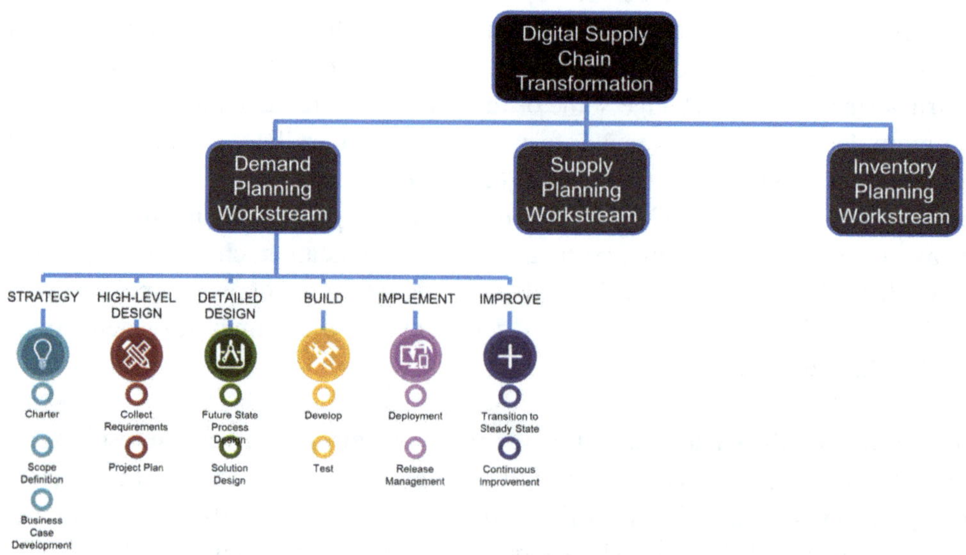

plexity of the supply chain transformation, with multiple workstreams working simultaneously, it is always challenging to maintain an updated comprehensive project plan. For this reason, it is recommended to utilize a cloud-based project management solution that keeps all project plans in a single place with real time updates. Below is an example Gantt chart from a cloud based project management solution called Clarizen.

Project management systems are also necessary to manage the interdependencies that commonly occur between workstreams in a supply chain transformation. For example, if there are data sets that must first be cleaned and validated by the Master Data Management workstream before system integration testing in the Demand Planning workstream can occur, then the project management system must link these tasks to ensure one is dependent upon the other finishing to completion. Additionally, these systems must be capable of identifying the critical path of the overall project. The critical path is the series of tasks that must finish on time for the entire project to finish on schedule. To emphasize, these system are absolutely critical for supply chain transformation to ensure there is one version of the truth for all schedules, activities and costs across all workstreams. If every workstream is "marching to their own beat," then the transformation will certainly fail (Brown, 2003).

4. **Cost Management Plan:** The Project Cost Management Plan is the outline of the project's estimation, allocation and control of costs for the required resources to complete the activities in the Integrated Project Plan. It is an absolutely essential part of this planning phase because it creates the safety net that guarantees that project cost is kept within the limits of the budget. Developing and executing the Cost Management Plan involves the following key steps:
    a. Estimating Costs – the process of developing an approximation of the funding needed for resources to conduct the activities in the Integrated Project Plan.
    b. Determine Budget – the process of aggregating the estimated costs of individual activities or workstreams to establish an authorized cost baseline.

Figure 2. Example of a project plan in Gantt chart format
(KPMG, 2017)

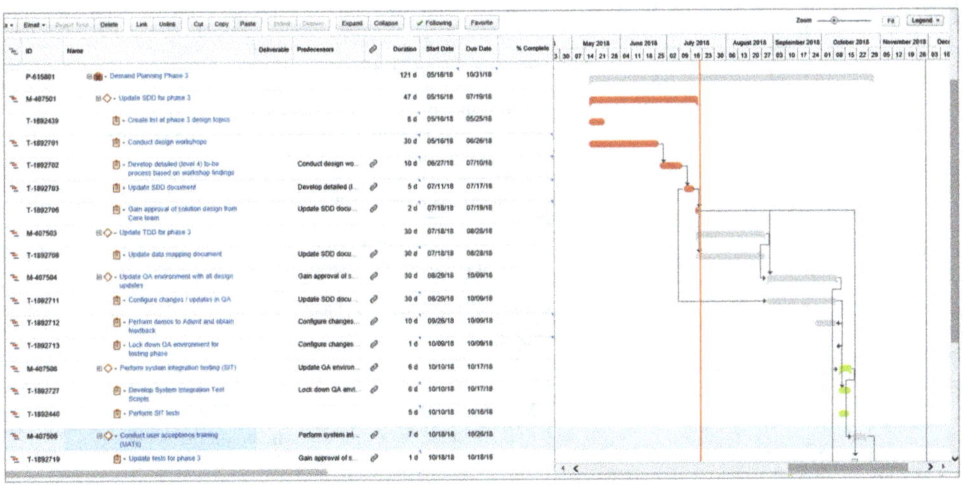

c. Control Costs – The process of monitoring the status of the project to update the project budget and managing changes to the cost baseline.

These steps can be iterative in nature. For example, in the initial stages of the project, project cost could have a rough order of magnitude (ROM) estimate in the range of +/-25%. Later in the project, as more information is known, estimates could narrow to a range of +/-10%. Throughout the project, the PMO must monitor the actual costs versus budget and the work that has actually been completed. Additionally, it is necessary to forecast actual costs and future budget variances.

Earned Value Management (EVM) is a commonly used method of performance measurement, but its specifics are beyond the objective of this text. In summary, it integrates project scope, cost and schedule measures to help the PMO assess and measure project performance and progress. This method develops and monitors three key dimensions for each major phase of work - planned value, earned value and actual costs. Table 1 summarizes the key terms and definitions of EVM (PMI, 2008).

5. **Project Quality Plan** – A Project Quality Plan address both the management of the project and the actual product of the project. Quality control for the project must measure compliance against its various other plans (PMI, 2008). Example activities in a Project Quality Plan include:
    a. Adherence to deliverable and milestone schedule
    b. Monitoring variances to scope, schedule and costs
    c. Adherence to the change control process and use of formal change requests
    d. Control of formal PMO documentation
    e. Updates to integrated project management plan

The Project Quality Plan also defines the quality control process for the solution itself. This is where functional unit testing (FUT), system integration testing (SIT) and user acceptance testing (UAT) will be fully defined. This will document:

Table 1. Summary of key terms for earned value management methodology

Term	Abbreviation	Definition	Formula
Planned Value	PV	This is simply the budget for a given phase or element of the WBS	-
Earned Value	EV	The value of the work completed for the WBS element. Most times it is simply the % completion of this element.	-
Actual Cost	AC	Total cost actually incurred for work performed	-
Schedule Variance	SV	Measures schedule performance. Indicates if a project is falling behind its baseline schedule.	EV-PV
Cost Variance	CV	Measures cost performance	EV-AC
Schedule Performance Index	SPI	Measure of progress achieved compared to progress planned on a project	EV/PV
Cost Performance Index	CPI	Measure of the value of work completed compared to the actual cost or progress made on the project	EV/AC

(PMI, 2008)

- The details of what is actually being tested and how it is tested
- The success criteria for each test
- Who will perform the testing
- Where the testing itself will be documented (typically a system designed for solution testing)
- How defects will be managed and documented

6. **Human Resources Plan** – The Human Resource Plan provides guidance on how project human resources should be defined, staffed, managed, controlled and eventually released. This plan will include descriptions of the roles and their specific responsibilities and accountabilities. A common tool to summarize the purpose of roles is the RACI diagram, which succinctly describes, by role, who is responsible (R), accountable (A), consulted (C), and informed (I) for each activity in the project and future state supply chain process (PMI, 2008). An example of this tool is shown in Figure 3 below.

Figure 3. Example of a RACI for a future state supply chain process
(KPMG, 2017)

R: Responsible
Person who performs the work
A: Accountable
Person who is ultimately responsible for the process to be executed as designed; accountable for the final decision
C: Consulted
Person who is consulted before completing the activity, generally a subject matter expert
I: Informed
Person who is informed after an activity is completed; generally someone who is dependent on the activity to be completed

			Core Team			Extended Team									
Process	#	Activities	Global Supply Chain Development / Global Planning	Demand Planning Lead	Supply Planning Lead	Customer Service	Customer Forecasting	Sales	Product Marketing	Product Development	Finance	Production (	Logistics	IT Systems/ Data	Procurement
Demand Planning	1	Generate a baseline (statistical) forecast	I	R				C	C					C	
	2	Generate Brand / Marketing forecast (quota)	I	I				C	R	C					
	3	Collaborate with Marketing to make any adjustments to the baseline forecast		R					C						
	4	Generate Customer forecast (ladder)	I	I			R								
	5	Generate Sales Field Forecast (SFF)	I	I				R							
	6	Publish Assumptions Package	A	R			C	C	C	C					
	7	Prepare for Consensus DP Meeting - review assumptions, forecast changes (cycle over cycle), forecast variances etc.	C	R			C	C	C						
	8	Conduct regional **Consensus Demand Meeting** - agree on an unconstrained consensus demand plan	A	R	I	I	C	C	C	I	I			C	
	9	Aggregate regional Consensus Demand Plans and publish Global Consensus Demand Plan	R	C	I	I	I	I	I	I	I	I			I
	10	Update financial forecast based on the unconstrained Consensus Demand Plan (in revenue)	C	C		I	I	I	I		R				
Supply Planning	11	Review Consensus Demand Plan changes cycle over cycle		C	R										
	12	Review major Assumptions driving the changes		C	R										
	13	Perform Forecast Consumption from customer orders		I	R	C		C							
	14	Compare inventory against target by product, by region	C		R										
	15	Perform Rough-cut capacity planning (RCCP)			R							C			
	16	Review and analyze Demand/Supply imbalances		I	R			I	I			C			
	17	Develop supply planning scenarios		I	R			I	I			C			
	18	Create Supply Planning Meeting agenda items		I	R							C			C
	19	Conduct **Supply Planning Meeting**	A	I	R							I		C	C
	20	Communicate initial Master Production Schedule (MPS) and Ship Plan	I	I	R							I			I
	21	Analyze MPS and Ship Plan and conduct detailed capacity planning to investigate other constraints			C							R			C
	22	Collaborate and adjust MPS and Ship Plan based on new constraints			I							R			C
	23	Analyze variances between original and adjusted MPS and Ship Plan			R							I			I
	24	Publish Final MPS, Ship Plan		I	R	I		I	I			I			
Executive S&OP	25	Create trade-off scenarios with financial impact based on published demand and known supply constraints	R,A	C	C						C				C
	26	Prepare for pre-S&OP meeting, develop draft S&OP deck	R,A	C	C						I				I
	27	Conduct **pre-S&OP meeting** & publish new actions	R,A	C	C			I	I	I	I	I	I	C	I
	28	Prepare for Executive S&OP meeting	R,A	C	C						C				
	29	Conduct **Executive S&OP meeting**	R,A	I	I			I	I	I	I	I	I	C	I
Weekly S&OP	30	Receive demand change signals (i.e.: orders, market changes)		R		C		C	C						
	31	Apply business rules to filter the key exceptions		R				C	C						
	32	Communicate key exceptions to supply planning		R	I										
	33	Determine feasibility of satisfying key exceptions		I	R							C			C
	34	Consolidate changes to supply plan for Weekly S&OP meeting review		I	R							C			
	35	Create Weekly S&OP Meeting agenda items	R,A	C	C							C			
	36	Conduct **Weekly S&OP Meeting** - Discuss and resolve short term demand / supply imbalances	R,A	C	C			I	I	I	I	C	I	C	C

Another key component of the Human Resources Plan is the staffing plan. The staffing plan identifies the number of hours per week required per role (or % dedication), how many individuals are in the role, when the role starts and stops, and overall cost of that role. The staffing model will need to be revisited and updated to react to resource and operations challenges of the supply chain transformation. The example staffing model in Figure 4 was used to show the percent dedication (expressed in decimals) by quarter, by role, by workstream, by phase for a supply chain transformation. The staffing plan is also a critical component of the Cost Management Plan.

The Human Resources Plan is also responsible for outlining the team location and segmentation of the PMO itself. PMO headquarters should have a single location, but for global transformations, additional PMO teams may be located in other countries. Proctor and Gamble executed this multiple location strategy in their massive 2009 replacement of their ordering, shipping and billing system and processes. P&G established a PMO in each country head office, but collocation was required for critical weeks such as training and integrated testing. The project ultimately proved successful for the $84 billion business (PMI, 2013).

7. **Communications Management Plan** - A communication plan is an approach to providing stakeholders with information. The plan formally defines who should be given specific information, when that information should be delivered and what communication channels will be used to deliver the information.

An effective communications management plan anticipates what information will need to be communicated to specific audience segments. The plan should also address who has the authority to communicate confidential or sensitive information and how information should be disseminated (email, websites, printed reports, and/or presentations). Finally, the plan should define what communication channels stakeholders will use to solicit feedback and how communication will be documented and archived.

Communication plans play an important role in the Change Management workstream. An effective communication strategy can help break down resistance to change by getting everyone on the same page and helping stakeholders become engaged and endorse the need for change and the steps being taken to

Figure 4. Example of a high level staffing plan
(KPMG, 2017)

		Phase 1		Phase 2		Phase 3			Phase 4			Phase 5		
Workstream	**Roles**	**Q3 17**	**Q4 17**	**Q1 18**	**Q2 18**	**Q3 18**	**Q4 18**	**Q1 19**	**Q2 19**	**Q3 19**	**Q4 19**	**Q1 20**	**Q2 20**	**Total**
PMO	Engagement Partner	0.0	0.1	0.4	0.4	0.4	0.4	0.4	0.4	0.2	0.1	0.1	0.1	3.0
	Program Manager and SME	0.5	0.9	0.9	0.9	0.9	0.9	0.9	0.9	0.9	0.6	0.5	0.5	9.2
	Delivery Project Executive	0.1	0.1	0.1	0.1	0.1	0.1	0.1	0.1	0.1	0.1	0.1	0.1	1.2
	Project Manager - Support	0.1	0.2	0.2	0.2	0.2	0.2	0.2	0.1	0.1	0.1	0.1	0.1	1.8
Business Process	Business / Functional Consultant - DP	0.5	1.0	1.0	1.0	1.0	1.0	1.0	1.0	1.0	1.0	1.0	1.0	11.5
	Business / Functional Consultant - SP & SC	0.5	2.0	1.0	1.0	1.0	1.0	1.0						7.5
	Business / Functional Consultant - S&OP							0.7	1.0	1.0				2.7
MDM	Data Analyst		1.0	1.0	1.0									3.0
	MDM and Integration Program Architect		1.0	1.0	1.0									3.0
Configuration	Solution Architect		1.0	1.0	1.0	1.0	1.0	1.0	1.0	1.0	1.0	1.0		10.0
	Technical Architect		1.0	0.3				1.0						2.3
	Application Consultant	0.5	1.0	1.0	1.0	1.0	1.0	1.0	1.0	1.0	1.0	1.0	1.0	11.5
	Technical Consultant	0.5	1.0	1.0										2.5
Change Mgmt	Change Management Consultant		1.0	1.0	1.0	1.0	1.0	1.0						6.0
	Training Lead			0.2				0.1				0.1		0.3
Grand Total		**2.6**	**11.3**	**10.1**	**8.6**	**6.6**	**6.6**	**8.3**	**5.5**	**5.3**	**3.9**	**3.8**	**2.8**	

bring it about. Standardization is important to communication management (PMI, 2008). To establish the standard methods, channels and audiences a table like Table 2 below should be constructed.

It is important to understand that these meetings must have strict schedules with the minimal resources necessary to be as efficient with time as possible. A 2014 study at a large company determined that a single weekly executive committee meeting consumed over 300,000 people-hours per year to support when it included all of the meetings, prep time and resources necessary to support it (Mankins, 2014).

8. **Risk Management Plan** - A risk management plan is a document that a project manager prepares to foresee risks, estimate impacts, and define responses to issues. A risk is "an uncertain event or condition that, if it occurs, has a positive or negative effect on a project's objectives." Risk is inherent with any project, and project managers should assess risks continually and develop plans to address them. The risk management plan contains an analysis of likely risks with both high and low impact, as well as mitigation strategies to help the project avoid being derailed should common problems arise. Risk management plans should be periodically reviewed by the project team to avoid having the analysis become stale and not reflective of actual potential project risks. The single document that houses all risks along with their details is called the Risk Register (PMI, 2008).
9. **Procurement Management Plan** – A Procurement Management Plan documents the process and policies necessary to acquire the supporting supply chain technology. This plan will have to specify the process by which technology vendors bid against a Request for Proposal (RFP) if required. Additionally, it will detail the selection criteria that the PMO will use to determine the best fit for the project. It is very important to link the selection criteria back to the original list of requirements to ensure the vendor is capable of meeting the business requirements (PMI, 2008).

The key concept in this Planning phase is to think the whole project through in advance to the extent possible. Doing so requires creating a variety of plans and considering all of the things that could potentially go wrong (risks). These plans provide the overriding governance of the transformation, and

Table 2. Summary of suggested meetings for supply chain transformation

Communication Type	Objective of Communication	Frequency	Audience	Owner
Kickoff Meeting for Phase	Introduce the project team and the project. Review project objectives and management approach.	Once per phase	• Project Sponsor • Project Team • Stakeholders	PMO
Workstream Status Reports	Review status of the project with each workstream	Weekly	• Project Team	PMO
Project Status Reports	Report the status of the project including activities, progress, costs and issues.	Weekly or Monthly	• Project Sponsor • Project Team • Stakeholders • PMO	PMO
Technical Design Meetings	Discuss and develop technical design solutions for the project.	As Needed	• Project Technical Staff	Technical Lead
Steering Committee	Report on the status of the project to management.	Monthly	• Project Sponsorship	PMO

(PMI, 2008)

provide much needed structure to the complexity of a supply chain transformation. Poor quality planning in this stage results in the age old adage: "Fail to plan, and you plan to fail."

Executing

In the Executing Phase, the team executes the plan and does the work to implement the technology, process and organizational changes for a supply chain transformation. The individual workstreams (e.g., Demand Planning, Supply Planning, etc.) actually do the work, while the PMO coordinates these resources.

A key role for the PMO during the execution phase is the management of the entire team. The PMO, working collaboratively with the Change Management workstream, must work to keep stakeholders engaged and working together as a team. This will require team building activities and constant communication to ensure alignment and trust. For digital transformations, in which concepts may be entirely new to the organization, the PMO is responsible for educating the team and making recommendations and judgements on key technology or configuration decisions that will affect the future state process. In stages where the technology is being implemented, the PMO will need to bridge the gap between the strictly technology-focused resources or contractors and the business users. This is going to require the workstream leads to constantly translate the information from solution and technical architects to the business and vice versa.

In the Executing Phase, the majority of work is performed and, therefore, the majority of the budget is spent. It is imperative to execute the Cost Management Plan to ensure project cost is tracking to budget. Additionally, change requests must go through the change control process, because as the project advances, changes are more expensive to adopt and implement. Not doing so will certainly result in scope creep. As the project is executed, it is important for the PMO to monitor the schedule and costs and adjust the plans if necessary based on how the project is progressing or any other issues going on with the business (PMI, 2008).

Monitoring and Controlling

The Monitoring and Controlling Phase is composed of processes to track the progress and performance of the project, identify any changes that need to occur to the plans, and then initiate the changes through the change control process. Digital supply chain transformations have many challenges to staying on track. Therefore, PMOs must have good processes for monitoring the schedule, cost, scope and deliverable production of the project and then make adjustments to the plans. To emphasize, all changes to these plans must go through the change control process which is ultimately governed by the PMO (PMI, 2008).

A key aspect of this part of the PMO governance is the routine status reports. These reports should be performed at the highest level of the Work Breakdown Structure. So, in the case of supply chain transformation, that would include separate status meetings for Demand Planning, Supply Planning and so on. The best practice is for these meetings to report out on progress against milestones in the schedule, report any risks that they are facing, and provide an overall self-assessment of where they are in terms of project schedule, resources and costs. The PMO must provide a common language for reporting status. A typical approach is to simply use a red, yellow and green rating for the entire workstream. PMOs should challenge workstreams to justify their rating. High visibility projects like supply chain transformations tend to result in too many overly optimistic green ratings, and the PMO will need to identify these situations and ensure the status definition is being applied fairly. However, PMOs must ensure they are not punishing those with red status. There is no greater example of this than at Ford Motor Company in 2006. During a difficult time of a program launch for the Ford Edge, Mark Fields showed the program status for the new Ford Edge as red. Historically, the program teams at Ford showed green statuses, even when there were issues, because of the history of consequences for showing red status. Fields' act drew praise from the CEO, and it is credited with being the tipping point for a turnaround at Ford, known as the "The Way Forward." Fields would later become CEO of Ford Motor Company (Sellers, 2013).

Closing

Closing the project is a formal process that involves getting sign-off and acceptance from the customer, performing a final reconciliation of cost actuals and budgets and rolling resources off the project. The PMO should formally close the project by archiving records, holding a lessons learned session, and celebrating the completion of the project. Additionally, all operational processes that had been performed by the project resources should be transitioned to the team that will perform the duties on a day-to-day basis. This certainly needs to include the management of an operational scorecard that tracks the savings or benefits from the transformation. These procedures should be fully documented, and a RACI should be delivered to document these responsibilities. The lessons learned should be documented and stored as a formal deliverable for future transformations (PMI, 2008).

Ensure a Highly Skilled Leadership Team Is Leading the PMO and Support It

It is an absolute must for PMOs to have executive support of the business. In a 2018 survey from PMI, one in four organizations reported that inadequate sponsorship was the root cause of a project's failure (PMI, 2018). Senior executives must publicly state the need for the structure of the PMO and the value it provides. In exchange for this support, executive leadership must hold the PMO accountable for delivering the improvement that is expected. To formalize this relationship between PMO and business leadership, the PMO should report directly into senior leaders. Companies have even started using the title "Chief Projects Officer," a position which can report directly to the CEO (Forrester, 2013). Below is a representation of the recommended level of the PMO leaders and to whom they report.

The organizational structure sets the tone in terms of support and authority by the PMO, but it is equally important to establish the PMO early on in the process and not after the charter has been established. It is much more effective to have the PMO play an integral role in the development of the business case and the set-up of the overall program resources and activity schedule. The PMO team should consist of individuals that are knowledgeable of both the overall business and its supply chain. Only high potential resources should be moved into and out of PMO roles. The PMO roles should be considered a high visibility career builder for the resource. Companies should never consider low or marginal performs for PMO roles. All of this ultimately helps to establish credibility for the PMO and to ensure it is not perceived as unnecessary overhead by the supply chain stakeholders.

After organizational alignment, it is important to understand the skills and training necessary for PMO resources. For a supply chain transformation, the competencies required are both in the realm of project management and supply chain management. For project management skills, it should be expected for leadership to have skills and accreditation in this area. The Project Management Professional (PMP) certification is an internationally recognized designation based on the Project Management Institute's Project Management Body of Knowledge (PMBOK). It is considered the best project management

Figure 5. Recommended alignment of PMO with senior leadership for digital supply chain transformation

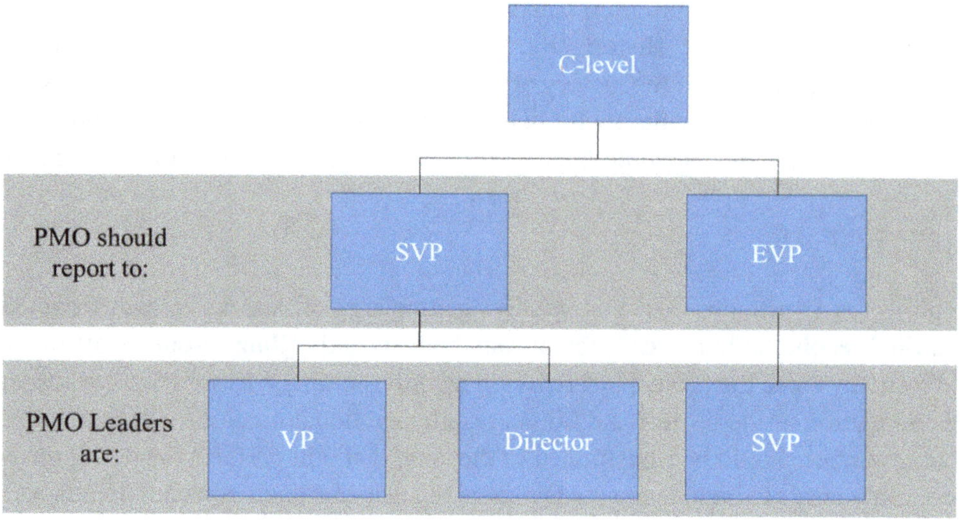

accreditation in the world. In a survey, 72% of PMO leaders felt certification is very relevant for mid-career project managers (PMI, 2018). There are other certifications available such Program Management Profession (PgMP), and Portfolio Management Professional (PfMP), but PMP is the most recognized and most popular. It is not entirely necessary for PMO leaders to possess the PMO designation, but it guarantees a high level of project management knowledge.

PMOs act as a central hub in an organization by interacting and building relationships inside and outside the business. They work with clients, senior leaders, rank and file managers, vendors and others, so they will need advanced communication skills. Yet, this is an area that is often neglected when it comes to professional development. It should be emphasized that the PMO have skills and experience with stakeholder management, negotiation, communication, presentation, group facilitation and coaching. These softer skills are every bit as important as the more technical project management, supply chain or digital transformation skills (Woerner and Aziz, 2007).

Create the Business Case and "Burning Platform" for Change

Projects like digital supply chain transformation that are long, complex and difficult will cause people at some point to ask the question "Why are we even doing this." The term "digital supply chain transformation" returns 31.7 million links when searched on Google, so clearly it is a popular topic, but it is important for firms to understand the value it drives to the actual business. Understanding and measure this value is a process known as benefits realization management. Once the PMO is able to quantify the savings in areas like inventory, premium freight, overtime and direct labor, they need to build a scorecard to actually measure them to ensure the savings are occurring after implementation has occurred. Then, this responsibility of measuring and managing the metrics has to be assigned to an actual person in the PMO. Finally, the metrics need to be built into the performance management process of leadership and supply chain stakeholders. Below are the details on each of these steps.

1. The first step is to identify the areas of the operation in which savings can actually occur. For supply chain initiatives, typical areas of expense saving are freight, premium freight, overtime or direct labor for planning, warehousing, logistics or other areas with redundancy. Growth metrics like service levels or on-time-in-full (OTIF) are areas that are difficult to translate into savings, but should be tracked nonetheless. Working capital, specifically inventory, should also be considered as a potential source of savings. The carrying cost of inventory (a minimum of 10%) should be considered an expense savings. The PMO must understand and quantify these baseline levels of expense and inventory and then estimate the percent improvement that can be made after the transformation is implemented. Operational budgets are often times used as baselines, but the authors urge caution here because budgets can sometimes vary significantly from actual performance. Therefore, it is recommended to develop these baselines based on the actual historical performance of these metrics. From the baseline, percent improvements are estimated. One way to generate these improvement estimates is to quantify the benefit associated with prior success stories using less sophisticated or home grown tools and then extrapolating to the entire scope of the operation. For example, if a plant or business unit recently developed an offline full truck load (FTL) optimizer spreadsheet to optimize truckloads, then the freight savings from this operation could be applied proportionally to the rest of the business, assuming the digital supply chain transformation will be providing this benefit as well. Once these savings are fully estimated, their realization should be scheduled based on the project plan. In the author's experience, at least 6 months should be planned between when the transformation is deployed to a certain scope element (e.g., business unit, geography, plant, etc.) and when that scope element actually starts to experience some savings. Additionally, the benefits need to be ramped up to their full estimation over a period of at least 1 year. As an example of a potential ramp-up schedule, if a solution was deployed to a business in January of 2018, benefits should not be scheduled to be realized until July of 2018, and full realization of steady state benefits will not occur until July of 2019. Once the schedule of benefits is understood, the PMO should perform the discounted cash flow analyses necessary to determine the Net Present Value (NPV) and the Internal Rate of Return (IRR). These are two very key values necessary to obtain and maintain support for senior C-suite level leadership.
2. Based off this quantified business case, an operational scorecard should be built to track these metrics. Operational KPIs for supply chain improvements must be kept simple. Developing too many KPIs will only dilute the message of the important few. Additionally, charts should be kept simple, straightforward and easy to understand. There should be absolutely no question as to what is being measured, what the values are and if it is improving. Once this scorecard is developed, it needs to be built into the overall balanced scorecard of the organization. If there is not a balanced scorecard established, the PMO must work to integrate these metrics into the overall DNA of the organization. Examples of ways to do this include building it into the monthly leadership message, posting it to an intranet portal or just scheduling meetings routinely to review it. The figure below is an example of an operations scorecard for a supply chain transformation.
3. Instead of just off-loading the responsibility of updating and managing the scorecard to a financial analyst, it needs to be owned specifically by someone in the PMO. In the largest of transformations, there are actual Benefits Realization Managers. In small projects, this is formally assigned to a project manager or other PMO staff. Once the transformation is completely implemented, this responsibility needs to be handed off to a specific supply chain stakeholder who will own the process of updating it and managing it going forward. 94% of highly mature organizations always formally

Figure 6. Example operations scorecard for benefits from supply chain transformation
(Wiseman, 2018)

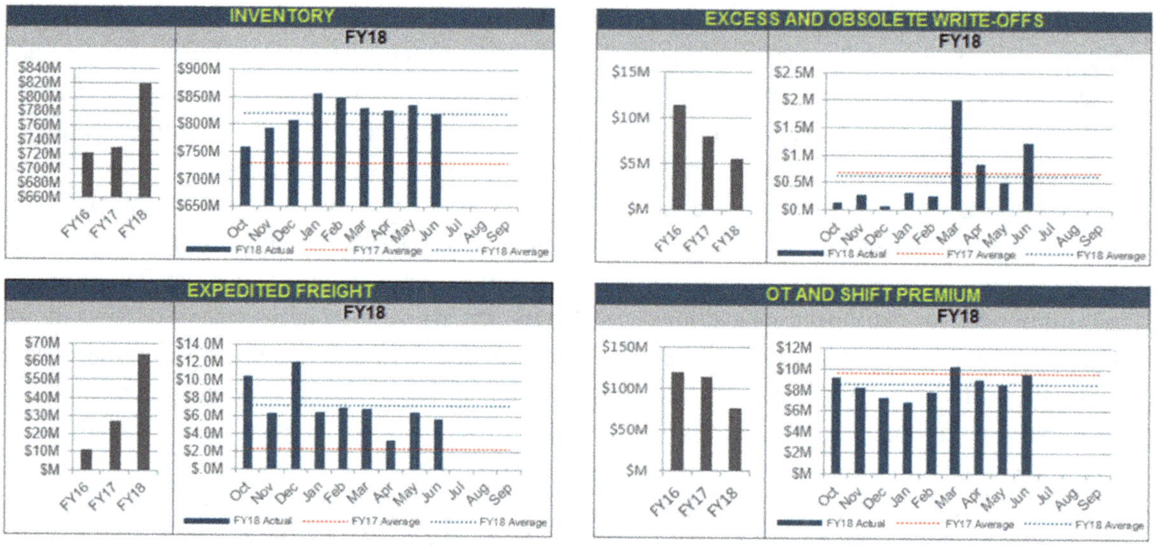

identify person(s) accountable for achieving business benefits versus 19% with low maturity (PMI, 2018). The key enabler for this accountability is owning the scorecard.

4. The final step of creating the burning platform for the digital supply chain transformation is to build these new metrics of supply chain improvements into the actual performance management process of leadership and supply chain stakeholders. If supply chain management is important enough to a firm to launch a digital supply chain transformation, then it needs to be reflected in what the organization considers important. To truly drive behavior that supports and owns the new capabilities from the transformation, the organization has to measure people in new ways that are aligned with the intended benefits of the project.

This process of benefits realization management is critical to achieving the transparency and credibility of the transformation. Symcor, a leading financial process services provider, measures projects based on the criteria in their corporate objectives: revenue, cost reductions, efficiencies and growth. Their Enterprise Project office then measures the achievement of these criteria against the cost to operate the project, and publishes the results in a document they call the business case analysis (BCA). Once a month, the BCA for each project in their portfolio is reviewed, allowing them to prioritize projects based on their return on investment. In some cases, projects were actually cancelled because they were operating at a loss. Symcor has attributed their benefits realization management process as a main reason for over $72 million in cost reductions and their overall strategic growth in recent years. Although their service is clearly different than that of a supply chain, they are recognized as a benchmark for benefits realization management (PMI, 2017).

FUTURE RESEARCH DIRECTIONS

Digital transformations are fundamentally different than other projects because the capabilities in data science have changed so much. The skills necessary to lead the PMO have therefore changed as well. As a result, PMO resources will eventually need to be proficient with predictive analytics, artificial intelligence (AI), machine learning and other advanced data science concepts. Project management systems themselves are actually starting to use AI to automate certain tasks like matching resources with tasks or compiling the knowledge management system for the project.

CONCLUSION

To summarize this chapter, the PMO is an integral part of major transformations. They become even more critical for supply chain transformations given the complexity, the number of functions involved, and the opportunity for significant reductions in working capital and expenses or improvements in service levels. If the PMO is constructed or managed poorly, it can be perceived as unnecessary overhead to an already expensive project. If it is not managed right, other initiatives within the organization can steal resources or funds away from the transformation. Additionally, poor change control processes can allow the project to take on unintended scope, which will result in the transformation not being able to address the objectives in the charter and ultimately running out of funding before the implementation is complete. A final key challenge reviewed here is the situation where there is a lack of integration between the workstreams, resulting in multiple independent "sub-projects" with minimal synchronization. To combat these challenges, the PMO must develop a highly structured set of deliverables to guide the project through the Initiating, Planning, Executing, Monitoring and Controlling, and Closing phases of the transformation. All along the way, it is critical that a highly skilled and trained PMO is perfectly aligned to the transformation sponsors and senior leadership. Finally, the PMO must build a solid business case and operational scorecard to socialize, track and ultimately prove that the transformation has been a success to the business.

REFERENCES

Brown, A. S. (2003). *Modeling tough scheduling problems with project management software.* Paper presented at PMI® Global Congress 2003—North America, Baltimore, MD.

Forrester Research, Inc. (2013). *Strategic PMOs Play a Vital Role in Driving Business Outcomes.* Author.

JDA Software Group, Inc. (2018). *Digital Supply Chain in Retail & Manufacturing: A State of the Industry Benchmark.* Retrieved from https://now.jda.com

KPMG, LLP. (2017). Transformation framework and select deliverable examples. New York, NY: Author.

Mankins, M. (2014). *This Weekly Meeting Took Up 300,000 Hours a Year.* Retrieved from http://hbr.org

Project Management Institute, Inc. (2008). *A Guide to the Project Management Body of Knowledge* (4th ed.). PMBOK Guide.

Project Management Institute, Inc. (2013). *Proctor & Gamble upgrades nearly 20-year-old software and work processes.* Author.

Project Management Institute, Inc. (2017). *Embracing Benefits Realization Management – An Essential Element in Achieving Project Management and Business Success.* Author.

Project Management Institute, Inc. (2018a). *PMI's Pulse of the Profession – 10th Global Project Management Survey 2018.* Author.

Project Management Institute, Inc. (2018b). *Establishing benefits ownership and accountability – Benefits Realization Management.* Author.

Sellers, P. (n.d.). *The "tipping point" in Ford's turnaround.* Retrieved from http://www.forbes.com

Wiseman, C. (2018). *Scorecards for supply chain transformations. Unpublished work. KPMG,* LLP.

Woerner, B., & Aziz, L. (2007). *PMO leadership—a catalyst for accelerating growth within the information technology project management office.* Paper presented at PMI® Global Congress 2007—North America, Atlanta, GA.

ADDITIONAL READING

Dittman, J. P. (2012). *Supply Chain Transformation: Building and Executing an Integrated Supply Chain Strategy.* New York, NY: McGraw-Hill Education.

JDA Software Group, Inc. *Digital Supply Chain in Retail & Manufacturing: A State of the Industry Benchmark.* Retrieved from https://now.jda.com

KPMG. LLP. *JDA, KPMG Supply Chain Survey Reveals Contrasting Digital Transformation Strategies for Retailers and Manufacturers.* Retrieved from https://home.kpmg.com/us

Person, R. (2009). *Balanced Scorecards & Operational Dashboards with Microsoft Excel.* Indianapolis, IN: Wiley Publishing, Inc.

Project Management Institute, Inc. (2008). *A Guide to the Project Management Body of Knowledge* (4th ed.). PMBOK Guide.

Project Management Institute, Inc. (2018). *PMI's Pulse of the Profession – 10th Global Project Management Survey 2018.*

Slone, R. E., Dittmann, J. P., Mentzer, J. T. (2010). *The New Supply Chain Agenda: The 5 Steps That Drive Real Value.* Boson, MA: Harvard Business School Publishing Corporation.

Woerner, B., & Aziz, L. (2007). *PMO leadership—a catalyst for accelerating growth within the information technology project management office.* Paper presented at PMI® Global Congress 2007—North America, Atlanta, GA. Newtown Square, PA: Project Management Institute.

KEY TERMS AND DEFINITIONS

Critical Path: The series of tasks that must finish on time for the entire project to finish on schedule. Each task on the critical path is a critical task. A project can go no faster than the critical path.

Integrated Change Control: Process performed by the PMO to evaluate new requirements or enhancements and then determine if they will be added to the scope of the project.

Integrated Project Plan: Document that contains all the activities necessary to perform the transformation. Typically, each workstream has its own project plan, but they are integrated into a single plan by the PMO.

Interdependencies: The relationships among tasks in different workstreams which determine the order in which activities need to be performed. Relationships between activities in the same workstream are dependencies, but if the activities are in different workstreams, they are referred to as interdependencies. There are four types of dependency relationships: finish to start, start to start, finish to finish, and start to finish.

Program Management Organization (PMO): A team of project managers and staff responsible for the centralization and coordination of the entire project. PMO can also stand for project management office when the project has a smaller scope and it can stand for Portfolio Management Office when the PMO is managing multiple projects or programs at the same time.

Project Management Body of Knowledge (PMBOK): A very comprehensive set of project management best practices published by the Project Management Institute. The PMBOK is the definitive standard for establishing and running PMOs.

Scope Creep: The phenomenon of adding features, functionality, geographies, business units, or anything else to the project that broadens the originally agreed upon scope that is documented in the charter. Scope creep occurs when the scope is not properly defined, or the change control process is not being enforced or it is incapable of detecting or monitoring the project.

Workstream: A work package of the project with its own resources, scope and objectives. Workstreams are the major components of a work breakdown structure. Typical workstreams for a digital supply chain transformation include demand planning, supply planning, inventory management, change management master data management, and integration.

Chapter 7
Supply Chain Performance Measurement and Organizational Alignment in the Digital World

Ehap Sabri
KPMG LLP, USA & University of Texas at Dallas, USA

Rohan Vishwasrao
JDA Software, USA

ABSTRACT

The authors describe how organizations can leverage the maturity model approach in conjunction with foundational concepts of perspective-based performance evaluation models like the balanced scorecard (BSC) to define a comprehensive performance measurement framework. A maturity model by design provides a road-map to the next level of performance. In this chapter, the authors propose using maturity models as a structured way of identifying current capability or maturity level of any supply chain. The authors provide guidance on selecting the right "causal linkages" between supply chain objectives and performance measures. They then define a mechanism for specifying even more granular definitions of measures linked to strategic objectives, as the level of maturity progresses. In this chapter, the authors survey widely used supply chain/business process maturity models and current practices related to measuring operational metric. And then present a tiered framework for operational metric alignment and KPI governance based on perspective-based modeling design principles.

INTRODUCTION

Financial metrics are useful lagging outcomes of the performance of an organization, but the operational metrics in-turn are leading indicators of an organizations future performance. Operational metrics, when correctly defined, act as guiding posts to the desired performance end state. Thus, the key question which we attempt to answer is; 'How to define metrics, which are aligned to the strategic context, as well as

DOI: 10.4018/978-1-5225-7700-3.ch007

Copyright © 2019, IGI Global. Copying or distributing in print or electronic forms without written permission of IGI Global is prohibited.

deployable in operational reality?' There are two aspects to this question; alignment to the strategy and operational deploy–ability. 'Operating metrics are often poorly understood and guidelines for the use of metrics are often poorly articulated' (Melnyk et al., 2005). The primary challenge is to define metrics such that they are consistent with the strategic objective and the activities at the execution level. Whereas, the secondary challenge then becomes, maintaining this alignment, in the dynamic operational context.

Performance management is a multi–step virtuous cycle that involves creating strategy and plans, monitoring the execution of those plans, and adjusting activity and objectives to achieve strategic goals. A performance management system, consisting of interlinked business architecture and IT architecture, should support this virtuous cycle (Wayne, 2009).

Over the years, a variety of performance measurement systems have been designed and studied by academics and consultants, but organizations struggle to leverage such systems effectively. Over a period of time, disconnect between strategy and metric deployment process are introduced due to changed operational realities both on the IT as well as on the business front. Sometime, minor changes to metric definitions – over-time – lead to incorrect understanding of the measures. To overcome these issues, we propose a comprehensive mechanism to maintain alignment between the operational metrics and organizational strategies, which will enable organizations to – proactively evolve performance management systems as they grow, implement better IT systems and refine operational processes. Subsequent sections of this chapter provide an overview of the fundamental building blocks of our proposed metrics alignment and governance framework. These building blocks are as follows: Balanced Scorecard, Supply Chain Maturity Models and Causal Loop Diagrams from System Dynamics for identifying 'causal linkages'.

Balanced Scorecard Fundamentals

The Balanced Scorecard (BSC) introduced by Kaplan and Norton in 1992, has been one of the most widely adopted management tools for describing, communicating and implementing strategy. BSC retains financial metrics as the ultimate outcome measures for company success, but supplements these with metrics from three additional perspectives; customer, internal process, and learning and growth as the drivers for creating long-term shareholder value (Kaplan, 2010).

Over the past two decades, BSC has evolved from being a tool to translate and communicate strategy, into a strategy management framework. It helps define strategy as a collection of 'strategic objectives' and provides a comprehensive measurement framework, that links operational performance improvements to customer and financial performance. "Operational effectiveness and strategy are both essential to superior performance, which, […], is the primary goal of any enterprise" (Porter, 1996). The success of Balance Scorecard is due to the fact that it provides an overarching view of both these key aspects in an easily comprehensible fashion. Of the three elements; Chance, Choice and Certainty, BSC helps map with *Certainty* the measures of operational effectiveness to those with the strategic objectives of an enterprise.

It is needless to say that when organizations change their strategies, though not a trivial or a frequent activity, the basic premise on which the BSC is designed for the organization, changes. A shift or change in strategy obviously calls for a re–design of the BSC for it to remain relevant in the changed context. But how does one go about accommodating the changing operational realities in the BSC system? As companies gain experience in execution, fine tune their processes and use better technologies, the premise on which operational effectiveness and corresponding measures are defined also change. These changes need to be accounted for in the BSC for it to remain relevant in the changed operational context. Changes in the operational contexts are more frequent, but might not be incorporated in the BSC if a formal structure for defining the improved or changed measures does not exist. This gap prompts us to think about the element of *Choice*; do organizations have a handle on how to define the changed operational context? Do they have a road-map to deliberately move to a better operational state?

Maturity Models: Concepts and Relevance

The aim of supply chain management is to optimize supply chain and gain competitive advantage. So, instead of striving for the highest level of performance for all processes, organizations must aim for the most optimal level of performance (van Looy 2013b). This is where capability maturity models provide pragmatic guidance by prescribing a road map for advancing or improving business processes. Typically maturity models have the following components; maturity levels, key process areas (level specific), key practices (level specific), specific goals and common features. The top most maturity level almost always characterizes all process being managed in the state of "deliberate process optimization/ improvement".

A variety of business process maturity models (BPMM) have been developed, some have been specifically designed with a Supply Chain focus. von Looy (2014) has provided the most comprehensive review of BPMM to date. In this survey von Looy (2014) lists 24 maturity models, some of which have been developed in the academia, while the rest by supply chain consulting firms. This survey includes the SCOR model, which is one of the most well-known and widely adopted supply chain business process reference models. According to the Supply Chain Council (2014); SCOR model provides a unique framework for defining and linking performance metrics, processes, best practices, and people into a unified structure. By definition, a process reference model provides domain specific generic constructs, which can be used in different models. The authors would like to highlight that, SCOR is a business process reference model and not a business process maturity model as classified by van Looy (2013a). The authors recommend Fettke et al. (2005), for a detailed survey of business process reference model across various domains like; information technology, enterprise systems, supply chain and management organization to name a few. Nevertheless, van Looy (2013a) provides a comprehensive set of maturity models to choose from.

Basic purpose of a maturity model is to give guidance on levels of maturity and maturations path. Typically set of measures, corresponding to respective stages, help identity the current and desired levels of maturity. While most SC maturity models cover the entire supply chain, there are others which focus on specific areas like: Logistics, Sustainability, Efficient Consumer Response and so on. With so many models to choose from, it can be a daunting task to evaluate and select the models most relevant to an organization. The question then become how does one '*Choose*' the right measures in a given context, so that one can answer with *Certainty*: Am I measuring the right variable? Is the factor that I am measuring, relevant to the organizations strategic objective? How is the variable being measured affects the outcomes or performance of my supply chain?

One key choice the authors will be making is that, irrespective of the maturity model being considered, for the development of their operational metrics alignment and governance framework, the authors will be leveraging the SCOR process reference model. The *Choose* the SCOR model for its depth of coverage and wide adoption, this model itself have hundreds of measures across the width of supply chain functional areas.

System Dynamics: Concepts and Relevance

System Dynamics is one of the six main disciplines (Operations Research/Information Technology, Logistics, Marketing, Organization and Strategy being the other five), that have contributed the most to the field of Supply Chain Management (Otto & Kotzab, 2003). It is a perspective-based methodology which uses information feedback and delays to understand the dynamic behavior of complex physical, biological, and social systems.

The causal loop diagrams (CLDs) which are used for system dynamics modeling are of particular interest to us. CLDs are used to create conceptual models, which represent the relationships between the variables in the system. They provide an understanding of the system structure as it identifies the important factors or variables influencing a system as well as the causal influence among these variables (Geethan et al., 2011).

From the point of view of evaluating performance of a supply chain, having a system dynamics perspective provides the proverbial 'most bang for the buck'. This is because causal loop diagrams can potentially provide answers to how certain variables influence the performance of a system, thereby providing insights on 'how' these 'key' variables influence the interconnected elements. A BSC on the other hand, in the context of a supply chain, simply provides information on how the performance measures roll-up or down the across the echelons of the organization. In the following section the authors, leverage the power of CLDs and BSC, in conjunction with the maturity model approach and propose a performance management framework which helps practitioners to deliberately manage the alignment of operational performance measures to the supply chain objectives in a dynamic operational context.

Proposal

Organizations employ strategies; define tactics and plans so that they know what choices to make in order to achieve their goals with some degree of certainty. BSC is a very effective tool to translate and communicate strategy, but it does not provide a mechanism for maintaining the relevance of defined measures. SCOR process model on the other hand adopts a building block approach and offers complete traceability (Thakkar et al., 2009). The SCOR–BSC framework developed by Thakkar et al. (2009) combines the salient features of performance management framework (BSC) and a supply chain specific process reference model (SCOR). The authors build upon the features of the SCOR–BSC framework by incorporating the salient features of capability maturity models, to enable organizations define operational tactics for processes at different levels of maturity and to provide guidance on improving supply chain processes, while maintaining alignment to corporate goals.

The proposed tiered framework, discussed in subsequent sections, for performance measurement and KPI governance is based on design principles rooted in perspective based models like Balanced Scorecard and the SCOR model. It is structured is similar in form to a capability maturity model, but the framework is agnostic to the maturity model selected. Additionally, the framework provides a toolkit which will enable practitioners to identify and define most relevant performance measures using the first principles of system dynamics, within the context of the supply chain objectives and key process area prescribed by the maturity model of their choice.

SURVEY, ANALYZE AND SYNTHESIZE

In this section we dive deeper into the three foundational themes of the proposed metrics alignment and governance framework; a) Supply Chain maturity models – selecting a relevant model, b) Performance measurement governance framework – combines features from Balanced Scorecard and Maturity models, and c) Identifying relevant performance measures – using Causal Loop Diagrams (CLDs). The objective of this section is to provide sufficient background on the building blocks of the framework.

Survey of Supply Chain Maturity Models

Origins of Business Process Maturity Models (BPMM) can be traced to the discipline of Software Engineering in the early 1980s and were strongly influenced by quality management principles of the day (van Looy, 2014). 'The need for BPMMs increased due to a software crisis that started in the 1970 – 1980s. Many IT projects faced great difficulties in delivering on time, on budget and within scope. Consequently, the first maturity models for software development processes emerged' (van Looy, 2013a). The Capability Maturity Model (initially referred as Process Maturity Framework) developed by Software Engineering Institute is arguably the most well-known and widely adopted maturity model. The success of this software engineering oriented process maturity model spawned a host of similar efforts for a variety of other business functions. The authors restrict their enquiry to Supply Chain domain specific maturity models. Supply chain specific business process maturity models, adapted from van Looy (2013a), have been listed in Table 1.

Table 1. Supply chain maturity models

#	Model Name	Author / Institution
1	SC Integration Maturity Model	Aryee, Naim & Lalwani
2	SC Integration Evaluation Tool & Maturity Model	Böhme & Childerhouse
3	SC Integration Enhancement Framework (SCIEF)	Campbell & Sankaran
4	SC Management Maturity Model	McCormack et al.
5	Web-enabled SC Integration Measurement Model	McLaren
6	21st Century Logistics Framework	Michigan State University
7	SC Maturity Assessment Test (SCMAT)	Netland, Alfnes & Fauske
8	SC Management – Technology Maturity Model	Riverola
9	Logistics Scorecard (LSC)	Tokyo Institute of Technology
10	Global SC Maturity Framework	Aberdeen Group
11	SC Continuum	Accenture
12	Global Scorecard for efficient consumer response capability	CGF, Consumer Goods Forum
13	SC Management Maturity Model	CGR Management Consulting
14	SC Maturity Model	Chicago Consulting
15	SC Maturity Model	CSC, SC Management Review Magazine & Michigan State University
16	SC Maturity Monitor (SCM^2)	eKNOWtion
17	SC Maturity Model	IBM
18	SC Maturity Scan	Jeroen van den Bergh Consulting & VU University Amsterdam
19	GAIA SC sustainability Maturity Model	LMI Research Institute
20	SC Compass	JDA Software
21	SC Maturity Model	PMG & PRTM
22	SCORmark Survey	SCC, Supply Chain Council & APQC
23	SC Management Maturity Model	Schoenfeldt
24	SC Integration Model	Stevens
25	SCM-CMM	Sun, Ren & Yeo

+Adapted fromvan Looy (2014)

Business processes are a reflection of the way an organization operates, while maturity models, as mentioned earlier, are a reflection how organizations evolve. Reiterating a key concept, the basic purpose of the maturity model is to outline the stages of maturation path. This includes the characteristics of each stage and the logical relationship between them. This has in the pas led to criticism of being "step–by–step recipes" that oversimplify reality (Röglinger et al., 2012), however if utilized rationally they can act as valuable guidelines. The maturity models listed in Table 1 are either collaboration focused (e.g.: SC Integration Model, Technology Maturity), or process focused (e.g.: Logistics, Customer Response, End 2 End Supply Chain). So from a practitioner's perspective the question then arises, 'Which model is best suited for their enterprise and what should be the evaluation criteria for selecting a "relevant" model'?

Selecting Relevant Process Maturity Model

To answer these questions the authors investigate two approaches; the first the one adopted by Röglinger et al., (2012); where they take the design approach to identify basic principles of a maturity model. These can be identified by answering the following three questions:

1. What are the improvement measures for each maturity level, and the level of granularity
2. What is the decision calculus for selecting improvement measures and
3. What is the adoption and/or assessment methodology (Röglinger et al., 2012)

The second approach proposed by van Looy (2014) is based on a Delphi study which resulted in 'criteria that must be strategically thought through' for selecting a business process maturity model. These questions are as follows:

1. "Which capability areas must be assessed and improved according to the organization's specific needs?
2. Must the BPMM define a roadmap per capability area, a roadmap for overall maturity, or both?
3. How much guidance must the BPMM give on your journey towards higher maturity?
4. Must the BPMM be generic (i.e. for business processes in general) or domain–specific (e.g. for business processes in supply chains or collaboration situations)?
5. Which type of data must be collected during an assessment?
6. How must information be collected during an assessment?
7. For which purpose must the BPMM be used?
8. Must evidence be explicitly given that the BPMM is able to assess maturity and helps to enhance the efficiency and effectiveness of business processes?
9. How many business processes must be assessed and improved?
10. How long must a particular assessment maximally take?
11. Must the assessment questions and corresponding level calculation be publicly available (instead of only known to the assessors)?
12. Must the BPMM explicitly recognize to include people from outside the assessed organization as respondents in the assessment?
13. How many questions must be maximally answered during an assessment?
14. Must the BPMM be free to access and use?" (van Looy, 2014)

The authors are confident that these two approaches will provide sufficient guidance to practitioners on the approach to defining business specific selection criteria. Using which, they would then be able to identify maturity models relevant to their specific supply chain needs. A business process maturity model 'smart selector' based on van Looy (2013a) approach is available at this uniform resource locator: http://smart-selector.amyvanlooy.eu/

As a closing remark to this subsection, the authors would like to specifically mention that the usefulness and elegance of the SCOR (Supply Chain Operation Reference), which lies in the form in which SCOR integrates Benchmarking, Performance measurement and Business process re–engineering across various entities in the Supply Chain. This process reference model provides over 140 measures across processes along pre–defined performance attributes. The question thus arises, 'How to identify and select the measure most relevant to a particular situation'? The authors attempt to answer this and related questions in the subsequent sections.

Performance Measurement Governance Framework

Metrics provide three basic functions; Control, Communication and Improvement (Melnyk, et al., 2004). It is important, however, to highlight the differences between a KPI, a metric, and a report — and to provide a common understanding of these three terms. Key Performance Indicator (KPI) is a metric, but not all metrics are necessarily KPIs. For a metric to be considered as a KPI, it should support *specific organizational goals* and strategy, be *accepted by senior management* and displayed on executive dashboards, and still *convey meaningful information* at all lower organizational levels. On the other hand a metric is derived from a report or set of reports. So a *Metric* must have 'a context and a target', is based on legitimate data, and should lead to tangible action or improvement. A perfect metric is characterized by; *being actionable*, having a *common interpretation*, being *transparent & simple to calculate*, and most importantly supported by *credible & accessible* data (Juice Analytics, 2009). Finally, *Reports* are defined as presentation of contextual data, either in aggregated or disaggregated form. By mapping Reports, Metrics and KPIs to the DIKW (Data–Information– Knowledge–Wisdom) framework one will notice that; Reports provide us with the contextual data, from which metrics and KPI, when designed smartly, provide us with useful information. The onus to derive 'knowledge and understanding' from such information lies with the practitioners and on the decision making tool they choose to employ. While deriving knowledge is a deterministic process dependent on decision support tools, understanding is largely driven by the mental models and experience of the practitioners. According to Russell Ackoff, knowledge transforms information into instructions (Wienberger, 2010).

Some Challenges in Measuring Performance Effectively

'Effective performance measurement and governance are crucial, as many companies measure too much or too little—or are measuring the wrong things' (Sabri, 2012). Supply chain performance measurement remains a challenge for most firms for the following reasons:

- There are too many choices, which causes difficulty when identifying metrics that will yield the most information for the least investment of time and effort
- Isolated metrics are functional or departmentally oriented and not aligned to corporate strategy

- There is a need for new metrics in today's business to complement traditional metrics. Firms require metrics that can measure lean, agile environments.
- Professionals cannot understand the trade–off and interrelation between metrics when coming up with a comprehensive list; for example, an increase in fill rate can be at the expense of inventory levels and cash cycle time.
- There is difficulty understanding root causes when key performance indicator (KPI) targets are not achieved. This can be a result of not tracking tier 2 metrics and unstructured governance for conducting root cause analysis or corrective action. In this case, the measurement itself can become a source of waste.
- There is lack of clear ownership for metrics and inability to drive good behavior.
- Consistently clean data are unavailable, which results in lack of confidence in the output.
- Due to a weak economy, there is an urgent need by senior management to review the quantitative business case or return on investment in order to approve the improvement program budget. But middle managers are unable to use metrics to come up with the business case due to previous challenges (Sabri, 2012).

Sabri (2012) proposes the use of a performance management framework which addresses these challenges. Such a framework enables practitioners to effectively analyze the impact of improving individual processes on the overall performance of the value chain, propagates objectives and metrics down to the operational level, and determines the success of corporate strategies. He then outlines a governance framework which is effective in achieving four key objectives: 1) Identify the right KPIs, 2) Establish root–cause analysis and ownership, 3) Systematically track KPIs and metrics and 4) Establish governance for KPI and metrics reviews (Sabri, 2012).

Benefits of Performance Management Frameworks

Historically, supply chain business function has been perceived from the cost reduction opportunity lens, but of late it is seen as an area to drive business growth, profitability, cash flow and asset utilization. Many studies have established a clear and direct link between supply chain excellence and financial performance. According to AMR-Gartner Research, companies with superior supply chain performance achieve better Earnings Per Share (EPS), Return on Assets (ROA) and Profit Margins than their peers. For example, Camerinelli and Cantu (2006) note that 10% improvement in perfect-order rating correlates with 50% better EPS and a 5% improvement in perfect-order rating leads to 25% improvement in ROA. Additionally, Camerinelli and Cantu (2006) found that 3% better perfect-order rating correlates with 1% additional profit margin. Sabri's KPI Governance Model (2012) has been implemented to define supply chain performance measurement systems across industries, i.e., from automotive manufacturing to retail pharmacy chains.

In the remainder of this sub-section the authors delve into establishing metrics governance and discuss how KPIs could be tracked using the performance measurement governance framework. Whereas, in the next section, a toolkit is discussed that will help practitioners identifying the right KPIs and establish traceability between Tier I & II metrics for the purpose of root cause analysis.

Framework for Effective KPI Governance

The framework for KPI Governance is based on the four key objectives discussed earlier, and its elements are structured in similar order. The first and foremost objective is to 'Identify the right KPIs'. Sabri (2012) suggests that practitioners consider the following three aspects; 1) Avoid Hammer's Deadly Sins of Performance Measurement, 2) Focus on a handful of KPIs that are most critical to the business and align them to corporate strategy and objective and 3) Define a target performance level for every KPI based on benchmarking with other companies or based on the company's own goals.

The next objective is to 'establish root cause analysis and ownership'. 'The proposed KPIs need to be aligned to supply chain strategic goals and should be able to measure their successes. For example, forecast accuracy can assess the success of an effective sales and operations planning meeting mechanism. Inventory turns can measure the success of network and inventory strategy. Because it is impractical to measure every activity, identifying a reasonable number of metrics (tier 2 metrics), that have a direct linkage to KPIs (tier 1 metrics) is a necessity' (Sabri, 2012). One way to identify tier 2 metrics is to conduct root cause analysis on the KPIs and investigate potential reasons for not achieving a certain target. The other method, discussed later in the chapter, is to map relevant factors in a systemic form and identify the factors/ variables influencing the performance indicator under consideration. 'Root causes can be broadly grouped into two categories: process design issues and policy (process enforcement) issues. In case of process design issues – the design of operating process or system simply does not allow it to operate at the target level. Therefore, a process or technology innovation enabler might be the right solution to reach the target. An example could be holistic redesign of the process is needed as corrective action' (Sabri, 2012). On the other hand, policy issues such as poorly trained or unmotivated workers can be resolved with effective change management. It is important to mention that process redesign will not help and will be a waste of time and money. More importantly, tracking metrics is not the goal; the goal is to enable improvement. With this level of granularity of investigation, ownership and corrective actions are just a consequence of the exercise. Figure 1 provides a graphical view of how one can communicate the alignment between Strategic Goals and KPIs, and the pairing of Tier I and II metrics for root cause investigation in the event of deviation of KPI from the agreed upon or expected range.

For effective governance of performance measurement, the key to success lies in clarity of definition, interpretation and ownership of the metrics. 'A metric must be well defined so there is no dispute about it. Otherwise, managers tend to interpret it in ways that work well for them but that might lead to conflict. For example, if not clearly defined, an on-time delivery performance metric can be interpreted by the supplier to be a shipping date, while the customer might assume the same metric represents a receiving date. A comprehensive set of metrics should be considered because improvement in one area is sometimes achieved at the expense of another. Also, metrics should stress results instead of activities' (Sabri, 2012).

'Identifying what needs to be measured is just the first step; finding the right way to measure and track is the next. Measuring at regular intervals is useful for base-lining the performance prior to a major transformation program and for getting a clear picture of the impact of the change on performance. Implementing a system which creates dashboards, on a periodic or as-needed basis, to sustain KPI tracking also is highly recommended' (Sabri, 2012). Table 2 provides a comprehensive list of parameters for tracking the KPIs and Tier I & II metrics from a governance perspective.

Figure 1. Aligning KPIs to corporate strategic goals

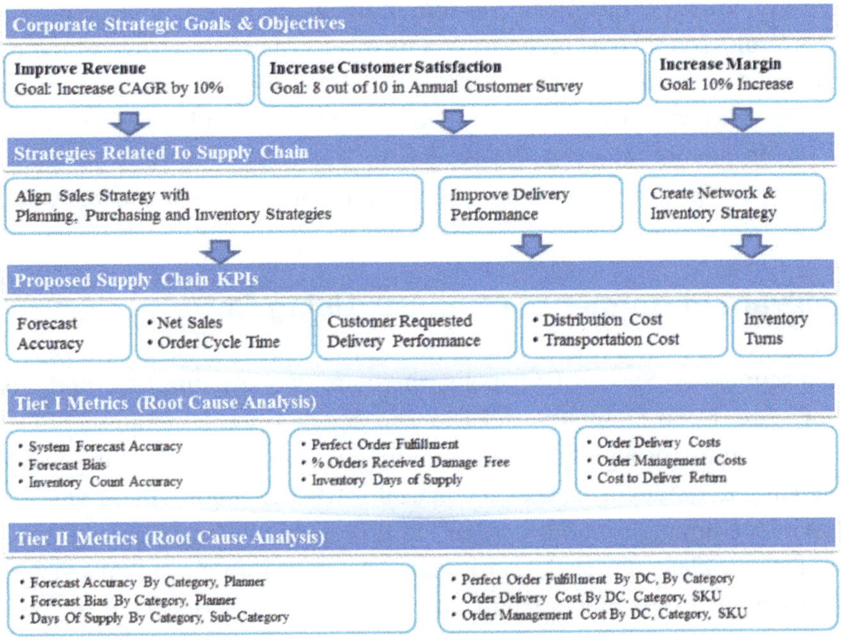

Table 2. Parameters for tracking metrics and KPI

Phase	Attribute	Description
Plan	Measure Name	A unique short name for the measure
	UoM	Unit of Measure
	Description	Brief description of usage and importance of the measure
	Granularity	Identify dimensions: potential grouping
	Interpretation	Interpretation of value & its evolution; optimum & limiting values, expected (statistical) dispersion
	Example	Supply examples including units and format
	Baseline	Past or current level of performance
	Target	Derived from and aligned to corporate goals
	Metric Owner	Role accountable for achieving the target for the defined measure
Do	Computation	How are values obtained? Formula and algorithms used, data source
	Data Source	Data repository which supplies the measure (or its components)
	Refresh Frequency	Frequency of data refresh
	Delivery Frequency	Frequency of re-calculation of the measure
	Delivery Mode	Means of consumption
	Calculation & Distribution Owner	Indicates team/ role responsible for generating and distributing the re-calculated measure
Check	Venue	Indicates where the measure will be discussed and used for deciding on corrective action, if any
	Audit Frequency	Scheduled frequency of review as the specified venue for oversight (?)
	Audience	Recipients and potential recipients of the measure
	Inter-relationship	Indicate other measures which: are antagonistic to the measure, can be used to improve interpretation, are someway related to the measure
Act	Corrective Action	Pointers to factors that may aid root cause analysis
	Timeline	Time window to act; begin at the point of problem identification
	Action Owner	Identify roles responsible & accountable for taking remedial actions, in case of deviations

Finally, to establish effective governance of performance measure reviews, establish a process to set targets, metrics without any target means no skin in the game. This can be achieved by defining the parameters in Table 2 and establish a processes that enables systematic review of the metric collection, communication and related corrective actions to enable (and or institute) continuous improvement. 'The highest level of maturity in establishing governance for measurement is to develop predefined corrective actions when targets are not achieved. This way firms can achieve sustainable gains and surpass the competition. Effective performance measurement and governance are at the heart of lasting success' (Sabri, 2012).

Identifying Relevant Performance Measure: Using CLDs

According to the discipline of System Dynamics, there are two structural methods for analyzing any dynamic system: Causal Loop Diagrams (CLDs) and Stock Flow Diagrams (SFDs). A CLD, also known as Influence Diagram, provides an understanding of the system structure as it identifies factors or variables influencing a system as well as the causal influence among these variables. It shows the governing inter–relations among a number of different variables using feedback mechanisms — the negative feedback loops (balancing) or the positive feedback (reinforcing) loops. Typically, a negative feedback loop indicates, goal–seeking behavior, i.e. the system or sub-system seeks equilibrium after a disturbance. Whereas, a positive feedback loop indicates an unstable system, i.e., initial disturbance leads to further changes to the state of the system.

According to Campuzano et al. (2008), CLDs play two important roles in System Dynamics; 'first, they serve as preliminary sketches of causal hypothesis during model development and second, they can simplify the representation of a model'. The authors recommend the use of group modelling approach to create CLDs in a collaborative manner. In the group modelling technique, the participants develop one or many models during structured sessions with the help of a facilitator, who must favor the elucidation of knowledge within the group. 'The highly interactive nature of the relationships both physical and interpersonal in supply chains makes the use of Group Modelling Techniques highly appropriate [...] The advantage of such a model is that it unearths the mental models of a range of decision makes, all whose decisions can influence the dynamics of the supply chain' (Bell et al., 2003).

Once a CLD or set of CLDs, has been developed by the group of stakeholders under the guidance of a facilitator, more often than not, the inter-dependencies and inter-relationship between various factors which previously were not obvious, will surface. This not only brings clarity to the group in terms of; insights into dynamics of the system as whole and but also reveals impact ones action can have on the supply chain objectives. This exercise if conducted properly will not only help define performance measures correctly, but will also be useful in eliminating potential issues arising out of selection of conflicting metrics.

Figure 2a exhibits a simple causal loop diagram which maps factors influencing Current Inventory, which is a key performance indicator at many organizations. Typically organizations will have many KPIs and a large variety of overlapping factors influencing various measures; the figure 2a is just a rudimentary illustration of how CLDs are to be utilized for; identifying Tier I and Tier II metrics which have a bearing on the KPIs, and to provide guidance on factors to investigate if interested in conducting Root Cause Analysis.

Figure 2a. Causal loop diagram

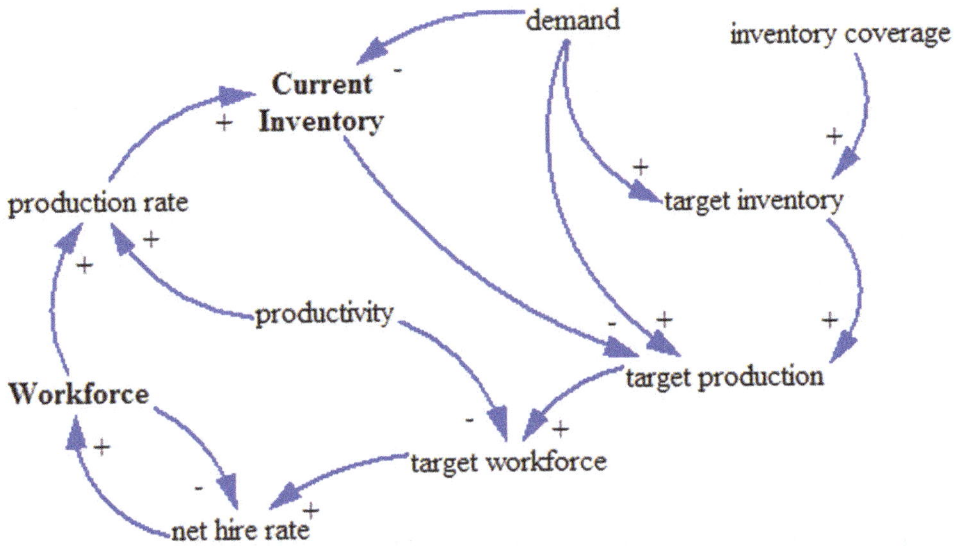

The method to interpret the CLD in Figure 2a is as follows; 'Current Inventory' which is the key performance indicator under consideration is influenced by Demand and Production Rate. The direction of influence line, indicate the direction of effect. Whereas, the polarity '+' or '-' indicate they type of effect, i.e., a '+' indicates that both the variables change in the same direction, otherwise the change in opposite directions. For example, if 'Demand' is increases 'Current Inventory' decreases (assuming all other variables remain constant). Similarly, when 'Production Rate' increases, 'Current Inventory' will also increase and the reverse will hold true. So in this rudimentary example, we can quickly identify that the KPI is Current Inventory for which, one of the Tier I metric is 'production rate', and the related Tier II metric is 'productivity' of the workforce. It goes without saying that when CLDs are developed in a rigorous group modeling setting, will yield more detailed information and generate valuable insights for the defining appropriate Tier I & II measures for all process areas and KPIs under consideration.

Assuming we continue using Systems Dynamics approach, the next logical step would be to create Stock Flow Diagrams (SFDs) based on the CLDs one develops, which help analyze systems in a more rigorous and quantitative fashion. One possible use of developing SFDs is to conduct simulation exercises in order to establish tolerance limits for variables. Such an exercise will help define operating limits for related measure, such that when the process variables operate within these boundaries will not affect the KPI adversely. Yet another useful exercise which might potentially help one study the behavior of the system over time is to identify feedback loops. According to System Theory, all systems exhibit one or more of the three possible structures: Independent Growth, Reinforcing Growth and Balancing Goal Seeking. Figure 2b show the SFD for the CLD presented above, one will notice concepts like stock variables – Inventory & Workforce, flow rates – production rate, new hire rate and influencing factors – productivity, target production etc., need explicit mathematical relations between them. Defining SFD for simulation is a non-trivial, but nevertheless rewarding task, from the point of view of insights it generates.

Figure 2b. Stock flow diagram

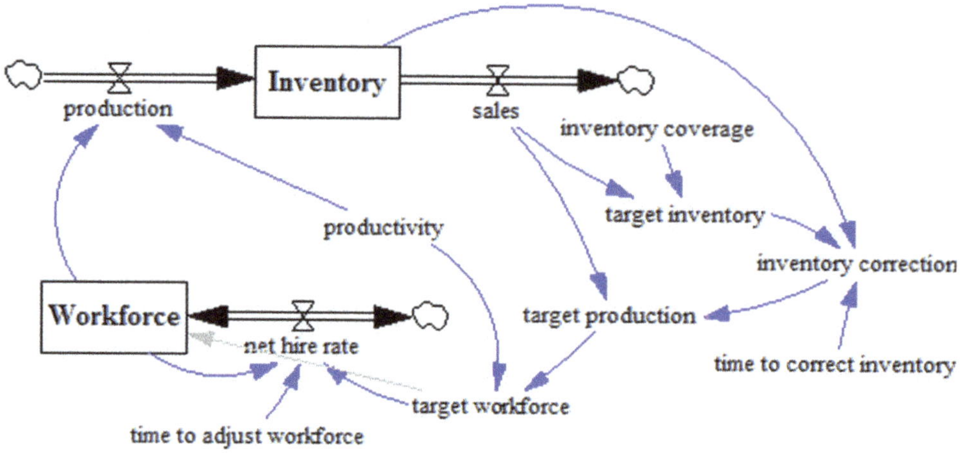

OPERATIONAL METRIC ALIGMENT AND GOVERNANCE FRAMEWORK

The three foundational themes of the framework: a) Supply Chain Maturity Models, b) Performance Measurement Governance and c) Identifying Performance Measures using Causal Loop Diagrams were surveyed in the previous sections. With this background, the authors now provide an outline of the tiered framework for supply chain performance measurement and governance of key performance indicators. An example explaining the salient feature of the framework and how it is applied to achieve the four key objectives of 1) Identify the right KPIs, 2) Establish root-cause analysis and ownership, 3) Systematically track KPIs and metrics and 4) Establish governance for KPI and metrics reviews, is also discussed next.

Figure 3. Performance measurement, alignment and governance framework

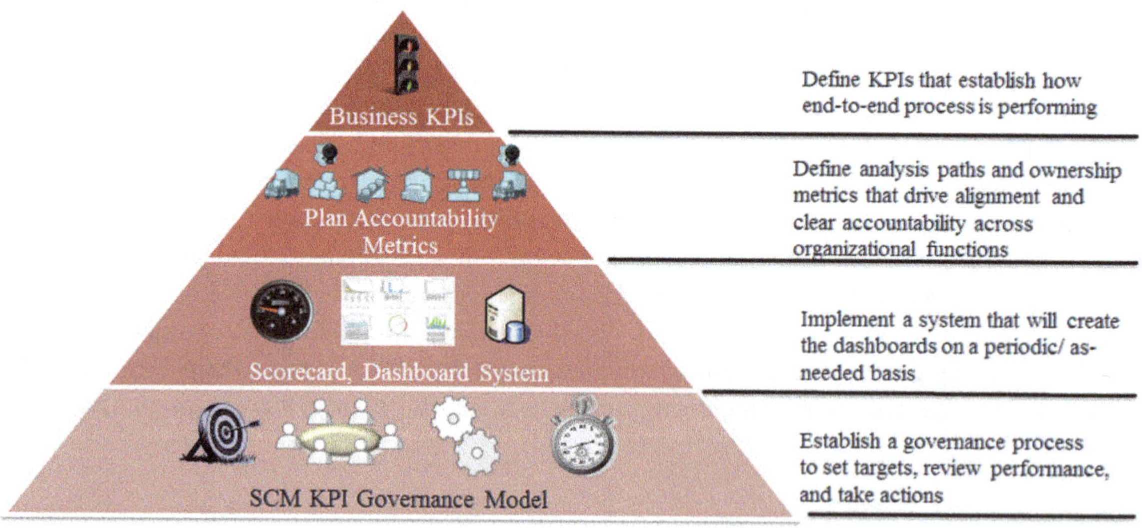

Table 3. Mapping echelons, objectives & foundational elements

Echelon	Objectives	Foundational Elements
Business KPIs	Identify the right KPIs	Causal Loop Diagrams
Plan Accountability Metrics	Establish root cause analysis & ownership	Maturity Models, CLDs
Scorecard, Dashboard System	Systematically track KPIs & metrics	Business Intelligence Tools*
KPI Governance Model	Establish governance for KPI & metrics reviews	Sabri's (2012) KPI Governance Model

* Subsequently discussed as part of the section on Reporting & Dashboards – An IT Perspective

* Subsequently discussed as part of the section on Reporting & Dashboards – An IT Perspective

The framework aims to provide executives with the means to propagate corporate objectives and define KPIs aligned to these objectives. The CLD technique when used in a group modelling setting provides managers with the means to effectively define non-conflicting measures and establish ownership and tie operational metrics with the KPIs. Such a structured approach not only helps in analyzing the impact of individual processes on the overall performance of the value chain, but also determines the success of corporate strategies, by establishing accountability and by aligning operational measured with the KPIs and corporate goals.

Figure 3 illustrates in a pictorial fashion the four echelons of the framework; 1) Business KPIs, which drives 2) Accountability Metrics, which in-turn are reflected on 3) Dashboards and Scorecards; these are monitored and controlled via a 4) KPI Governance Model.

Each of these echelons (tentatively) map to the four objectives of a performance governance framework, which the authors have outlined previously. These echelons are anchored in the foundational blocks discussed in the previous sections. Table 3 provides a mapping of these echelons to the objectives and corresponding foundational elements of the metrics alignment and governance framework.

In Figure 4 a high-level workflow has been depicted for implementing the framework; for identifying, aligning and governing supply chain performance measures. Some of the elements like 'Selecting Relevant Maturity Model' (E2.0) and 'KPI Governance Model' (E3.0) have been discussed briefly in the previous sections. Before delving into an end-to-end example about the usage of this framework, the authors will discuss the two key elements of the (arguably) most important echelon – Plan Accountability Metrics, i.e., Identifying Current Maturity Level (E2.1) and Identifying & Defining Level I & II Operational Metrics (E2.2 & E2.3). Then from an IT implementation perspective the authors will highlight factors to be considered while 'Identifying and Defining Reporting and Dashboard Needs' (E4.0)

Identifying Current Maturity Level

The essence of any maturity assessment procedure is essentially benchmarking, where the industry best practice and related goals form the highest level of maturity, while the current state of a process area indicates the level of maturity, as defined by the model selected. Let's first reiterate the key components of a maturity model; key process areas (level specific), key practices, specific goals and common features for a given maturity level. A key point to be noted is that one needs measures – qualitative or quantitative, for each process area and the corresponding highest level of maturity indicator, i.e., the industry

Figure 4. Framework implementation workflow

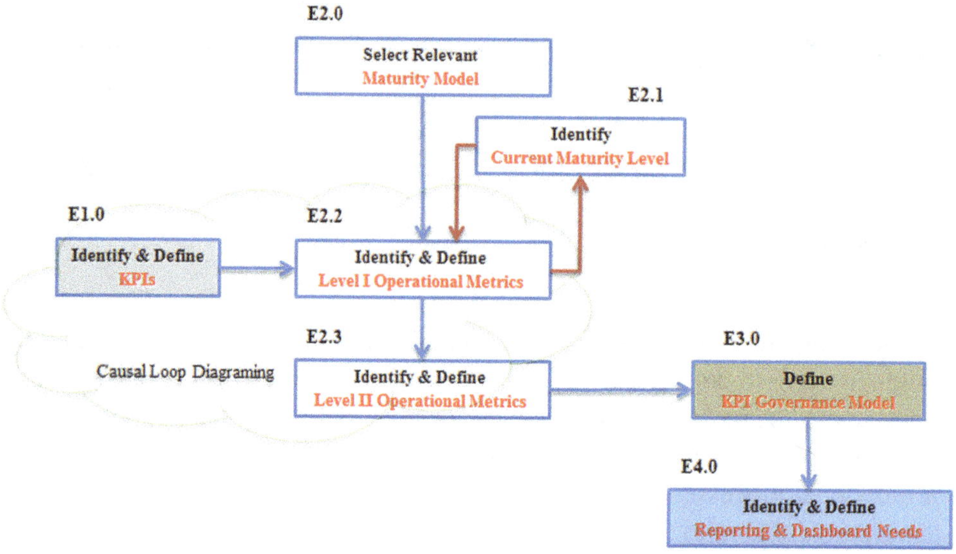

best-practice. In addition to the best practices prescribed in the maturity model selected, Netland et al. (2007) provide three more sources of Best Practice repositories which one might want to consider. These are 1) SCOR Model's Best Practices Appendix, 2) Best Manufacturing Practices Center of Excellence (BMPCOE) and 3) European Foundation for Quality Management's (EFQM) Excellence Model.

We draw upon Netland et al. (2007) approach for assessing the maturity of a company's supply chain operations. Netland and Alfnes (2008) suggest that there are five types of test procedure for identifying the current state of an organizations supply chain: a) Standard maturity self-assessment, b) Gap–analysis (as–is and to–be), c) Counterpart triangulation, d) Third-party triangulation and e) Maturity benchmark study. Though these procedures are discussed in the light of the SCMAT Maturity Model (see Table 1, Row 7), they are generic in nature and can be used with any supply chain maturity model. Further they define these test procedures as follows:

- Standard Maturity Self-assessment – 'The test is carried out by a team of company representatives either alone or with the facilitation of researchers or consultants' (Netland and Alfnes, 2008). Current maturity is determined by qualitative experienced based responses for each of the key practice areas.
- Gap Analysis – The evaluation team (of company representatives) attempt to answer two questions for each of the process areas on a scale of 1 to 5 on the SCMAT Maturity Scale, to identify the largest improvement gaps. The first question (as–is) is phrased as: "To which extent does our supply chain use best practice stated?" (Netland and Alfnes, 2008), whereas the second question (to–be) is phrased as: "To which extent does our supply chain aim to use the best practice stated five years from now?" (Netland and Alfnes, 2008).
- Counterpart Triangulation – In this procedure the organizations upstream (vendors) and downstream (customers) supply chain partners are challenged to evaluate the organizations maturity across relevant process areas. This exercise may provide interesting insights from the point of view of key stakeholders.

- Third-party triangulation – similar to counterpart triangulation, third party consultants or researcher are challenged to evaluate the organizations maturity across key process areas. This exercise is aimed at leveraging the extensive and broad experience and expertise these consultant and researchers may have and may provide a fresh and valuable perspective.

We want to emphasize that selecting the right set performance measures are critical for making the correct assessment of the maturity of supply chain processes. Also, the fundamental reason for adopting maturity models is to "aid companies in benchmarking the maturity of their operations relative to industry best practice" (Netland et al., 2007). Akyuz and Erkan (2010) note that in recent years, the SCOR model has gained increased adoption and have contributed to the development of performance management systems and maturity models for the following reasons:

- 'Provides a standardized way of viewing the supply chain (cross-industry standard)
- Offers a consistent 'scorecard' framework for development of performance
- Emphasizes process orientation and de-emphasizes functional orientation
- Enables cross-industry benchmarks' (Akyuz & Erkan, 2010)

We discuss the usage of metrics as defined by the Supply Chain Operations Reference (SCOR) Model, with respect to the proposed framework in greater details next.

Plan Accountability Metrics Echelon

Akyuz and Erkan (2010) identified the need for 'developing measurement and performance systems in the form of new maturity models supported by SCOR, to enable benchmarking'. Najmi et al. (2013) provides a detailed survey of the adoption of the SCOR model by various researchers in performance measurement system of supply chains. Considering the needs identified in previous research, the authors decided on taking the current approach of incorporating the SCOR performance measure into the structure of a maturity model. 'Plan Accountability Metrics' echelon can be viewed as being at the crux of the metrics alignment exercise. Planning for 'accountability metrics' essentially has two–stages of selection; first stage is selecting the appropriate maturity model. All that a maturity model provides are the process areas of interest and the objectives or levels of performance expected at a particular stage of maturity. The second–stage then entails selecting appropriate set of measures to ensure they provide 'coverage' for the process areas of interest.

Example: Echelon 2 – From Maturity Model to Level II Metrics Selection

Let's assume that, a manufacturer of widgets, who also sell widgets through its own retail stores, wants to align its supply chain operational metrics to its corporate goals. Management's stated goal for the company is to; *increase market share by keeping its customers satisfied and expand customer, thereby increasing revenue and improve profitability.* An external consultant has been hired to achieved this goal of metrics alignment and she decides to use the proposed 'operational metrics alignment and governance framework'.

Also, assume that the consultant has identified all the key stakeholders and has set expectation with the stakeholders on the outcomes, time–lines and the process to be followed (group modelling and workshops) for achieving the goal of aligning operational measures to the corporate objectives. Until this point, after due consideration (and using guidelines provided earlier) it has been determined by all the stakeholders involved that, SCM–CMM model which considers 'Process, People and Technology triangle, across five levels of maturity' (Sun et al., 2005), is the most relevant maturity model for 'evolving' the company's supply chain. And on conducting a detailed assessment of their supply chain processes, it was concluded that *most* of the processes were at SCM–CMM Maturity Level 3.

The next critical task for the stakeholders is to prepare detailed design for developing 'accountability metrics' for all the key processes areas at SCM–CMM Maturity Level 3. Doing so will help them first define in details the expectation for processes at Level 3 maturity and overtime validate, their hypothesis that their processes are indeed at Level 3 maturity. In this sub–section, the authors describe the outline of the process these stakeholders would have followed to prepare detailed design (stage 2 of echelon 2) for the 'Customer Service and Delivery' which is one of the process areas of SCM–CMM Level 3.

The procedure to prepare detailed design for all the key process areas at a maturity level is as follows:

0. Select the desired maturity level as defined by the maturity model
1. Identify the defining characteristics of the maturity level and related facets
2. Select a key process area
    a. Identify facet objectives vis-à-vis maturity level
    b. Map facet objectives (at the maturity level) to the supply chain strategies
    c. Identify KPIs relevant to both supply chain strategies and facet objectives
3. Identify key influencing factors and related SCOR measures
4. Determine parameter values for tracking metrics (refer to Table 2)
5. Repeat steps 2 to step 4, until all key process areas are covered
6. Begin at step 1, and repeat until all maturity level are covered

Note: In case of SCM–CMM, the facets are: People, Process and Technology. And Maturity Levels are: 1) Ad hoc, 2) Initial, 3) Defined, 4) Extended and 5) Networked.

As discussed several times in the previous sections, the authors strongly recommend taking a group modelling approach for creating the detailed design of accountability metric echelon. The idea is to enable participants develop the detailed design during structured sessions with the help of a facilitator. Such an approach will not just ensure collaboration, but at the same time will resolve potential conflicts by avoiding selection/ definition of overlapping performance measures and generate insights into the dynamics of the supply chain system as whole. The core steps of the procedure are discussed next.

Step 1: Identify Characteristics and Facet Objectives for a Given Maturity Level

According to Sun et al. (2005), Level 3 of the SCM–CMM "is the breakthrough level. Managers employ SCM with strategic intent and results. Cooperation between intra-company functions, vendors and customers takes form of teams that share common SCM measures and goals that reach horizontally across the supply chain [...] the SCM function becomes a serious part of the firm's strategic framework". The defining characteristic of an organization at this level of maturity is to '*Achieve logistics capability*'. The SCM–CMM Level 3 objectives for each of the process, people and technology facets can then be described as follows.

- Process – Well-defined demand/supply balancing process which combine forecasting and planning with sourcing and manufacturing are implemented. Advanced planning and scheduling (APS) begins to occur at this level.
- People – Become more responsive to customer requests and service level
- Technology – Software programs are applied to determine where the warehousing should be located, how much space should be involved, how much inventory is required to meet demand, how the goods should be stored and retrieved.

Once, the level objectives have been identified clearly, the next step is to quantify these in terms of metrics and targets.

Step 2: Align Facet and Organizational Objectives

Sub–Step 2a: Identify Facet Objectives vis-à-vis Maturity Level

SCM–CMM Level 3 has three key process areas: *Customer Service and Delivery*, *Advanced Planning & Scheduling (APS)* and *Network Planning*. In real life it is advisable to consider these three key areas together for the detailed design, for the purpose of illustration; we choose to focus on the '*Customer Service and Delivery*' process area. With respect to this particular process area, from the *People* facet perspective the objective is to "focus on customer satisfaction and service level", from the *Process* facet perspective the objectives would be: "Being Responsive To Customer Request", "Being Responsive To Service Levels", "Focus on Inventory needed for meeting demand" and finally "Supply & Demand Balancing". The *Technology* facet is primarily an enabler, and is useful for identifying "decision support" requirements. Once the facet objectives have been listed, move to the next sub–step.

Sub–Step 2b: Map Level Objectives to Supply Chain Strategy

Before mapping the level objective identified in the previous step, one needs to know the specific supply chain strategies that help drive the corporate goals. This is required so that one can align level objectives to the supply chain strategies, which is turn, are derived from the corporate goals themselves. The supply chain strategies relevant to the example have been briefly mentioned in Figure 1, but first let's review those in the context of the corporate goals. The company's stated goal can be translated into the following specific objectives: a) increasing market share, b) improve customer satisfaction, c) increase revenue and d) improve profitability. As noted in Figure 1, these goals can be achieved by employing these Supply Chain strategies: i) Align sales strategy with planning, purchasing and inventory strategies, ii) Improve delivery performance and iii) Create network & inventory strategy.

Sub–Step 2c: Identify Relevant KPIs

Next step then would be to identify the set of KPIs (Key Performance Indicators) which would accurately reflect the quantification of one or more goals. Typically companywide KPIs would be derived from a BSC exercise, if the organization does not have a BSC or similar practice, then it is recommended that the KPI should be selected in such that they can be derived directly (as much as possible) from the measures which are relevant and acceptable to all the stakeholders. In the Table 4 the corporate objectives, corresponding supply chain strategies have been mapped to some of the Level 3 objectives. Additionally,

Table 4. Mapping corporate goals to level objectives

Corporate Goals	Supply Chain Strategies	Level 3 Objectives	Key Performance Indicators
• Improve Revenue • Increase Customer Satisfaction • Increase Margin	• Create Network & Inventory Strategy • Align Sales Strategy with Planning, Purchasing & Inventory Strategies • Improve Delivery Performance	• Institute Supply & Demand Balancing Process • Coordinate MRP & Handling, Manufacturing & Planning • Focus on Inventory needed To Satisfy Demand • Be Responsive To Customer Requests • Be Responsive To Service Levels	• Net Sales • Forecast Accuracy • Customer Requested Delivery Performance • Order Cycle Time • Distribution Cost • Transportation Cost • Inventory Turns

some KPIs relevant to these supply chain strategies and level objectives have been identified; some of these would be potentially used during detailed design.

Step 3: Identify Influencing Factors and Related Measures

Arguably the most important step is to identify all possible factors, which have influence on the process area under consideration. This is where authors make use of a powerful tool know as influence diagram (also called as causal loop diagrams), to map the causal influence among various factors and uncover the system structure. Figure 5 indicates one possible way to map the influence of the factors affecting the objectives under consideration which are represented by a measure or combination of measures. The authors would like to highlight a note of caution i.e., for the sake of illustration, they have taken a narrow view of the influencing factors, and have limited the scope of investigation to just one of the three key processes areas at this level. In a practical setting it is advised that practitioner take a broader view for the sake of complete coverage and in order to avoid missing any important influencing factors.

In the causal loop diagram illustrated in Figure 5, the authors have identifying the factors that influence three elements Revenue, Margin and Customer Satisfaction (which are corporate goals) from the 'Customer Service and Delivery' point of view (SCM–CMM Level 3 key process area). One will note that if the other two key process areas are considered, i.e., Network Planning and Advanced Planning & Scheduling, it will lead to additional factors being considered for mapping their influencing these three elements of the core corporate goals. Defining boundaries for identifying influencing factors is an important consideration, and generating consensus on the same during group modeling workshops, will help avoid potential adoption issues in the future.

Step 4: Define Tier I and Tier II Metrics

One of the important outcomes of rigorous group modelling exercise for developing CLDs would be consensus on: a) the KPIs and 2) Related pairing of Tier I and Tier II measures. The authors have provided a comprehensive list of parameters for tracking metrics as described in Table 2 follow the PDCA

Figure 5. Causal loop diagram for level 3 customer service and delivery process area

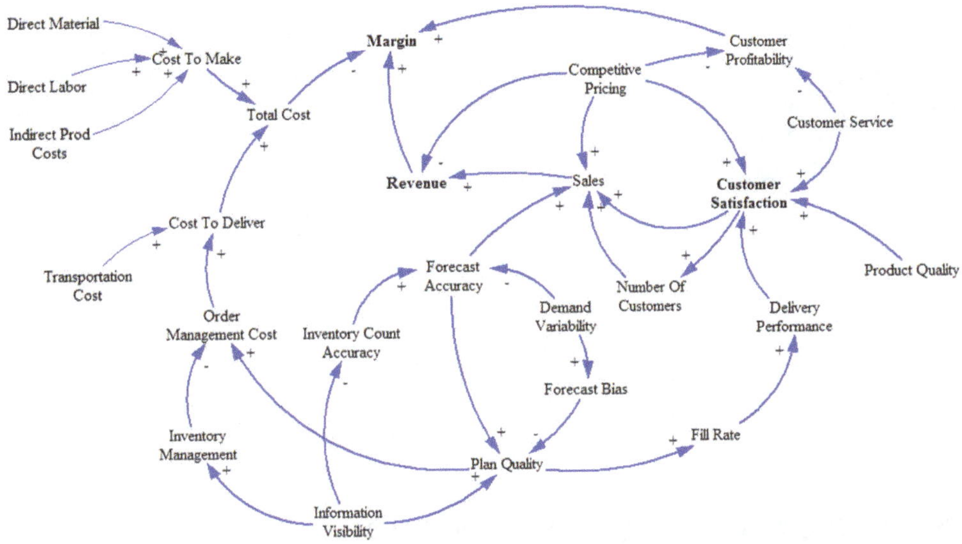

format. The 'plan' parameters define how the metric is to be interpreted and identifies the owner. 'Do' parameters explicitly define the formula, frequency and role responsible for calculating and maintaining the metric definition. 'Check' parameters establish the governance details like venue, frequency and audience responsible for review of the measure. And finally the 'act' parameters define roles responsible for taking corrective action in case of deviations, the suggested corrective actions and the associated timeline. While the exact mechanism for establishing a governance structure has not been defined in this chapter, the authors believe that the outcome of step 4 essentially prepares ground work for establishing the foundation for governance as part of the metrics definition phase itself. To continue with the earlier example, from the CLD in Figure 5, consider the KPI 'Net Sales', the corresponding Tier I metrics in this case would be; Customer Satisfaction and Forecast Accuracy, while the Tier II metric have be shown in Table 5. Those interested can work through the parameters from Table 2 to continue working on the detailed design for these metrics.

Figure 6 is an attempt to show pictorially the composition of Echelon 2, vis-à-vis the maturity levels of a maturity model (in this case Level 3 to Level 5 of the SCM-CMM) and the linkages between corresponding KPIs and Tier I & Tier II metrics. In this figure only one KPI (Net Sales) has been shown and its corresponding Tier I and Tier II measures.

Table 5. Accountability metrics design example

<table>
<tr><th colspan="3">Stage I</th><th colspan="2">Stage II</th></tr>
<tr><th>Maturity Model</th><th>Process Area</th><th>KPI</th><th>Tier I Metric</th><th>Tier II Metric</th></tr>
<tr><td rowspan="5">SCM CMM</td><td rowspan="5">Level 3 Process Area:
Customer Service & Delivery</td><td rowspan="5">Net Sales</td><td rowspan="3">Customer Satisfaction</td><td>Delivery Performance</td></tr>
<tr><td>Product Quality</td></tr>
<tr><td>Customer Service</td></tr>
<tr><td rowspan="2">Forecast Accuracy</td><td>Demand Variability</td></tr>
<tr><td>Inventory Count Accuracy</td></tr>
</table>

Figure 6. Echelon 2 schematic

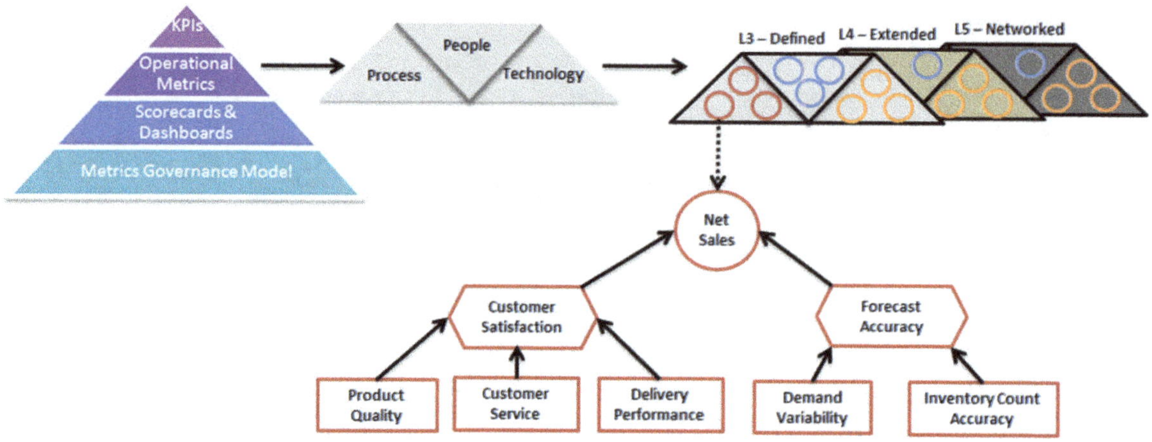

REPORTING AND DASHBOARDS: INFORMATION TECHNOLOGY PERSPECTIVE

In the previous sections the authors have noted that when viewed from the DIKW (Data–Information–Knowledge–Wisdom) framework perspective; Reports provide contextual data, while Metrics and KPIs provide potentially actionable information. The purpose of generating this information is to gain insights into the health of an enterprise, but more importantly support decision making. INFORMS defines 'Analytics as the scientific process of transforming data into insight for making better decisions'. Whereas, dashboard on the other hand is a business tool that displays, a set of performance indicators, KPIs and any other relevant information to a business user. The primary purpose of a dashboard thus can be stated as that of providing users with insights for the purpose of decision support. With this in mind the authors will discuss the design principles and factors to be considered while designing dashboards for business users.

Information Technology Building Blocks

In real–life business settings, the operational raw data generated by most organizations is massive and warranty the use of specialized software for functions like storage, retrieval, reporting and analytics. 'Business Intelligence (BI) is an umbrella term that refers to a variety of software applications used to analyze an organization's raw data. BI as a discipline is made up of several related activities, including data mining, online analytical processing, querying and reporting' (Mulcahy, 2010). This discipline provides us with techniques to define the requirements for the design of Dashboards (echelon 3 of the metrics alignment and governance framework). To understand the basic building blocks of this discipline, the authors turn to the Business Intelligence Continuum developed by a consultancy called Enterprise Management Associates. As shown is Figure 7 the EMA BI Continuum, is a set of related features and functions organized into five categories to act as a framework for classifying enterprise business intelligence platforms (EMA 2012). This framework provides an end-to-end view of all the critical factors to be considered (see Table 6) while defining requirements for dashboard design, i.e., right from planning

Figure 7. EMA business intelligence continuum

*Table 6. 'Factors to be considered' by design category**

Data Acquisition	Data Sources – Single, Multiple
	Source Data Formats – OLTP, OLAP
	Target Data Formats
	Data Acquisition Method – Auto, Scripts
Data Management	Data Model Engine – Auto Discovery, Manual Design
	Data Model and Storage Configuration Method – Auto, Script
	Data Storage Style – In-Memory, Disk
	Data Storage Scale – Peta-, Tera-, Gigabyte
Business Analytics	Multi-Dimensional Analysis – OLAP
	Simple Query Results – SQL
	Dynamic Forecasting – What if?, Linear projection
	Descriptive Modeling – Classification, Regression Trees
	Predictive Modeling – Neural Networks, Radial basis functions, Naïve Bayes
Knowledge Delivery	Visualization – Dashboards / Charts, Scorecards, Geo/Mapping
	Reports – Pixel Perfect, Prebuilt Templates
	Distribution – Manual Push, Manual Pull, Automated Publish/ Subscribe
	Delivery Channel – Web-Based, Mobile, PDF, Office Doc, Collaborative
Actionable Intelligence	Alerts
	Work-flow Engine

*Adapted from Business Intelligence Platforms for Mid-size Organizations: Comparing Birst, MicroStrategy, Oracle and SAP BusinessObjects

to sourcing, storing and managing the operational data, all the way to generating alerts for enabling management by exception.

Dashboard Design Consideration

Information is useful only when provided in the right context. Similarly, dashboards are effective only when they provide 'business role specific' contextual information. For example, a Plant Manager will be interested in metrics like Capacity Utilization, Throughput, etc., whereas, a Financial Controller might be interested in measures like Asset Utilization, COGS, and so on, for the same plant. On the other hand her boss the CFO will be interested in P&L specific measures at both the organization as well as plant level. Certain roles might be interested in 'digging deep' through the information provided, while others would rely on the dashboards for identifying exceptions. Wilson (2012) provides some guidance on how practitioners can approach the design of dashboards as follows:

- Who are you trying to impress?
    - What decisions do they make?
    - What questions do they need answered?

- Select the right type of dashboard
    - Operational: Think of it as monitoring the nerve center of operations
    - Strategic: Provide executives with a high-level overview of the state of the business
    - Analytical: Allows user to explore more of the data and get different insights
- Group data logically
    - Structure the information to make it super easy to answer high priority questions
- Make the data relevant to the audience
    - In what context will they be reviewing the dashboard?
    - Clearly define the boundaries of information by user roles
- Don't clutter your dashboard – Less Is More
- How often does the data really need to be refreshed
    - Operational dashboard's require data in real-time or near real-time
    - Strategic dashboard's require data refreshed on a less frequent basis

Potential Challenges: Implementation and Adoption

One common mistake practitioners tend to make is that they do not differentiate between reporting and analytics. Dykes (2011) states that, the purpose of reporting is to translate raw data into information, that in–turn should result in users raising questions about the business. Whereas, the purpose of analytics is to transforms data and information into insights. 'The goal of analytics is to answer questions by interpreting the data at a deeper level and providing actionable recommendations' (Dykes, 2011). In other words, 'reporting shows you what is happening (numbers) and analysis focuses on explaining why it is happening and how you can act on it (words)' (Dykes, 2011). The end result or presentation of data or information may look similar, i.e., lots of charts, graphs and tables, but on a deeper look the differences will be evident. The most important differences being; approach to delivery and underlying technical design. Reporting generally follows the push approach, where reports in the form of alerts, canned reports and dashboards are passively pushed to users. They are then expected to extract meaningful insights and take appropriate actions (Dykes, 2011). Analytics on the other hand is context driven and hence tends to follow the pull approach, i.e., the users pull the required data to answer a specific business question or hypothesis, by interpreting data, generating insight and ultimately recommend action. On the technical front, an analytical tool is designed to work through multi-dimensional data and help users isolate the sub-set of interest based on multiple data attributes. Typically reporting tools also provides filtering and slice-n-dice capabilities, but the features are limited due to its design and purpose.

The environment in which businesses operate is changing at rapid pace. Factors which are important today might become irrelevant a few weeks from now. Businesses have to react at the same pace to such changing influences to remain competitive. Hence, it becomes imperative that the decision models which enable users to make decision should be update at the same pace or faster, to stay relevant. Business users can no longer remain depended on support function like IT to intervene and update dashboards, reports and such, as it not only add to the response lag, but also increases the chances of taking decision based on obsolete or incorrect decision models. One potential solution is to empower business users by transferring the control of creating dashboards and reports from IT to the actual users under pre-defined guidelines. More often than not, crucial tasks like Data Management which needs specialized skills will not be performed by business users, but by IT specialists.

But, a more optimal solution would be to create an analytics center of excellence, like Davenport states in his article '*Competing on Analytics*' (Davenport, 2006), 'Place all data-collection and analysis activities under a common leadership, with common technology and tools'. Organization, sooner or later, have to acknowledge the fact that analytics, like IT is not a supporting tool, but a strategic weapon and that they need to organize people, process and their responses to meet the continuously evolving decision making process.

CONCLUSION AND FURTHER RESEARCH OPPORTUNITIES

In this chapter the authors have presented a framework for the alignment and governance of supply chain operational metrics. Operational metrics are the leading indicators of an organizations future financial performance and are crucial from the stand point of providing guidance on changing operational dynamics and identify opportunities for improving supply chain processes. The authors have developed this comprehensive framework by incorporating the salient features of capability maturity models into the SCOR–BSC framework. The frameworks enable organizations define operational tactics for processes at different levels of maturity and also provides guidance on improving supply chain processes (depending on the maturity model selected), while maintaining alignment to corporate goals.

In addition to the proposed framework the authors have presented a case for the use of 'system dynamic' tools like influence diagrams (or CLDs) using group modeling formats, which are very effective for developing conceptual models of an organizations' supply chain in a collaborative fashion. The authors believe that such an approach will not only generate insights into the dynamics of the supply chain, but will also promote collaboration and avoid conflicting objectives and strategies across various functions. These techniques when used effectively will result in increased visibility, improved transparency and better governance of supply chain processes across levels of management.

The authors, for the purpose of enabling the implementation of this framework, have provided guidance on; designing selection criteria of maturity models, a comprehensive list for detailed metric definition and governance and last but not the least factors to be considered for designing dashboard. They have also recognized the fact that IT is a critical enabler for the effective roll out of any performance management system and have provided design considerations for both business and IT users from the DIKW (Data–Information–Knowledge–Wisdom) perspective for identifying the requirements. Finally, the authors then discuss the potential challenges in adoption and implementation of a business intelligence system.

Future Research Opportunities

Over the past decade researchers have approached supply chain performance measurement with a variety of methods; process based, six-sigma oriented, perspective based and even utility theory oriented techniques (Najmi et al., 2013). But not enough research has been conducted on the application of system dynamic principles in supply chain performance management. Modeling supply chains and measuring their performance from a 'System Dynamics' perspective has the potential to add immense value. The following are the main guidelines identified for future research:

- Develop Stock Flow simulation models for supply chain what–if analysis
    - To examine the dynamics of the supply chain
    - To define operating tolerances for various factors influencing the performance of a supply chain
- Need for examining factors that influence various supply chain strategies
    - To establish 'metric pairs' for key influencing factors
    - Define 'metric pairs' either by key process areas and maturity levels or by industry characteristics

The authors firmly believe that there is much value in investigating these areas from a practical standpoint, as they prompt researcher to look deeper into the dynamics of the supply chains and can potentially provide much needed guidance to practitioner, on industry or strategy specific situations, for implementing operational performance measurement in a rigorous fashion.

NOTE

This work was previously published in *Optimization of Supply Chain Management in Contemporary Organization*, edited by Ehap Sabri, pp. 148-176, copyright 2015 by IGI Publishing (an imprint of IGI Global).

REFERENCES

Akyuz, G., & Erkan, T. (2010). Supply chain performance measurement: A literature review. *International Journal of Production Research*, *48*(17), 5137–5155. doi:10.1080/00207540903089536

Analytics, J. (2009). *White Paper: A Guide To Creating Dashboards People Love to Use*. Retrieved from: http://goo.gl/QGGHty

Bell, C., Higgs, R., Vickers, S., Toncinich, S., & Haslett, T. (2003). *Using System modelling to understand the dynamics of supply chains*. Monash University. Working Paper 70/03.

Bernard, M. (2012). *Key Performance Indicators (KPIs): The 75 Measures Every Manager Needs To Know*. FT Press. Retrieved from: http://goo.gl/v7r4hZ

Camerinelli, E., & Cantu, A. (2006). Measuring the Value of the Supply Chain: A Framework. *Supply Chain Practice*, *8*(2), 40–59.

Campuzano Bolarín, F., Lisec, A., & Esteban, F. (2008). Inventory cost consequences of variability demand process with a multi-echelon supply chain. *Logistics & Sustainable Transport.*, *1*(3), 1–12.

Davenport, T. (2006, January). Competing on Analytics. *Harvard Business Review*.

Dundas. (n.d.). *Dashboards Demystified*. Retrieved from: http://goo.gl/OriOSu

Dykes, B. (2011). *Web Analytics Action Hero: Using Analysis to Gain Insight and Optimize Your Business*. Adobe Press. Retrieved from: http://goo.gl/OWZSKn

Eckerson, W. (2009). *Performance Management Strategies: How to Create and Deploy Effective Metrics*. TDWI Best Practices Report Q1 2009.

Enterprise Management Associates. (2012). *White Paper: Business Intelligence Platforms for Mid-size Organizations: Comparing Birst, MicroStrategy, Oracle and SAP BusinessObjects*. Retrieved from: http://goo.gl/lm2XRC

Fettke, P., Loos, P., & Zwicker, J. (2005). *Business Process Reference Models: Survey and Classification*. Third International Conference on Business Process Management (BPM), Nancy, France. Retrieved from: http://goo.gl/TQILgk

Geethan, K. A. V., Jose, S., Koshy, A., & Samuel, A. B. (2011). Methodology for Study of Characteristics and Time Reduction in Reverse Supply Chain Using System Dynamics. *International Conference on Sociality and Economics Development, 10*.

INFORMS. (n.d.). *What is Analytics?* Retrieved from: http://goo.gl/odWhqS

Kaplan, R. S. (2010). *Conceptual Foundations of the Balanced Scorecard*. Harvard Business School Accounting & Management Unit Working Paper No. 10-074. Retrieved from: http://ssrn.com/abstract=1562586

Melnyk, S., Stewart, D., & Swink, M. (2004). Metrics and performance measurement in operations management: Dealing with the metrics maze. *Journal of Operations Management*, *22*(3), 209–217. doi:10.1016/j.jom.2004.01.004

Melnyk, S. A., Calantone, R. J., Luft, J., Stewart, D. M., Zsidisin, G. A., Hanson, J., & Burns, L. (2005). An empirical investigation of metrics alignment process. *International Journal of Productivity and Performance Management*, *54*(5/6), 312–324. doi:10.1108/17410400510604494

Mulcahy, R. (2010). Business Intelligence Definitions and Solutions. *CIO Magazine*. Retrieved from: http://goo.gl/VA8Wzx

Najmi, A., Gholamian, M., & Makui, A. (2013). Supply chain performance models: A literature review on approaches, techniques, and criteria. *Journal of Operations and Supply Chain Management*, *6*(2), 94–113. doi:10.12660/joscmv6n2p94-113

Netland, T., & Alfnes, E. (2008). *A practical tool for supply chain improvement – experiences with the supply chain maturity assessment test (SCMAT)*. EurOMA/POMS/JOMSA Conference, Tokyo, Japan.

Netland, T. H., Alfnes, E., & Fauske, H. (2007). How mature is your supply chain? A supply chain maturity assessment test. EurOMA Conference, Ankara, Turkey.

Otto, A., & Kotzab, H. (2003). Does supply chain management really pay? Six perspectives to measure the performance of managing a supply chain. *European Journal of Operational Research*, *144*(2), 306–320. doi:10.1016/S0377-2217(02)00396-X

Porter, M. E. (1996, November). What Is Strategy? *Harvard Business Review*, 4. PMID:10158475

Pruyt, E. (2013). *Small System Dynamics Models for Big Issues: Triple Jump towards Real – World Complexity*. Delft: TU Delft Library. Retrieved from http://goo.gl/ge98Wt

Röglinger, M., Pöppelbuß, J., & Becker, J. (2012). Maturity Models in Business Process Management. *Business Process Management Journal*, *18*(2), 328–346. doi:10.1108/14637151211225225

Sabri, E. (2012, September). Enduring Transformation. *APICS Magazine*, 45 – 47.

Sun, H., Ren, Y., & Yeo, K. (2005). *Capability Maturity Model for Supply Chain Management. International Conference on Management Science and Applications*, Chengdu, China.

Supply Chain Council (SCC). (2014). Retrieved from: https://supply-chain.org/

Thakkar, J., Kanda, A., & Deshmukh, S. (2009). Supply chain performance measurement framework for small and medium scale enterprises. Benchmarking. *International Journal (Toronto, Ont.)*, *16*(5), 702–723.

van Looy, A. (2013a). *BPMM Sample (N=69).* Retrieved from: http://goo.gl/dbiVkQ

van Looy, A. (2013b). Which Business Process Maturity Model Best Fits Your Organization? *BPTrends*. Retrieved from: http://goo.gl/1yCkEA

van Looy, A. (2014). *Business Process Maturity: A Comparative Study on a Sample of Business Process Maturity Models*. Springer. doi:10.1007/978-3-319-04202-2

Wienberger, D. (2010). The Problem with the Data–Information–Knowledge–Wisdom Hierarchy. *HBR Blog Network*. Retrieved from: http://goo.gl/tDtQQD

Wilson, G. (2012). Designing and Building Great Dashboards - 6 Golden Rules to Successful Dashboard Design. *Geckoboard Blog*. Retrieved from: http://goo.gl/cJLCLK

Section 3

Recipe for Success for Optimizing Certain Supply Chain Processes in the Digital World

Chapter 8
Cognitive Integrated Business Planning

Salim Shaikh
JDA Software, USA

ABSTRACT

Supply chains of the 21st century are becoming exponentially more complex due to increased mergers and acquisitions, the omni-channel conflict, direct-to-consumer, rapid proliferation of product configurations, same-day delivery, the recall management problem, shrinking product lifecycles, and market volatility. Moreover, today's consumers are increasingly demanding a personalized, consistent, and seamless experience across retail, online, and mobile. To be able to serve this diverse spectrum of customers, products, markets, and channels and at the same time do so in a win-win profitable manner, organizations need a cognitive integrated business planning process, which has the ability to act with speed, agility, responsiveness, and flexibility, leveraging machine learning and artificial intelligence for predictive and prescriptive analytics, thereby enabling organizations to realign their plans quickly through an always-on, self-learning, and autonomous integrated business planning process.

INTRODUCTION

Following the industrial revolution, over the last 35 years the supply chain has gone through a linear evolution process, spanning material requirements planning (MRP), manufacturing resource planning (MRP II), distribution requirements planning (DRP), lean, vendor managed inventory (VMI), collaborative planning, forecasting and replenishment (CPFR), and business-unit sales and operations planning (S&OP). These improvements were successful and appropriate as supply chains evolved, but companies today are operating in a new world. The very backbone of the supply chain has been shaken by the digital revolution, which is characterized by innovations such as the Internet of Things (IoT), social, news, events, and weather (SNEW) data, 3D printing, quantum computing, robotics, demand sensing, artificial intelligence (AI), machine learning (ML), and neural networks, among other things.

DOI: 10.4018/978-1-5225-7700-3.ch008

Copyright © 2019, IGI Global. Copying or distributing in print or electronic forms without written permission of IGI Global is prohibited.

Supply chains of the 21st century are becoming exponentially more complex due to increased mergers and acquisitions, omni-channel conflict, direct-to-consumer channels, rapid proliferation of product configurations, same-day delivery requirements, the recall management problem, shrinking product lifecycles, and market volatility. The outsourcing and globalization culture has resulted in an explosion of the number of supply chain nodes, creating a multi-dimensional supply grid that represents a highly diversified and complex network of connection points in terms of physical assets, processes and stakeholders. The globalization culture of buy anywhere, make anywhere and sell anywhere has its benefits in terms of sourcing the best materials from across the globe, producing them at the cheapest locations and then distributing them to consumers across the world. However, globalization brings with it negative effects such as increased risk associated with natural calamities, labor unrest, tariffs, currency fluctuations, geo-political situations, litigation and trade sanctions. As a result, there is huge pressure to reduce supply chain risks, and the risk of business disruption or failure increasingly worries global firms. Current political, environmental and economic events like tariffs, Brexit, trade wars, flooding in Thailand, and the geopolitical instability in the Middle East have exposed the shortcomings of globalization. Donald Allan, chief financial officer at tool maker Stanley Black & Decker Inc., said the uncertainty surrounding tariffs and trade in the U.S. and globally has roughly doubled the time he spends on contingency planning. (Ezequiel Minaya, Tatyana Shumsky and Nina Trentmann, 2017)

Moreover, today's consumers are increasingly demanding a personalized, consistent and seamless experience across retail, online and mobile. To be able to serve this diverse spectrum of customers, products, markets and channels, and at the same time do so in a win-win profitable manner, organizations need a cognitive integrated business planning (IBP) process that has the ability to act with speed, agility, responsiveness and flexibility, leveraging ML and AI for predictive and prescriptive analytics, thereby enabling organizations to realign their plans quickly through a continuous closed-loop replanning process. AI and ML have become an integral part of our lives whether we know it or not; personalized product recommendations from Amazon, movie recommendations from Netflix, personalized news feeds from Google, and social network recommendations from LinkedIn or Facebook are all examples of AI and ML. AI and ML help people understand the patterns behind the data – because AI and ML now transcend human computational intelligence across many fields – and leverage those insights to redefine and reimagine an organizations' demand planning, master planning, inventory planning and IBP processes for competitive advantage. By storing the efficacy of planners' historical actions, prescriptive and predictive analytics can proactively automate and improve recommended actions in the future. Companies also need exception management capabilities, which will allow organizations to prioritize responses to current and predicted disruptions based on severity and impact, as well as run what-if scenario analysis using real-time insights to better understand trade-offs. Real-time collaboration with trading partners will help organizations resolve exceptions and execute decisions across the supply chain and extended network. Thus, cognitive IBP is infused with AI, which can analyze existing supply chain strategies and data to learn what factors lead to supply chain failures. This knowledge is used to predict future supply chain problems and proactively prescribe or autonomously execute resolutions. This will help organizations make faster and better decisions, which will drive superior customer experiences and significant competitive advantage.

BACKGROUND

What Is Cognitive IBP?

Cognitive IBP involves a closed-loop continuous process, where different internal and external stakeholders from sales, marketing, development, operations, sourcing, finance and trading partners come together in a formal structured process to create an integrated company game plan that reconciles the views of all functional areas at the same time making sure that this plan is in alignment with the strategic business plan. In today's fast-paced, media-driven world, the IBP process needs to leverage SNEW data to get a real-time pulse of the market and connect with customers and clients. As supply chains merge with IoT and big data, the volume, velocity and frequency of data has increased exponentially. It is becoming increasingly important for companies to be able to see, analyze and act on information across the supply chain in real time, and then learn from those experiences to become better at sensing and responding to supply chain risks and opportunities. A cognitive IBP process has the ability to ingest real-time signals (from the digital edge via SNEW data and competitor promotions, as well as from physical assets like smartphones, sensors, radars and satellites), provide predictive visibility to warn or sense a disruption before it happens, and then leverage prescriptive analytics to manage the unpredictable through risk mitigation plans. If a company isn't agile and is unable to respond to supply chain disruptions and market volatility, demand will exceed supply, resulting in reduced customer service, expediting and overtime. Similarly, if supply exceeds demand, it will lead to excess inventories, obsolescence, price cuts and discounts. Hence, controlling and managing the impact of variability is critical for the success of any firm.

As part of the Intelligent Manufacturing survey (JDA 2018 Intelligent Manufacturing), JDA collected responses from 271 U.S.-based professionals across the manufacturing and wholesale distribution industries. From the survey it was clear that nearly half of the companies surveyed are aggressively pursuing supply chain digitalization strategies and technologies as a major initiative in 2018 for enhancing and redefining their supply chains. Manufacturers have also reported a current investment in digital strategies and solutions, such as:

- IoT (57 percent)
- Cloud-based applications (47 percent)
- Mobile applications (47 percent)
- Software as a Service (42 percent)
- Integration platform as a Service (40 percent)
- Advanced analytics (46 percent)
- Digital data hub (44 percent)

Nearly a third (31 percent) of manufacturing respondents revealed a commitment to integrated planning, wherein their long- and mid-term planning process is integrated with tactical execution through a single, connected technology accessed by users across the supply chain function. The survey found that organizations who implemented an integrated planning approach reported benefits such as greater profitability (61 percent), increased customer service levels (49 percent) and reduced spend (48 percent).

In the past, organizations have been able to throw inventory, capacity and planners at the problems created by siloed planning, but in today's world of shrinking margins and cutthroat competition where profitability is key, this will no longer be sustainable. Sabri and Shaikh (2010), in their book "Lean & Agile Value Chain Management (LAVCM): A Guide to the Next Level of Improvement," introduce the following LAVCM guiding principles. Cognitive IBP leverages the same foundation principles and augments them with ingestion of real-time signals to provide predictive visibility using AI, ML to warn or sense a disruption before it happens, and then leverage prescriptive analytics to manage the unpredictable through risk mitigation plans. Hence, Cognitive IBP is dramatic differentiator that drives revenue and market share growth.

GUIDING PRINCIPLES OF COGNITIVE IBP

Principle 1: Focus on Customer Success

This principle stresses aligning and synchronizing the entire organization to meet the customers' needs. This includes: moving away from a product or channel focus to instead focus on the most important reason for having supply chains — to satisfy customer demand; understanding evolving needs of customers across different markets and improving visibility into changing customer demand; and ingesting digital data signals into your Cognitive IBP process to be able to better respond to customers' changing needs.

Principle 2: Create a Win-Win and Trusted Environment for all Stakeholders

Based on the author's experience, typically, only a few percent of the stakeholders agree that their current key performance indicators (KPIs) were driving the right behaviors. This is because a lot of organizations use metrics that will inevitably make the organization and its people look good. This is primarily because the bonuses and promotions of different stakeholders are usually tied to results measured in terms of "feel good" performance metrics. For instance, in the area of sales it is quite common for "sandbagging" to occur, where a sales executive has a lower forecast toward the end of the year when his quota for the next year is getting finalized, which is then immediately followed by an increase in his forecast at the beginning of the following year to make sure that he has enough supply to meet his quota Cognitive IBP is a cross-functional process, and this principle encourages organizations to look beyond local, compartmentalized performance metrics and focus on an organizational performance measurement system that creates a win-win for all stakeholders while at the same time is in alignment with the business plan. This involves: selecting the right things to measure, those aspects of organizational performance that are both controllable and important in achieving enterprise success and creating an organizational culture and value system that encourages the use of metrics so that they are part of the corporate bloodstream.

Principle 3: Eliminate Waste and Reduce Non-Value-Added Activities

This principle encourages firms to become operationally efficient and lean by eliminating wasteful activities, thereby freeing up resources to focus on value-added activities like collaboration and coming up with risk mitigation what-if scenarios. For example, by leveraging technology and standardization of processes, stakeholders can spend more time on solving real-world problems, thereby making Cognitive IBP an executive decision-making process as opposed to a wasteful activity of just collating data from multiple places and making it a reporting exercise. Technology has come a long way and ML can be used to store outcomes and institutionalize resolution workflows to solve pervasive and persistent problems in an automated fashion.

Principle 4: Institutionalize Continuous Improvement

A disciplined, structured Cognitive IBP process on a repeatable cadence, which rewards continuous improvement and management by exception, should be institutionalized so that it becomes a part of the organization's DNA.

Principle 5: Close the Loop Between Planning and Execution

This principle emphasizes a "one-number" plan that the whole organization marches toward through continuous closed-loop, vertical integration between strategic, tactical and operational planning, linking the Cognitive IBP process to annual budgets and daily execution. Markets have become more volatile and supply chains more subject to risk in recent decades, and business agility is a direct reaction to the instability of the global economy.

ML and AI technology can be used to drive automation and agility and mitigate risk through rapid prescriptive and predictive what-if scenario analysis. Also, positioning suitable capacity and inventory buffers and multi-sourcing to guard against uncertainty enables organizations to become more flexible, agile and responsive.

MATURITY LEVELS

A recent survey on IBP practices was conducted across a spectrum of industries in discrete manufacturing (high-tech, semiconductor, auto, industrial, metals, diversified manufacturing, and aerospace and

Figure 1. Maturity levels

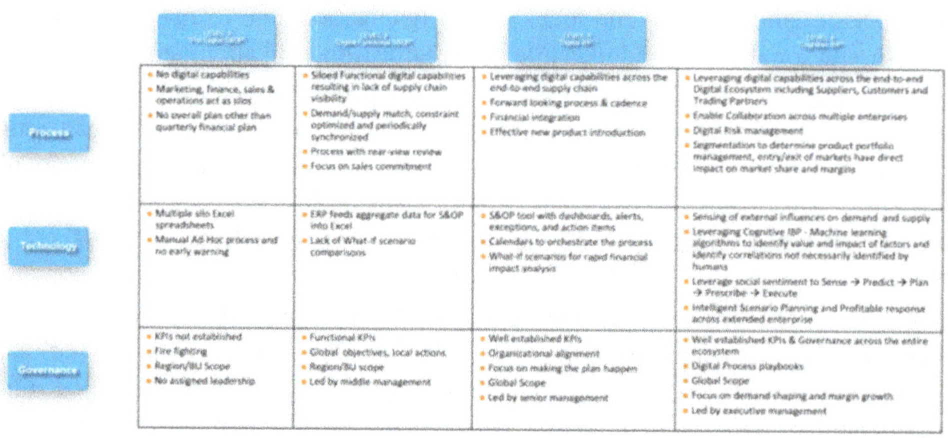

defense) and process manufacturing (chemical, consumer packaged goods, pharmaceuticals, and food and beverage). Some key findings from the survey highlighted that more than 50 percent of the companies were still using spreadsheet-based technology to orchestrate their IBP processes. Though Excel-based spreadsheets are good for rendering data, they are unable to provide the necessary support for what-if scenarios, data aggregation and analysis across multiple plans. In addition, the respondents also highlighted that some of the key challenges in their current IBP processes included the lack of suitable technology to provide end-to-end visibility and transparency, conduct what-if scenario analysis to explore trade-offs and formulate risk mitigation strategies, as well as an inability to link plans from different stakeholders and a lack of executive sponsorship. Gaining effective cross-functional team alignment was highlighted as a major shortcoming by close to 90 percent of the respondents. Process orchestration using calendars, plan visibility across different stakeholders, and capability to aggregate/disaggregate data across different levels in the hierarchy were highlighted as other important functional requirements.

Though most companies are doing IBP in some way, they are not getting the maximum value because they are either at Level 1 (Pre-Digital S&OP), or at the most, they are at Level 2 of process maturity (Digital Functional S&OP). In these companies, there is typically budgeted revenue and profit established at the beginning of the year, and at some point in the middle of the year, a gap starts to emerge between budgets and actuals. The most common questions are: "Will we hit budget? How will we close the gap?" Up until that point there is hope and reassurance that the company will be able to get back on track and close the gap. But eventually reality and panic sets in, and the question becomes: "How do we cut costs to meet budget?"

Improving the existing IBP process and moving to higher levels of maturity is not a cliff event; it's a marathon and not a sprint. Typically, the organization's "as-is" IBP process maturity level is assessed, and existing gaps identified. After careful analysis and scrutiny, an improvement plan is developed to take the organization through a step-by-step journey to elevate the organization to higher stages of "to-be" process maturity, finally culminating in Level 4 (Cognitive IBP), the highest level of IBP process maturity and excellence. The maturity model can be used as a blueprint for organizations who want to move to higher levels of IBP maturity.

Level 1: Pre-Digital S&OP

At the Pre-Digital S&OP level, the supply chain has no digital capabilities to improve functional and end-to-end performance. It is characterized by different stakeholders operating in silos, entrenched in resolving day-to-day priorities, constant firefighting and knee-jerk responses to issues without any assigned leadership. Every department has its own ad hoc manual processes and its own version of the plan and makes decisions as an independent functional group, resulting in a lot of non-value-added activities and goes against Principle 3 (Eliminate waste and reduce non-value-added activities). There is no overarching plan other than a quarterly financial plan. Demand and supply signals come through nondigital mediums, such as electronic data interchange (EDI), phone or fax, resulting in lack of visibility. The S&OP process is plagued with challenges as it entails using an "over the wall" approach between the different S&OP process steps. Also, business processes are not standardized throughout the organization, and every department has its own way of getting things done. This leads to redundancy and duplication of effort and goes against Principle 4 (Institutionalize continuous improvement). There are no KPIs established even at the departmental level and no plan ownership, which often results in the blame game and finger-pointing.

Level 2: Digital Functional S&OP

Digital Functional S&OP is characterized by siloed digital capabilities and the absence of a common end-to-end supply chain focus. For example, an organization could be leveraging IoT capabilities, with the primary focus on predictive maintenance and production monitoring, with the goal of maximizing asset utilization. Every department focuses on its own operational efficiency, priorities and goals and that ends up taking precedence over what the customer wants and hence goes against Principle 1 (Focus on customer success). Though the demand signals might be captured digitally through customer portals or EDI, the supply chain organization is still siloed, which means digital demand signals are not shared across the supply chain to create an integrated supply response. Similarly, supply signals are not fully shared consistently with other supply chain functions, resulting in a lack of end-to-end supply chain visibility. Often companies may be very efficient at doing sales planning, operations planning and financial planning, but the problem is that those processes are not connected. The result is a plethora of siloed plans, with an associated myopic performance measurement for each functional area. This leads to gaming behavior and second guessing where the person who yells the loudest is usually the winner. At this level, the focus is on the tactical short term and disconnected from the organization's overall business strategy. The majority of time and effort is spent on analyzing past performance as opposed to focusing on forward-looking plans and long-term visibility. Also, there are large disconnects between aggregate and detailed plans since the data is spread across multiple systems. This results in a disproportionate amount of time spent on collating data from multiple systems and creating meaningful reports rather than analyzing the data, which goes against Principle 3 (Eliminate waste and reduce non-value-added activities). Though the organization might succeed in achieving a demand supply balance through a lot of blood, sweat and tears, it might fail when it comes to meeting what it has committed to the market from a business plan perspective.

Additionally, organizations at Level 2 leverage technology in a limited way; typically, technology is used to aggregate S&OP data from ERP feeds into Excel, but it lacks what-if scenario comparison capabilities.

Level 3: Digital IBP

Digital IBP is characterized by leveraging digital capabilities across the end-to-end supply chain. For example, demand signals from consumer mobile devices are used to sense demand, sharing this data throughout the supply chain and taking into account cost-service trade-offs across the supply chain to profitably respond to or shape demand. It includes a structured IBP process led by senior management, which transcends departmental silos and leads to cross-functional synchronization, aligning with Principle 1 (Focus on customer success). At this level, there is financial reconciliation across all the demand and supply processes and a longer-term focus. There are also well-established cross-functional KPIs that are in alignment with the organizational goals, which aligns with Principle 2 (Create a win-win and trusted environment for all stakeholders). Organizations at Level 3 leverage technology to enable dashboards, alerts, exceptions, action items, calendars, and what-if scenarios for rapid financial impact analysis to orchestrate the IBP process. Leveraging technology as an enabler for automation aligns with Principle 3 (Eliminate waste and reduce non-value-added activities). However, as organizations face increasingly volatile economic and market conditions, this IBP maturity level lacks the predicative visibility leveraging ML, AI, automation, flexibility and responsiveness to recalibrate plans across the extended enterprise, including customers and suppliers, when inevitable surprises occur (related to personnel, materials, capacity or demand), disrupting even the most efficient supply chains.

In a recent survey of supply chain executives, more than 60 percent of respondents indicated that sudden market pattern changes caused key disruptions, and more than 70 percent pointed to supply-side issues as the primary reason for supply chain disruptions. One of the automotive original equipment manufacturers I interacted with recently mentioned that it had to expedite two million pounds of steel from Germany because of lack of visibility from its trading partners. Companies need the ability to capture and comprehend demand and supply variability as quickly as possible, and then be able to rapidly assess the end-to-end impact of those changes throughout the end-to-end supply chain.

Level 4: Cognitive IBP

Cognitive IBP is the highest level of process maturity and leverages the five guiding principles, aligning and synchronizing the entire organization to meet customer needs, reinforcing Principle 1. Relying on digital capabilities, the supply chain collaborates with customers, suppliers and trading partners to sense, shape and respond to demand. For example, Under Armour orchestrates collaborative relationships with its trading partners like Fitbit and Zappos. Under Armour uses Fitbit to collect demand signals and predict future footwear demand. This information is then sent to Zappos, so that the online retailer can fulfill and shape that demand. At this highest level of maturity, the Cognitive IBP process is used as a lynchpin between strategic business planning, tactical planning and execution, underscoring Principle 5 and creating a closed-loop continuous strategy deployment tool rather than just balancing demand, supply and inventory.

The Cognitive IBP process provides executives with an overall snapshot of business and supply chain health. Executive management leads the process and defines the roles and responsibilities clearly and concisely. There are holistic cross-functional and cross-organizational KPIs that are geared toward internal and external collaboration, motivating people to act in a certain direction that is aligned with the corporate goals, rather than myopic and conflicting departmental goals, and aligning with Principle 2. The metrics are embedded in the organization's DNA, and there is a target performance level for each metric and an individual process owner who is accountable and responsible. This individual constantly tracks the performance against the target, and as soon as a gap starts to emerge, the individual finds the root cause of the deviation and proactively resolves it to get back on track. Most of the time and effort is spent on forward-looking product launches, market trends, competition and new markets rather than just analyzing past variances to budget. Senior management rewards managers who use the right metrics and communicates an executive commitment to meaningful metrics across all channels and to all facets of the organization.

Rather than use a "peanut butter spread" approach, segmentation is leveraged, based on attributes like risk, margins, criticality, revenue, volume, lead times, life cycle stage, etc., which helps the organization put more emphasis and resources on key customers and products and make decisions on product portfolio management, as well as entry/exit of markets. In the future, unsupervised ML could be used to mine unstructured data and automatically create clusters with meaningful patterns in the data. The power of machine learning is to be able to segment not with just one or two features, but with dozens of features in an automated fashion.

Generous use of state-of-the-art technology like ML and AI are leveraged to automate and eliminate repetitive tasks, which enables automation and eliminates of lot of the non-value-added activities (in alignment with Principle 3), so that stakeholders can spend their time on more value-added activities like collaboration and what-if scenario analysis. The cognitive IBP process has the ability to ingest real-time digital signals – from external sources such as SNEW data, competitor promotions, smartphones, sensors, radars, satellites and more – to provide predictive visibility to sense a disruption before it happens and then leverage prescriptive analytics to mitigate the risk.

With AI and ML embedded in the self-learning supply chain, machines will be able to examine supply chain strategies to determine where supply chain failures have occurred in the past and determine what combination of external factors — such as loyalty, inventory levels, weather, competitor events, market performance, socio-economic events, etc. — contributed to those supply chain failures. ML algorithms will then sift through this data to learn how these factors interact to result in a high probability of a supply chain failure. In the future, this type of self-learning supply chain will be able to tell a planner that when a certain combination of events occurs at the same time it is predictive of a supply chain failure. The machine will then be able to prevent the failure by moving inventory to a new location, or it will alert the planner to respond to the problem (Baumann Fred 2018) (http://www.supplychainquarterly.com/news/20180330-a-look-into-the-future-the-self-learning-supply-chain/)

Additionally, social sentiment data from Twitter feeds, Facebook and Instagram posts and Google searches are leveraged to incorporate unstructured data in ideation, new product introduction, demand sensing, marketing and crowdsourcing to get better customer insights and then recalibrate plans and respond with agility based on customer feedback. ML can help understand the patterns behind the data and establish correlations between those patterns, so that if an event happens today then another event will happen in the future. Deep-learning algorithms will drive the supply chains of the future. They will be able to analyze all these combinations of factors, determine which of these items are predictive of a service failure, and build risk mitigation strategies to avoid them at the lowest possible cost. By establishing correlations between unstructured data like internet searches and structured data like actual sales, it is now possible to predict sales well in advance. For example, a well-known toy manufacturer is now using unstructured, social sentiment like Instagram chatter to gauge if a toy it is planning to launch in the market will be a star or a bust.

By storing the efficacy of past outcomes, ML can also be used for automation of proactive issue resolution. Calendarization and orchestration capability ensures process compliance and repeatability of the process steps, which help bring discipline and structure to the process. Technology is also leveraged for audit trails of meetings held, action items, action item assignments, and statuses. All the assumptions, risks and opportunities of different resolution options are documented and tracked so that there is transparency and accountability. This type of top-down, middle-out and bottom-up reconciliation allows different stakeholders to enter inputs at different levels of the flexible hierarchy while at the same time ensuring that everybody is working toward the same overarching corporate strategy.

Cognitive IBP is an exception-driven S&OP process that increases stakeholder efficiency (Principle 3) by allowing stakeholders to triage exceptions and proactively detect, analyze and resolve gaps, with a focus on the plan-do-check-act framework for continuous improvement. Digital process playbooks with associated lever libraries are ingrained structurally into the organization's culture. For example, if a gap has started to emerge between Budget Revenue and Actuals, the digital process playbook would identify the root causes as competitor action, macroeconomic trend, or wrong product mix. Based on the root cause identified, the possible resolution levers could be to launch a promotion, pull in a new product launch, enhance customer collaboration, increase forecast accuracy to optimize the product mix, or alter pricing.

Recently, a semiconductor company that operates in an industry known for its demand variability and long product lead times embarked on a journey to transform its end-to-end supply chain planning processes and tools to ensure that it could respond more swiftly to market changes. The company has been able to move from Level 1 (Pre-Digital S&OP) to Level 3 (Digital IBP) and has the roadmap to get to Level 4 (Cognitive IBP). When the company started its transformation journey, it was using homegrown S&OP tools and was not able to sustain a dynamic business environment because of limitations in scalability and integration. Moreover, it followed a sequential planning process between sales, marketing, supply chain and production, which resulted in a lot of manual ad hoc firefighting and wasteful activities, which went against Principle 3 (Eliminate waste and reduce non-value-added activities).

Since completing the transformation to Level 3 (Digital IBP), the company has been able to re-engineer its end-to-end planning processes and tools to ensure that it could respond more quickly to market changes. The organization has achieved a broad range of results across various dimensions of its business, including reducing its planning effort and errors, improving forecast accuracy and reducing lead times. Technology is being leveraged as an enabler to synchronize supply, demand and capacity across strategic, tactical and execution levels and orchestrate this best-practice continuous and collaborative process. Technology has also been used to facilitate rapid response demand realization simulations and capacity expansion simulations to see the impact on operational and financial plans, ensuring the entire organization can react to changing market conditions with agility and take appropriate actions like adding or offloading extra capacity when necessary.

CONCLUSION

To summarize, companies now operate with an Amazon-era mentality, where deliveries are expected to be made in hours and days rather than weeks and months. Consumers want instant gratification and fast responses. How well a company can sense and respond intelligently to consumers' needs has become a key differentiator for survival and success. Customers now expect more choices, more options and at the same time immediate shipments, with 100 percent product availability 24/7. Any delivery miss is considered a performance failure. This change in customers' expectations is shaping what businesses now expect from their supply chain teams. Companies need to continuously learn to become better at sensing and responding to risks and opportunities. Hence, embarking on cognitive IBP has become a strategic mandate. Because of the exponential increase in the volume, variety, frequency and velocity of big data, companies now have more opportunities to gain a deeper understanding of their customers. By deploying a cognitive IBP process, companies can leverage real-time digital data signals to predict a disruption before it happens, and then use prescriptive analytics to mitigate the risk. This closed-loop continuous process brings together different internal and external stakeholders, including sales, marketing, development, operations, sourcing, finance and trading partners, in a formal and structured way; in doing so, it enables the business to create an integrated game plan that reconciles the views of all functional areas while at the same time making sure that the plan is in alignment with the overarching, strategic business plan.

Cognitive IBP encompasses and augments the five core principles: Focus on customer success; create a win-win and trusted environment for all stakeholders; eliminate waste and reduce non-value-added activities; institutionalize continuous improvement; and close the loop between planning and execution. The path forward to cognitive IBP begins with an assessment of "as is" business processes, outlining how the organization's processes and technology work together and where the company is on the IBP maturity scale. The next step involves iteratively debating where improvements are needed (this is considered the to-be state), isolating a set of practical decisions to unify strategy across all levels of the business. Uncertainty and variability will continue to exist but can be managed through agility and responsiveness by exploring what-if scenarios (i.e., by making changes to key variables like volumes, capacity, mix and price, seeing its impact on bottom-line costs and top-line revenues, and developing contingency plans). Using process playbooks, multiple courses of action can be explored and compared, enabling the company to arrive at an integrated game plan that reconciles the views of all functional areas while at the same time making sure that the plan is in alignment with corporate strategy.

Technology advancements in AI and ML make it possible for companies to analyze vast amounts of data to predict events, spot trends and anomalies; analyze any correlations between patterns and variables; understand the ramifications of different response options; and provide recommendations. Now with the ability to analyze outcomes (including consumer insights and past behavior) and adjust supply parameters, companies can be armed with better decision support. As part of the cognitive IBP process, responses to internal and external disruptions are coordinated across the supply chain instead of managed within individual business units. Additionally, the ability to sense demand and supply changes based on information or data analysis and then incorporate that data into a company's planning processes can make it easier for a company to connect to its consumers' unique needs. This not only helps an organization make faster, better and more profitable decisions, but it also reduces costs and waste across the supply chain. With a digitally-enabled supply chain, companies now have the opportunity to leapfrog existing frameworks to predictive/cognitive models that mitigate risk and reduce variability.

Thus, in order to compete in today's global marketplace of increased market volatility, uncertainty, shrinking product lifecycles, omni-channel fulfillment, direct-to-consumer channels, and same-day delivery, Cognitive IBP will surface as perhaps the most compelling enabler for enterprise excellence because of its ability to not only cut waste and increase efficiency but also provide flexibility, responsiveness and risk management to changing business conditions. Embarking on a cognitive IBP journey can have a positive impact on various facets of the organization, providing benefits such as better forecast accuracy, better asset utilization, increased supply chain visibility, higher on-time delivery performance, improved margins, reduced costs, improved profitability, quicker response time, faster time to market and higher shareholder value.

REFERENCES

Fred, B. (2018). *A look into the future: The self-learning supply chain*. Retrieved from (http://www.supplychainquarterly.com/news/20180330-a-look-into-the-future-the-self-learning-supply-chain/)

JDA. (2018). *Intelligent Manufacturing Survey*. Retrieved from https://jda.com/knowledge-center/collateral/2018-intelligent-manufacturing-survey-exec-summary

Minaya, E., Shumsky, T., & Trentmann, N. (2017). Retrieved from https://www.wsj.com/articles/executives-fear-trade-conflicts-could-dent-economic-growth-1529227800?mod=djemlogistics_h

Sabri, E., & Shaikh, S. (2010). *Lean & Agile Value Chain Management (LAVCM): A Guide to the Next Level of Improvement. J.* Ross Publishing.

ADDITIONAL READING

Sabri, E., & Shaikh, S. (2010). *Lean & Agile Value Chain Management (LAVCM): A Guide to the Next Level of Improvement. J.* Ross Publishing.

Shaikh, S., Sabri, E., & Esturi, S. (2017). Making the journey to a multimodal, segmented supply chain. Retrieved from http://www.supplychainquarterly.com/topics/Strategy/20170626-making-the-journey-to-a-multimodal-segmented-supply-chain/

KEY TERMS AND DEFINITIONS

Agile: Agile is the process of increasing flexibility and responsiveness.

Change Management: Managing people/teams/organization and transitioning them from the current AS-IS state to a future TO-BE state.

Cognitive Integrated Business Planning: Cognitive IBP involves a closed-loop continuous process, where different internal and external stakeholders from sales, marketing, development, operations, sourcing, finance, and trading partners come together in a formal structured process to create an integrated company game plan that reconciles the views of all functional areas at the same time making sure that this plan is in alignment with the strategic business plan. A cognitive IBP process has the ability to ingest real-time signals (from the digital edge via SNEW data and competitor promotions, as well as from physical assets like smartphones, sensors, radars, and satellites), provide predictive visibility to warn or sense a disruption before it happens, and then leverage prescriptive analytics to manage the unpredictable through risk mitigation plans.

Lean: Lean is a process of waste elimination and increasing operational efficiency.

Machine Learning: Machine learning is a field of artificial intelligence that uses statistical techniques to understand the patterns behind the data, establish co-relation between those patterns and "learn" from data, without being explicitly programmed.

Risk Management: Risk management is the process of doing what-if scenarios to enable risk mitigation strategies so as to minimize the impact of unfortunate events.

Segmentation: Segmentation is the process of stratifying the portfolio (product, market, channel etc.) into clusters based on attributes like risk, margins, criticality, revenue, volume, lead times, life cycle stage, etc., which helps the organization put more emphasis and resources on key customers and products and make decisions on product portfolio management, as well as entry/exit of markets to enable an organization to offer differentiated service treatment to certain groups.

SNEW: The ability to ingest real-time digital signals – from external sources such as SNEW (social, news, events, and weather data) can help provide predictive visibility to sense an event/disruption before it happens with the goal of making better and faster decisions.

Chapter 9
Impact of Digitalization on Category Management

Arif Mohammed
JDA Software, USA

Ricardo Cesar Panserini
JDA Software, Brazil

ABSTRACT

The discipline of category management has always played an important role within retailers as well as their CPG manufacturer suppliers. While the eight steps within the category management process (category definition, category role, category assessment, category scorecard, category strategies, category tactics, category implementation, and category review) have remained the same, with digitalization the discipline is undergoing a massive transformation, and the approach to the process is getting disrupted through the availability of huge volumes of transactional data, customer loyalty data; advancement in hardware technology through better scanners, image recognition devices, sensors and IoT devices and machine learning, and artificial intelligence. In this chapter, the authors take a closer look at the eight-step category management process, the traditional approach, the enabler for disruption, the new approach, and its benefits and what the future may hold.

INTRODUCTION

Category Management is the discipline of managing a related group of products as a category or a business unit whereby its performance with respect to metrics such as sales velocity, margin, revenue, market share, etc., are closely monitored to meet the overall objectives of the business. While there are several reasons for the existence of this discipline, one of the primary reasons is that it allows retailers to take a holistic view of their categories rather than a brand-centric or a product-centric view thereby promoting better alignment with corporate financial objectives. Also, it enables retailers and suppliers to collaborate enabling them to take advantage of each other's strengths, for instance retailers have plethora of data on shopper insights whereas the suppliers have deep expertise related to the products.

DOI: 10.4018/978-1-5225-7700-3.ch009

Copyright © 2019, IGI Global. Copying or distributing in print or electronic forms without written permission of IGI Global is prohibited.

Although this practice has been in existence for centuries, the term Category Management was formally coined in 1989 by Dr. Brian Harris, co-founder of The Partnering Group. Over the years, this concept has received several definitions. According to the Category Management Report (1995) published by the Joint Industry Project on Efficient Consumer Response, or ECR, it may be defined as "*The distributor/supplier process of managing categories as strategic business units, producing enhanced business results by focusing on delivering consumer value*". Nielsen (1992) takes a slightly different approach - "*Category management is a process that involves managing product categories as business units and customizing them [on a store by store basis] to satisfy customer needs.*"

Although Catman (Category Management abbreviation) has evolved significantly over the last thirty years, it still retains its fundamental purpose to push manufacturers and retailers to work collaboratively to grow categories by understanding and responding to market trends and shopper needs. This evolution has been driven in great part by two important factors, first the needs and challenges of the retailers and second advancement in technology, especially Digitalization. More than ever, technology is allowing retailers to address historic problems or even recreate some market ecosystems. It is important to mention here a few of these aspects to provide some perspective on how the consumer landscape is evolving and how it is important for the Catman process to be adapted to these new circumstances. In the article "Retail Trends 2018 – A transformative time for retail" published by Deloitte (2018), the authors highlight 3 important "themes" which every retailer should be aware of and suggest they have a clear set of actions to address the same. The themes highlighted are as follows:

- First, stores need to be reinvent themselves to be more than stores, providing also customer experiences. They need to be able to "put digital in the physical" by making digital part of the core, replicating part of the ecommerce experience in the offline environment.
- Second, innovation needs to be applied though experiments, since new technologies such as augmented / virtual reality, artificial intelligence and others will demand a "trial and error" approach in order to find the right balance in every company.
- Third, companies should be willing to transform their businesses, since customer, competition and culture are constantly changing. Trends like "Try before you buy", "Direct to consumer" and "Brand purpose" need to be understood, evaluated and applied carefully.

Catman practice needs to rapidly reinvent itself to keep up with these changes and to be able to support retailers and manufactures with all these challenges. This chapter will focus on analyzing how digitalization has impacted the practice of Category Management. This chapter has 8 sections focusing on the steps of the Catman process, as defined by ECR (Figure 1). Within every section we will provide a brief description of the process, review the traditional approach and how it has been impacted by digitalization. Finally we wrap up this Chapter with a conclusion and our predictions about how this practice will continue to evolve in the near future.

Category Definition

This is step one of the Catman process. As highlighted by ECR (2000), Category definition answers the following question: "*How should the SKUs within the category be segmented, based on consumer decision trees and therefore what SKUs should be included in the category?*". To address this question, Nielsen (2014) proposed the following: "*Define a distinct, measurable and manageable grouping*

Figure 1. 8 Step category management process

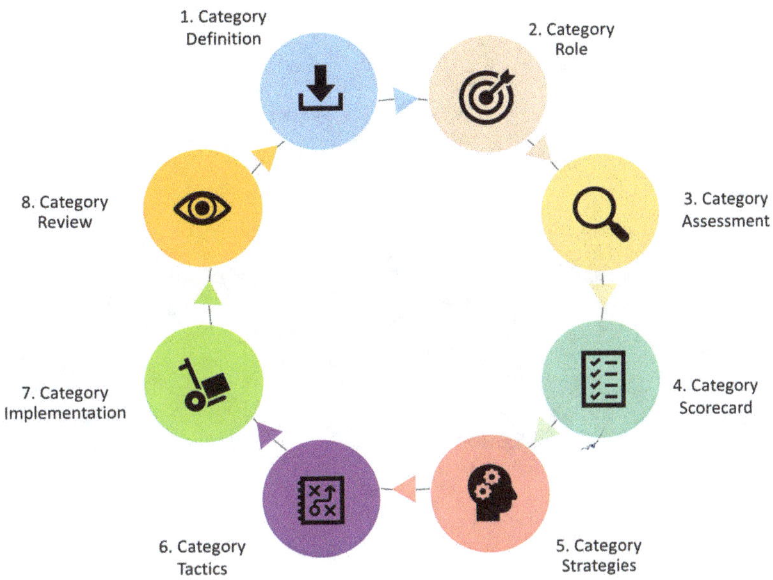

of products that the retailer and manufacturer will optimize by increasing their understanding of and meeting the needs of shoppers."

Traditionally retailers have defined categories by grouping products by function and packaging. For instance, for the longest time most general merchandise retailers have had a category called 'Deodorants' that included products that contained some information on its packaging with a related meaning. However more recently the tendency has been to define the category more holistically as 'Personal Care' to include soaps, shampoos, shaving creams, razors along with deodorants for the specific shopper group. This shift in category definition has been driven by better sources of information and shopper insights available through digitalization that is allowing Category Managers to be more detailed and precise. Loyalty card data is one such example of new data available. Every time a shopper informs his/her loyalty number that transaction can be identified and grouped with the other purchases in that shopper's history. The analysis of these patterns generates important insights that can help Category Managers to define categories using attributes such as rate of substitution, basket correlation, source of volume, etc., that can help correlate products to each other, identifying how much one product can be substituted by another or how likely it is for items A and B to be in the same transaction. Using insights from this type of data it is possible to construct customer decision trees (CDT) that not only "group" all related products from the point of view of the shopper but also organize and segment them according to substitutability and basket correlation. For example, a traditional approach to category definition might organize a soft beverage category as shown in Figure 2, grouping products by their brands. However, based on CDT studies powered by data that has now been made available by digitalization and advancements in technology to observe shopper behavior, it has been found that shoppers are actually more likely to substitute light products by another light product and not for a regular from the same brand.

This insight would suggest that products within the same type should be closer in the structure than products within the same brand. In other words, the Brand > Type structure should be altered to Type > Brand. The redesign of the Baby Care category by leading CPG manufacturers Johnson & Johnson

Figure 2. Example of category decision tree

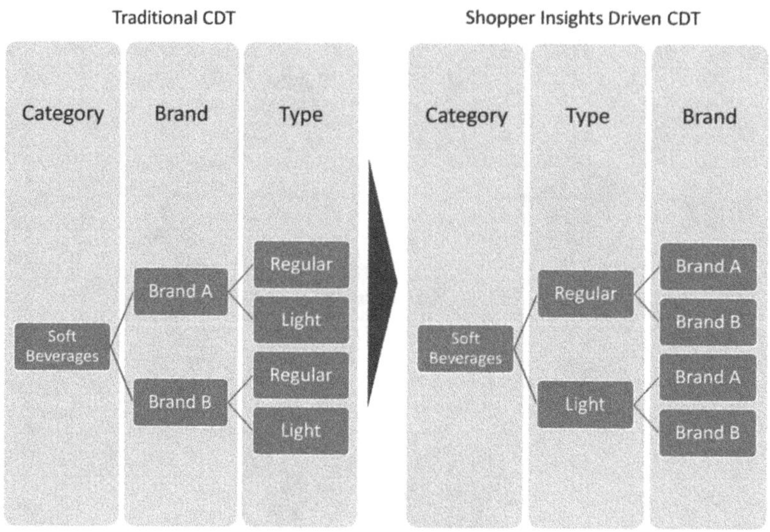

and P&G is a good illustration of this improved way to group, organize and define categories. The basis of the restructuring of Category Definition was deep understanding of the shopper profile and behavior that revealed that the shopper is usually a woman who is buying not necessarily based on the product (shampoo, conditioner, wipes, etc.) but mostly using age and moments as the driving factor for purchase. Age is related to the fact that some products are aimed at recently born (< 1 year) and others at toddlers while moments refers to the task involved, for example "am I looking for products for bath, for changing or some other use during the day?". These insights have led CPG companies and retailers to reorganize the Baby Care category based on these aspects, not just in the category definition but in other processes as well such as assortment planning, merchandising and promotions (2013). Although many retailers have shifted to the new category definition approach, it still common to see traditional category definition being applied, mostly because it is simpler to execute and manage.

Although there is steady growth in adoption of shopper insights driven category definition, this approach relies on the existence of customer loyalty data and transaction logs, which is a challenge for many retailers. However, there is growth in new sources of data through monitoring of shopper behavior online. Unlike brick and mortar stores where even for loyalty card customers only limited information can be monitored, online stores allow every movement to be tracked and measured. Retailers are now able to track several metrics for a high number of customers opening the doors to a new world of analytical possibilities to answer questions such as:

- What brought the shopper to the store? Facebook ad, email promotion, web promotion, etc.
- What is the common browsing behavior for a product, what products are usually co-searched, compared and co-shopped?
- The moment of shopping card abandonment (i.e., what led them to leave, out of stock of a product they searched, price of a product, etc.).
- What is the average purchasing history for a customer looking for a specific product, for instance what are the average number of units typically purchased and the average dollars spent.

Digitalization is helping provide answers to these and many other questions, enabling a level of understanding about how shoppers group products that was inconceivable to earlier generations of category managers. Another influencing factor has been the advancement in technologies that are being used to track how shoppers "navigate" within a physical store. IoT (Internet of Things) devices, in-store localization, beacons and intelligent IR (image recognition) cameras can now easily map the path taken by shoppers, producing new insights on how different items and categories interact and complement each other. Today it is very common to see retailers define categories at a company level which makes the flawed assumption that shoppers group the products in the same way, regardless of whether they are in an urban convenience store or doing a monthly stock-up at a Cash & Carry. However, with an enhanced level of understanding of shoppers enabled through digitalization, categories can be defined, segmented and organized at a more granular level. Today we could define categories in a hyper-personalized manner at an individual shopper level, especially in ecommerce however that must be balanced with the complexity of execution and usually there is a sweet spot somewhere in between.

Category Roles

This is second step of the eight step Catman process. Within this step the retailers express the strategy that will guide the deployment of assets in order to reach the overall company's plan, as defined by CMA (2016). According to ECR (2000), categories can be defined to have one of the following roles as shown in Table 1.

Nielsen (2014) proposes that this step *"Outlines the role that each category plays in the retailer according to the type of store and target shopper. This process can explain the reason why some categories have clearance sales, while other categories are always priced on higher margin"*. Although this definition is an important step in the Catman process, traditionally more than half of the categories have been labeled 'routine', and therefore have been receiving generic recommendations such as:

- Be an important source of products to the shopper
- Help build retailer's image
- Deliver competitive value
- Secondary on the generation of profit

Table 1. Category roles, adapted from ECR (2000)

Role	Objectives
Destination	• Defines the image of the retailer • Very important to target shoppers • Leads all categories in terms of sales growth • High percentage of resources
Routine	• Provides a balance between value, growth and profit • Important to consumers as part of their everyday grocery needs
Convenience	• Provides opportunity for additional 'convenience' purchase • Reinforces the image of the retailer as a one-stop shop • Provides opportunity for profit growth
Seasonal	• Similar to Destination, but for limited periods of the year • Creation of excitement and traffic

As highlighted by Ruttenberg (2018) from Dunnhumby, global leader in data sciences and customer analytics, *"Effective category management requires more than generic templates and processes"*. Roger Jackson, from Shopper Intelligence (largest international program of systematic shopper insights), also argues that "*The absence of hard data on the issue ends up becoming a dialogue of opinion, not fact. In reality, this is a very nuanced debate*". Using shopper behavior, market and social data, retailers will be able, and pushed, to be more specific, not in just creating different roles, but also clearly defining what it means to be assigned to one of them. Shopper Intelligence proposes the following 7 category roles as shown in Table 2.

These are examples of different approaches a retailer could take when defining an underlying strategic purpose to its categories. It is perfectly valid to come up with other roles based on recent trends. Some examples include "Private label focused", "in-store experience", "internet price matching", etc. To better design category roles and to improve the strategy behind each one of them, it is essential to understand the key drivers in each category, since none of them will react in the same way to price in-

Table 2. Category groups, as adapted from shopper intelligence mindset model

Segment	Insight	Strategies
Everyday Regulars	Shoppers buy their usual items on auto pilot, so in store activity is less likely to be effective, but these are categories that can effectively drive store choice	• Promotions to win traffic • Advertising • Theme promotions
"Must Get it" Item	It is likely that the shopper has a particular item in mind decided even before the trip, and it is already known to them, but they might buy more than planned	• Multibuy • Avoid deep discount • Differentiated range
Get my usual	The key difference here compared to "Must get it" item is a willingness to trade up. These are categories where Premium in particular can win loyalty. Familiarity with the product would mean that the shoppers would want to find their chosen item quickly.	• Trade up • Invest in Premium • Display • Make easier to find
Stocking up	This mindset is about hunting for deals on regular, high value purchases. There is an opportunity to drive volume since these are regularly consumed, and via range/merch create a point of difference to win loyalty	• Multibuy • Great range • Differentiate & Innovate • Make easier to find
Find my choice	This mindset is about personal choice, these are range based categories that require engagement and selection and are more interesting/enjoyable. An opportunity to trade up.	• Incentivize premium products and bigger baskets
Grab it now	This is the treating / snacking mindset around familiar regular purchases. Since it is an 'of the moment' decision display and themed activity should be used to add to basket size	• Secondary display • Easy to find • Full price where possible • Visibility promotions
Find Something nice	It is all about things shoppers buy for an occasion, often for dinner, with a slightly indulgent mindset. They browse looking for something they fancy or for a promotion that catches their eye. Good categories to use for differentiation	• Invest in premium range • POS display • Innovate

centives, promotions, assortment, space and other tactics. This knowledge will help managers avoid a common trap wherein traditionally destination categories were designed to have the broadest assortment but with highly competitive prices and lower than average margin. Dunnhumby calls “CATEGORY DNA” the combination of these drivers and exemplifies this concept with a contrast between two types of categories: Fresh and Alcohol. The first being very sensitive to price and promotion with low response to changes in space. The second with high engagement for innovation and low importance of private label. In a related study, Dunnhumby proposed to a non-disclosed large European retailer the following process to define category roles. All categories were measured in terms of importance to the customer (hi / low) and to the retailer (hi / low), therefore creating 4 types of roles: Control, Protect, Develop and Win. This definition was the basis for an assortment simplification process that reduced duplication up to 30% in some cases, while retaining market-leading products. This initiative generated a 2% uplift in sales, driven by a better shopper experience and shopper availability. Figure 3 illustrates these 4 possible roles based on their importance to the customer and to the retailer.

Case in point, a clear understanding of how to define and plan for category roles allowed a mid-western retailer to completely revitalize the wine category. By defining it as one of the 5 destination categories, the company created a very specific set of strategies and tactics in order to achieve its goals. They realized this category is extremely complex in which the shopper demands education at the point of sale, prompting the idea to hire a wine specialist to be at the shelf helping customers to choose and showing them the new brands available (CMA, 2016). This was just one of the very customized tactics implemented, that were only possible because the retailer had a deep understanding of the category`s role and DNA.

Although this level of category role definition remains uncommon, the increasing popularity of big data and “testing mindset” will enable retailers to reach new standards within this step of the process, especially in online/mobile channels, as the cost and complexity to test and learn are significantly lower.

Figure 3. Category roles, extracted from Dunnhumby (2017)

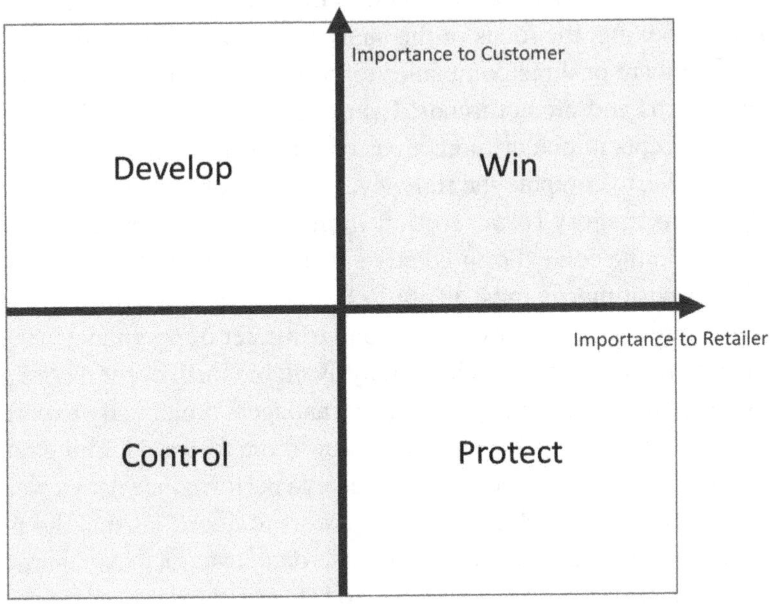

Category Assessment

This is third step of the Catman process. Traditionally in this step, managers understand what is happening in the category or, more likely, what has happened, since a great part of the analysis has traditionally been performed looking backwards into the data. A common expected output of this stage is a comparative evaluation of key metrics of the retailer, consumer, market and suppliers, showing for example, how the category is performing internally vs competitors. Digitalization is already impacting the way managers perform this assessment and it will enable even drastic changes as new technologies became available and are implemented. The data available today has exponentially increased in terms of the level of detail, frequency, source and type. Wade (2016), from CMA, highlights also that today retailers and CPG companies have a "Tsunami' of data, which no Catman practitioner has been able to integrate yet. Wade also adds that, fortunately, new sophisticated analytics have appeared to *"make sense of the data and their implications"*. Multi-variate regressions, that reveal the relative response of many concurrent factors can now be acquired off-the-shelf, increasing the applicability of the available data. Machine Learning and Artificial Intelligence (AI) also are changing the game and have huge potential to impact even more as retailers and manufactures understand and implement initiatives based on these concepts. A good example of a multi-variate regressions being applied in this context is the Marketing Mix Modeling (MMM). Although this concept was not created recently, new conditions stated before are turning these models more accessible to a larger number of companies. MMM is used on a sales time series to calculate the impact of several marketing / trade marketing / commercial investments such as advertising, promotion, prices and many others. This concept was developed by econometricians and its first use dates back to the early 1990s to help executives understand how to better channel their investment and achieve optimal business results.

This combination of huge amounts of data and new analytical tools are enabling category managers to ask not just the "what" question, but also the "why". "Why the shopper is motivated to behave in this specific manner?". The answer to these questions will provide insights that will, *permit grocers to develop solutions and offer experiences far superior to cold, impersonal crates shipped from distant warehouses"*, Dudlicek (2016). As mentioned earlier, as the traditional analytics approach was intrinsically static and backward looking, the focus of the analytics was mostly diagnostic. Digitalization and the new market environment are pushing companies to implement a more prescriptive approach, which is capable to identify patterns and predict trends. Every year there is a steady increase in the number of retailers using these concepts in one or more areas of the advance analytics, for instance to forecast consumer probability to leave, to compute the right level of inventory, to create targeted promotions and several other applications. In Category Tactics section, more uses of this type of analysis will be discussed.

An interesting example in the context of predictive analytics is that of a giant US retailer using data science to predict when a customer is most likely to be pregnant and using this information to send coupons and offers to capture the customer in her second trimester of pregnancy ahead of other retailers who may only find out about the event through publicly available birth event record giving them a competitive advantage. Another important change category managers are already experiencing is that with instant and near real time access to data, the analysis is now more forward looking rather than historical. Earlier it was common for category managers to only receive performance data a week after the close of the month and most of the times leadership received answers to questions that did not make sense anymore. With the decrease in latency and real time access to data, category managers are able to shift the question from "How did the category do last month?" to "How is the category performing right now?".

With the explosion in sources of data available, it is easy for category managers to be overwhelmed with information and suffer from data overload. For instance, today they could be receiving syndicated market data, customer loyalty data, online browsing data, qualitative shopper studies, search engine results, social network data, execution compliance metrics, macroeconomic and demographics data, etc. To avoid being overwhelmed by this influx of data, a best practice framework should be followed to plan how categories should be assessed as outlined below:

- Start with well-defined and clear objectives, making it easier for the team to organize a response plan.
- Focus on a manageable number of KPIs that are important to each business or categories being analyzed.
- Discard information that is not relevant, filtering only relevant data to do the analysis.
- Standardize to have a common template set, not just to collect data but also for other steps of the analytical process.
- Apply communication techniques such as SBAR (situation, background, assessment and recommendation) to be as concise as possible yet comprehensive.

An important issue that needs to be highlighted in this context is the training and preparedness of Catman personnel to work with such advanced data. Recent studies from ShopperVista have shown that only half of the category managers have had a structured training on data analysis, with many staff members having no training at all. The same report also shows that only 1 in 10 had any formal external training on insight generation. The advent of new technologies and the shift in the business environment will demand a change in the skill set required to work and be successful as a category manager. Although these professionals still need to combine hard and soft skills and only organization, category knowledge and communication skills will not be enough. As advanced analytics becomes a required skill, Catman areas should start to hire more from statistics and mathematics background. Additionally, given the challenges in hiring candidates externally, companies will also have to design comprehensive retraining programs to prepare the personnel for the demands of the job.

Category Scorecard

This is the fourth step of the Catman process. After defining the category, its role in the organization and assessing its performance, category managers have to define their objectives for the category through a scorecard. This scorecard will serve as a link between the assessment phase, where the objective of the category is defined and the next two steps: strategy and tactics, where the plan to reach that objective are fleshed out. This scorecard will not just define what is success, but also how it will be measured, clearly stating which metrics will be used. Traditionally the set of variables used contained several aspects such as financial (sales, profit, margin), competitive (market share, penetration), development (sales growth), operational (return on inventory, wastage, days on hand) and even shopper metrics (satisfaction, basket size). Digitalization is impacting this step in three different ways: metrics, frequency and granularity. The Tsunami of data mentioned in the prior section is allowing managers to establish an extremely detailed scorecard, especially in online channels where it is possible to measure conversion rate, traffic, time spent on the web site and other metrics. Also, in-store monitoring technologies are enabling physical stores to track similar indicators. As illustrated in the Figure 4, for modern Catman it is not enough to establish

Figure 4. Traditional and Extended Scorecards

Traditional SCORECARD

CaT	KPI 1	KPI 2
Cat 1	3%	1%
Cat 2	2%	5%
Cat 3	4%	3%

Extended SCORECARD

		Region 1			Region 2			Region 3		
Category	Sub Cat	KPI 1	KPI 2	KPI 3	KPI 1	KPI 2	KPI 3	KPI 1	KPI 2	KPI 3
Cat 1	Sub A	3%	5%	5%	3%	1%	4%	5%	1%	2%
	Sub B	1%	5%	5%	2%	5%	5%	1%	5%	4%
Cat 2	Sub C	4%	3%	4%	3%	4%	3%	2%	3%	5%
	Sub D	4%	4%	5%	2%	3%	2%	3%	1%	3%
Cat 3	Sub E	2%	5%	1%	2%	2%	1%	2%	1%	2%
	Sub F	4%	3%	1%	3%	4%	1%	4%	3%	1%

that category X must grow 5% year over year, instead as already leveraged by market leading retailers, Category Scorecards need to be more detailed at cluster or even store level with targets at SKU level.

Category Strategy

This is step five of the Catman process. In this step the strategy that will be used to reach the objectives of the category scorecard will be defined which is strongly influenced by the category assessment step as well. Traditionally, managers have six strategies to mix and match when selecting a category plan:

- **Traffic Building:** The main objective of this strategy is to attract shoppers to the store and the category. Usually price sensitive products with high household penetration are included in this strategy.
- **Transaction Building:** The goal of the strategy is to increase the spend of the shoppers by stimulating them to spend more by buying more units of the same product or by buying complementary products, essentially increasing the transaction size.
- **Profit Generating:** This strategy focuses on increasing the share of products/brands with high profit margin, usually by positioning them close to traffic builders.
- **Turf Defending:** This strategy is applied to protect the company's market share from competitors through an aggressive price/promotion positioning although it is usually detrimental to the category's profit margins.
- **Excitement Generating:** Best suited for seasonal products or categories with new products, this strategy relies on creating a sense of opportunity or urgency by communicating innovation and limited edition.
- **Image Enhancing:** Not necessarily focusing on short term objectives, this strategy helps the retailer to align its image with attributes such as "exclusive brand", "healthy" or "complete assortment".

The selection of one or more of these strategies to be applied to a category is greatly influenced by the role performed by it. For example, it is practically impossible to have a destination category executing a profit generating strategy since several of the requirements of this role will usually decrease the average margin. Another important connection between these two concepts (Category Role and Category Strategy) is that a successful result will demand from the Catman team a balanced combination of the several roles and strategies available. Thanks to digitalization, Category Managers now have access to advanced results from the assessment phase and can be more creative and insightful when defining strategies, relying less on pre-defined generic options. Following a similar approach described in the Category Role section, digitalization will enable and facilitate a deeper, complex and customized strategy definition.

The advent of new technologies within the business environment is also changing strategy definition in two other dimensions - Time and Organization. On the time dimension while companies and categories will still need to have term 1-3 year strategy plans as their north star, market dynamics will necessitate frequent reviews, say on a monthly basis. Amazon, for example, to enable this new frequency of strategy reassessment, created an atmosphere where associates feel comfortable with failing fast, giving the ability to quickly change direction, taking more risks and learning from them. Amazon managed this by "coding" every decision into two types: one-way i.e. difficult to reverse and two-way where choices need to be made fast, even with limited information, allowing Amazon to regularly adjust category strategy (Harrison & O'Nell, 2017).

On the organizational dimension the role of strategists needs to evolve from being merely top down rules communicators to influencers with high degree of autonomy and flexibility that can react quickly to changes in the market. As a result of these trends category managers will have to review and adapt the way they define, communicate and update their strategy plans, because now these individuals have to deliver a better, personalized and constantly updated category plans that need to be understood, adjusted and executed by other groups within the organization.

Category Tactics

This is step six of the Catman process. In this step category managers define specifically what actions will be implemented in order to achieve the goals of the Category strategy. For example, if the category was chosen to be Destination and Transaction Building, some of the tactics will include broad assortment coverage and competitive price positioning. Digitalization is having a significant impact on the tactics available to achieve category goals which we will review within the famous 5Ps framework: Product, Place, Pricing, Promotion and People.

Product

In 1998 ECR proposed that *"The proper mix of SKUs that best meets target consumer needs affects virtually every aspect of both the supply and the demand side. By definition, consumer needs are better satisfied when the right products are available at the lowest possible cost. Moreover, when assortments are optimized within the specific parameters of the category role strategies provided by a Category Management process, the entire business system can work faster, better and more efficiently"*. Although ECR's proposition still represents a remarkably good aspiration, the complexity involved in the process have changed dramatically over the last 20 years. Digitalization is pushing retailers and manufacturers to move away from siloed gut feeling assortment decisions to a more scientific interconnect approach based on advanced analytics and a clear sense of strategy. Kent Ruesink from JDA (global leader in supply chain and retail) also emphasizes that *"With new products constantly hitting the market, retailers are challenged to satisfy and retain shoppers with shifts in in-store layouts, an ideal mix of new products, best sellers and private labels within limited shelf space"*.

Two very important tasks that have been disrupted because of the new technologies available are 'add and delete' of products in the current assortment. This is a highly complex activity and depending on how well it is done it can greatly impact the overall performance of a category. As discussed in Category Assessment section, loyalty card data can help category managers understand several aspects of customer behavior that were unavailable previously. Using loyalty card data, category managers have access to analytics that are critical when evaluating any potential new product addition or deletion. The main objective is to add products with a low potential for cannibalization of existing products and to delete products that shoppers can easily substitute for another existing one. Another criterion is to ensure high coverage of products bought by high value and loyal shoppers. CMA proposes the following parameters as the basis for these decisions:

- **Loyalty:** This metric expresses how much a product is switched by another product in the same category. If a shopper usually decides to not buy anything when a product is not available, it indicates a high degree of loyalty.
- **Shopper Worth:** This refers to how much a shopper spends throughout the year, not just on a specific trip to the supermarket. This is important because Category managers should avoid excluding items commonly encountered in the baskets of shoppers high on this metric, since losing this shopper would impact not just the category, but potentially the whole store.
- **Substitutability:** This measure denotes the level of substitution between one or more products, which helps managers decide, especially when the space is limited, to have products with a low level of substitutability. An extreme case of Substitutability is Exclusivity where a subset of the customers is so loyal that they do not substitute for any other product at all.

The understanding of product similarities can be identified by applying Natural Language Processing (NLP) in the search patterns of ecommerce. NLP is a branch of Artificial Intelligence (IA) that deals with the interactions between computers and humans, specifically aimed at configuring software to process and analyze huge amounts of natural language data, for example, words written or spoken by humans. Although there are several applications of this technology, in the context of assortment definition NLP is commonly used by ecommerce platforms to come up recommendations such as "people who bought this product also bought…". This knowledge can be used not just to understand complementary or substitute products, but also to automatically select a similar product when fulfilling ecommerce orders for an out of stock product. Another important information that can be used in order to understand product similarity is online browsing behavior. Flow visualization tools, for example, from google analytics can show how shoppers interact with one or more products before making a decision. If a product X page is almost always seen before or after the Product Y page, category managers can associate the two products to have correlation, being substitutes or complementary to each other

Online data can help with not just the mapping of similarities between products, but also how help planners to understand shopper preferences at a store level, even for products currently not selling at the store. For example, in order to create a "store of the community, Walmart uses, along with other inputs, Facebook and other social media data to understand emerging local trends and offer products that shoppers want to buy. More information about this case can be found in the article from Bhatia (2017) in analytics India.

This increase in the customization of the assortment and configuration of the offering of the stores based on store demographics is called localization, a response to dissatisfied shoppers that started to rebel against the one-size-fits-all retailing model. However, localization has its limitations. Even with unlimited data, it is not possible for a company to customize all pieces of its business in every point of sale, mostly because the multiplication of complexity and the costs associated with it. In order to benefit from localization but to avoid the complexity, companies are using data science algorithms to cluster stores by buying behavior attribute, which creates a relatively small number of variables and enables a simplified decision process. A popular statistical technique used to group similar stores is known as CHAID, short for chi-squared automatic interaction detection, a method that was originally proposed in 1980 by G. V. Kass but only now is being implemented as widely, thanks to democratization of data due to digitalization. An application of this type of clusterization was applied by giant electronics retailer Best Buy when remodeling a good part of their stores to be more customer-centric and have a better fit with the local community. Best Buy found 5 relevant and very different types of customer personas: busy mother & head of the family, technology driven junkie, time-constrained successful professional, family man on a restricted budget and finally business customers. This customization by cluster allowed the company to deliver tailored customer-centric service without losing the benefits of economies of scale. The results were clear, the stores where this strategy was applied posted sales gains two times the company average. Even though clusterization reduces the number of variables, any localization strategy increases the complexity of the assortment process making it nearly impossible to be conducted manually or using spreadsheets. The need for this shift was observed in a recently conducted JDA "Voice of the Category Manager" survey that that showed that 59% of the retailers are planning to move away from traditional spread-sheet based solutions to advanced software options. To serve this need of retailers, there are many packaged software solutions available in the market that can provide intelligent assortment recommendations.

Place

In this step, managers are responsible to define how much space will be allocated for each category and where in the store they should be placed to ensure maximum shopper satisfaction and to meet company objectives such as development of key categories and the reduction of out of stocks. Although the objectives have remained more of less the same, the science behind these definitions has advanced in the digitalization era. To be effective, Space and Assortment definitions must be planned together, not as separate or disconnected process which is still unfortunately common in a great number of organizations. Both activities need to be tightly coupled with inputs and feedback from each other generating not just a space-aware product mix, but also an assortment-aware visual merchandising plan at the point of sale. This alignment is even more important in today's scenario where due to the change in role of the store, the shopping space in physical stores is being reduced by new activities such as Click & Collect and ecommerce order fulfillment. This transformation of stores to mini "distribution centers" further increases the importance of using advanced techniques for design of the space within the store.

The development of automation tools is transforming how companies are creating, updating and distributing planograms throughout the organization. Traditionally this task was very manual and did not allow creation of store specific planograms but now it possible to automatically create localized shelf space plans in an automated fashion, thereby allowing planners to focus on more strategic and value add activities. Figure 5 illustrates a planogram generated through JDA software than can be configured to automatically generate localized shelf space plans.

While it is natural to expect that an increase in the number of facings in the shelf for a product or in the floor area for a category will increase its sales, given the limited space availability the challenge is identifying what products will have the best return to investment in space. One essential metric for this is the space elasticity factor, a coefficient that expresses how the sales of a product/brand/segment will change as its space is changed. If ΔSpace is the percentage variation in space and ΔSales is the percentage variation in sales after that change in the space, SE (space elasticity) can be calculated using the formula:

$$SE = \frac{\Delta Sales(\%)}{\Delta Space(\%)}$$

A coefficient of one signifies that for each 1% increase in the category space, sales will increase by a similar amount. However, this coefficient will vary depending on how much space has already been allocated. For example, for categories with very little space in the store, any small increment will create an important impact in its performance. The effect however may not be the same when the category already has a considerable amount of space in the store. This is because space, together with other types of stimulus, generally has a diminishing return on investment, as illustrated in Figure 6:

In the above example it is possible to analyze the different space elasticities that decrease and after a point incremental space will not generate any incremental sale. This approach is preferred rather than the traditional productivity metric (sales/m^2), which may be misleading since it will recommend allocating more space to high performance categories, but this extra space may not necessarily result in increase

Figure 5. Example of planogram

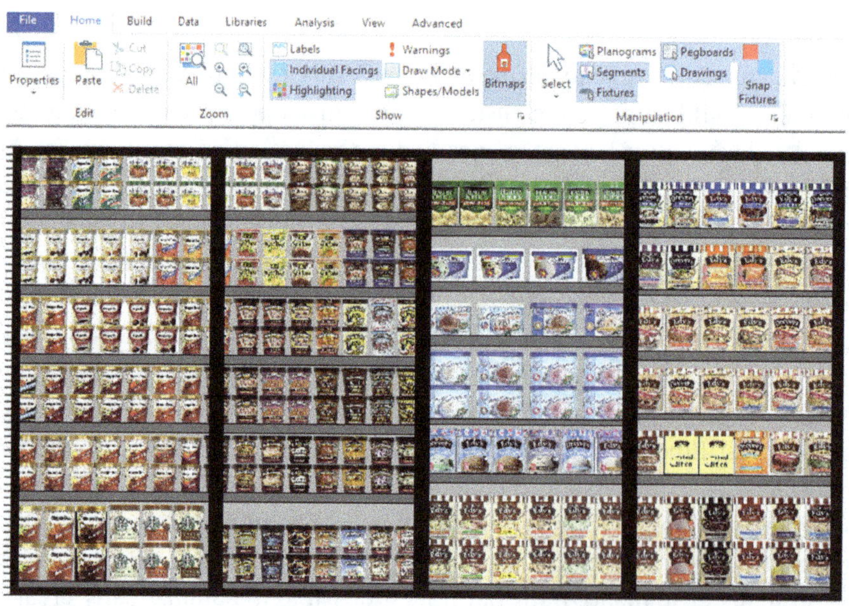

Figure 6. Relationship between sales and space

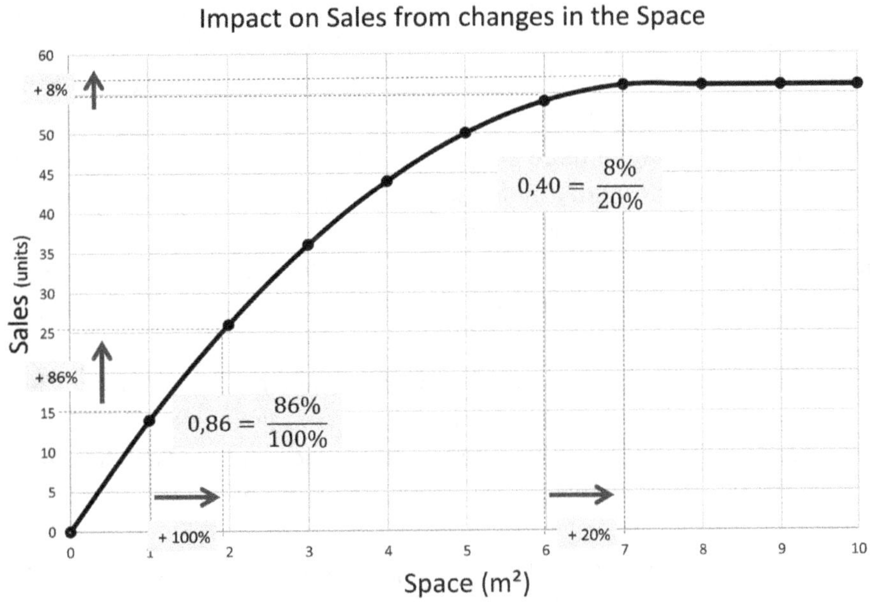

in sales. Digitalization is not just popularizing the algorithms and techniques applied to calculate these curves, it is also giving managers better means to evaluate or predict the impact of changes on the store layout or visualize how products are organized in the shelves. Virtual Reality (VR) technologies, for example, are becoming more accessible as more companies start to offer this type of service. As shown in Figure 7, *Google Maps Business View* can be used to map the inside of a store using the same technology as *Street View.*

Figure 7. Google maps business view

VR can also be used to create complete virtual stores, allowing managers to track user movement through aisles, measure traffic flow, A/B test alternative layouts and several other scenarios before incurring any expensive construction and layout costs. Food and Beverage leader Nestle used this technology to answer a question posed by a retailer about the placement of its new line of ice cream cups - "Now that this subcategory (cups) will have critical mass, should it be merchandised in dedicated freezer doors, or should each cup line stay in its respective brand space?". In other words, should a category that traditionally was organized primarily by brand change and create a sub-area dedicated just for the cup format, now that this sub-category has become more important?

The company had no time to go over traditional A/B store testing and decided to use VR to test different options of product placement and pricing in virtual stores, allowing it to quickly make an informed decision (CMA,2016).

Not just understanding how the shopper would eventually walk through the store, VR devices can also track eye movement, giving information about how customers are reacting to communication stimulus or how they are "screening" the shelfs when looking for a product. These visual heatmaps (Figure 8) are crucial to either confirm the well-established traditional shopper knowledge or challenge it with fresh and more precise data.

Although it is important to define the quantum of space to be given to a category or a product, it is not the only space related decision to be made. It is also crucial to define where these products will be located and how they will be visually displayed. An essential input to this task is the understanding of shopper's behavior obtained traditionally, but not exclusively, through a very costly and time-consuming research method where the shopper is recorded and the data is later analyzed. Several tracking technologies such as Image Recognition (IR), Wifi localization and Bluetooth beacons are automating the process of monitoring shoppers' movements inside the store, identifying the most common paths, how much they interact with products and other questions that were impossible or very expensive to answer before the popularization of these new research methods. A good example of these applications is Carrefour in France, that is using more than 600 beacons spread among 28 stores to communicate with shoppers

Figure 8. Virtual eye tracking of the shopper

sending personalized in-store routes and promotions. By doing this, the company is also able to monitor shopper behavior and continuously improve store layout and operations (Deloitte, 2017).

All these new technologies are allowing category managers to design better layouts and planograms not just to please shoppers but also to avoid a very common performance detractor: out of stocks (OOS). Although varying by region and industry, it is common to see OOS indexes close to 10%, which creates a negative impact not just on the immediate sale, but also on the overall shopper's satisfaction. Digitalization is providing means to improve this metric. One example is the increasing application of advanced algorithms to predict demand by leveraging AI and Big data. These technologies can absorb and process an infinite, multi-sourced array of data and instantly react to changes in any part of the complex ecosystem of the business. For example, a change in temperature can lead to an increase in the demand for soft drinks in stores, which will mean more space needs to be allocated in the shelfs to stock these products. Case in point, leading UK based retailer Tesco is feeding weather data into its predictive analytics system in order to predict demand for products such as coleslaw and ice cream. This initiative is helping right size inventory thereby reducing out of stock and also overstock, not only resulting in revenue lift but also helping reduce $140 million in spoilage (Arkenberg, 2017). Digitalization is allowing companies to implement these strategies in real-time, connected and at store level as opposed to a reactive, siloed and uniform approach.

Price

Traditionally Price and Promotions were not areas of focus for Catman Managers and this area was mostly handled by marketing and commercial teams. However, the new market landscape is forcing Catman to be more connected with these areas and now Pricing and Promotions is considered an integral part of Catman. Digitalization has helped markets become competitive by enabling perfect information from a price perspective. While it is common knowledge that it is very easy to price shop online, even brick and mortar shoppers today have the ability to compare prices by scanning bar codes using their mobile phones and even finding where else the product is being sold in their neighborhood. This reality puts a great deal of pressure on category planners to first understand precisely how their consumers react to price changes and second develop intelligent strategies to create product differentiation and avoid price wars.

On the first topic, the combination of information and new technologies available are enabling companies to understand elasticity (own and cross) with higher precision. Using advanced analytics and computer algorithms, it is possible to instantly predict the store/SKU impact of a price reduction applied by a competitor. These algorithms can also dynamically recommend (or automatically apply) a price correction to optimize sales performance. An extreme example of dynamic price changes is Amazon, which by some estimates has more than 2.5 million price updates per day, while may annoy some customers but has resulted in a profit increase of 25%. This "changing speed" is 50 times faster than Walmart and Best Buy (Business Insider, 2018), the question is how much closer to this performance traditional Brick & Mortar retailers can get, considering all their challenges, the costs of switching prices being one of them.

On the subject of differentiation, it is more important than ever for companies to create a holistic plan and not to rely just on price reductions to increase sales and reach targets. This broader strategy needs to include a positioning/communication plan that frames the product/brand uniquely to set it apart from its competitors. It should prevent the shopper from easily creating a price reference because of the differentiation of the offering (size, quantity, bundle, coupon, etc.).

Not only in the planning stage, digitalization is also impacting how prices are monitored and executed. Several retailers have not implemented digital price tags that allow automatic price updates as the central system is updated, avoiding common non-compliance issues and reducing implementation labor costs.

Promotion

Apart from regular price definition, digitalization is also completely revolutionizing how promotion is designed and executed. Retailers are migrating from mass promotion, that reduces the price for the same product for all shoppers to targeted shopper specific promotions, where only the most appealing SKUs (based on that shopper's behavior) are promoted based on algorithms that optimize the return on the promotion investment by lowering the price only to the individuals that would not buy at the same price otherwise, reducing the number of unnecessary promotions. A great example of this concept is personalized discount coupons that are generated at checkout based on customer's loyalty membership data. These coupons can be personalized at a shopper level and can be filled with promotions based on one or more purposes. For example, the promotion could be selected based on the items the shopper used to buy in the past but has stopped, meaning that he or she might be buying from the competitor, thereby attempting to perform a "recovery" strategy. Another example is supplier sponsored discounts, where CPG companies instead of mass promotion, identify select customers based on their shopping profile for targeted promotions. Figure 9 illustrates the use of such strategy by Tesco.

Customization and personalization is not the only aspect of promotion affected by recent technologies. Virtual and augmented reality are disrupting the experience of shoppers at the store. For example, as shown in Figure 10, using their cellphone camera shoppers can unveil additional information about products, from clearance price signs to a recipe book showing recommendations on how to use the product, to product manual.

Figure 9. Examples of personalized discount coupons

Figure 10. Augmented reality enhancing in-store shopper experience

Internet of Things (IoT) devices have increased the potential touch points between companies and shoppers, thereby multiplying possibilities for sending and receiving promotion stimulus. In-store beacons, for example, can be used to send personalized messages to shoppers approaching some endcap or promotion display. Once the shopper's attention has been "grabbed", customized apps can recommend additional products and show product reviews. This extreme level of traceability is also enabling companies to monitor and analyze the impact of the investment done on promotions. It was always a challenge to understand the ROI for different types of tactics since it is almost impossible to perform promotion effectiveness analysis using just using POS data. Using GPS location data, sensors and image recognition, category managers can precisely identify the level of attraction and conversation each promotion stimulus is creating. Digitalization is giving the tools needed for companies to finally answer strategic questions that were impossible to be tackled before and allowing planners to spend scarce promotional dollars in a smarter way.

People

As mentioned in the Category Assessment section, the profile of Category Manager is likely to change dramatically with the increase in adoption of digitalization in the organization. Both technical skills and soft skills required for the job will be impacted. On the technical skills, specialization will become the norm as the domain knowledge required to master the complexities of any part of the sub-process, i.e. space planning, assortment planning, pricing, promotions, etc., will make it nearly impossible for one associate to master and be responsible for all subjects, especially in large companies. Also, it is becoming increasingly common for Catman discipline to bring statisticians, mathematicians and data scientists to the team. With the popularization of automation software, manual tasks with low value add will be reduced or eliminated, pushing the teams to be more strategic and less operational and there will be an increased emphasis on collaboration with other roles within the organization. For example, for a precise definition of an assortment, the Assortment Planner will have to work with other departments from Buyers to Marketing to Store Operations in order to understand the big picture. Today, some large companies use scores to identify people with reasonably advanced planogram skills. Acosta a North American firm that supports Category Management processes, has more than 310 space management experts and attributes its success to the ability to make sure that the entire team is "keeping up" with all software developments related to the market (CMA, 2016).

Category Implementation

This is step 7 of the Catman process and this is where the rubber meets the road. Communicating the plan developed in the head office by the Catman team to the stores and to execute it has always been and is still is a major challenge for every company. For example, it is not uncommon to observe that the stores only adhere to planogram specifications less than 50%, a factor tracked as planogram compliance rate. The lack of good communication systems and excessive reliance on manual labor are two important factors for this low compliance. Digitalization is helping companies to shorten the distance from headquarters to the point of sale by providing intuitive, real-time and seamless information interchange platforms connecting associates in different parts of the organization in an efficient way. Store managers can now receive messages on their smartphones about an urgent planogram reset, with the new shelf layouts attached. In one click, the manager can send this task to the employees that will execute this reset and report back when it is done. Business rules can be programmed for the standard process and category managers only need to deal with the exceptions.

Although many companies are still to implement fully streamlined workflow previously described, increasingly more and more CPG companies and retailers are implementing these systems as they get cheaper due to increased adoption. Some pioneering companies have gone even further in the automation of this process by using robots to scan the aisles for planogram compliance and for detecting events such as out of stock or price errors. Walmart already has 50 stores testing an autonomous robot equipped with wheels and cameras as show in Figure 11 that can spot shelving errors using image recognition technologies that are able to identify out-of-stocks, incorrect prices, products in the wrong place and even generate a compliance score that can inform associates that, for example, the coffee category is only 60% correctly executed. This is certainly just the beginning as other retailers are also testing similar technologies to improve store execution using drones and intelligent cameras to automatically monitor every aspect of execution within store and point of sale. These new capabilities, while having a huge impact on processes such as store security, fulfilment, offer customization task generation and others, are also greatly improving Catman implementation success rates.

Category Review

In this last step of the Catman process, day-to-day Category Management comes to life through the monitoring of key performance metrics that may indicate that the execution is not going as planned and something may need to be fixed quickly. This phase can be designed to be driven based on alerts configured in the scorecard or it could take place in planned periods throughout the year, where the performance of the period can be evaluated in order to course correct and ensure the results are on track. Digitalization is impacting the review phase in many aspects. First, the frequency of these revisions has increased (it is not happening just 1 or 2 times a year anymore) since automation tools can now reduce the time not just to assess the scenario but also to act on it. For example, based on changes in the assortment or commercial agreements, updated planograms could be generated in minutes, not weeks like it was common previously. Second, the level of manual effort involved in understanding the scenario and addressing the same can be reduced dramatically by the use of Artificial Intelligence and Machine Learning.

Figure 11. Walmart robots scanning the isles for compliance

CONCLUSION

In this chapter we have reviewed the 8 steps of the traditional Catman process and how it has been disrupted by digitalization. We strongly believe that the transformation of Catman process is in its nascent stage and it will continue to evolve in the coming years in the increasingly digital world. Below are our top three predictions for Catman of the future.

First, siloes will continue to be broken and the discipline of Category Management will interoperate closely with other disciplines such as Supply Chain & Logistics, Marketing, Buying, Finance, Operations, etc. For instance, the expectation will be that the optimal promotion plan will not be theoretical and can be fulfilled by Supply Chain & Logistics in a timely manner. Similarly, Buyers will only buy what can be displayed and assorted for a store.

Second, organizations will start to make more use of data during the Catman process. While many organizations have access to data such as price history, promotions, weather, competitor price, new product introduction information, etc., it is seldom used to draw insights. Also, IoT and edge computing opens the doors to new sources of data, the use of which will be the norm in the Catman process of the future.

Third, the role of Catman process will be elevated from support function producing stale planograms to strategic function helping provide key insights on gaining market share, improving margins and lifting revenue. This will also require Catman personnel to acquire deep analytical, statistical, ML/AI and other relevant skills.

REFERENCES

Arkenberg, C. (2017). *Intelligent Logistics*. Retrieved from https://towardsdatascience.com/intelligent-logistics-e85de07c3570

Bhatia, R. (2017). *Analytics India.* Retrieved from http://analyticsindiamag.com/inside-walmartlabs-indian-operations-fuelling-online-growth-global-retail-giant

CMA. (2016). *Catman 2.0 - Driving Growth in a Shopper-Centric World.* Category Management Association.

Deloitte. (2017). *Disruptions in retail through digital transformation.* Retrieved from https://www2.deloitte.com/content/dam/Deloitte/in/Documents/CIP/in-cip-disruptions-in-retail-noexp.pdf

Deloitte. (2018). Retrieved from https://www2.deloitte.com/uk/en/pages/consumer-business/articles/retail-trends.html#

Dudlicek, J. (2016, December). Shoppers in Need Are Friends Indeed. *Progressive Grocer*, p. 4.

Harrison & O'Nell. (2017). *3 Changes Retailers Need to Make to Survive.* Retrieved from https://hbr.org/2017/11/3-changes-retailers-need-to-make-to-survive

Insider, B. (2018). *Amazon changes prices on its products about every 10 minutes.* Retrieved from https://www.businessinsider.com/amazon-price-changes-2018-8

Jackson, R. (2012). *Category Role - at the heart of category management for 20 years, but until now vague and even prejudiced?* Retrieved from http://www.shopperintelligence.com/wp-content/uploads/whitepapers/Category_Role.pdf

JDA. (2017). *JDA Delivers Transformational Assortment Optimization.* Retrieved from https://jda.com/knowledge-center/press-release/jda-delivers-transformational-assortment-optimization-powered-by-dunnhumby

JDA Voice of the customer. (2017). Retrieved from jda.com: https://jda.com/-/media/jda/knowledge-center/thought-leadership/voice-of-the-category-manager-executive-summary1.ashx

Nielsen. (2014). *Category management – common language between retailers and manufacturers.* Nielsen.

Nielsen Marketing Research. (1992). *Category Management: Positioning Your Organization to Win.* NTC Business Books.

RuttenbergR. (2018). Retrieved from https://www.dunnhumby.com/re-inventing-category-management

Wade, G. (2016, December). The More You Know. *Progressive Grocer*, pp. 6-8.

KEY TERMS AND DEFINITIONS

A/B Test: Also known as split testing, is an experiment comparing two versions of a single strategy, typically by testing a subject's response to variant A against variant B and determining which of the two variants is more effective. This can be used, for example, to compare different versions of a promotion that were implemented in two distinct store groups.

Cannibalization: In the category management context, this term denotes a negative impact a new product has on the sales performance of its related products. When this happens, the demand from existing products shift to the newly introduced product potentially reducing overall sales.

Cash and Carry: It is a store format resembling a wholesaler which originally used to focus on B2B but is also now available to end consumers. Its hallmark characteristics are low prices and limited assortment and services.

Click and Collect: Is a hybrid e-commerce model in which people place orders online and go to physical location to collect which could be stores or parking lot or any other location.

Conversion Rate: In the category management context refers to the percentage of people entering the store that have bought something.

Customer Decision Tree (CDT): It refers to graphical representation of a customer's buying decision process expressed in a tree format. For example, when a customer is choosing an ice cream an example of the decision tree could be size, followed by flavor followed by brand.

House Panels: Group of houses that routinely participate in surveys and research to answer questions related to wide ranging topics from political inclination to consumer preferences.

IoT Devices: IoT is short for internet of things and refers to a growing network of physical devices featuring internet connectivity using with they can communicate with other devices and programs.

Perfect Information: Economic term to define a competition scenario where all consumers and producers have perfect and instantaneous knowledge of all market prices and other important information.

Planogram: Also known as plan-o-grams or POGs. They are visual representations of store products and their shelves, strategically organized in order to achieve category goals.

POS: Short for point of sale. POS display refers to merchandising structures strategically placed inside the store.

Shopper Behavior: Actions taken by consumers at the point of sales or while shopping online. Not to be mistaken by consumer behavior, since the person buying a product is not necessarily the same who will use it afterwards.

Social Sentiment: It is a way to measure the emotion behind mentions on social media. It is important to understand not just if some subject, brand or person is "trending" but also in which direction, positive, negative, or neutral.

Trade Up: Category strategy where the retailer tries to encourage current customers to spend more by changing products in their baskets to bigger sizes and/or premium versions.

Chapter 10
Digital Inventory Optimization:
A Practitioner's Guide to Transform Your Organization

Andreas Werner
KPMG LLP, USA

ABSTRACT

This chapter provides an overview of select inventory optimization (IO) techniques for single and multi-echelon optimization. The main goal is to familiarize the reader with various IO models by providing a clearly structured approach, improving the reader's understanding of the mathematical concepts, and by providing an ample number of examples. Furthermore, the guaranteed service model for a three stage serial supply chain is introduced to show the effects of keeping inventory at different echelons in the supply chain in regards to total cost. Lastly an inventory planning maturity model is presented to show actionable next steps to the practitioner.

INTRODUCTION

Inventory reduction remains one of the key targets of companies to reduce working capital and its associated costs which leads to improved cash flow. At the same time customers are demanding higher service levels and increased convenience for example shorter lead times. To achieve these seemingly conflicting objectives is a great challenge for many companies on their digital journey, however, inventory optimization (IO) has proven that it can achieve an increase in customer service while reducing safety stock (Farasyn et al., 2011). Surprisingly, most companies are not yet taking advantage of inventory optimization, especially of multi-echelon inventory optimization (MEIO). Only 21% of consumer goods companies surveyed reported that they perform multi-echelon inventory optimization to some extent (Romanow, 2014). Another study found that a MEIO implementation can increase service levels by 3% while reducing the cash-to-cash cycle by 15% (Aberdeen group, 2012).

DOI: 10.4018/978-1-5225-7700-3.ch010

Copyright © 2019, IGI Global. Copying or distributing in print or electronic forms without written permission of IGI Global is prohibited.

The main value proposition of the following chapter is providing the reader and supply chain practitioner an overview of the IO basics including mathematical concepts which enables them to understand important details for a digital transformation journey. MEIO is the focus of the main chapter since the author feels that the greatest opportunity for many companies exists in this area. The target audience for this chapter is knowledgeable in supply chain management and undergraduate level statistics but not an expert in inventory optimization. Most existing literature can be categorized into either of the following.

- Academic articles focused on the mathematical aspect of inventory optimization, e.g. operations research
- Articles focusing on the qualitative aspects of inventory optimization, e.g. defining the approaches, best practices and laying out the observed benefits of an inventory optimization implementation

This chapter seeks to strike a balance between both worlds and is structured in the following way. Firstly, select literature is reviewed that provides the foundation to understand the further sections. After that, the main section explains the mathematical background of single- and multi-echelon inventory optimization. The goal of which is to provide the mathematical basics and an understanding of the general IO concepts and common formulas. After this, the context of inventory optimization within the overall supply chain planning function is explained to help the reader understand the big picture and the fit of IO within their organization's supply chain functions. Lastly, a maturity model for inventory planning is introduced to enable the reader to articulate the gaps and opportunities within their organization and help with the next steps.

BACKGROUND

The following will provide a literature review on select articles that the author deems important to understand the main section of this chapter. Table 1 shows an overview of the sources reviewed in the literature review alongside for their reasoning of being included in the background section.

Table 1. Literature reviewed

Literature reviewed	Category	Reasoning
Farasyn et al. (2011)	Case study of inventory optimization	Qualitative study to showcase results of single- and multi-echelon inventory optimization.
Graves and Willems (2003)	Mathematical modeling of MEIO	Comparison of MEIO techniques: GSM and SSM. Includes details of GSM that are used later in the chapter. Also explains solving the supply chain configuration problem which simultaneously makes sourcing and inventory decisions
Klosterhalfen, Minner and Willems (2014)	Mathematical modeling of MEIO	Example of an extension to the GSM model (dual supply) and its benefits
Eruguz et al. (2016)	Mathematical modeling of MEIO	Overview of various GSM models

Farasyn et al. (2011) describe the benefits of applying inventory optimization at Procter and Gamble. Procter and Gamble (P&G) is a large consumer packed goods (CPG) company with a revenue of more than 65 billion USD in 2017. The author describes a decision framework that P&G uses to decide between deploying a single or multi-echelon approach across their different businesses. The framework promotes the use of single echelon optimization in the form of spreadsheets for their simpler supply chains in terms of number of SKUs and network stages.

The company achieved between 10% and 50% in total inventory reduction with the help of single echelon inventory optimization. Farasyn, Perkoz and Van de Velde (2008) go into more detail on the single echelon spreadsheet approach. Multi-echelon optimization is deployed in their more complex businesses, for example, Beauty & Grooming. An average network model is described as having 4,000 – 5,000 stages and 6,000 – 10,000 arcs. Based on a guaranteed service (GS) multi-echelon algorithm, the realized benefits are described as a total inventory reduction of 7% across their North America cosmetics supply chain while simultaneously increasing service levels.

Graves and Willems (2003) compare the guaranteed service model (GSM) and stochastic service model (SSM) in their chapter on supply chain design. They derive the respective models based on the following assumptions:

- The supply chain represents a generic network as opposed to a distribution network or assembly system. This assumption makes the models applicable to most real-world supply chains.
- The focus is on finding an optimized safety stock placement in the supply chain based on demand uncertainty. Other variables for example lead time, lead time variability or capacity uncertainties are not considered.
- The authors further assume that placement of safety stock is not constrained by e.g. warehouse space at different nodes since the safety stock problem falls under supply chain design in the authors' framework.
- Stages place a replenishment order to the supplier equal to the demand which means that there are no hedging or lot sizing effects in place
- Every stage has a deterministic processing time

The above represents the most important assumptions based on which the GSM and SSM models are derived. The SSM takes a service target level for the external customer as an input and provides service target levels for internal customers as an output when used in an optimization context. The replenishment time τ_j at any stage *j* of the network is equal to the constant processing lead time L_j plus any delay from upstream stages. The following equation for the expected replenishment lead time is derived, assuming a maximum of one supplier will experience a stock-out per period and defining π_{ij} as the probability of stage *i* causing a stock-out at stage *j*.

$$E\left[\tau_j\right] = L_j + \sum_{i:(i,j)\in A} \pi_{ij} L_i$$

Graves and Willems further derive the objective function for the SSM assuming normally distributed demand and considering holding costs.

The main part of this chapter focuses on the GSM, so it will be explained in more detail based on the definition in Graves and Willems (2003). The key characteristic of the GSM is that it eliminates probability by assuming a 100% service level if demand stays within the defined boundary. In case of a normally distributed demand, the boundary D_j can be set by defining a customer service level with an appropriate z score.

$$D_j\left(t\right) = t\mu_j + k_j\sigma_j\sqrt{t}$$

where

t = Number of time periods
μ_j =Mean demand per period
k_j = z score of customer service level
σ_j =Standard deviation of the demand per period

Every stage j will quote an outgoing service time s_j^{out} to their customers and receive incoming goods with a service time s_j^{in} and processing lead time L_j. Then the replenishment time τ_j equals

$$\tau_j = s_j^{in} + L_j$$

Since this is a deterministic equation it is easy to define the net replenishment lead time as $s_J^{in} + L_j - s_j^{out}$. The base stock B_i of a node i, which is the inventory at time 0, needs to cover the demand within the replenishment lead time. Using the demand bound equation from earlier we can see that

$$B = \left(s_J^{in} + L_j - s_j^{out}\right)\mu_j + k_j\sigma_j\sqrt{s_J^{in} + L_j - s_j^{out}}$$

Using this formula Graves and Willems define an objective function with the goal of minimizing the inventory holding costs per unit C_j^s for the network.

$$\min\sum_{j=1}^{N} C_j^s k_j \sigma_j \sqrt{s_J^{in} + L_j - s_j^{out}}$$

Later in this chapter, we will see examples that use the formulas and definitions of this basic GSM model. After deriving the models, they are applied to two real-world examples: Bulldozer assembly and Battery manufacturing and distribution. A simplified network is depicted for both supply chains and the underlying modeling assumptions are highlighted. In contrast to the assumptions listed earlier, these assumptions are related to the specific supply chains. The total supply chain costs are then compared. The SSM leads to higher costs across all end customer service levels less than 100%. The authors explain this behavior with the different underlying assumptions of GSM and SSM. While the SSM's countermeasure to stockout is more inventory, the GSM assumes that demand that exceeds the defined boundary is considered either lost or is being fulfilled by taking extraordinary measures, e.g. premium freight or overtime.

The chapter continues with a modified version of the safety stock problem called supply chain configuration problem. Configuration decisions are sourcing decisions in the Graves and Willems' model. The example is that a local high-cost supplier has a shorter lead time compared to a global, low-cost supplier which reduces safety stock costs. Other costs that are considered in the model are the cost of goods sold and pipeline stock costs. The GSM is used as a basis and expanded with the sourcing options. The resulting non-linear mixed integer programming problem is solved in the bulldozer supply chain example. The sourcing options and their related costs are created based on observations from the industrial manufacturing industry. After solving the example the authors conclude that significant additional cost savings can be realized by looking at supply chain configuration and safety stock placement holistically.

Klosterhalfen, Minner and Willems (2014) extend the GSM framework with an exact model for static dual supply in general acyclic N-echelon network structure. The author can show a 9.1% cost savings compared to approximate results from previously published solutions. Dual- or multi-sourcing can be an important part of a companies' supply chain strategy to mitigate the risk of being dependent on a single supplier. Another consideration is that supply chain agility is increased when sourcing from multiple suppliers by being able to secure upside demand. The trade-off compared to single sourcing is usually increased costs since smaller order quantities are placed with the different suppliers.

The model presented in the paper is based on the following assumptions:

- Stages place a replenishment order to the supplier equal to the demand which means that there are no hedging or lot sizing effects
- Every stage has a deterministic processing time
- Allocations between the suppliers are static, e.g. one supplier receives 30% of the demand another one receives 70%.

Eruguz et al. (2016) provide an overview of the various extensions to the original GSM while looking at three different angles:

- Modeling assumptions such as deterministic vs. stochastic lead times
- Solution methodologies and optimality/network configuration/objective function
- Industry applications and results

The author of this chapter recommends a review of Eruguz et al. (2016) to anyone planning to implement a GSM in their organization since it provides guidance on the mathematical models that are currently available.

TYPES AND PURPOSES OF INVENTORY

The lean principle taught us that unnecessary inventory is one of the seven types of waste. The question arises what constitutes as unnecessary inventory and what does not, in other words: What is the purpose of inventory?

To answer this question the following types of inventory or stock are defined and examples are given:

- Cycle stock
- Safety stock (sometimes: Buffer stock)
- Tactical and Strategic stock

All the inventory types shown in figure 1 can be present at any level in the supply chain, e.g. at raw material, sub-assembly, or finished good level.

Cycle Stock

The American Production and Inventory Control Society (APICS) defines cycle and safety stock as follows.

One of two main conceptual components of any item inventory, the cycle stock is the most active component. The cycle stock depletes gradually as customer orders are received and is replenished cyclically when supplier orders are received. The other conceptual component of the item inventory is the safety stock, which is a cushion o protection against uncertainty in the demand or in the replenishment lead time. (Pittman, P., Blackstone, J.H., & Atwater, J.B., 2016)

So cycle stock represents the amount of inventory that is kept to fulfill the demand of the downstream stage until the product is replenished.

Ideally the cycle stock amount matches the replenished stock. This requires the future demand picture or forecast to be 100% accurate to avoid stock-outs. Since this is not achievable in reality, safety stock is kept. Figure 1 shows the relationship between replenishment time and cycle stock. The longer it takes to replenish the inventory, the more amount of cycle stock is necessary to be kept. In practice the cycle stock quantity is often calculated using the *Economic Order Quantity (EOQ)* formula which provides a solution for the purchasing and manufacturing lot size problem.

Figure 1. Idealized sawtooth pattern showing the three types of inventory over time

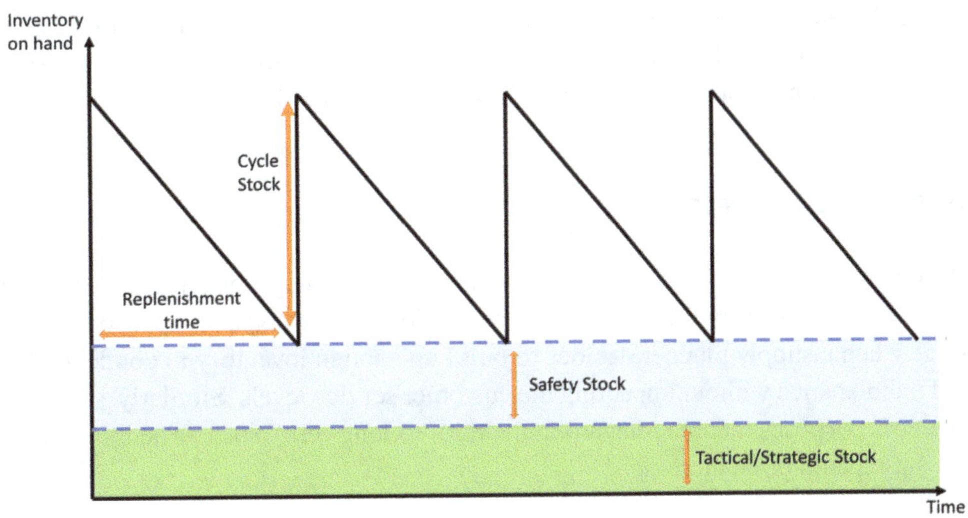

In case of a manufactured product choosing the cycle stock quantity or lot size is often a trade-off between changeover costs and inventory holding costs. Changeover cost represents the cost it takes to manufacture a different product on the same machine. They can vary widely depending on the type of products. Inventory holding cost consists of two main components: The first component of inventory holding cost is the cost of capital tied up in inventory. This represents the opportunity cost of not being able to invest the money elsewhere. Typically, it is calculated by multiplying the standard cost of the product with the cost of capital percentage of the organization.

The second component of inventory holding cost are the warehousing costs. Depending on the size and shape of the product a different portion of personnel costs to handle the product, rent costs of the facility, utility costs, inventory shrinkage, insurance costs, taxes etc. can be assigned to a product. Due to the difficulty of this calculation, some implementations only consider the cost of capital to optimize their inventory. Implicitly, this assumes that the warehousing costs are proportional to the cost of the product which might not be true for all products, e.g. bulky low-cost products like bottled water.

Safety Stock

Safety stock is used as a buffer against uncertainty. Without safety stock at the customer facing echelon of the supply chain, a decrease of the anticipated supply or an increase of the anticipated demand of the product would lead to a guaranteed stock-out and a decrease in customer service level – unless extraordinary measures like premium freight are taken. Demand-side uncertainties typically account for the largest portion of the total safety stock. Examples of demand changes are inaccurate forecast or changing customer orders. Examples on the supply-side are variability in the manufacturing process, e.g. a lower than expected yield of a production run. Another supply-side example could be variability in the lead time of the incoming products needed to manufacture the outgoing products. E.g. bad weather causes a shipment from overseas to be delayed. However, if there was no uncertainty on both the supply- and demand-side no safety stock would be necessary. Make-to-order products represent another scenario where no safety stock of the finished good is kept. The decision of where in the supply chain make to order or make to stock should be used is one of the questions that MEIO can help answer.

An important concept is that safety stock only has to cover for the net replenishment lead time. If a customer's expectation is to receive an order within 10 days of placing it and it only takes 9 days for the supplier to order and receive materials, manufacture the product, and transport it, then there is no need to keep any inventory (make to order). But if the customer requires the product to arrive within 6 days, inventory needs to be kept to account for 9 -6 = 3 days' worth of demand plus demand and supply variability.

Tactical and Strategic Stock

Tactical and strategic stock is inventory build on top of cycle and safety stock. It can serve a multitude of purposes. Tactical inventory is build up in the short- to mid-term for a specific purpose. An example of tactical stock is when a supply planner decides to build up enough inventory to conduct a full machine shutdown and maintenance without impacting the customer service levels. Similarly, strategic inventory can fulfill business purposes that are relevant in the mid- to long-term, such as hedging raw material to counteract an anticipated price increase.

To summarize inventory is kept for a variety of reasons that are legitimate. Any inventory on top of the described purposes is excess inventory that does not serve any purpose and reduces the working capital of the organization. Furthermore, inventory needs to be kept at the right stage in the supply chain. To answer these two questions of where to store inventory and how much of it, the optimization piece of this book chapter will focus on the latest research in safety stock optimization. However, the other components of inventory shall not be underestimated as there can also be significant benefits in optimizing cycle stock and tactical/strategic stock.

Figure 2 depicts the author's view of an inventory optimization maturity model. In contrast to a maturity model presented later in this chapter it focuses only on the optimization piece of the whole inventory planning process.

SINGLE ECHELON INVENTORY OPTIMIZATION

The calculation of single echelon safety and cycle stock quantities will be the primary topic of discussion in the following sections. The author sees a lot of importance in the understanding of the mathematical background for anyone implementing supply chain inventory optimization (IO). In its core every IO transformation will be based on a mathematical model and even though there are many other aspects to a successful transformation, the proper design of the IO software represents one of the most important ones.

In the following paragraphs definition and examples of these important IO concepts will be given:

1. Economic order quantity (EOQ) calculation
2. Type 1 and type 2 service level definition
3. Type 1 service level calculation
4. Type 2 service level calculation
5. Type 1 service level calculation including lead time variability

Figure 2. Inventory optimization maturity model

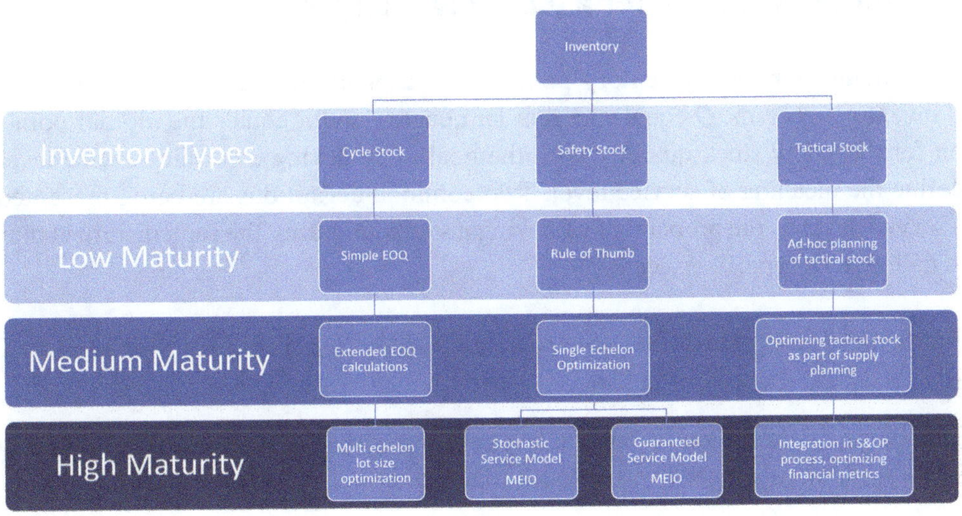

Applying single echelon optimization techniques in an organization can be realized with spreadsheets or specialized software. One example for a successful spreadsheet implementation is shown in the literature research part of this chapter (Farasyn et al. 2008).

The Economic Order Quantity

The economic order quantity (EOQ) is a very popular rule of thumb to quantify the reorder amount. It optimizes the relationship of ordering cost and holding cost. Ordering costs are the fixed costs per order and typically include the cost of transportation and handling. The formula to determine the EOQ is the following:

$$Q = \sqrt{\frac{2DK}{h}}$$

where

Q = Economic Order quantity
D = Demand quantity over the reviewed period
K = fixed cost per order
h = holding cost per unit over the reviewed period

The formula assumes that the demand stays constant within the reviewed period and each replenishment is delivered on time and in full (OTIF). As a result the optimal quantity Q is independent of the unit cost. The resulting order quantity is generally considered a robust solution, however research has shown that it can be sensitive to forecast errors (Mykytka and Ramberg, 1984).

The EOQ is a highly researched topic and various extensions to the EOQ formula exist to consider quantity discounts, one-time discounts, stochastic lead time, finite replenishment (Zipkin 2000), fuzzy costs (Vujošević, Petrović and Petrović, 1996) and more.

Single Echelon Optimization for a (Q,R) Inventory Policy

The (Q,R) or continuous review inventory policy is widespread in industry and is the basis of many commercial inventory systems. *Q* equals the reorder quantity and *R* equals the reorder point. To define a calculation for the safety stock quantity with the goal of achieving a certain service level goal, one must first define the meaning of service level. Two common definitions are being presented. The first one defines service level as the probability of having a stockout during the replenishment duration. This definition is called α- or type 1 service level.

$$\alpha = P\left(Cum.demand\, in\, replenishment\, period \leq Inventory\, at\, beginning\, of\, repl.\, period\right)$$

The second common definition of service level considers the fill rate instead of a binary stock-out situation. So, it gives more weight to a stock-out that results in a significant backlog quantity and less weight to a stock-out that results in only a few units of backlog. The β- or type 2 service level measures the portion of the demand that is met on time:

$$\beta = 1 - \frac{Demand\,not\,filled\,during\,repl.\,period}{Demand\,during\,repl.\,period}$$

The choice of service level measurement is important because it changes the calculation methods and the level of safety stock kept. Comparing the definitions makes it clear that $\alpha \leq \beta$ and sometimes they can differ considerably. Even if a single unit of product is missed during the period, the service level is set to zero in the case of the α-service level. So the same (Q,R) inventory policy could lead to an 85% α-service level, but a 99% β-service level.

The α-service level is more appropriate if a stock-out has severe consequences regardless of quantity. An example is an automotive tier 1 supplier that needs to make sure not to run out of stock to avoid disrupting the OEM production line or inventory of a life-saving medicine. However, in the consumer-packaged goods (CPG) industry the β-service level might be more appropriate since the consequences of missing an order are mostly missed revenue which is proportional to the quantity missed.

In case of the α-service level it can be shown that the EOQ provides the optimal reorder order quantity Q. Considering only demand variability for normally distributed demand the reorder point R can be determined by applying the following formula

$$R = k\sigma + \mu$$

where

k = z score of customer service level
σ = standard deviation of the total demand within the replenishment lead time
μ = mean of the total demand within the replenishment lead time

The safety stock portion of the reorder point equals $k\sigma$.

Example 1: Type 1 service level and random demand:

A product has normally distributed weekly demand with mean $\mu = 100$ units and standard deviation $\sigma = 20$. The lead time is 1 week. The fixed cost per order K = \$20, the product cost equals \$5 and the holding costs h are based on a 10% annual interest rate. The α-service customer service level should be 95%. First, the EOQ is computed to

$$Q = \sqrt{\frac{2DK}{h}} = \sqrt{\frac{2 * 100 * 52 * \$20}{\$5 * 0.1}} \approx 645$$

Second, the reorder point R is computed.

$$R = k\sigma + \mu = 1.64 * 20 + 100 \approx 133$$

The total inventory policy is (645,133) for a type α-service level and the safety stock equals 33 units.

Example 2: Type 2 service level and random demand:

Looking at the β-service level we must use a different formula. The approach presented by Silver et al. (1998, pp.269) is to calculate the inventory policy iteratively although alternative, approximate calculations are available, see for example Vasconcelos and Marques (2000), that might be easier to implement. The increased complexity stems from the fact that Q and R, or cycle stock and safety stock, are no longer independent of each other. Intuitively, this becomes clear by looking at the implicitly assumed shortage cost. Every time a stock-out occurs shortage cost are proportional to the shortage quantity. The bigger Q, the lower the shortage costs become and thus R can be set lower while achieving the same service level.

The calculation uses the standard loss function L(z) and assumes the same service level as in the type 1 example above. Starting off with a Q_0 equal to the EOQ, R is calculated with the following formula:

$$L(z_0) = \frac{(1-\beta)Q_0}{\sigma} = \frac{(1-0.95) * 645}{20} \Rightarrow z_0 = -1.6$$

$$R_0 = z_0\sigma + \mu = -1.6 * 20 + 100 = 68$$

Now Q_1 is calculated based on R_0. $F(z)$ represents the standard cumulative distribution.

$$Q_1 = \frac{(1-\beta)Q_0}{1-F(z_0)} + \sqrt{\frac{2Kd}{h} + \left(\frac{(1-\beta)Q_0}{1-F(z_0)}\right)^2} = \frac{(1-0.95) * 645}{1-F(-1.6)} + \sqrt{\frac{2 * 100 * 52 * \$20}{\$5 * 0.1} + \left(\frac{(1-0.95) * 645}{1-F(-1.6)}\right)^2} \approx 680$$

For the next iteration Q_1 is used to calculate z_1 and then computed as in the example above. See table 2 for the results of the iterative calculations.

Table 2. Iterations for a type 2 service level continuous review policy

Iteration i	Q_i	R_i
0	645 (EOQ)	68
1	680	66
2	681	66

After two iterations R is converging to 66. This results in the final inventory policy of (681,66). As expected compared to the type 1 service level of (645, 133) R decreased drastically and Q slightly increased. This example shows that choosing a type 1 or type 2 service type definition results in significantly different outcomes of the required safety stock quantity.

The standard deviation has been used in the examples above. Organizations of a certain maturity level will provide a forecasted demand picture instead of assuming the demand will follow the average demand for past periods. Only demand quantities that are deviating from the provided forecast need to be considered for safety stock purposes. In this case the standard deviation of forecast and actual demand should be provided for safety stock calculation purposes. Some software vendors use an approximation by applying a conversion factor to the forecast accuracy metric MAD (mean absolute deviation) to come up with the standard deviation of the forecast (Silver et al, 1998). The following formula is an estimate for the standard deviation assuming the normal distribution is appropriate.

$$\sigma = \sqrt{\pi / 2} * MAD$$

Another choice that presents itself to the practitioner is the choice of forecast lag. The question is which cycle's forecast should be used to determine the deviation between forecast and actuals. A common practice is to set the forecast lag equal to the top 5% lead time of purchased goods in the supply chain.

Examples 1 and 2 only considered demand variation as an input factor to safety stock. However often supply variability represents a challenge as well as shown in figure 3 b) and c). Supply variability can occur at every echelon. At the raw material level the supply variability includes the lead time it takes the supplier to respond to the order and ship a product. Transportation processes can include significant variability, especially oversea shipments. If the supplier operates make to order, the supplier manufacturing lead time and lead time variability also needs to be considered. At finished good level the internal manufacturing lead time might vary as well, sometimes considerably in case of machine outages.

Figure 3. Inventory patterns with and without variability

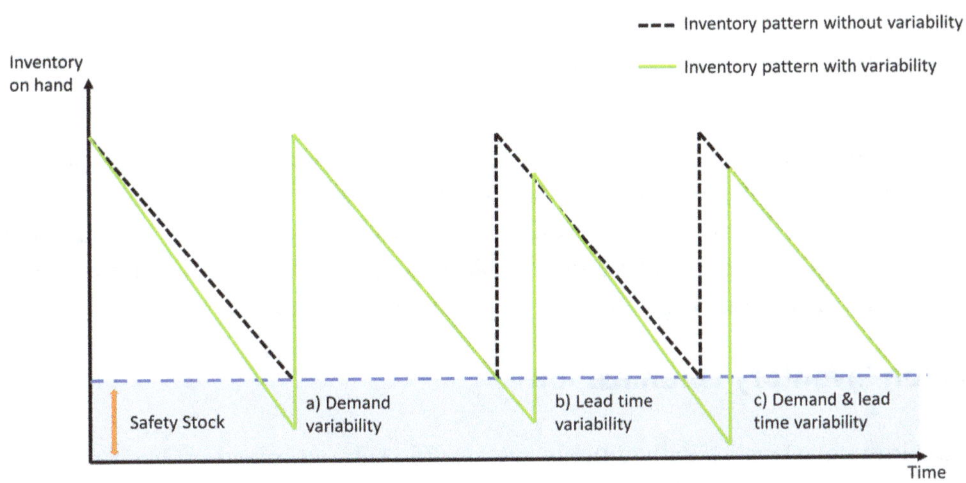

The following formula applies to normally distributed and independent demand and supply variability for a type 1 service level. The first sum inside the square root accounts for lead time variability and the second part accounts for the demand variability as illustrated in figure 3.

$$Safety\,Stock = k * \sqrt{\mu_D^2 * \sigma_L^2 + \mu_L * \sigma_D^2}$$

where

k = z score of customer service level
μ_D = mean of the demand in each period
σ_L = standard deviation of the lead time duration
μ_L = mean of the lead time duration
σ_D = standard deviation of the demand in each period

Example 3: Type 1 service level and random demand & lead time:

A product has normally distributed weekly demand with mean $\mu_D = 100$ units and standard deviation $\sigma_D = 20$ as in example 1. The lead time is now a random variable. To be able to compare it to example 1 we set the lead time to $\mu_L = 1 week$. The standard deviation of the lead time shall be Ã$_L$ = 2 days = 2/7 weeks. The α-service customer service level should be 95%.

$$Safety\,Stock = k * \sqrt{\mu_D^2 * \sigma_L^2 + \mu_L * \sigma_D^2} = 1.64 * \sqrt{100^2 * \left(\frac{2}{7}\right)^2 + 1 * 20^2} \approx 57$$

The reorder point R is computed to

$$R = \mu_D * \mu_L + Safety\,Stock = 100 * 1 + 57 = 157$$

Comparing this result to the inventory policy from example 1 we see that there is an increase of 24 units or 72% in safety stock when considering lead time variability.

It should be noted that the calculations presented in this section apply mostly to fast-moving items for which normally distributed demand is a reasonable assumption. Other distributions need to be taken into consideration for slower moving items, e.g. the gamma distribution (Burgin, 1975).

Multi-Echelon Inventory Optimization

Optimizing the inventory levels locally will always result in sub-optimization. Each echelon is focused on maintaining a customer service level that their immediate downstream customer demands, but for an optimized solution the focus should be on the end customer and inventory decisions should be made based on the end customer service requirements. For that reason, multi-echelon inventory optimization can achieve significant cost savings, especially in complex supply chains, even if a sophisticated single echelon optimization is already in place.

Generally, MEIO is not implemented in the form of spreadsheets, but instead with the help of specialized software since the model and calculations can be too complex and the data volume too big for spreadsheet software to handle. That means to achieve the next level of inventory optimization maturity an investment must be made by the company including an underlying business case. Businesses might have a different set of requirements and being able to understand and challenge the software vendor's proposed solution can be advantageous to the success of the project. It also becomes important during the vendor selection process to inquire about specific capabilities on the IO software.

There are mainly two different approaches to MEIO. The guaranteed service model (GSM) and the stochastic service model (SSM). The differences are discussed in more detail in Graves and Willems (2003) and also in the background section of this chapter. The following section will give the reader an overview and understanding of the basic GSM as presented in the literature review (Graves and Willems, 2000). The GS service model was the focus of extensive research in the last decade. Multiple extensions to the basic GS have been made in recent years and it has been applied at many large companies, e.g. Procter and Gamble, Eastman Kodak, Hewlett Packard, Intel, and Microsoft (Eruguz et al., 2016). For this chapter, two GS spreadsheet models are developed and the results are presented with different input values. Each of these scenarios will serve to increase the reader's understanding of the basic GSM and the factors and decisions to make as part of MEIO in general.

Model 1: 2 Stage GSM

In the first example a 2-step manufacturing process is analyzed. This is common in the CPG industry. Typically, the first step is the bulk production of a product and the second step is packaging the bulk product into the final product that is shipped to the distribution center or retail store. Looking at the example in Figure 4 the following parameters are given.

Looking at the service times, s_1^{in} equals the total supplier lead time of the product that is transformed in the manufacturing process. As per the assumptions of the basic GSM, all service times are deterministic in nature and the only decision variable in our 2 stage model is s_1^{out} which is equal to s_2^{in}. The customer service time is s_2^{out}. The GSM will determine the optimal inventory level at stages 1 and 2 given all these constraints. This is done by solving for s_1^{out}. This becomes clear by looking at low and

Figure 4. Two stage manufacturing example

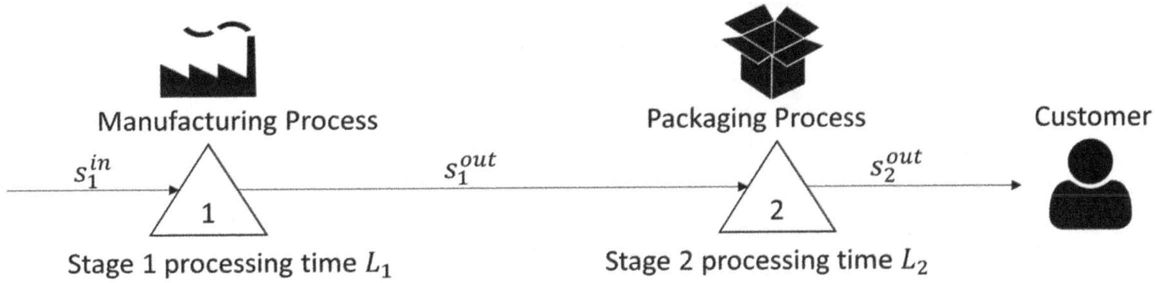

high values for s_1^{out}. In case of a low value for s_1^{out} a higher amount of inventory has to be stocked at stage 1 in order to be able to fulfill the demand with a shorter service time. Similarly, if the optimal s_1^{out} value turns out to be a high value, a small amount of inventory has to be kept.

Note that there are no transportation stages modeled. Stages 1 and 2 have deterministic processing times L_1 and L_2. This is the time it takes from receiving the incoming product to making the product available to the downstream stage. Thus, all lead times that are modeled at a stage *i* need to be summed and included in L_i such as goods received time, manufacturing lead time, transportation lead time, etc.

In the basic GSM the demand from the customer is stationary. This means that the mean demand μ and standard deviation σ do not vary over time. k represents the z score of the service level which the model is achieving by calculating the upper demand bound. For a given value of customer service lead time s_2^{out} the model will achieve 100% service level as long as the demand is not exceeding the demand bound. As explained in (Graves and Willems 2000) should the demand increase beyond this upper limit extraordinary measures have to be taken to fulfill the demand. The usual ways that an organization can avoid lowering their customer service level in this case are expediting freight, run overtime, and ad-hoc subcontracting, all of which incur a premium cost.

C_1 and C_2 represent the inventory holding costs. The input parameters shown in table 3 are used in the first scenario for model number 1.

Based on the demand parameters the upper demand bound calculates to $D_j\left(s_2^{out}\right) = s_2^{out}\mu_j + k_j\sigma_j\sqrt{t} = 1*10 + 1.64*4*\sqrt{1} = 16.56$ units per day.

Only 1 decision variable exists in this two-stage network which is the service time s_1^{out}. Based on the parameters above s_1^{out} is bounded by 0 on the low end since service times cannot be negative. The upper

Table 3. Input parameters for model 1, scenario 1

Parameter	Value	
s_1^{in}	8	Total supplier lead time in days
s_2^{out}	1	Customer service time commitment in days
L_1	5	Stage 1 lead time in days
L_2	2	Stage 2 lead time in days
C_1	1	Holding cost per unit at stage 1 in USD
C_2	1.2	Holding cost per unit at stage 2 in USD
μ	10	Mean customer demand per day at stage 2 in units
σ	4	Standard deviation of daily customer demand at stage 2 in units
k	1.64	Z score of a 95% customer service level

bound equals 13 days because having a service time of 13 days means that stage 1 operates as make to order ($s_1^{in} + L_1$). Additional service lead time on top of the 13 days is unnecessary.

Computing all possible combinations results in the safety stock quantities and costs at stages 1 and 2 pictured in figure 5.

The optimum safety stock configuration in this network is achieved by setting $s_1^{out} = 13$. As a result all safety stock is kept at stage 2 and stage 1 becomes a make to order process without any safety stock.

A second scenario is created in figure 6 by increasing the inventory holding costs C_2 to \$1.4.

In this case it is most cost-effective to set $s_1^{out} = 0$. However, there is still safety stock kept at stage 2. This is necessary because the lead time L_2 is smaller than the customer service time s_2^{out}, so some inventory needs to be kept at stage 2 to achieve the service level. The last scenario for this supply chain network will now look at the effect of a decreased lead time $L_2 = 1$. All other input parameters are the same as in scenario 2.

Figure 7 shows the result. As expected the optimal s_1^{out} is still 0, however, now no inventory is required at stage 2 as it becomes a make to order process. This strategy is also called *postponement.* In this example it means that the product is stored in bulk and only packed once the order has been placed by the customer. In this example it results in significant inventory holding cost savings going from \$32.84 to \$23.65 (28%).

Figure 5. Costs and safety stock quantities for scenario 1

s_1^{out}	0	1	2	3	4	5	6	7	8	9	10	11	12	13
SS Qty Stage 1	23.65	22.72	21.76	20.74	19.68	18.55	17.36	16.07	14.67	13.12	11.36	9.28	6.56	0.00
SS Qty Stage 2	6.56	9.28	11.36	13.12	14.67	16.07	17.36	18.55	19.68	20.74	21.76	22.72	23.65	24.55
Costs	\$ 31.52	\$ 33.86	\$ 35.39	\$ 36.49	\$ 37.28	\$ 37.84	\$ 38.18	\$ 38.33	\$ 38.28	\$ 38.01	\$ 37.47	\$ 36.55	\$ 34.94	\$ 29.45

Figure 6. Costs and safety stock quantities for scenario 2

s_1^{out}	0	1	2	3	4	5	6	7	8	9	10	11	12	13
SS Qty Stage 1	23.65	22.72	21.76	20.74	19.68	18.55	17.36	16.07	14.67	13.12	11.36	9.28	6.56	0.00
SS Qty Stage 2	6.56	9.28	11.36	13.12	14.67	16.07	17.36	18.55	19.68	20.74	21.76	22.72	23.65	24.55
Costs	\$ 32.84	\$ 35.71	\$ 37.66	\$ 39.11	\$ 40.22	\$ 41.05	\$ 41.65	\$ 42.04	\$ 42.22	\$ 42.16	\$ 41.82	\$ 41.09	\$ 39.67	\$ 34.36

Figure 7. Costs and safety stock quantities for scenario 3

s_1^{out}	0	1	2	3	4	5	6	7	8	9	10	11	12	13
SS Qty Stage 1	23.65	22.72	21.76	20.74	19.68	18.55	17.36	16.07	14.67	13.12	11.36	9.28	6.56	0.00
SS Qty Stage 2	0.00	6.56	9.28	11.36	13.12	14.67	16.07	17.36	18.55	19.68	20.74	21.76	22.72	23.65
Costs	\$ 23.65	\$ 31.91	\$ 34.75	\$ 36.65	\$ 38.05	\$ 39.09	\$ 39.85	\$ 40.37	\$ 40.64	\$ 40.67	\$ 40.40	\$ 39.74	\$ 38.37	\$ 33.11

Model 2: 3-Stage GSM

A 3-stage supply chain network is examined next. The 2-stage model is extended by including a warehouse process with a lead time L_3 shown in figure 8.

Now two decision variables are present in the model. In addition to s_1^{out} the internal service time of stage 2 serving stage 3, namely s_2^{out}, is to be determined.

The customer service time commitment has been lowered to zero. This means that inventory must be immediately available at stage 3 to fulfill the customer demand. The bounds for s_1^{out} are the same as in the previous model. For s_2^{out} the upper bound depends on the choice of s_1^{out} plus L_2. The results of the cost calculation with all instances within the bound are displayed in figure 9.

Figure 8. 3-stage supply chain network

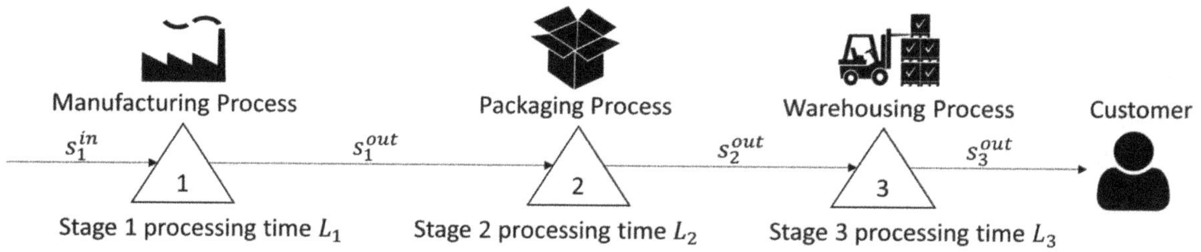

Table 4. Input parameters for model 2, scenario 1

Parameter	Value	
s_1^{in}	8	Total supplier lead time in days
s_3^{out}	0	Customer service time commitment in days
L_1	5	Stage 1 lead time in days
L_2	2	Stage 2 lead time in days
L_3	1	Stage 3 lead time in days
C_1	1	Holding cost per unit at stage 1 in USD
C_2	1.2	Holding cost per unit at stage 2 in USD
C_3	1.3	Holding cost per unit at stage 3 in USD
μ	10	Mean customer demand per day at stage 2 in units
σ	4	Standard deviation of daily customer demand at stage 2 in units
k	1.64	Z score of a 95% customer service level

Figure 9. Costs for 3-stage supply chain network

s_1^{out} (columns) → ; s_2^{out} (rows) ↓

Costs	0	1	2	3	4	5	6	7	8	9	10	11	12	13
0	$61.54	$63.77	$65.39	$66.60	$67.47	$68.07	$68.41	$68.50	$68.32	$67.85	$67.00	$65.62	$63.28	$55.43
1	$61.92	$65.24	$67.42	$68.98	$70.10	$70.89	$71.38	$71.60	$71.53	$71.14	$70.37	$69.06	$66.78	$58.98
2	$54.59	$64.45	$67.71	$69.83	$71.31	$72.35	$73.04	$73.40	$73.46	$73.18	$72.50	$71.26	$69.05	$61.31
3		$56.52	$66.33	$69.52	$71.56	$72.96	$73.90	$74.46	$74.66	$74.51	$73.93	$72.78	$70.65	$62.97
4			$58.00	$67.75	$70.87	$72.82	$74.12	$74.93	$75.33	$75.32	$74.87	$73.82	$71.78	$64.19
5				$59.15	$68.82	$71.86	$73.71	$74.88	$75.53	$75.71	$75.41	$74.49	$72.55	$65.04
6					$60.02	$69.60	$72.53	$74.26	$75.26	$75.70	$75.59	$74.83	$73.01	$65.61
7						$60.63	$70.11	$72.92	$74.48	$75.28	$75.42	$74.84	$73.18	$65.90
8							$61.01	$70.36	$73.00	$74.36	$74.86	$74.54	$73.06	$65.94
9								$61.14	$70.34	$72.77	$73.83	$73.86	$72.64	$65.71
10									$61.02	$70.01	$72.14	$72.74	$71.87	$65.19
11										$60.61	$69.30	$70.97	$70.66	$64.34
12											$59.83	$68.05	$68.82	$63.06
13												$58.51	$65.84	$61.15
14													$56.25	$58.11
15														$48.46

The optimal solution in this example occurs for $s_1^{out} = 13$ and $s_2^{out} = 15$. This means that all safety stock inventory of the supply chain is stored at stage 3. As seen in this example and the examples of model 1, the optimal solution seems to be an extreme point. That means that the optimal solution dictates that each stage either has a service time equal to its net replenishment lead time or a service time of zero. This has been established as true for all concave cost functions in the basic GSM (Humair and Willems, 2006). Figure 9 shows further the power of MEIO. If each stage is determining their own safety stock quantities in a single echelon calculation, sub-optimization will most likely occur (red area). Only a holistic view of the supply chain enables the supply chain manager to find the optimal solution.

In practice the extreme point property of the GSM can lead to some challenges especially if the organization is operating in silos. Let each stage in our example represent a different plant that belongs to a different business unit and thus reports to different management within an organization. If the results of the MEIO calculation were followed, then one stage would take all the burden of the inventory and would have significantly worse inventory key performance indicators (KPIs). On the other hand, the other stages would drastically reduce their customer service KPIs, e.g. on time in full (OTIF). As seen in the examples, MEIO can help to answer the strategic questions of push or pull. To achieve alignment, support for the MEIO initiative in an organization must be at the C-level in the organization. Furthermore, it requires a restructuring of the KPIs for plant management. Instead of focusing on lower inventory at a single echelon the new KPI could measure the adherence to the safety stock target instead and so ensure that the output of the MEIO calculation becomes reality.

So far, the examples have been simple serial supply chain networks. But real-world supply chains are often general acyclic networks or even cyclic networks as seen in following figure 10 a and b. Solving for cyclic networks has not been subject to much research so there might be a need to break up the supply chain model to avoid creating cyclic relationships.

Figure 10. a) General acyclic network b) cyclic network

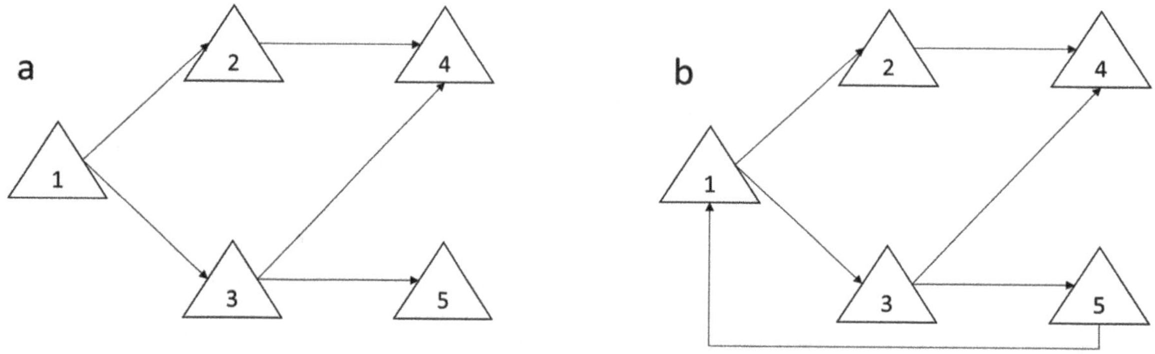

Risk Pooling

Looking at node 3 in figure 10 a) one can see that it serves the two downstream nodes 4 and 5. This could be a common subassembly or component for a finished product. Now assume that the two downstream nodes are producing different products and the two products have independent demand. In this case it can be shown how through risk pooling the safety stock inventory can be lowered substantially.

Stages 4 and 5 have a demand random variable X_4 and X_5. Then the mean demand at stage 3 is

$$E(X_3) = E\left(X_4 + X_5\right) = E\left(X_4\right) + E\left(X_5\right)$$

This represents a simple addition of the mean demand at the downstream stages. It seems intuitive and does not contribute to the risk pooling effect. However, looking at the demand variance shows a different picture:

$$VAR\left(X_3\right) = VAR\left(X_4 + X_5\right) = VAR\left(X_4\right) + VAR\left(X_5\right) + 2Cov\left(X_4, X_5\right)$$

Equation 1: Variance of Summation of Two Random Variables

The total demand variability at stage 3 depends on the covariance of the downstream demand. Figure 12 shows two common cases of demand covariance.

If the demand for the two end products is positively correlated (positive covariance), for example, demand for pens and notebooks at a retail store, the positive effects of risk pooling are reduced. However, if the products are negatively correlated (negative covariance), e.g. 2 similar products that cannibalize each other, then the positive effect of risk pooling is increased. Going forward the assumption is that the random variables X_4 and X_5 are independent from each other which represents a neutral situation, i.e. the covariance equals zero and the covariance term in equation 1 can be ignored.

$$VAR\left(X_3\right) = VAR\left(X_4 + X_5\right) = VAR\left(X_4\right) + VAR\left(X_5\right)$$

Figure 11. Positively and negatively correlated demand patterns

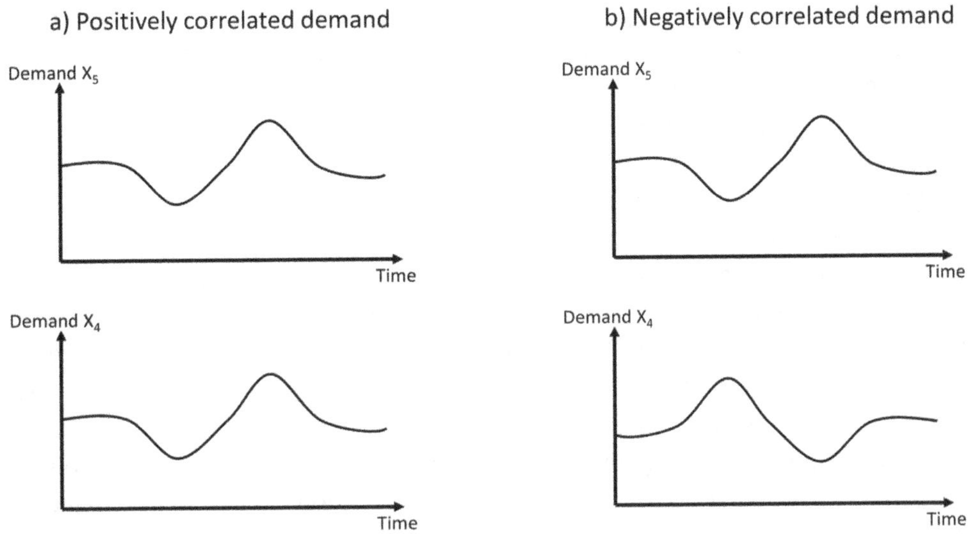

To illustrate the implications of this equation an example is shown. Let X_4 and X_5 be normally distributed demand with standard deviations of $\sigma_4 = 5$ and $\sigma_5 = 6$. Then

$$\sigma_3 = \sqrt{\sigma_4^2 + \sigma_5^2} = \sqrt{25 + 36} \approx 7.81$$

So instead of having to account with safety stock for a standard deviation of the demand of 11 ($\sigma_4 + \sigma_5$) only 7.81 needs to be considered. This effect allows the company to carry significantly less safety stock while keeping the same customer service level. Practically the risk pooling effects need to be considered when making decisions on warehouse consolidation (Eppen, 1979) or postponement of the finished good assembly to keep inventory at a common subassembly stage.

INVENTORY PLANNING PROCESS AND MATURITY MODEL

Now that the reader is familiar with the basic mathematical concepts the broader scope of inventory optimization will be discussed in the form of the inventory planning process. The main goal of the inventory planning process is to provide the safety and sometimes cycle stock parameters to other planning functions, namely:

1. Production scheduling and material requirements planning (MRP)
2. Master planning and rough-cut capacity planning (RCCP)
3. Sales and operations planning (S&OP)

The following describes the general relationship between inventory planning and the planning functions above. It should be noted that the interconnection of these processes can vary by organization based on business model, maturity, and system architecture. The production scheduling and MRP processes have the goal to create a feasible, short-term production schedule for shop floor execution to fulfill the customer orders while balancing costs such as stock-out, overtime and inventory holding costs. The output of the inventory planning process has to be an input to this process or otherwise the computed safety and cycle stock targets will not be realized.

The master planning and RCCP process has the goal to achieve a balance of demand and supply based on capacity constraints and planning parameters that have been deemed important to model for a mid-term horizon. As such it usually represents an input to the production scheduling process to bring in the information of a tactical buildup of inventory, level loading of production lines, etc. As such the computed safety and cycle stock targets need to be provided as an input as well. Similarly, the S&OP process seeks to balance demand and supply on a mid to long-term basis. The focus in the S&OP process is on strategic challenges and aligning all departments within an organization towards a common goal. Scenarios based on strategic investments, e.g. new production lines are created and evaluated on their financial KPI.

Figure 12 depicts the author's view of an inventory planning maturity model. The higher levels of maturity encompass all positive characteristics of the lower levels. Governance, technology, and process are the three dimensions of inventory planning. It is possible to have a different maturity level in each of the dimensions, for example an organization might have a high technology, but a lower governance maturity. With any kind of business transformation, it is important to know what maturity level represents the starting point and then define what level should be achieved based on the business case.

Figure 12. Inventory planning maturity model

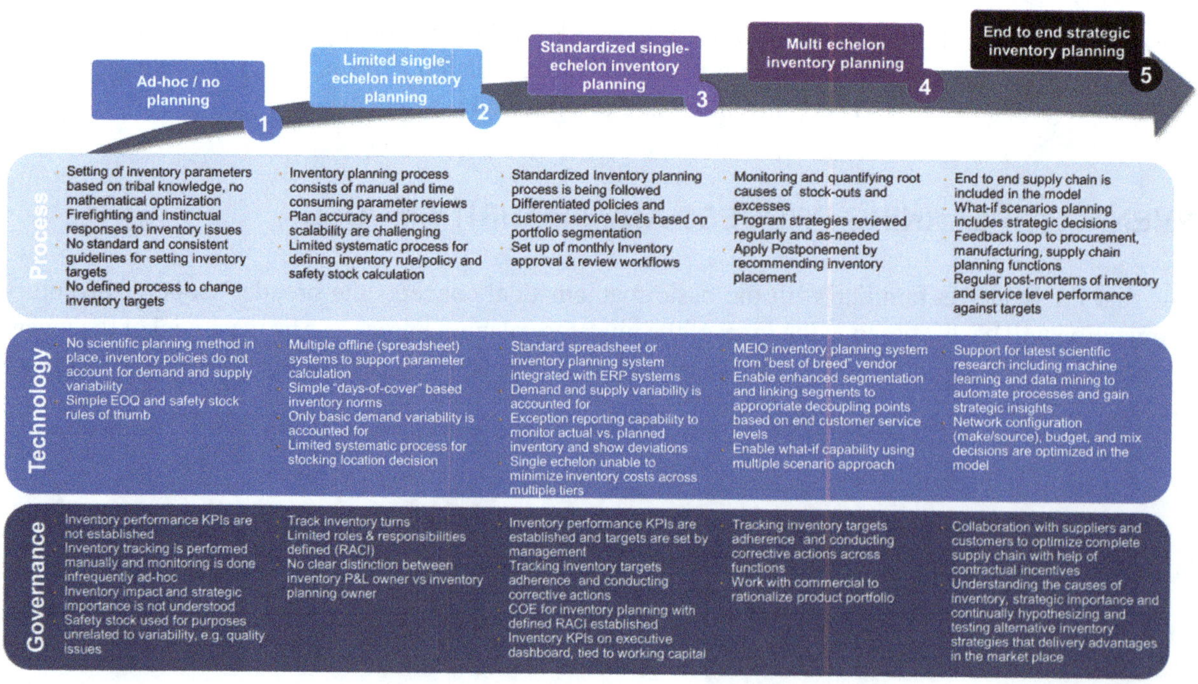

Thus, the first step is to take an unbiased look at the current inventory planning process, technology and governance to determine the current levels. Common techniques to achieve this first step is to analyze inventory parameter data and conducting interviews with the inventory planning stakeholders. The levels are described as the following.

The first level of the maturity model describes an ad-hoc or "no planning" state of inventory planning. There is no defined process to set inventory parameters in the system of record. Rules of thumb are used instead which leads to a circle of trial and error. Even the rules of thumb might vary across silos of the organization and the process cadence is not defined. As such the IO supporting technology is sparse to non-existent. In terms of governance, the KPIs are not established and tracking of actuals is not done consistently. Overall the importance of inventory is not well understood.

The second level is called "Limited Single Echelon Inventory Planning". As improvements compared to level 1, the process is now defined, but might vary across business units. Inventory parameters are reviewed one by one since no exception capabilities are present. As a result the process is not scalable. The technology at this level consists of offline, non-standardized spreadsheets. They might include some of the formulas presented in the "Single Echelon Optimization for a (Q,R) inventory policy" section of this chapter. Since the IO system is not integrated with the ERP, simple day of cover policies are being used to avoid entering time-phased safety stock numbers. The governance includes tracking of inventory turns and a limited definition of roles and responsibilities.

The third level is still operating with a single echelon optimization model, but the overall maturity is improved in many ways. The inventory planning process and its cadence is fully standardized, documented, and adhered to. Portfolio segmentation exists to focus on the inventory issues of high value first. Technology-wise the single echelon approach can still be implemented as a spreadsheet solution or alternatively a specialized planning system is used. The output of the tool is integrated with the ERP system and exception reporting exists, which makes the solution scalable. Leadership is fully aware of the importance of inventory and KPI targets are being dictated.

The fourth level of inventory planning maturity adds the element of regular root cause analysis of stock out and excess inventory. MEIO enables the scientific application of postponement and inventory placement. The system is fully integrated with the source and target systems and allows for cost based optimization through mathematical programming. What-if scenarios are possible to model the inventory impact of new product introduction, inventory impact of a new sourcing method, changes in demand variability, etc. Inventory target adherence is tracked and root causes are identified, documented, and a plan is created on how to avoid non-adherence in the future. Cross functional initiatives on rationalizing the product portfolio might be included in the IO scope based on a total cost of ownership approach.

The final stage of inventory planning maturity is called "End-to-end strategic inventory planning". The end-to-end supply chain is included in the maturity model including external suppliers, customers, and their suppliers and customers. The holistic approach requires sharing of information across the different organizations that could be achieved with incentivized contracts. Machine learning and data mining is used to predict the optimal future network configuration. The scope of IO is extended to also include network configuration aspects, for example sourcing decisions.

FUTURE RESEARCH DIRECTIONS

The author identifies research opportunities in the areas of

1. Inventory optimization surveys. The latest survey on IO tool and process adoption that the author was able to identify is from 2014. Given the rapid increased usage of digital technology, the numbers might look different at the present time. The survey should contain a variety of industries to show the differences in IO adoption.
2. SSM versus GSM. Although this chapter focused on the GSM, the SSM is a proven MEIO tool to provide safety stocks across the network. The different assumptions of both models might make one more applicable than the other depending on industry, supply chain network, computational costs, or other considerations. Developing a decision framework represents an opportunity for research. Other questions that could be answered in this framework are: Is the investment in MEIO worth it for a simple supply chain and what is the complexity threshold? What are industry best practices in terms of IO tool configuration?
3. Machine learning applied to inventory optimization. The traditional IO models are limited to a defined set of input parameters, for example demand and supply variability. Typically the historical variability is used as an indicator for the future. However each of these parameters could instead be predicted with machine learning techniques depending on input parameters such as the weather, port closure information, point of sales data, social media input, etc.

CONCLUSION

There is an opportunity for inventory optimization in many organizations that handle physical goods. Even the most advanced organizations that are known for their supply chain capabilities have not yet mastered all aspects of inventory planning maturity (Farasyn et al., 2011). The author is confident that using the inventory optimization tools presented in this chapter and combining them with transformation guidelines presented in the rest of this book will set up the supply chain practitioner for success and wishes the reader best of luck on their digital supply chain journey.

REFERENCES

Aberdeen Group. (2012). *Inventory Optimization – Impact of a Multi-Echelon Approach.* Boston: Aberdeen Group.

Burgin, T. (1975). The Gamma Distribution and Inventory Control. *Operational Research Quarterly, 26*(3), 507.

Eppen, G. D. (1979). Effects of centralization on expected costs in a multi-location newsboy problem. *Management Science, 25*(5), 498–501. doi:10.1287/mnsc.25.5.498

Eruguz, A., Sahin, E., Jemai, Z., & Dallery, Y. (2016). A comprehensive survey of guaranteed-service models for multi-echelon inventory optimization. *International Journal of Production Economics, 172*, 110–125. doi:10.1016/j.ijpe.2015.11.017

Farasyn, I., Humair, S., Kahn, J., Neale, J., Rosen, O., Ruark, J., ... Willems, S. (2011). Inventory Optimization at Procter & Gamble: Achieving Real Benefits Through User Adoption of Inventory Tools. *Interfaces, 41*(1), 66–78. doi:10.1287/inte.1100.0546

Farasyn, I., Perkoz, K., & Van de Velde, W. (2008). Spreadsheet Models for Inventory Target Setting at Procter & Gamble. *Interfaces, 38*(4), 241–250. doi:10.1287/inte.1080.0345

Graves, S., & Willems, S. (2003). *Supply chain design: safety stock placement and supply chain configuration*. Academic Press.

Humair, S., & Willems, S. (2006). Optimizing Strategic Safety Stock Placement in Supply Chains with Clusters of Commonality. *Operations Research, 54*(4), 725–742. doi:10.1287/opre.1060.0313

Klosterhalfen, S., Minner, S., & Willems, S. (2014). Strategic Safety Stock Placement in Supply Networks with Static Dual Supply. *Manufacturing & Service Operations Management: M & SOM, 16*(2), 204–219. doi:10.1287/msom.2013.0472

Mykytka, E., & Ramberg, J. (1984). On the Sensitivity of the EOQ to Errors in the Forecast of Demand. *IIE Transactions, 16*(2), 144–151. doi:10.1080/07408178408974679

Pittman, P., Blackstone, J. H., & Atwater, J. B. (2016). *APICS Dictionary* (15th ed.). APICS.

Romanow, K. (2014). *Custom Research Inventory Optimization*. Retrieved from: http://www.consumergoods.com

Silver, E., Pyke, D., & Peterson, R. (1998). *Inventory management and production planning and scheduling*. New York: Wiley.

Vujošević, M., Petrović, D., & Petrović, R. (1996). EOQ formula when inventory cost is fuzzy. *International Journal of Production Economics, 45*(1-3), 499–504. doi:10.1016/0925-5273(95)00149-2

Zipkin, P. (2000). *Foundations of inventory management*. Boston: McGraw-Hill.

KEY TERMS AND DEFINITIONS

Arc: Connection between stages/nodes. It can, for example, represent a relationship defined in a bill of material or a transportation network.

BOM: Bill of material.

CPG: Consumer packaged goods.

EOQ: Economic order quantity.

GSM: Guaranteed service model.

IO: Inventory optimization.

KPI: Key performance indicator.

MAD: Mean absolute deviation.

MEIO: Multi-echelon inventory optimization.

MRP: Material requirements planning.

OTIF: On time in full. It represents a KPI for delivery performance and is typically calculated by dividing the number of deliveries delivered on time in full by the total number of deliveries.

RCCP: Rough-cut capacity planning.

S&OP: Sales and operations planning.

SSM: Stochastic service model.

Stage/Node: A stage in the supply chain. It can represent a manufacturing operation or a warehousing process.

Chapter 11
Capacity Planning in Digital Age:
A Process to Prepare to Meet the Volatile Demand

Amit Gupta
KPMG LLP, USA

ABSTRACT

This chapter answers the following questions: 1) What is the capacity planning process? 2) Why do companies need to perform capacity planning? 3) What are current challenges in the capacity planning process? 4) What are different levels in the capacity planning? 5) What are planning zones? 6) How does capacity planning implementation journey look like? In the chapter, the author touches some of the basics of the capacity planning and then goes into advance level in the capacity planning. The chapter expects readers to have a basic knowledge of the capacity planning.

LITERATURE REVIEW

Capacity planning has been around for a very long time; earlier businesses used to plan factory throughput or the number of customers they can serve to buy equipment or hire labor. Initially, capacity planning span was a factory to a workstation. When supply chains began to move out of organizations' four walls, a need for holistic capacity planning manifested, with several challenges. The long lead time associated with outsourcing introduced limited flexibility and higher inventory, for both safety stock and cycle stock. Global footprints led to inconsistent factory utilization, which highlighted the need for global planning and visibility; however, with limited software sophistication, the focus remained on optimizing a factory and pressure feeding-plants and suppliers to support the plan. With today's digital capabilities, an organization can not only link its strategic plan to a detailed execution-level capacity plan, but also gain visibility outside its four walls to ensure the complete network can support its strategic plan.

DOI: 10.4018/978-1-5225-7700-3.ch011

Copyright © 2019, IGI Global. Copying or distributing in print or electronic forms without written permission of IGI Global is prohibited.

To link the strategic plan to the operational plan and support specific decision needs, the capacity planning process has broken into multiple levels. Each level has different granularity and frequency and has a distinct purpose. While APICS divides end-to-end capacity planning into four levels (resources requirement planning, rough-cut capacity planning, capacity requirement planning, and input/output control), this chapter divides end-to-end capacity planning into five levels with strategic capacity planning as an additional level to align corporate objectives with the execution plan. The variations in the number of levels have existed; for example, Bram Desmet of Solventure and Adrian Bentley of McBride divided the capacity planning process into five levels in a webinar[1]. The picture below shows the proposed five levels of capacity planning.

Five levels in the capacity planning provide a holistic, top-down view of the capacity—validating and verifying the process's end goal at each stage and disseminating the information to the next level to make execution-level decisions. For example, leadership defined a long-term goal in strategic capacity planning that is disaggregated into a yearly plan considering market conditions in the annual budget planning process. Following the budget, rough-cut capacity planning and capacity requirement planning generate and track a tactical plan to achieve the annual plan. Finally, detailed production planning adds execution-level detail for day-to-day execution. The level of sophistication and need of supporting technology increase as the process moves from level 1 to level 5.

A subsequent section provides background information, and after the background, the chapter expands five levels of capacity planning process and provides a maturity model for organizations to assess their capabilities.

Figure 1. Capacity planning levels

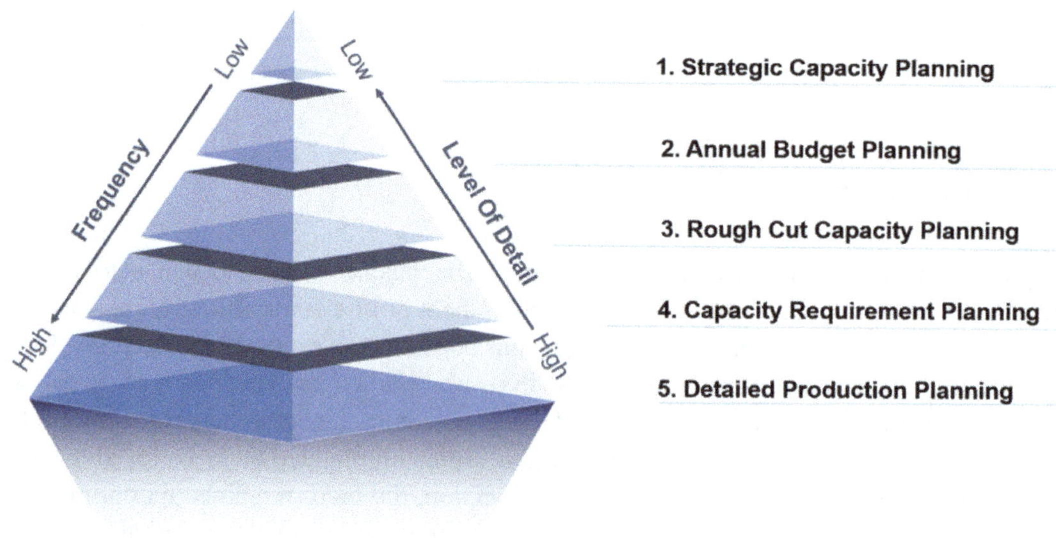

BACKGROUND

Capacity Definition

Capacity is the output of a resource for a period. A resource can be a manufacturing plant, an assembly line, warehouse space, a truck, or any equipment that assists in producing a product or delivering a service. Resources can exist within an organization's four walls or at companies supplying components, raw materials, or supporting select operations. For example, Samsung© builds components for its Galaxy© product line at its facilities in South Korea while it also uses Foxconn© for assembly operations in China; therefore, Samsung has internal capacities in South Korea and external capacities at Foxconn in China.

The following diagram shows a simple linear supply chain with five nodes—supplier, manufacturing, transportation, warehouse, and store. Each node in this supply chain has one or more capacities. For example, the raw material supplier, a mining company, has capacity in the form of labor and heavy machinery to extract ore, such as an earthmover that can move 1,000-tons of dirt per hour. The transportation company has trucking capacities to support the movement of the goods, such as a truck that has a total of 1,000 cubic feet of space or can move a 25-ton weight.

Capacity Planning

Capacity planning is a technique to plan optimum resource levels to meet future demand in all market conditions. The key to effective capacity planning is the optimal level of resources because excess capacity reduces investment available to other functions, while inadequate capacity causes lost sales and unhappy customers.

Organizations can make minor capacity adjustments through overtime, idle time, or lower run rate to respond to short-term demand variations. On the other hand, large capacity variations, such as opening a distribution center to add storage space or shutting down a plant to eliminate excess capacity, are done only in large chunks with an associated long lead time—a few months to several years.

Figure 2. Different types of capacities in the supply chain

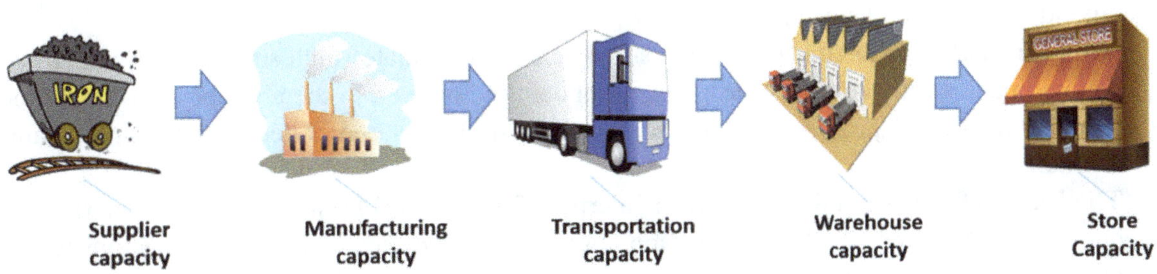

Most of the examples and concepts in this chapter are manufacturing-organization focused; however, similar concepts are applicable to service organizations. Additionally, a majority of the concepts mentioned in the chapter are aligned with APICS[2] definitions with some variations based on the author's 15 years of experience in the field at various organizations.

Now, with the basic understating of capacity planning, the discussion is moved to understand the need for a capacity planning process and the implications when the process is not executed aptly.

Need for Capacity Planning

If demand was uniform or resources were unconstrained, the capacity planning process would be a trivial task; however, except for a few government agencies, such as tax authorities, product or service forecast has low accuracy and high volatility with access to only finite resources to meet this demand. Coping with demand volatility and making long-term decisions with hundreds of unknowns while mitigating risks make the capacity planning process challenging. Some of the challenges of capacity decisions are as follows:

- **Volatile demand:** As mentioned previously, except for a few government agencies, organizations deal with demand volatility (peaks and troughs) and timing and accuracy. In current market conditions, where shorter product life cycles are becoming the norm and threatening previously optimized flows, achieving a comfortable demand accuracy for a sustained period is turning out to be more challenging; as a result, companies need to be prepared, on the supply side, to absorb some of the demand challenges.
- **SKU proliferation:** Online sales channels offering customized products with unprecedented choices are leaving both online and offline players with a large number of products to manage. On the supply side, additional product variations complicate the capacity planning process because factories now needed to run a large number of products leveraging the same resources while minimizing changeovers. With SKU proliferation, lack of a defined capacity planning process and the absence of an enabling technology to execute the process may lead to higher costs and lost sales.
- **Shorter product life cycle:** It is not obvious, but a shorter product life cycle has large implications for capacity planning as supply organization constantly need to refresh capacities to phase out old products and launch new products.
- **Need for visibility:** Digitization of the supply chain necessitates high supply chain visibility so that companies can commit to customers confidently; however, in the absence of the right tools together with SKU proliferation, providing true visibility to end nodes in the supply chain is challenging.
- **The influx of new digital capabilities:** Internet of Things (IoT) sensors in machines, radio-frequency identification (RFID), and collaboration technologies are enabling organizations to share and receive information to respond better to market needs; however, many organizations are not prepared to harness the new information that may cause them to lose to a competitor who built these capabilities.

Given the challenges outlined above and their implications for the prospects of the organization, a better capacity planning process can not only boost revenue and lower capital requirement, but also provide a true competitive advantage.

Challenges in Capacity Planning

Realizing the importance of capacity planning, many organizations have begun focusing on improving the capacity planning process; however, organizations are facing several challenges in managing the process efficiently. The list below highlights some of the challenges.

1. **Defining the right level for planning:** Every organization performs capacity planning in some shape or form; however, conducting at a level that puts forth the right detail to support leadership to make the right decisions is the ultimate objective of the process. This may sound simple, but not many organizations are able to achieve it. For example, capacity planning for high-level resources, such as total factory capacity to make shoes at a shoe manufacturer, can be used to determine the need to build a new factory or expand the factory; however, this high-level information cannot help in answering if the company can deliver 10,000 shoes in the month of July. Many companies are performing capacity planning either at a very high level for long-range strategic planning or performing at a detailed factory planning level, which is a complex, resource-intensive process and challenging to rapidly respond to market fluctuations. Defining the right levels for capacity planning is vital to support the right decisions.
2. **Availability of the right data:** The capacity planning process relies heavily on having the right data with sufficient detail to support the process, such as time-phased capacity information for resources, products capacity usage etc. In the absence of correct data, the process generates inaccurate results leading to wrong decisions.
3. **Defining the right hierarchy:** To perform capacity planning at different levels of aggregation to support different decisions, organizations need the right levels in the product, location, geography, and time hierarchies. Right levels in the hierarchies enable aggregation and disaggregation for different functional groups to view the same information at a different level. For example, Finance views total revenue at the business unit level while the S&OP team views revenue by product lines.
4. **Set up the right organization:** Many organizations lack a dedicated group to manage the complete capacity planning process. Several groups support part of the process, but a single group does not cover the holistic capacity picture, which cuts through cross-functional boundaries. Lack of the right organization structure leaves the organization with localized suboptimal results.

Capacity Planning Levels, Maturity, and Implementation

Before discussing each level of capacity planning mentioned in Figure 1, it is important to understand some of the concepts related to capacity planning.

Capacity Unit of Measure

Capacity is measured using various units of measure. Three commonly used measures are as follows:

1. **Run rate:** Run rate for a machine is defined as total output produced in a defined time, for example, 200 units/minute for an injection-modeling machine or 40 tons of steel per hour. Run rate is mostly used to quote capacity for resources producing a single line of product. For example, a simple one-liter water bottle filling machine can fill 4,000 bottles in an hour.

2. **Total available time:** Some resources can produce a variety of products, and each product can have a different run rate on the resource. For example, a lathe machine can produce 20 small gears per hour, while it can produce only 2 pistons per hour. Depending on the type of product, the resource's run rate can vary; therefore, instead of quoting the resource's capacity as multiple run rates, the resource's capacity can be quoted as total available hours, such as 18 available hours per day.
3. **Space:** Capacity of warehouses, retail stores, service organizations, etc., are defined in square feet.

Capacity Calendar

Due to maintenance activity or operator's availability, or various other reasons, a resource's capacity can vary week over week. To represent capacity variations, capacity is defined in a calendar format, which provides the flexibility to maintain different capacity for different periods. For example, a gear-cutting machine can be available 18 hours per day for most days, but for a few days, due to maintenance and operators' availability, it can be available only for 8 hours.

Additionally, resources have two types of capacities—design capacity and effective capacity. Design capacity is the maximum output of the resource while effective capacity is the capacity that can be generated consistently over a long period. The reason for two different types of capacities is that resources can run at maximum capacity only for a short time as running at maximum capacity for a prolonged time may cause breakage, which results in downtime or reduced capacity. For resource load planning, effective capacity is used. The table below shows an example of an effective capacity calendar of a lathe machine.

Planning Horizon and Planning Buckets

The planning horizon is the period of time in the future that an organization plans capacity. Planning horizon can be 4 weeks to 5+ years, depending on the level of the capacity planning. The planning horizon is divided into planning buckets. Planning buckets can be daily, weekly, monthly, quarterly, or yearly. Most often, daily and weekly planning buckets are used for short-term planning, such as detailed production at Level 5 in Figure 1, where detailed information is necessary to execute orders in a factory or place a raw material order to support production. Monthly and quarterly buckets are used primarily for a medium-term planning horizon, while yearly buckets are used for long-term planning. Based on the organization structure and product type, organizations can define the length of the planning horizon and planning bucket.

The following picture shows the five-year planning horizon with weekly, monthly, and quarterly buckets. Different planning buckets in the same horizon are called a mixed bucket horizon or telescoping buckets—more detail in near-term and time aggregation later to reduce uncertainty.

Table 1. Capacity calendar

Lathe capacity	Week 1	Week 2	Week 3	Week 4	Week 5	Week 6	Week 7	Week 8
Hour per day	18	18	18	18	10	10	12	18
Number of days	5	5	5	4	4	4	5	5
Total weekly capacity (hours)	**90**	**90**	**90**	**72**	**40**	**40**	**60**	**90**

Figure 3. Planning horizon and planning buckets

2018								2019				2020				2021				2022			
Weekly					Monthly							Quarterly											
W1	W2	W3	W4	W5	Feb	...	Dec	Jan	Feb	...	Dec	Jan	Apr	July	Oct	Jan	Apr	July	Oct	Jan	Apr	July	Oct

Top-Down Approach to Capacity Planning

At the beginning of the chapter, Figure 1 introduced five levels of capacity planning. Each level of capacity planning is done to meet a specific objective and to make specific decisions. The section provides detail of each level.

- **Strategic Capacity Planning:** Strategic capacity planning is tied to the organization's strategic planning process, which defines strategic direction for the next 3 to 5+ years. As a part of the strategic planning process, strategic capacity planning helps in understanding the total capacity required to achieve the organization's long-term growth plan. Strategic capacity planning is performed for overall capability considering plants', subcontractors', and suppliers' capacity to understand, at a high level, if the supply chain has the required throughput to support the growth plan. Strategic capacity planning is performed yearly for a 3 to 5-year planning horizon (in the case of auto OEM, 5 to 10 years) in quarterly or yearly planning buckets. The objective of strategic capacity planning is to enable leadership to make large capital investment decisions, such as opening a new factory or building new supplier capability in 2 years, etc.

For example, a shoe manufacturer has \$5 billion in annual revenue and has factories to fulfill \$5.5 billion revenue to accommodate growth. A new CEO joins the company and sets up a new target for the next five years: achieve 4 percent compounded growth year over year to achieve \$6 billion in revenue by the fifth year. To support this long-term growth plan, in the strategic capacity planning process, leadership validates the supply organization's capability to support the growth and makes capital investment decisions to fill the gap. Based on revenue projections year-over-year for five years (Table 2), the organization will face a \$500 million revenue shortfall for the fifth year and total \$870 million cumulative revenue gaps over 5 years due to capacity shortages. To fill these capacity shortages, leadership has multiple options: expand capacity at the beginning of year 2, buy a supplier in year 3, open a new factory in year 3, improve performance of existing capacity, and so on.

- **Annual Budget Planning:** Annual budget planning or annual operating planning occurs yearly to define goals and the operating plan for the whole organization for the upcoming financial year. It is an organization-wide process with the supply chain group as one of the participants. Finance typically leads the process with inputs from various business units and functional groups. In this process, the leadership defines revenue targets, which translate into demand targets for different business units to achieve the collective annual plan. Based on demand targets, the supply planning group identifies, in collaboration with procurement, an operating plan to fulfill the demand and gaps in current capacities. The supply planning group presents the operating plan and capacity

Table 2. Strategic capacity planning analysis example and resolution options

	Current year	Year 1	Year 2	Year 3	Year 4	Year 5
Revenue	$5.0B	$5.2B	$5.41B	$5.62B	$5.85B	$6.0B
Supply capacity	$5.5B	$5.5B	$5.50B	$5.50B	$5.50B	$5.5B
Shortfall				($120M)	($250M)	($500M)
Cumulative shortfall				($120M)	($370M)	($870M)
Plan to fill the shortfall		Initiate improvement	Expand the plant	Buy a supplier		

gaps to the supply chain leadership to obtain the operating budget and investment to fill any capacity gaps, such as for acquiring a new machine, hiring additional labor, etc. Annual budget planning is performed in quarterly buckets and tracked to quarter-ends in a financial year.

For example, this year, the shoe manufacturer in the previous example is targeting to achieve $5.2 billion in revenue, 4 percent or $200 million above last year's plan. To meet the additional revenue goal, the organization is planning to introduce a new product line. The supply planning group, responsible for capacity, determines that the organization would need to expand capacity of three assembly lines and buy three new machines to support the additional revenue. During the annual budget planning process, the supply planning group will produce the plan to expand capacity to the leadership. Based on the proposal, leadership may assign capital budget to expand the capacity.

- **Rough-Cut Capacity Planning:** Rough-cut capacity planning (RCCP) is part of a mature monthly sales and operation (S&OP) process. A key objective of S&OP is to get the product volume right considering consensus demand and available capacity; therefore, RCCP, which assists the S&OP team in validating capacity, is done at an aggregated level, such as at the product family level. Since RCCP is performed at an aggregated level, resources in RCCP are also aggregated to enable the S&OP team to make tradeoffs among product families to maximize fill rate, increase margin, and fill any gaps between the annual operating plan and current operational plan. Here is a guideline to select resources for RCCP.
- Factory throughput can be one of the constraints.
- For select strategic products, overall output can be a constraint.
- Overall product output can be a constraint when a product is sourced from more than one source.
- An aggregated resource, which dictates a factory or product output; for example, Bliss press capacity in forging operation or molding capacity for a foundry or plastic part manufacturing

RCCP is performed in monthly buckets for the next 18- to 24-month planning horizon, and if the horizon is longer than 24 months, then in quarterly buckets. The aim of RCCP is to highlight demand/supply gaps in midterm (outside of the 3-month horizon) and assist in filling the gaps using different strategies, such as prebuilding to accommodate peak demand, offloading volume to suppliers, etc. The output of the RCCP is called production requirements.

RCCP is one of the parts of the larger monthly S&OP process and S&OP is a large topic in itself. Without going into detail of S&OP, the following depiction will expand the shoe manufacturer example to demonstrate RCCP briefly.

Sales, operations, marketing, and finance together finalize the annual plan and break it into a monthly or quarterly plan for execution and tracking. Additionally, to plan for the longer term, the planning horizon is extended to 2 years using projections considering the strategic plan, demand history, product roadmap, and market conductions.

In RCCP, first demand planning and supply planning bring their best plan along with several scenarios to fill any revenue gaps or eliminate supply shortages. For the review meeting with leadership, the demand plan is aggregated to Business Units (BU) and families to assess the gap between unconstrained demand plan and annual plan and supply plan is aggregated to view supply shortages for a BU and a family.

Table 4 shows demand, supply, and supply gaps for one product family, Sports Shoe, in both units and dollars. Showing the demand plan in both units and dollars is important because different groups talk in a different unit of measure. For example, Finance cares about revenue while demand planning cares about units; therefore, aligning groups in showing the plan in their unit of measure helps in making quick decisions.

In the leadership review meeting, apart from highlighting supply gaps, the supply planning group proposes various scenarios to fill those gaps, such as run plants overtime for three days in a month, or if plants are already running at the maximum capacity, shift the load to a supplier, and so on.

After resolving supply gaps for individual families, leadership reviews revenue gaps between the demand plan and annual plan (an example is shown in Table 5) and reviews proposed options to fill gaps, such as run a promotion to close revenue gaps or launch a product early, etc. After the review, leadership approves a plan for the execution.

Table 3. Annual plan example

In million $	M1	M2	M3	M4	M5	M6	..	M23	M24
Annual plan	$100	$100	$100	$110	$110	$110	..	..	..

Table 4. Family level supply gaps example

Sports shoe	M1	M2	M3	M4	M5	M6	..	M23	M24
Demand plan ($)	$30M	$35M	$33M	$34M	$36M	$37M	...	...	...
Demand plan (units)	1.2M	1.4M	1.32M	1.36M	1.44M	1.48M	...	...	...
Supply plan unit ($)	$30M	$32.5M	$32.5M	$32.5M	$32.5M	$35M	...	...	...
Supply plan unit(s)	1.2M	1.3M	1.3M	1.3M	1.3M	1.4M	...	...	...
Supply gap ($)		($2.5M)	($0.5M)	($1.5M)	($3.5M)	($2M)	...	...	...
Supply gap (units)		(0.1M)	(0.02M)	(0.06M)	(0.14M)	(0.08M)	...	...	...

Table 5. Revenue gaps example

	M1	M2	M3	M4	M5	M6	..	M23	M24
Sport shoe	$30M	$32.5M	$32.5M	$32.5M	$32.5M	$35.0M	…	…	…
Formal shoe	$20M	$25.0M	$30.0M	$35.0M	$35.0M	$34.0M	…	…	…
Casual shoe	$52M	$40.0M	$39.0M	$39.0M	$38.0M	$38.0M	…	…	…
Total plan	$102M	$97.5M	$101.5M	$106.5M	$105.5M	$107M	…	…	…
Annual plan	$100	$100	$100	$110	$110	$110	…	…	…
Gap	$2M	($2.5M)	$1.5M	($3.5M)	($4.5M)	($3.0M)	…	…	…
Cumulative gap	$2M	($0.5M)	$1.0M	($2.5M)	($7.0M)	($10.0M)	…	…	…

- **Capacity Requirement Planning:** Capacity requirement planning (CRP) is performed as a part of the master planning process. In master planning, the output of RCCP—production requirement at an aggregated volume level—is used to plan individual products to drive a master production schedule (MPS) at an item or SKU level. At an aggregate level, MPS should match with the production requirement of the S&OP process. CRP considers only key bottleneck resources; therefore, it should not be confused with detailed production planning. The number of resources in CRP is generally more than RCCP but fewer than the detailed production planning process, which considers most of the resources. For example, RCCP may consider total molding capacity as a consolidated capacity constraint, while CRP may further divide molding into three constraints, divided by tonnages, such as 1000 ton, 2000 ton, or 5000 ton. Unlike RCCP, CRP can plan some of the detailed capacities because the demand in CRP is at item level; thus, the load on an individual machine can be determined to identify load on the capacity.

CRP is performed in weekly buckets for next the 2- to 6-month planning horizon, and monthly buckets following the weekly buckets. Since CRP input—production plan—is in monthly buckets, it needs to be broken into weekly buckets for the first few weekly buckets. Monthly bucket to weekly buckets can be done in different ways; for example, equally to all weeks or a specific percentage for each week.

The aim of CRP is to understand the short-term production plan for the next few months so that procurement can order materials and resources. The output of CRP—MPS—is used for alignment between sales and production—the customer representative team uses it to make customer promises while plants and vendors use it as an expected production plan to prepare raw materials and resources.

A question that is most often asked about CRP is "Which resources should be the part of the CRP process?" A simple guideline is to include the constraints that can give sufficient confidence in committing the production plan to the sales team while avoiding getting into the complex details of production planning. Here are a few additional guidelines to select resources for CRP:

- Consider bottleneck resources that often hit their ceiling.
- Plan resources at an aggregated level, not at an individual tool level.
- Avoid labor as a constraint; however, if labor is a major roadblock, consider leveraging it in some other form, such as a total number of hours.
- Consider selected long lead-time parts or raw materials that often pose scheduling challenges.

In CRP, and also in RCCP and detailed production planning, resource constraints are applied in two ways: soft constraints and hard constraints. The difference between two types of constraints is overloading—hard constraints cannot be loaded more than 100 percent while soft constraints can be loaded more than 100 percent. The reason for overloading soft constraints is to alert the planners to overloading and have the planner identify an alternate, which can be expediting material by paying premium freight or using another supplier, etc. In the case of hard constraints, if the constraint hits 100 percent, the system seeks for unused capacity in adjacent planning buckets, and if it cannot find available capacity, it alerts the planner to unresolved capacity gaps.

The output of the CRP process is MPS, which feeds the detailed production planning process. Additionally, MPS drives material requirement planning (MRP) to release purchase orders to suppliers or change existing purchase order, for example – push out, pull in, or cancel a purchase order. The CRP process is demonstrated using the shoe manufacturing company.

In CRP, production plan of families—sports shoes, formal shoes, and casual shoes—is disaggregated into the product-level production plan to model and validate selected critical bottleneck resources. The table below shows CRP analysis on sewing capacity. While weeks 2 and 3 have excess capacity, weeks 4, 5, 7, and 8 have a capacity shortage. To balance the capacity load, the capacity planner may pull forward some load of week 4 to weeks 2 and 3, week 7 load to week 6, and run overtime or extra shifts in week 8. While this example shows manual capacity balancing, modern capacity planning systems can perform this task automatically.

After balancing the bottleneck critical resources, the final master production schedule (MPS) is released to detailed production planning for execution.

- **Detailed Production Planning:** Detailed production planning uses MPS as an input and develops a production plan at the daily-level detail. In detailed production planning, all major resources are considered to plan a full production day. Detailed production planning runs weekly (rerun daily for production misses and for minor changes) to plan for the whole week in daily or weekly planning buckets. The output of detailed production planning is shared with the shop floor to schedule production, which drives material release orders to warehouses to draw the material. Detailed production planning is a time- and resource-intensive process; therefore, the focus on detailed production planning is only 2 to 5 weeks planning horizon in daily buckets.

Table 6. Resource capacity example

Sewing capacity (hrs.)	Wk 1	Wk 2	Wk 3	Wk 4	Wk 5	Wk 6	Wk 7	Wk 8	..	M 23	M 24
Available capacity	20k	20k	20k	20k	20k	20k	20k	20k	…	…	…
Required load	20k	19k	19k	22k	21k	19k	21k	22k	…	…	…
Gap		1k	1k	(2k)	(1k)	1k	(1k)	(2k)	…	…	…
Cumulative gap		1k	2k	0	(1k)	0	(1k)	(3k)	…	…	…

Figure 4. Capacity balancing

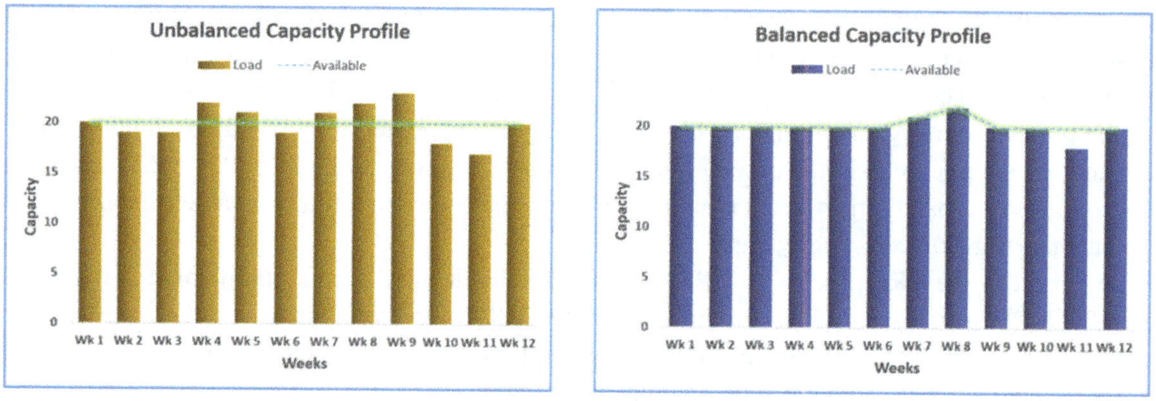

Some smaller companies or companies with simpler manufacturing skip detailed production planning and move to factory scheduling directly. If these companies have a sophisticated system that incorporates the detailed production planning in the CRP, they can execute the process; however, if they are planning manually, they will eventually spend more time in CRP to balance the plan, which makes the process rigid to respond to the market demand.

Using the shoe manufacturer example, the detailed production planning process is illustrated subsequently.

After receiving MPS for a specific shoe, the production planner creates a short-term production plan for 4 to 5 weeks in daily buckets. In detailed production planning, the production planner checks capacities of major factory resources that may constrain the plan including labor resources to run lines.

In Table 7, due to sewing capacity shortage on D2, the production planner can move some of the units to D1 and D3.

Planning Zones and Controls

With the different planning levels, a discussion on planning zones cannot be omitted as the zones drive change types in the capacity plan. The planning organization defines rules for making changes in the plan in a planning zone and establishes governance to manage the zones. A planning horizon can be divided into three planning zones:—frozen, firm, and free—with a varying time horizon for each zone. Three planning zones are tied to the last three levels of capacity planning levels—detailed production planning to frozen zone, master production planning to firm zone, and RCCP with free zone.

Table 7. Detailed capacity example

RS-001XBND	D1	D2	D3	D4	D5	D6	..	D27	D28
Production plan	1,000	1,000	1,000	1,000	1,000	1,000	…	…	…
Sewing requirement	83h	83h	83h	83h	83h	83h	…	…	…
Sewing available	200h	10h	100h	80h	100h	100h			
Assembly hours required	167h	167h	167h	167h	167h	167h	…	…	…
Assembly hours available	200h	100h	200h	200h	200h	200h			

Figure 5: Planning Zones

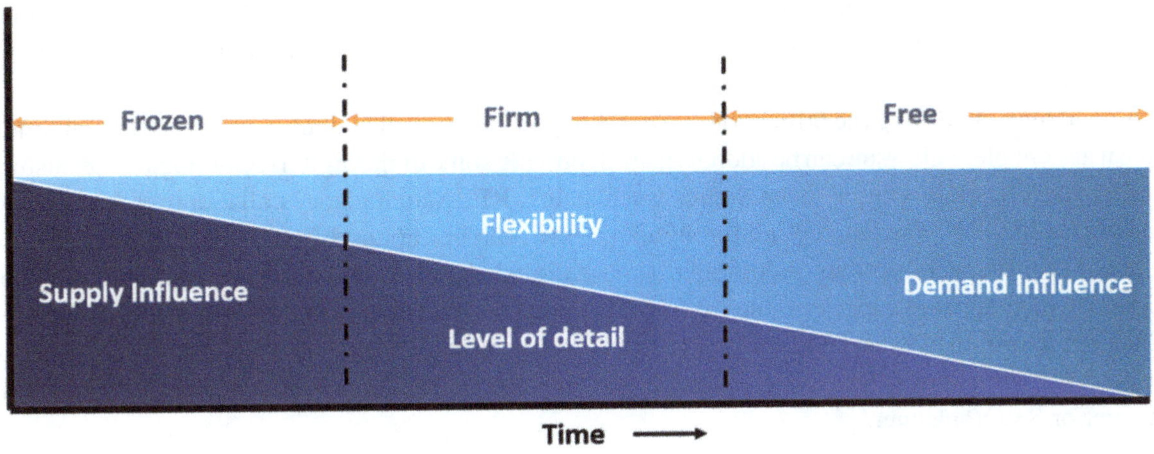

- **Frozen Zone:** Frozen zone, as the name suggests, does not allow too many changes. Production planned in the frozen zone, once committed, mostly remains unchanged with some exceptions with a valid reason and approvals. Frozen production plan in the short term provides the manufacturing stability to commit resources internally and externally. Production planner and production managers control the frozen zone. Any change in a quantity larger than a certain percentage in the frozen zone needs production manager approval.
- **Firm Zone:** Firm zone provides a little flexibility to accommodate a moderate amount of changes because not all sources in the firm zone duration are committed to the production; however, the long lead-time materials are already ordered for the production in the firm zone that restricts large changes without expediting material. Master planners, jointly with production managers and procurement managers, control the firm zone. Tactical demand and supply weekly/bi-weekly meetings with sales and marketing perspective provide guidelines and ensure both manufacturing and customer priorities stay in equilibrium.
- **Free Zone:** Free zone is for long-term planning and visibility. No commitments are made in the free zone and the majority of the changes, within the overall capacity level, can be accommodated. Supply chain leadership controls the free zone and manages through the monthly S&OP process.

In frozen and firm zones, available and committed supply influences the demand (what can be fulfilled based on available resources), while in the free zone, demand influences supply (what supply should be arranged).

Capacity Utilization Tracking and Identifying Resources for Planning

Resources capacity is measured in utilization percentages; the higher the utilization the better the cost efficiencies; however, utilization above 90 percent denotes close to full utilization and inability to accommodate any maintenance downtime or short-term demand changes.

Resource utilization = (Used capacity/Available capacity) * 100

In capacity planning, keeping a history of resource utilization month over month is useful in identifying a trend in resource loading, which can help in identifying resources for RCCP and CRP. Maintaining the history of both high utilization and low utilization is also useful in determining the list of resources for the planning.

A challenge in tracking the utilization is identifying the right level and measuring in near real time to make it actionable. This issue can be addressed by deploying some of the digital technologies and business intelligence (BI) tools. Digital technologies, such as IoT, RFID, and factory collaboration, can provide constant availability of resources and throughput, which can be captured in BI tools and displayed in a dashboard for planners' actions. Additionally, these digital signals can be fed into the planning system to identify the impact of capacity issues in fulfilled demands. To measure at the right level, it is better to collect the data at the lowest level and leverage BI tools to provide planners capabilities to view metrics at different aggregations; for example, at line level for production planner and at plant level for plant manager or S&OP planner.

Implement the Capacity Planning Process

This section provides a high-level capacity planning maturity model for companies to assess their current maturity level and a brief implementation approach for them to move to a higher level. Since the maturity model in this chapter considered only high-level processes, companies will be benefitted by further assessing their maturity within each level on four dimensions—process, system, organization, and delivery model. Detailed maturity model and detailed implementation approach are out of scope for this chapter.

Capacity Planning Process Maturity Model

Most companies, small or large, benefit from performing all five levels of planning as each level has a distinct objective and associated decisions. The following diagram shows the capacity planning maturity model.

Figure 6. Capacity planning maturity model

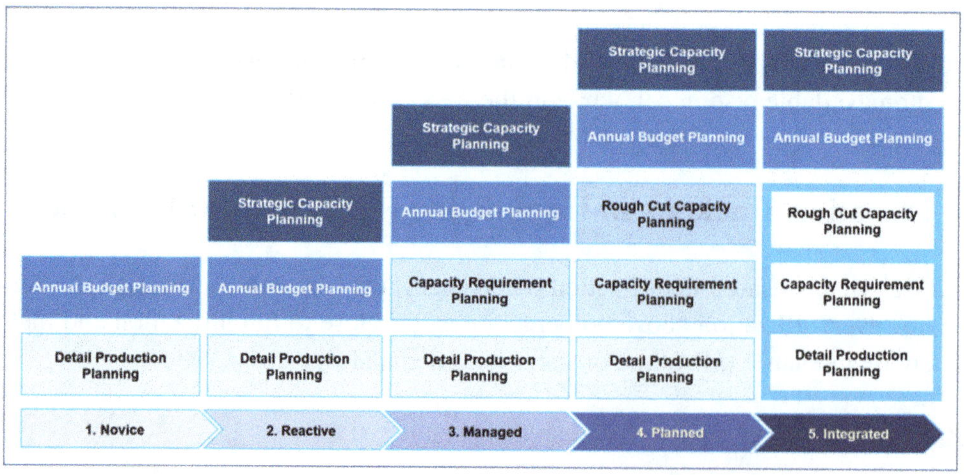

Many job shops or small companies perform only basic capacity planning that focuses on planning for a week's work or plan a job. These companies, which perform only ad hoc capacity planning, will fall at Level 1 or novice maturity.

All medium and large companies are at least at the level-two maturity level, which includes strategic capacity planning, annual budget planning, and detailed production planning because all three processes are part of the basic planning process; however, level of maturity and process efficiency among companies varies widely, which requires a separate discussion. Each subsequent maturity level adds an additional level of capacity planning. At maturity level five, boundaries among the last three levels start disappearing. Additionally, level five requires a sophisticated system that can run RCCP, CRP, and detailed planning in a single model with different aggregation and disaggregation logic catering to the needs of different levels.

Implementation

To implement an effective capacity planning process, the first step is to understand the planning organization's current process maturity level, solution capabilities, and nature of the business. After that, evaluate the current capabilities with the desired capabilities to identify the gaps to fill. Following the gap identification, create a roadmap to bridge the gaps in phases—attain one maturity level and move to another.

As previously discussed, the capacity planning process relies heavily on data—the right process but the incorrect data will lead to a failure; lack of trust in results will cause a relapse into silo processes and broken links in the top-down process. A data assessment prior to implementation will provide insight into data quality and data gaps. For example, assess product, customer, and location hierarchies to understand if hierarchies are consistently maintained across product lines and business units. Additionally, assess if the same hierarchies and hierarchy levels are used across functional areas, such as finance, sales, marketing, demand planning, supply planning, etc. If differences exist, consider harmonizing hierarchies to bring all groups to use one hierarchy.

In large implementations, running a pilot program always pays off down the line. A pilot program allows the implementation team to establish and test the new processes with a business unit and a selected product type to identify the challenges at a smaller, manageable level and resolve them before rolling out the process to the broader organization. After a successful pilot, the organization can begin adding products and regions to the program.

CONCLUSION

While most medium and large companies run some capacity planning process, companies need to give capacity planning processes a holistic view—implementing five levels in the capacity planning process—looking from the strategic level at corporate headquarters to detailed daily-level scheduling at factories while integrating other groups in the levels in between. Additionally, digitalization of the supply chain has bestowed powerful capabilities, such as Artificial Intelligence and Machine Learning in planning tools and control towers enabling organizations to run self-healing processes with reduced human intervention.

Transforming the organization to build a robust capacity planning process is a long journey and the organization can begin the journey by first enabling the fundamental processes to support higher maturity in the future. A five-level capacity planning maturity model assists organizations in setting up those basic processes and helps ensure that a foundation has been established before moving to the next level. A robust multilevel capacity planning process prepares the organization to control the supply chain and respond to uncertainty in the new digital age.

ADDITIONAL READING

APICS. (n.d.). *Rough-Cut capacity planning*. Retrieved from http://apicsforum.com/ebook/capacity_planning

SolventureS.Rough Cut Capacity PlanningO. P. (n.d.). Retrieved from https://www.solventuregroup.com/content/rough-cut-capacity-planning/

Chapter 12
Green Supply Chain Management Practices and Digital Technology:
A Qualitative Study

Michael Sony
Namibia University of Science and Technology, Namibia

ABSTRACT

Modern day organizations have begun to implement the green supply chain management (GSCM) practices in response to demand from various stakeholders which includes customers to create products and services that are environmentally sustainable. The digital technology has been a boon in erstwhile supply chain management practices. However, the impact of digital technology on various dimensions of GSCM practices are not yet studied. This chapter explores the impact of digital technology on green supply chain management practices. A qualitative study is conducted on managers working in organizations using GSCM. The data is analyzed in line with interpretative phenomenology analysis approach. The impact of digital technology is analyzed on the five dimensions of GSCM practices suggested in earlier research. The research propositions are developed, and future research opportunities are identified.

INTRODUCTION

Supply chain management (SCM) needs the integration and coordination of business processes and strategy alignment throughout the supply chain. The main purpose for the need for integration and coordination is satisfying the final customers of the supply chain. Customer satisfaction is the most important success factor for any business to be successful(Green Jr *et al.*, 2012). In order to satisfy the customer, there should be integration and coordination of the business process, in addition to strategic alignment. The components of business processes which should be integrated and aligned, and it includes purchasing, manufacturing, marketing, logistics, and information systems. In terms of strategy, all the components of business processes should be aligned to customer focus, efficiency, quality, and

DOI: 10.4018/978-1-5225-7700-3.ch012

Copyright © 2019, IGI Global. Copying or distributing in print or electronic forms without written permission of IGI Global is prohibited.

responsiveness(Zelbst *et al.*, 2010). Nevertheless, more recently another aspect which has surfaced in addition to the above-discussed factors and it is environmental sustainability (Govindan *et al.*, 2017; Longoni and Cagliano, 2018). Environmental sustainability means a systematic approach that allows economic activities to be bounded by environmental limits(Holland, 2003). In other words, all economic function happens within the boundary of environmental limits. These limits if exceeded will cause a detrimental impact to the future generations. In supply chain perspective, the integration & coordination of business processes should be also be aligned to environmental sustainability in addition to efficiency, quality, and responsiveness. However, the degree of alignment with respect to these factors will, in turn, decide how successful the business will be in future. There are many reasons due to which the organizations will try to integrate the business processes to environmental sustainability. Some of the prominent reasons which were dominant in the past studies were regulation, legislation and cost savings. It was realised that just meeting these environmental regulations is not enough to stay competitive in the business. This has led organizations into pollution prevention and monitoring for effective operations (Famiyeh, Kwarteng, *et al.*, 2018). Green supply chain management (GSCM) is one such initiative in which organizations bring in environmental thinking into their erstwhile supply chain management perspective. The other aspects of SCM like product design, material sourcing, and selection, manufacturing processes, delivery of the final product to the consumers as well as end-of-life management of the product after its useful life (Srivastava, 2007) are also aligned to environmental sustainability. It is done so that all aspects of the supply chain are touched with green initiatives. Supply chain is a series link and all elements should be given equal importance to achieve the objective of GSCM. Now a question arises why should organizations indulge in GSCM? The organizations will adopt GSCM if its adoption will lead to specific financial and operational benefits. Financial benefits in terms of investment recovery and profits. Such initiatives will benefit to the organization. In terms of operations benefit, in addition to operational advantages it also should consider the environmental sustainability. Therefore, it is relevant at this juncture to ask an important question. Does going green really pays of the organizations? The answer to the question is inconclusive as previous research is divided on this matter (King and Lenox, 2001; Rao and Holt, 2005; Zhu and Sarkis, 2006; Stefan and Paul, 2008). It is also questioned in previous studies that adoption of green results in win-win situations for all partners in the supply chain or does it lead to environmental and economical trade-off for specific supply chain partners. It is a relevant point to consider because if adopting GSCM is not beneficial to all elements in the supply chain, then the sustainability of this strategy, in the long run, will be questionable(Wong, Wong and Boon-itt, 2018). Modern day business is far complex and competitive to maintain its position in the market place. The entry barriers are crumbling in the market place as firms from less developed countries are entering the market place. This results into fierce competition. Consequently, the market place is dominated by firms that can introduce new products and services faster and cheaper. The increased capability of digital technologies coupled with the reduction in investment cost allow capital and information flow to any part of the world. The consumers, on the other hand, are becoming even more demanding and discriminating. Therefore, supply chain management (SCM) is recognized as an important area for digital technology innovation and investment. With the advent of fourth industrial revolution the integration of cyber-physical systems within and external to the organization has resulted in immense challenges for the supply chain management(Ivanov *et al.*, 2016; Douaioui, Fri and Mabroukki, 2018).The erstwhile the narrow focus of managers and the confrontational relationships between logistics providers, suppliers, and customers are replaced by broad thinking within the supply chain networks from digitisation to sharing of sensitive information. It results in strategic alliances and long-term cooperative relationships and viewing suppliers and customers as partners instead of adversaries. The SCM infuses thinking of maximizing competitiveness and profitability for the company as well as the whole supply chain network including the end-customer. By adoption of digital technology, there is better information exchange between the partners. It gives up to date information exchange between the partners. Such information exchange results in better decision making opportunity. To cite an instance up to date information leads to more accurate inventory responses to changes in demand and thus more appropriate inventory levels throughout the supply chain. Besides the other benefits of up to date information includes minimizing the bullwhip effect, maximizing the efficiency of conducting activities along the supply chain, minimizing inventories along the supply chain, minimizing cycle times along the supply chain, achieving an acceptable level of quality along the supply chain(Patterson, Grimm and Corsi, 2003; Khan *et al.*, 2018; Tseng *et al.*, 2018). Digital technologies can also improve agility in supply chain to meet the speed of change and the accelerating competition in markets (Brusset, 2016). In a normal supply chain digital technology are used as transaction execution, collaboration and coordination and decision support. Green supply chain practices revolve around the five dimensions. The dimensions are a)Internal Environment Management b) Green purchasing c) Customer cooperation d) Investment recovery e) Eco-design. However, the impact of digital technologies on each Green Supply Chain Management practice dimension is yet to be studied. It is important because such studies will help to clarify how organizations should use digital technologies while implementing GSCM. This chapter is designed to explore the impact of digital technologies on Green Supply Chain management practices. The main research question is to study the impact of digital technology on GSCM practices. Hence, the research question is *how do digital technologies impact GSCM practices especially on Internal Environment Management, Green purchasing, Customer cooperation, Investment recovery and Eco-design*? A qualitative study is envisaged along with literature evidence to build a substantive theory about the use of technology in GSCM practices. The chapter is detailed as follows: First in this chapter background theories are examined. Subsequently the focus of the chapter is explicitly stated. The research aims, objectives and methodology of the study is explicated. The solutions and recommendations are offered. At last the future research and conclusion are expounded.

BACKGROUND THEORY

As per Council of Supply Chain Management Professionals, (2008) the SCM is defined as an integration of planning, analysing, coordinating and scheduling of every activity involved in "sourcing and procurement, conversion and logistics management activities"(Jaggernath and Khan, 2015). It requires an association among resource suppliers, merchants, middlemen, third-party service providers, agents, distributors, and customers. According to the Council of Supply Chain Management Professionals (2008), SCM is the desegregation of "supply and demand management within and across companies" into a cohesive and high-performing business model which encompasses all logistics management activities and manufacturing operations, as well as drives coordination of processes and activities with and across marketing, sales, product design, finance and information technology (Jaggernath and Khan, 2015).Supply chains struggle to keep internal health and environmental sustainability using the capability to self-correct based on information from the external environment. As the demand for products and services that do not damage the environment increases, organizations will make decisions that support the integration and coordination of GSCM practices throughout the supply chain. In addition, to the requirement of meeting the customer demand, those organizations can gain competitive advantage by being the first to adopt environmental sustainability and implement GSCM practices(Green Jr *et al.*, 2012). The twenty first century has seen the integration of Green to erstwhile supply chain management.

GSCM reduces environmental impacts of sourcing, production, and distribution activities along the supply chain. GSCM is becoming an important component of the sustainability of supply chain management. It is thus relevant to examine the definitions of GSCM. GSCM is defined as "*the strategic, transparent integration and achievement of an organization's social, environmental, and economic goals in the systemic coordination of key inter-organizational business processes for improving the long-term economic performance of the individual company and its supply chains*"(Carter and Rogers, 2008). Another comprehensive definition is "*as integrating environmental thinking into supply chain management, including product design, material sourcing, and selection, manufacturing processes, delivery of the final product to the consumers as well as end-of-life management of the product after its useful life*" (Srivastava, 2007). The two definitions transpire the importance of environmental perspectives besides others while designing a supply chain. There has been a lot of study on the importance of environmental issues. Due to increased environmental concerns expressed by various sections of the society the importance of GSCM has increased. The environmental concerns include environmental pollution resulting from production and consumption issues around the world, diminishing raw material resources, overflowing waste sites, and increasing levels of pollution (Srivastava, 2007). Supply chains and organizations can gain a competitive advantage by being the first to adopt environmental sustainability and implement GSCM practices (Sen, 2009). An important framework for classifying GSCM practices is by Zhu and Sarkis (2004) and Zhu et al. (2008).

The GSCM practices are classified into five categories. The five principles of green supply chain practices are a) *Internal Environment Management* - The major components under this dimension include commitment of GSCM from senior managers, support for GSCM from mid-level managers, cross-functional cooperation for environmental improvements, total quality environmental management, Environmental compliance and auditing programs, ISO 14001 certification, Environmental Management Systems etc. b) *Green purchasing* is the second dimension, it includes components like providing design specification to suppliers that include environmental requirements for purchased item, Cooperation with suppliers for environmental objectives, Environmental audit for supplier's internal management, Suppliers' ISO14000 certification, Second-tier supplier environmentally friendly practice evaluation c) *Customer cooperation* is the third component. It includes aspects like Cooperation with customer for eco-design, Cooperation with customers for cleaner production, Cooperation with customers for green packaging, Cooperation with customers for using less energy during product transportation d) *Investment recovery* e.g. Investment recovery (sale) of excess inventories/materials, Sale of scrap and used materials, Sale of excess capital equipment e) *Eco-design* is the fifth dimension, it includes components like design of products for reduced consumption of material/energy, Design of products for reuse, recycle, recovery of material, component parts, Design of products to avoid or reduce use of hazardous of products and/or their manufacturing process (Zhu and Sarkis, 2004; Zhu, Sarkis and Lai, 2008; Famiyeh, Adaku, *et al.*, 2018). Figure 1 depicts the five-principle classification of GSCM practices. These five dimensions substantiates the green practices in important functions in the organization. The broad perspective of GSCM which include both internal and external practices play an important role in greening the supply chain and these five dimensions incorporates this philosophy in totality. In addition, these five GSCM practices are integrative and need cross-functional cooperation rather than oriented towards a single function or department. Internal environmental management is a key to improving enterprises' perfor-

Figure 1.

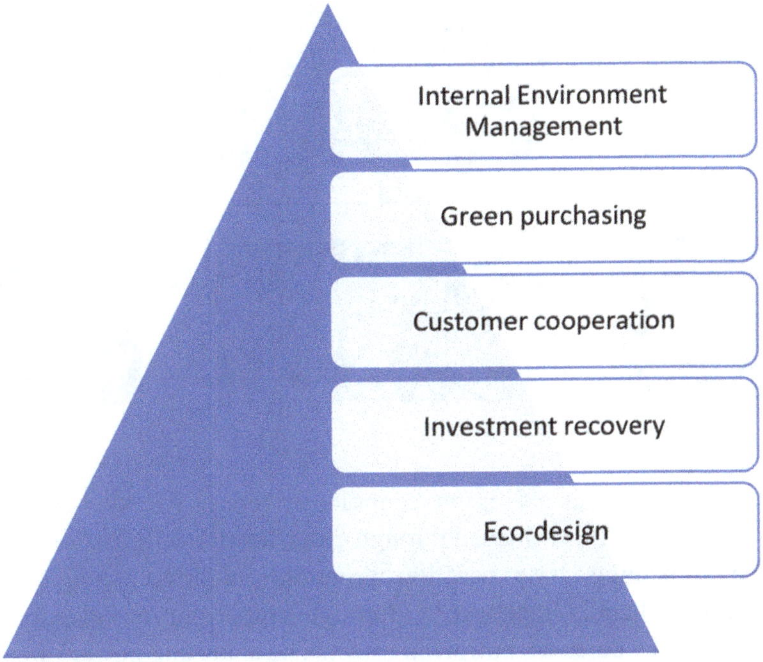

mance and external GSCM relationships and eco-design are important in any organization. Investment recovery is the aim of any investment an organization undertakes. For any greening practices to be successful customer cooperation is of paramount importance. Therefore, five dimensions captures all the important aspects of GSCM practices.

Digital technologies are used in supply chain management for various reasons 1) providing information availability and visibility 2) enabling a single point of contact for data 3) allowing decisions based on total supply chain information; and 4) enabling collaboration with supply chain partners (Auramo, Kauremaa and Tanskanen, 2005). Digital technologies in SCM gives a reduction in cycle time, a reduction of inventories, a minimization of the bullwhip effect, and improvement in the effectiveness of distribution channels (Levary, 2000). The recent advances in information technology, particularly in the e-business arena, are enabling firms to rethink their supply chain strategies and explore new avenues for inter-organizational cooperation. However, an incomplete understanding of the value of information sharing and physical flow coordination hinder these efforts (Sahin and Robinson, 2002; Arunkumar, 2018; Oguz *et al.*, 2018). It is wrong to assume that digital technological resource alone adds value to Supply chain. In fact, managerial skills, which enable adaptations on supply chain processes and corporate strategy to accommodate the use of IT, are shown to play the strongest role in IT value creation(Sindi and Roe, 2017). Furthermore, backend integration and managerial skills are found to be more valuable in more competitive environments. While commodity-like resources have diminishing value under competition, integrational and managerial resources become even stronger(Dong, Xu and Zhu, 2009). Thus, the benefits of digital technologies in SCM are manifold and can vary according to the implementation method. The functional role of digital technologies includes a) transaction execution b) collaboration and coordination c) decision support. Figure 2 depicts the role of IT in SCM.

Figure 2.

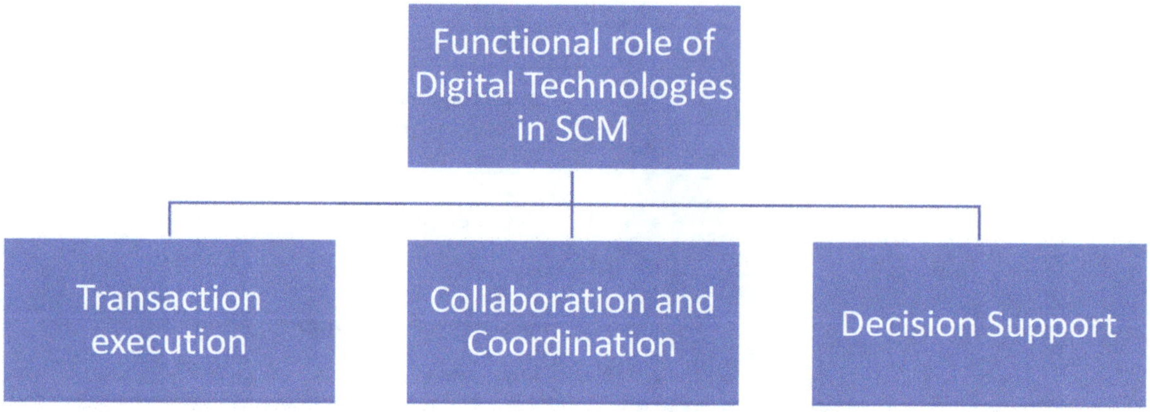

The transaction execution aspects of digital technologies reduce friction between different partners or elements in the supply chain. It is achieved through cost effective information flow with various elements in the supply chain enabling easy transaction execution(Laudon and Laudon, 2015). Collaboration and coordination in supply chain is implemented through supporting role of information sharing. For e.g. information is one the key cures for bull whip effect. The analysing power of computers is used for making better decision making(Auramo, Kauremaa and Tanskanen, 2005; Thoni and Tjoa, 2017; Vanpoucke, Vereecke and Muylle, 2017). The literature review identifies that digital technology is expected to have a pivotal role in managing supply chains, now and in the future(Kochan *et al.*, 2018; Oguz *et al.*, 2018). In fact, it seems that the use of digital technology is crucial, especially in fast-moving industries, and particularly for managing contemporary supply networks(Moreira and Tjahjono, 2016; Kache and Seuring, 2017). Moreover, the close relationship of the two concepts of GSCM and digital technology sometimes makes it hard to assess which one contributes what benefits. Though there are many studies on the impact of digital technologies on the supply chain, there are hardly any studies which studies the relationship of digital technologies on GSCM practices across all elements of the supply chain. It is important to study this relationship as with the advent of fourth industrial revolution, the supply chains are getting smarter(Lee, Bagheri and Kao, 2015; Ivanov *et al.*, 2016). The digitization of supply chain will result in optimization of supply chain networks along various parameters which was unthought of earlier(Ivanov *et al.*, 2016; Douaioui, Fri and Mabroukki, 2018). One of the important parameters which can be optimised in this process due to digitization, is greening all the elements of supply chain(Duarte and Cruz-Machado, 2017). Therefore, this chapter intends to study the impact of digital technology on GSCM practices across the supply chain.

MAIN FOCUS OF THE CHAPTER

Supply chain management is documented as a significant area for digital technology innovation and investment. The erstwhile the narrow focus of managers and the argumentative associations between logistics providers, suppliers, and customers are substituted by supply chain management holistic thinking. This holistic rational has led to strategic alliances and long-term cooperative relationships and viewing suppliers and customers as partners instead of opponents. GSCM brings in environmental sustainability in addition to SCM factors. Thus, GSCM reduces environmental impacts of sourcing, production, and distribution activities along the supply chain. GSCM is basically becoming an important component of the sustainability of supply chain management. In the existing literature the GSCM practices are classified into five categories. a)Internal Environment Management b) Green purchasing c) Customer cooperation d) Investment recovery e) Eco-design(Zhu and Sarkis, 2004; Zhu, Sarkis and Lai, 2008). The digital technologies are used in supply chain management for various reasons 1) providing information availability and visibility 2) enabling a single point of contact for data 3) allowing decisions based on total supply chain information; and 4) enabling collaboration with supply chain partners. The three functional roles digital technologies play in the GSCM are transaction execution, collaboration and coordination and decision support (Auramo, Kauremaa and Tanskanen, 2005). The earlier studies have studied the general impact of IT on SCM, however, there is a lack of study which deals with the impact of Digital technology on GSCM practices. Thus, it is pertinent to analyse the impact of digital technology on GSCM especially a)Internal Environment Management b) Green purchasing c) Customer cooperation d) Investment recovery e) Eco-design. This chapter will thus add to the academic body of knowledge of GSCM, which will clarify whether the impact of digital technologies on Green Supply Chain Management practices. Besides, being a qualitative study, it will enable the further building of knowledge in this area.

Objective

The study was designed to explore the lived experience of managers who are working at Organizations where GSCM are promoted. The primary objective of the study was to explore the impact of digital technology on GSCM practices. This study is intended to add to the knowledge and understanding of this complex phenomenon of the role of digital technology on various aspects of GSCM practices especially on Internal Environment Management, Green purchasing, Customer cooperation, Investment recovery and Eco-design. In this study the Green supply chain management refers to the way in which innovations in supply chain management is considered in the context of the environment leading to impact in Internal Environment Management, Green purchasing, Customer cooperation, Investment recovery and Eco-design. Digital technologies are defined as digital technologies used in supply chain management for providing information availability and visibility, enabling a single point of contact for data, allowing decisions based on total supply chain information, and enabling collaboration with supply chain partners. The functional role of digital technologies in the supply chain includes a) transaction execution b) collaboration and coordination c) decision support

Methodology

The research question directed the researchers to design a study that explored the lived experience of managers working in organizations that promote GSCM. Managers have lived through the experience of implanting GSCM practices in organizations. Hence, elicitation of their experience is a lived-in experience. Therefore, an interpretative (IPA) research approach was used for this study. IPA offers insights into how the participant in a in a given context, make sense out of given phenomenon(Smith and Osborn, 2004; Eatough and Smith, 2017). IPA further recognizes that different people perceive the world in very different ways, dependent on their personalities, prior life experiences and motivations.

The technique also tries to explore/understand/make sense of the subjective meanings of events/experiences/states of the individual participants themselves. In addition, IPA is chosen when the topic under study is novel or under explored, the issues are complex or ambiguous and at last where the focus is on understanding something about the process(Smith and Osborn, 2004). IPA was selected among other qualitative research methods as the study involves both analysing and interpreting the phenomena of GSCM practices in context of digital technologies used within and external to the organizations which was complex phenomenon to study due to various factors involved. In addition, a second reason for choosing the IPA was because it views the analytic outcome as resulting from an interaction between participant's accounts and the researcher's frameworks of meaning which will help better understanding of this complex phenomenon of the impact of Digital Technology on GSCM practices.

Selection of Participants

IPA warrants the use of purposive sampling. The participants were recruited through a personal contact using the snowballing method(Larkin and Thompson, 2012). The potential participants were first approached for a casual discussion and the nature of the research with its agenda was explicitly expressed. The main criterion for participant's inclusion was participants themselves describing them to be working in the Organization where GSCM is practiced. Besides they should be willing to talk in depth about their experiences with working with GSCM practices. The samples in IPA(interpretative phenomenological analysis) studies are generally small. This enables a detailed and very time-consuming case-by-case analysis. Besides, there are studies conducted using IPA, for example, one, four, nine and fifteen. Though the large sample size is possible but is less common (Pietkiewicz and Smith, 2014; Sony, Mekoth and Therisa, 2018). In this study we wanted an in-depth analysis, hence we choose a sample size for 9. Nine participants took part in this study through a telephonic interview: 4 females and 5 male participants with an age range from 24 to 48. Participants' mean age was 38.9 years (SD 5.2). The managers had qualification graduate and above. During the interviews, in order to remove this bias, the first author attempted as far as possible to remain led by the participant. So that to avoid imposing his own beliefs and ideas on the interview process. This included encouraging the participants in the study to explicate the concepts in detail that seemed clear from the viewpoint of the first author to ensure that assumptions were not being made. A number of studies have advocated this methodology(Cassar and Shinebourne, 2012; Sony and Mekoth, 2014; Sony, Mekoth and Therisa, 2018).

Interviews

The IPA methodology provides flexible guidelines to be adopted by researchers as per the aims of the research(Larkin and Thompson, 2012). Semi-structured interviews were conducted by the first author telephonically as per the convenient time and date decided by the managers. Mostly, the telephonic interviews were conducted on the weekends as per the convenience of the managers. Usually, on weekends, they are free and uninterrupted telephonic interviews are possible without any hindrances. Primarily questions focused on the experiences of the participants as regards to the use of digital technologies in GSCM practices. In order to bring in structure to the interview the five categories of GSCM were used as a guidepost. The five categories included Internal Environment Management, Green purchasing, Customer cooperation, Investment recovery and Eco-design. The sample questions were *What digital technologies for managing GSCM in your organization? How does this digital technology improve your*

GSCM? How do you think the digital technology used in your organization improve the internal environment management?...... In addition, the participants were asked the demographical questions first to make them comfortable. To enable analysis, the interviews were tape recorded using the record feature on the phone. This was deliberately done so as to bring in structure to the interview process (Creswell and Miller, 2000). Likewise, such a strategy will bring in focus from the diffused thinking. As the managers were apprehensive about tape recording, they were assured that the participant nor their organization would be identified, and excerpts of this interview would be used to make a theoretical contribution. The participants were given Pseudo names to enable anonymity of respondents. Subsequently, on a next convenient date given by the participants were telephoned again and transcripts were read to them to make the data more credible and trustworthy(Corbin and Strauss, 2008).

Plan of Data Analysis

Computer assisted data analysis software packages were not used because of the a) The software was costly and this was not a funded project b) Coding and retrieval of data using the software is criticized by some for fragmenting it in such a way that the narrative and context is lost(Spencer, Ritchie, & O'Connor, 2003) c) The coding and automatic retrieval of coded fragments according to categories makes quantification of the data possible, which may present the temptation of shifting to a quantitative approach(Mikheenkova, 2011). We used Microsoft Excel(Meyer & Avery, 2009), for managing the meaning units from the transcripts with appropriate line number from the interviews. These concepts helped us to further link, these meaning units into themes and master themes. The memo for the meaning units, themes and master themes was done using the add comment feature of MS excel. In order to create visual networks for better analysis, shapes feature of Excel was used. The analysis of the data was conducted in several stages. In the first stage written description and the transcript of the first participant were read many times to become immersed in the data and to get theoretical sensitivity. Care was taken during reading to take notes or comments which appear significant or interesting were recorded in the transcript. In the second stage, the written description and transcript transformed into initial notes were classified into emerging themes or concepts. However, care was taken not to lose the connection between the participant's own words and the researcher's interpretations. The third stage consisted of examining the emerging themes during the second phase and trying to cluster them together based on the conceptual similarities. The emerging clusters were given a descriptive label which was selectively chosen to convey the conceptual nature of the themes for each cluster. The written description and the transcript were checked to ensure that the connection with what the participant has said was maintained as the clusters of themes starts emerging. In the final stage, a tabulation of themes was undertaken.

SOLUTIONS AND RECOMMENDATIONS

The analysis of transcripts revealed that themes on the impact of digital technology were revolving around five principle dimensions of Green practices.

Digital Technology and Internal Environment Management

Internal environment management is related to the organization is a factor internally related to the organization. The managers were of the view that digital technology can be used successfully for practices of GSCM related to internal environment Management. The excerpts from the interview were:

I feel digital technology can be used to implement the environmental management system of the company. It will help a lot with data collection and analysis. While implementing environmental management systems we need to play with a large amount of data. Hence digital technologies can be a boon. Besides, the drudgery of data collection will be eliminated totally, leaving one time for doing something worthwhile. To conclude I feel that digital technologies should be implemented within the companies while using quality management practises in environmental management

Digital technologies can be used effectively in total quality environmental management systems. The information technology plays a major role in implementation of total quality environmental management system (Borri and Boccaletti, 1995). Thus, it is proposed that

Proposition 1: Digital technology will be beneficial to manage the Internal Environment Management within the organization particularly while implementing total quality environmental management systems.

Digital technologies will also play a major role in environmental compliance and auditing programs. Data is the primary requirement for environmental compliance /auditing programs and Environmental Management Systems. With the development in IT and data analytics, a large amount of real-time data is at the disposal of organizations(McAfee *et al.*, 2012). Therefore, digital technology will play a major in the environmental compliance and auditing programs. Thus, it is proposed that

Proposition 2: Digital technology will be beneficial to manage the Internal Environment within the organization especially during environmental compliance and auditing programs

In a seminal paper, it was found using systems model that properties such as 'emergence', 'hierarchy', 'communication' and 'control' can help top managers with process thinking. Such a thinking will make them feel more confident about committing to any change (Mackness, 1991). The implied argument from this study is that unless defensible statements can be made about all four properties described above, commitment from top management cannot be assumed to exist. In order to get defensible statements, top management needs data in the real-time which will help in the process of emergence, hierarchy, communication, and control. Thus, digital technologies will help the top management to get real time data and it can ensure top management commitment. One of the managers during the interview also suggested,

You get support from the top if your actions are supported by facts and figures, not some whimsical thinking. If you say that going green will improve customer satisfaction, the top management will ask you the basis by which you are making this statement. I have seen that management always supports initiatives which are based on facts or data.

The previous research and interview when analysed in together makes one hypothesize that

Proposition 3: Digital technologies will result in a large amount of real-time data; which will enable the top management to support or contradict the GSCM practices using facts-based analogy.

It is therefore recommended that digital technologies related to data acquisition, data dissemination will help to manage the internal environment of the organization. The organization before implementing an environmental management system should critically analyse the type of digital technology one would use in acquiring, processing and transmitting information. Figure 3 depicts the positive impact of digital technology on internal environment.

Digital Technology and Green Purchasing

Green Purchasing denotes the procurement of products and services that have a lesser or reduced effect on human health and the environment compared with rival products or services that attend the same purpose. Green purchasing involves providing design specification to suppliers which also include environmental requirements for purchased item, cooperation with suppliers for environmental objectives, environmental audit for supplier's internal management, suppliers' ISO14000 certification, second-tier supplier environmentally friendly practice evaluation (Zhu, Sarkis and Lai, 2008). In this research, the managers expressed explicitly that digital technologies will play a major role in implementing GSCM practice of Green Purchasing.

Digital technologies impact the green purchase decisions. In any transaction, an organization undertakes information exchange is a significant feature. Especially in Green purchasing the information is required on specifications which are related to environment etc. Besides, information on existing environmental practices in supplier's companies will be beneficial to make purchase decisions. Hence I feel digital technology will be a huge success in green purchasing

Figure 3.

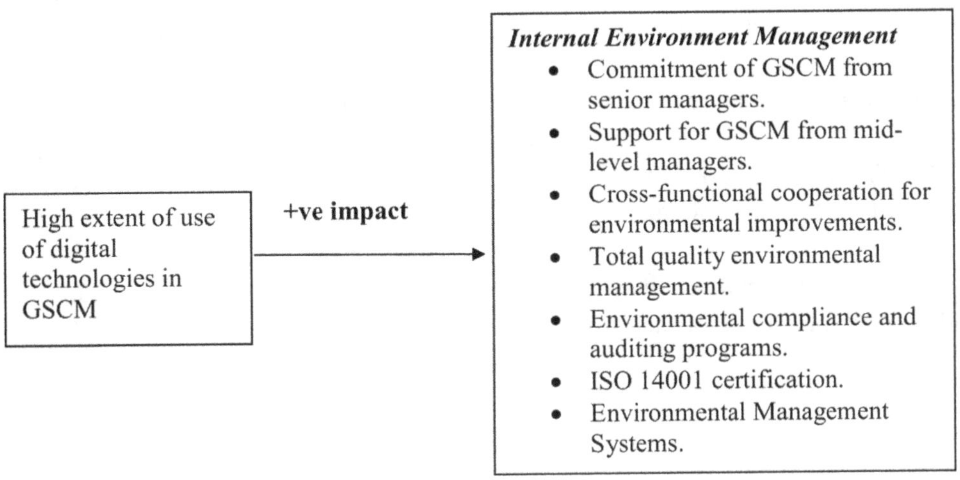

Green consciousness plays a foremost role for green purchase decisions. For developing green consciousness information related to environmental concerns helps in developing green consciousness (Lafuente and Sánchez, 2010). It is seen from previous studies that green consciousness in companies results in green purchase decisions (Min and Galle, 2001). Digital technologies will help in information acquisition, processing, and dissemination. Companies using digital technology will be better placed to implement GSCM practices related to green purchasing.

Proposition 4: Digital technologies will enable companies in information acquisition, processing, and dissemination to successfully implement green purchasing.

In modern-day businesses, firms cannot ignore environmental issues. There is increasing government regulation and stronger public mandates for environmental accountability. It has brought these issues into the executive's minds, and also strategic planning agendas. Also, the companies are integrating their supply chain processes to lower costs and better serve customers. These two trends are not independent; companies must involve suppliers and purchasers to meet and even exceed the environmental expectations of their customers and their governments (Walton, Handfield and Melnyk, 1998). Digital technologies will play a major role to integrate suppliers in the supply chain process to serve the customers.

Proposition 5: Digital technologies with high information acquisition, processing, and dissemination capabilities will empower companies to involve suppliers and purchasers to meet and even exceed the environmental expectations of their customers and their governments.

Gradually, purchasing managers are being asked to integrate environmental issues in their decisions in addition to strategic functions. Introducing the environmental dimension into purchasing decisions results in a new set of trade-offs in the decision, complicating the decision-making process with both qualitative and quantitative factors (Handfield *et al.*, 2002). One of most common criterion considered for green supplier selection was "environmental management systems"(Govindan *et al.*, 2015). In the implementation of the environmental management system, digital technologies play a major role. Hence it is important to consider the usage of digital technologies for the GSCM practice of supplier selection.

Proposition 6: Digital technologies with high information acquisition, processing, dissemination, and intelligent decision-making models will help in the Green supplier selection.

Technology plays a pivotal role in the implementation of ISO 14000. Environmental quality management systems like ISO 14000 plays a major role in green purchasing behaviour. The supplier information of ISO 14000 will be greatly impacted by digital technologies(Chen, 2005). Hence using digital technologies, the ISO 14000 implementation will be easier.

Proposition 7: Digital technology with high information acquisition, processing, and dissemination capabilities will play a major factor in the implementation of ISO 14000 at supplier side.

It is recommended that digital technologies should be used by organizations in green purchase decisions. These technologies will help first in creating an environmental consciousness within the organizations thus resulting in green purchase decisions. It can also help to integrate various elements across the GSCM. Besides, digital technology can be used as an aid for green supplier choice. Such technology will aid in convincing suppliers with realistic data to implement quality management systems like ISO 14000. Figure 4 depicts the positive impact of digital technology on green purchasing.

Digital Technology and Customer Cooperation

The customer is an important element in any business venture. In order for a business to be successful customers need to co-operate. The customer cooperation in terms of eco-design, cooperation with customers for cleaner production, cooperation with customers for green packaging, cooperation with customers for using less energy during product transportation etc. Large customers exert pressure on the companies which result in green practices among various elements in the supply chain. In this research, one of the managers remarked.

Green practices will be implemented in the supply chain if the customer demands it. You can see an immediate change if customers demand products which are environment friendly. In any thing we do throughout the supply chain the customer cooperation is very important. If we tell other elements to implement green practices they will not do it. However, if customer request you can see the change happening fast

Eco-friendly design brings in many advantages and disadvantages like increased cost. In order for such a design to be successful customer, cooperation is the key element (Jin Gam, 2011). The green practices will be successful across the supply chain if customer cooperates. Using digital technology will result in great information exchange between customer and other elements in the supply chain leading to greater cooperation.

Figure 4.

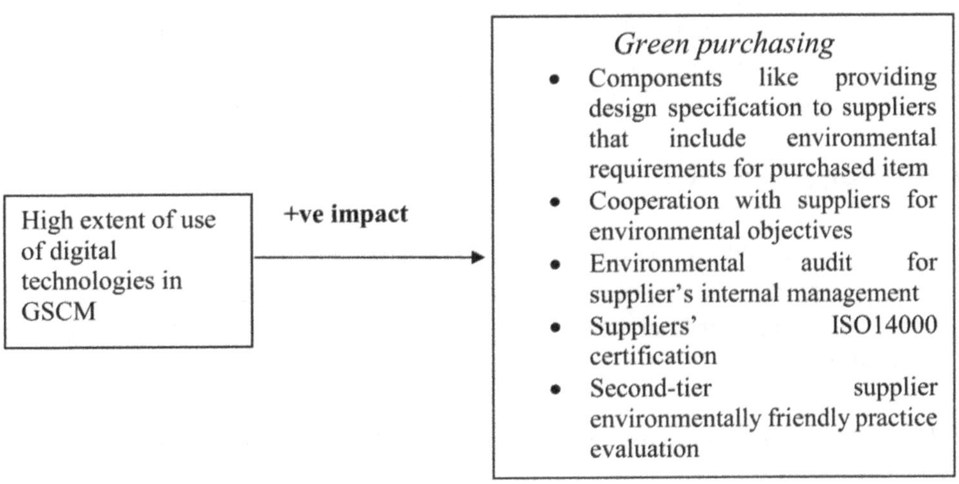

Proposition 8: Digital technology will enable information exchange for customer cooperation while using eco-friendly design in the supply chain.

Cleaner production is a preventive strategy which results in a company-specific environmental protection initiative. The purpose is to minimize waste and emissions and maximize product output. Cleaner production is a strategy to prevent emissions at the source and to start a continuous preventive improvement of environmental performance of organizations. In terms of Cleaner production, the focus of management should be on prevention rather than on cure in avoiding environmental problems (Fresner, 1998). Such a phenomenon should be recognised and valued by the customer. Digital technologies will play a major role in this regard.

Proposition 9: Digital technology with high information acquisition, processing, dissemination, and intelligent decision-making models will permit information exchange for customer cooperation for cleaner production strategies in the supply chain

A consumer environmental choice is studied by analysing the relative importance of green packaging when compared with other relevant product attributes (Rokka and Uusitalo, 2008). Green package can also be called " *ecological package*" or "environmental friendly package", is defined as environmental friendly package, which is completely made by natural plants, can be circle or second use, be prone to degradation and promote sustainable development, even during its whole lifecycle, it is hurtless to environment as well as to human body and livestock's health. In short, green packaging is the proper packaging that can be reused, recycled or degradation, corruption and does not cause pollution in humans and the environment during the product life cycle (Zhang and Zhao, 2012). For a firm to indulge in green packaging customer cooperation is most important. In order for this to happen, the customer should be aware of this packing strategy and how it might benefit the environment. Digital technologies will help to disseminate the information in the real-time with the customers resulting in better cooperation.

Proposition 10: Digital technology with high information acquisition, processing, dissemination, and intelligent decision-making models for better customer cooperation for green packing.

It is recommended that digital technologies can help in customer cooperation. The increased contact level a customer has through the digital medium can make them cooperate. The increased cooperation can result in eco-design, cleaner production or convincing the customer for green packaging. Figure 5 depicts the positive impact of digital technology on customer cooperation.

Digital Technology and Investment Recovery

Digital technology can be used for green supply chain management for Investment recovery e.g. Investment recovery with respect to the sale of excess inventories/materials, Sale of scrap and used materials, Sale of excess capital equipment is mostly used in organizations. However, during the interviews, the managers expressed that

Using digital technologies may help to identify excess inventory. Usually, inventory should be mapped across the supply chain. It is difficult to pin point inventory at each level. Technology will help to map

Figure 5.

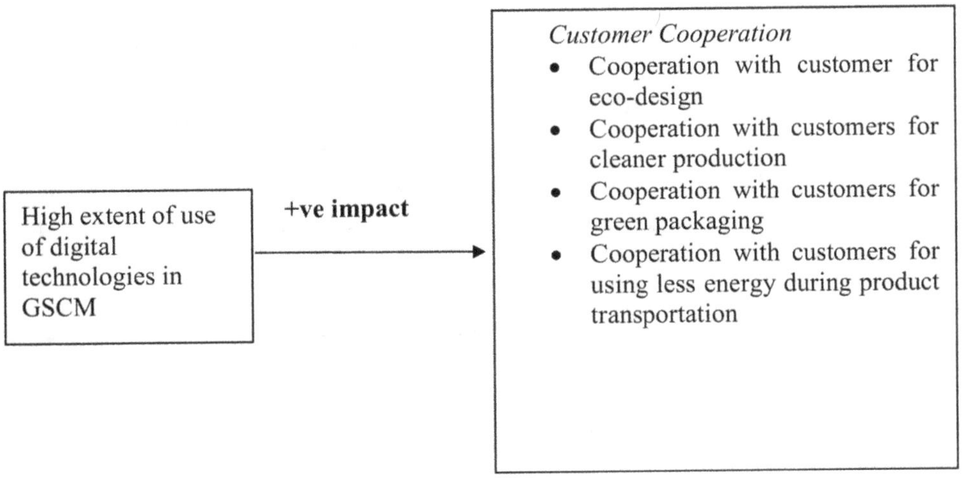

the inventories across all the levels in a supply chain. Our main motto is to reduce inventory across the supply chain. Sometimes it is difficult to point out where the inventory lies. Using technology one can map it easily.

In traditional supply chain inventory management, orders are the only information firms exchange, but digital technology now allows firms to share demand and inventory data quickly and inexpensively(Cachon and Fisher, 2000). In a GSCM environmental impact are also shared between various elements in a supply chain. Digital technology will help in data sharing across various elements in the supply chain for better inventory management across the supply chain.

Proposition 11: Digital technology which with capability to allows firms to share demand and inventory data quickly and inexpensively will help in better inventory management leading to reduction in inventory cost in the Green supply chain.

Digital technologies will help to locate the scrap or reject or used materials and inventory them across the supply chain. Such an inventory database across the supply chain will enable green initiatives like recycle, reuse etc. Also, it will help in selling the excess raw materials. Hence, it is proposed

Proposition 12: Digital technology will help to record the scrap, reject or used material across the supply chain, thereby enabling ease in using green initiatives for its disposal.

Thus, it is proposed that using digital technology will help to implement GSCM practice which are related to investment recovery. The organizations can make use of technology for mapping the inventories across the supply chain. Technologies like Radio frequency identification or Global positioning system can be integrated in the existing software's to create a visual flow of materials and inventories across the supply chain. Figure 6 depicts the positive impact of digital technology on internal environment. Figure 6 depicts the positive impact of digital technology on investment recovery.

Figure 6.

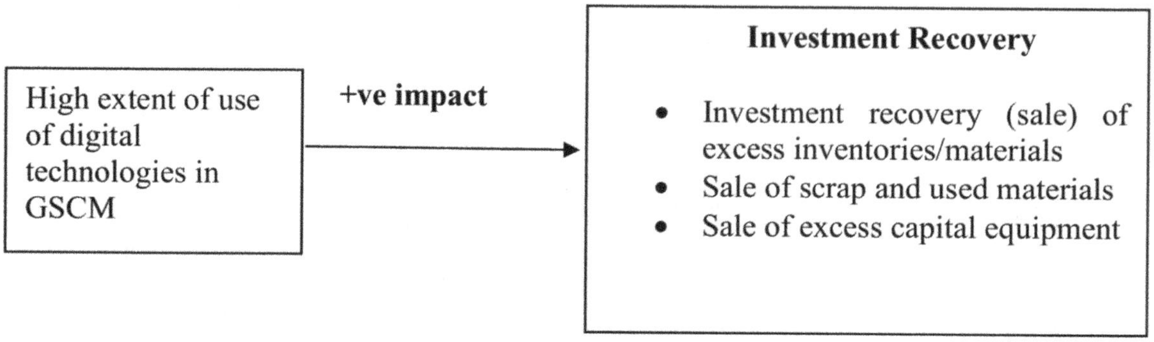

Digital Technology and Eco-Design

Digital technologies will help in Eco-design of products and processes across the supply chain. Products consume material during the design stage. Energy is consumed both during the design and operation stage. Hence, it is relevant to reduce the consumption of energy and material during the design and operation stage which in turn will help in the green initiative. Technology will help in better auditing of materials balance. Judicious use of materials will help in the green initiatives across the supply chain (Kenney, 2012). Energy balance is one of the most important aspects while designing and manufacturing a product. Digital technologies will help in energy monitoring across various stages and thereby help in energy balance. During the interview one of the managers have proposed that,

It is difficult to convince all the members across the supply chain about the dangers of using a particular material or process. But, if someone takes an action by not using it, then other members question why you are not using this cheap material and so on. One way you can solve this issue is by giving them data on the dangers of the materials or process. So, if you use technology it will help in making the other members understand the importance of not using the materials. Besides, it will also help in locating a use of dangerous material and other members can try to influence the using member from not using it

Thus, it is proposed as:

Proposition 13: Digital technology with high information acquisition, processing, dissemination capabilities as regards to material, energy, and other parameters during design and operation stage which will help in judicious use of material and energy to design eco-friendly products.

Digital technologies will help in the design of products for reuse, recycle, recovery of material, component parts. Digital technologies will also help in mapping the materials for its reuse, recycle, recovery of material and component parts. In addition to mapping, it will also help to share information in specifications, type, function etc. Thus, it is proposed that

Proposition 14: Digital technology with high information acquisition, processing, dissemination capabilities will help in reuse, recycle, recovery of material, component parts across the supply chain.

While implementing green initiatives it is important to design products which avoid or reduce the use of hazardous materials and/or their manufacturing process. During the design process, it is important that the required information is available to the designers across the supply chain about the hazardousness of products at various stages of design and manufacture. Thus, it is proposed that,

Proposition 15: Digital technology will help in the reduction or elimination use of hazardous materials and /or manufacturing process by creating awareness across all the elements of the supply chain. Figure 7 depicts the positive impact of digital technology on Eco-design.

FUTURE RESEARCH DIRECTIONS

This chapter has proposed that digital technology will be useful while implementing GSCM practices related to Internal Environment Management. Future studies can explore in detail how technology can be used to implement total quality environmental management systems. Case studies may be conducted to study the critical success factors for implementation of total quality environmental management systems using the aid of technology. Studies may also explore the impact digital technology may have on the impact of on environmental compliance and auditing programs. The impact may also be classified into internal and external audits for better understanding the effects of technology. Future studies may also discover the impact of digital data and top management to support GSCM practices. Qualitative studies may study how large data sets will help the top management in the fact-based support for GSCM practices.

Another research areas would be to study in detail the impact of digital technologies on green purchasing. Technology as an antecedent to green purchasing may be studied in detail to explore the mediation and moderating variables. A qualitative research will be suitable as there is a need to develop a process model. The research can further diversify into studying how technology may help supplier coordination and co-operation. Further studies can also explore how technology can affect green supplier choice. Choosing a green supplier who meets the needs of the organization is a cumbersome task. Digitization's results in vendor or supplier management within the organizations in an intelligent manner. Future research offers a huge opportunity in this regard. Customer cooperation for green practices

Figure 7.

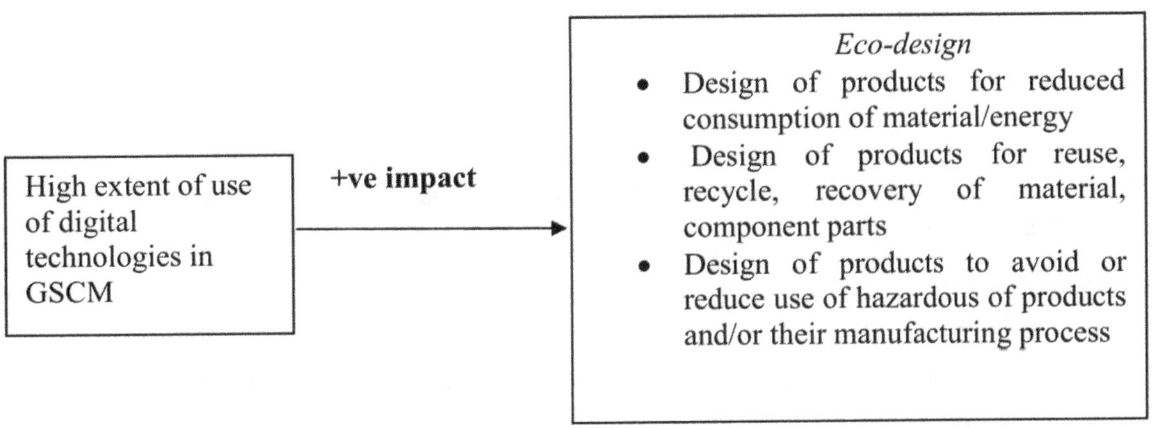

is particularly important. Technology can play a major part in seeking customer cooperation. Research may be conducted on the impact of digital technology on GSCM practices related to customer cooperation. Customer cooperation is a multidimensional concept. Customer cooperation may be studied in terms of eco-design, clean production, and green packaging. The extent of digitization and the impact of customer cooperation in the above areas will be an interesting area to explore.Recovery of investment is important for any GSCM practices. Technology can act as a boon for the investment recovery. There is a need for studies on how digital technologies will help in inventory management. Quantitative and Qualitative studies may be conducted in this regard as this area needs further studies for understanding the benefits in terms of investment recovery for GSCM practices. Eco-design is one of the most widely GSCM practices. Technology can be a boon in this regard. Thus, it is proposed that future studies may explore the specific impact of technology on judicious use of material and energy to design eco-friendly products. Besides studies may be also be directed at reuse, recycle, recovery of material, component parts across the supply chain. Similarly, one of the important aspects of GSCM is the reduction or elimination use of hazardous materials and /or manufacturing process by creating awareness across all the elements of the supply chain. Qualitative studies may be conducted in this area to enlarge our spectrum of understanding on the reduction of use of the hazardous element in terms environment.

CONCLUSION

This chapter discussed the impact of green supply chain management practices and the digital technology. The impact of digital technology was critically analysed first using the extant literature on all the five dimensions of green supply chain management practices. The five dimensions proposed by Zhou et al (2008) are a) Internal Environment Management b) Green purchasing c) Customer cooperation d) Investment recovery e) Eco-design. Simultaneously the data of qualitative study was analysed in detail with the procedures of qualitative analysis to substantiate the viewpoints in the literature. The qualitative study was conducted on managers working in organizations where green supply chain management was undertaken. A snowball sampling methodology was used to locate the participants and data was analysed in line interpretative phenomenology approach. Around 15 research propositions were developed as a guide for future researchers. Future research directions are given so guidance of researchers. Since the study was conducted in Africa, cultural variables may have influenced the respondent's responses. A similar study in a different context will help to clarify the impact.

REFERENCES

Auramo, J., Kauremaa, J., & Tanskanen, K. (2005). Benefits of IT in supply chain management: An explorative study of progressive companies. *International Journal of Physical Distribution & Logistics Management*, *35*(2), 82–100.

Borri, F., & Boccaletti, G. (1995). From total quality management to total quality environmental management. *The TQM Magazine*, *7*(5), 38–42.

Brusset, X. (2016). Does supply chain visibility enhance agility? *International Journal of Production Economics. Elsevier*, *171*, 46–59. doi:10.1016/j.ijpe.2015.10.005

Carter, C. R., & Rogers, D. S. (2008). A framework of sustainable supply chain management: Moving toward new theory. *International Journal of Physical Distribution & Logistics Management, 38*(5), 360–387.

Cassar, S., & Shinebourne, P. (2012). What does spirituality mean to you? An Interpretative Phenomenological Analysis of the experience of spirituality. *Existential Analysis, 23*(1), 133–149.

Corbin, J., & Strauss, A. (2008) Basics of Qualitative Research: Techniques and Procedures for Developing Grounded Theory (3rd ed.). SAGE Publications, Inc. doi:10.4135/9781452230153

Dong, S., Xu, S. X., & Zhu, K. X. (2009). Research note—information technology in supply chains: The value of it-enabled resources under competition. *Information Systems Research, 20*(1), 18–32.

Famiyeh, S. (2018). Green supply chain management initiatives and operational competitive performance. *Benchmarking: An International Journal, 25*(2), 607–631.

Govindan, K. (2017). Eco-efficiency based green supply chain management: Current status and opportunities. *European Journal of Operational Research, 10*, 57.

Govindan, K., Rajendran, S., Sarkis, J., & Murugesan, P. (2015). Multi criteria decision making approaches for green supplier evaluation and selection: A literature review. *Journal of Cleaner Production. Elsevier, 98*, 66–83. doi:10.1016/j.jclepro.2013.06.046

Green, K. W. Jr. (2012). Green supply chain management practices: impact on performance. *Supply Chain Management: An International Journal, 17*(3), 290–305.

Handfield, R. (2002). Applying environmental criteria to supplier assessment: A study in the application of the Analytical Hierarchy Process. *European Journal of Operational Research, 141*(1), 70–87.

Holland, L. (2003). Can the principle of the ecological footprint be applied to measure the environmental sustainability of business? *Corporate Social Responsibility and Environmental Management, 10*(4), 224–232.

King, A. A., & Lenox, M. J. (2001). Does it really pay to be green? An empirical study of firm environmental and financial performance: An empirical study of firm environmental and financial performance. *Journal of Industrial Ecology, 5*(1), 105–116.

Lafuente, R., & Sánchez, M. J. (2010). Defining and measuring environmental consciousness. *Revista Internacional de Sociologia, 68*(3), 731–755. doi:10.3989/ris.2008.11.03

Larkin, M., & Thompson, A. (2012). Interpretative phenomenological analysis. In Qualitative research methods in mental health and psychotherapy: A guide for students and practitioners. John Wiley & Sons.

Levary, R. R. (2000). Better supply chains through information technology. *Industrial Management, 42*(3), 24.

Mackness, J. (1991). Top Management Commitment? In *Achieving Competitive Edge Getting Ahead Through Technology and People* (pp. 167–171). Springer. doi:10.1007/978-1-4471-1904-3_28

McAfee, A. (2012). Big data: The management revolution. *Harvard Business Review, 90*(10), 60–68. PMID:23074865

Min, H., & Galle, W. P. (2001). Green purchasing practices of US firms. *International Journal of Operations & Production Management, 21*(9), 1222–1238.

Patterson, K. A., Grimm, C. M., & Corsi, T. M. (2003). Adopting new technologies for supply chain management. *Transportation Research Part E. Logistics and Transportation Review, 39*(2), 95–121. doi:10.1016/S1366-5545(02)00041-8

Pietkiewicz, I., & Smith, J. A. (2014). A practical guide to using interpretative phenomenological analysis in qualitative research psychology. *Psychological Journal, 20*(1), 7–14.

Rao, P., & Holt, D. (2005). Do green supply chains lead to competitiveness and economic performance? *International Journal of Operations & Production Management, 25*(9), 898–916.

Sahin, F., & Robinson, E. P. (2002). Flow coordination and information sharing in supply chains: Review, implications, and directions for future research. *Decision Sciences, 33*(4), 505–536.

Sen, S. (2009). Linking Green Supply Chain Management and Shareholder Value Creation. *IUP Journal of Supply Chain Management*, 6.

Sony, M., & Mekoth, N. (2014). The dimensions of frontline employee adaptability in power sector: A grounded theory approach. *International Journal of Energy Sector*. Available at: http://www.emeraldinsight.com/doi/abs/10.1108/IJESM-03-2013-0008

Sony, M., Mekoth, N., & Therisa, K. K. (2018). Understanding nature of empathy through the lens of service encounter: A phenomenological study on FLE's. *International Journal of Productivity and Quality Management, 23*(1), 55–73.

Srivastava, S. K. (2007). Green supply-chain management: A state-of-the-art literature review. *International Journal of Management Reviews, 9*(1), 53–80.

Stefan, A., & Paul, L. (2008). Does it pay to be green? A systematic overview. *Academy of Management Journal, 22*(4), 45–62.

Walton, S. V., Handfield, R. B., & Melnyk, S. A. (1998). The green supply chain: Integrating suppliers into environmental management processes. *Journal of Supply Chain Management, 34*(1), 2–11.

Zelbst, P. J. (2010). Relationships among market orientation, JIT, TQM, and agility. *Industrial Management & Data Systems, 110*(5), 637–658.

Zhu, Q., & Sarkis, J. (2004). Relationships between operational practices and performance among early adopters of green supply chain management practices in Chinese manufacturing enterprises. *Journal of Operations Management, 22*(3), 265–289.

Zhu, Q., & Sarkis, J. (2006). An inter-sectoral comparison of green supply chain management in China: drivers and practices. *Journal of Cleaner Production, 14*(5), 472–486.

Zhu, Q., Sarkis, J., & Lai, K. (2008). Green supply chain management implications for "closing the loop". *Transportation Research Part E. Logistics and Transportation Review, 44*(1), 1–18. doi:10.1016/j.tre.2006.06.003

ADDITIONAL READING

Bag, S., Anand, N., & Pandey, K. K. (2017). Green Supply Chain Management Model for Sustainable Manufacturing Practices. In Green Supply Chain Management for Sustainable Business Practice (pp. 153-189). IGI Global.

Green, K. W. Jr, Zelbst, P. J., Meacham, J., & Bhadauria, V. S. (2012). Green supply chain management practices: Impact on performance. *Supply Chain Management*, *17*(3), 290–305. doi:10.1108/13598541211227126

Sarkis, J., Zhu, Q., & Lai, K. H. (2011). An organizational theoretic review of green supply chain management literature. *International Journal of Production Economics*, *130*(1), 1–15. doi:10.1016/j.ijpe.2010.11.010

Zhu, Q., Sarkis, J., & Lai, K. H. (2012). Examining the effects of green supply chain management practices and their mediations on performance improvements. *International Journal of Production Research*, *50*(5), 1377–1394. doi:10.1080/00207543.2011.571937

KEY TERMS AND DEFINITIONS

Customer Cooperation: Is the customer cooperation for the green supply chain management initiatives. It is process perspective, which concerns types of customer relationships that occur in green supply chain management. Customer pressure is a primary driver for enterprises to improve their environmental image and practices.

Digital Technology: The branch of scientific or engineering knowledge that deals with the creation and practical use of digital or computerized devices, methods, systems, etc.

Eco-Design: Is ecologically friendly design of products. RCO-design or design for environment (DfE) is an important and emerging GSCM practice to improve companies.

Environmental Sustainability: Means a systematic approach that allows economic activities to be bounded by environmental limits.

Green Purchasing: Green purchasing practice focuses on the inbound or upstream segment of a product's and organization's supply chain. It includes environmental requirements for purchased items, cooperation with suppliers for environmental objectives, environmental audits for supplier's internal management, and suppliers ISO14001 certification.

Green Supply Chain Management: The strategic, transparent integration and achievement of an organization's social, environmental, and economic goals in the systemic coordination of key interorganizational business processes for improving the long-term economic performance of the individual company and its supply chains.

Internal Environmental Management: Is defined as improving organizational environmental performance. Top management support is necessary of improving environmental performance.

Interpretative Phenomenological Analysis: (IPA): Is a method of qualitative research with an idiographic focus. The main aim is to give insights into how a given person, in a given context, makes sense of a given phenomenon under study. Usually these phenomena relate to experiences like in this case green supply chain management practices.

Investment Recovery: Is recovery of investments already made for green supply chain management. Investment recovery typically occurs at the back end of the supply chain cycle or as a method to "close the loop."

Lived Experience: Refers to a depiction of the experiences and choices of a given participant, and the knowledge that they gain from these experiences and choices.

Supply Chain Management: The management of the flow of goods and services. It involves the movement and storage of raw materials or WIP (work in process) or finished goods from suppliers (point of origin) to customers (point of consumption). In other words, it included interconnected or interlinked networks, channels and node businesses, which combine altogether in the provision of products and services required by end customers in a supply chain.

Section 4
Key Enablers for Digital Supply Chain Transformation

Chapter 13
Digital Transformation:
Impact of 5G Technology in Supply Chain Industry

Likhit Verma
Ericsson, USA

Mohit Lalwani
Oracle, USA

ABSTRACT

Supply chain industry is undergoing massive digital transformation. However, the pace of transformation has been rather slow. One of the challenges in the transformation is that there is so much dependency among various digital technologies that if one is implemented without the other, it might lead to no value creation at all. Furthermore, some of these technologies are dependent on other technologies that are still in its early phase of adoption. The existing technologies (namely artificial intelligence, machine learning, augmented reality, internet of things, virtual reality, big data) are critical enablers for the digital supply chain network; however, to unleash the full potential of these technologies, an extensive data sharing and analysis is required. This will only be possible if there is a robust telecom network. 5G with its features of low latency, high bandwidth, higher speeds, and low power requirements is expected to fill the void and hence expedite the digital supply chain transformation.

INTRODUCTION

Leaders win through logistics. Vision, sure. Strategy, yes. But when you go to war, you need to have both toilet paper and bullets in the right place at the right time. In other words, you must win through superior logistics. ~ Tom Peters

In today's globalized world, organizational success is not just dependent on its own internal efforts, but it also largely depends on how effectively the organization can orchestrate a vast, global network of supply chain to deliver goods and services to its consumers. With the growing complexity of supply chains,

DOI: 10.4018/978-1-5225-7700-3.ch013

Copyright © 2019, IGI Global. Copying or distributing in print or electronic forms without written permission of IGI Global is prohibited.

and the number of stakeholders involved, it is even more important to be able to track products in real time by accessing data and making a quick decision within the supply chain. This requires a massive transformation of the supply chain network.

Supply Chain Visibility Platforms, Big Data Analytics, IoT and Cloud technologies are some of the technologies that are leading the change in this Digital Supply chain transformation. However, the change has been rather slow. According to a survey by Capgemini Consulting and GT Nexus, 70% of executives mentioned that they have started a digital supply chain transformation, but only 5% are very satisfied with progress so far (Nextus, 2016).

One of the challenges in the transformation is that there is so much dependency among these various technologies that if one is implemented without the other, it might lead to no value creation at all. Furthermore, some of these technologies are dependent on other technologies that are still in its early phase of adoption.

In this chapter, we not only discuss the role of these existing technologies (namely Artificial Intelligence, Machine Learning, Augmented reality, Internet of Things, Virtual reality, Big Data) in digital supply chain transformation but also describe an upcoming technology that is expected to impact these technologies and hence in the transformation of next-generation Digital Supply Chain – 5G.

The flow of the chapter is as follows:

- Digital supply chain transformation
- Key technologies that are enabling digital supply chain transformation (along with its use cases).
- Next generation wireless technology: 5G and how it impacts the digital supply chain transformation and its applications in supply chain industry
- 5G as an enabler to other Digital Supply chain technologies

DIGITAL SUPPLY CHAIN TRANSFORMATION

Beginning from the first industrial revolution until now, various industries including the supply chain have gone through various transformations. Refer to Figure 1 for various stages of the industrial revolution.

- **Industry 1.0:** It was all about manual labor. Water-and steam-powered machines were used to help workers perform their job.
- **Industry 2.0:** Electricity became the prime source of power for industries. Mass production of goods using assembly lines became a commonplace
- **Industry 3.0:** Inventions of computers and software lead to the automation of tasks that were previously performed by humans.
- **Industry 4.0:** Connects the internet of things (IOT) with manufacturing techniques to enable systems to share information, analyze it and use it to guide intelligent actions. It incorporates technologies including Big Data, artificial intelligence and other cognitive technologies, advanced materials, and augmented reality.

Figure 1. Stages of industrial revolution
Source: Wikipedia Christoph Roser at AllAboutLean.com

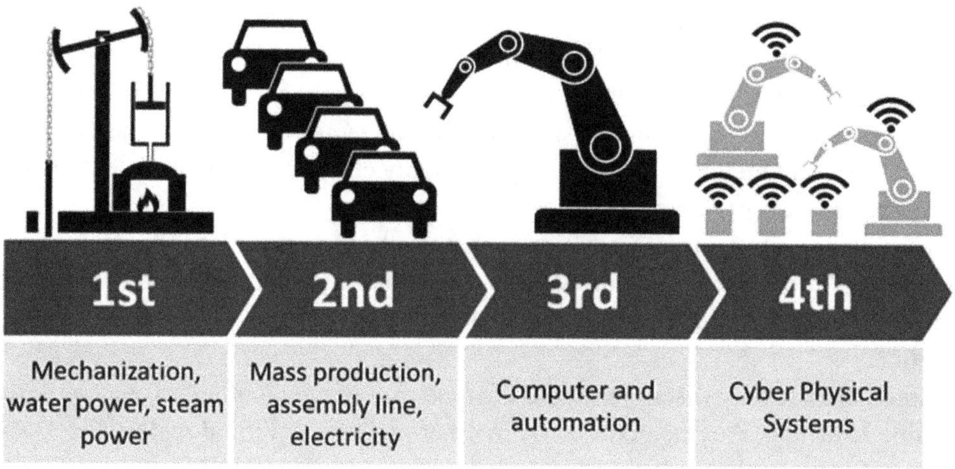

Today we are at the beginning of the 4th industrial revolution. Industry 4.0 is all about connecting the digital and physical worlds. Before Industry 4.0, industries have been able to automate routine activities, expand the capabilities of existing systems, and even perform analytical actions. However, with the introduction of new technologies in 4.0, these industries can make significant improvements in performance that were not possible before.

Industry 4.0 is already having a huge impact on Supply chain. In fact, Industry 4.0 represents the fourth industrial revolution in discrete and process manufacturing, logistics and supply chain referred to as Logistics 4.0. With the connected infrastructure enabled by Logistics 4.0, supply chain applications like Predictive Inbound Logistics management, no warehouse in supply chain, Predictive Delivery management, Autonomous Transportation vehicle / Equipment (China, n.d.) are becoming reality.

The next section of this chapter discusses the various technologies that authors believe will achieve the Digital transformation as imagined in Industry 4.0/Logistics 4.0

KEY TECHNOLOGY ENABLERS IN DIGITAL SUPPLY CHAIN

There are numerous digital technology enablement options available today, However, identifying the right option has always been a challenging task. In 2016 SC Digest conducted survey (Jda, 2016) to look at the current approach supply chain companies are taking to prioritize digital initiatives for the future. 58.6% of the respondents believe 'Real-time inventory visibility' and 'Understanding of product flows' have the highest impact on supply chain performance. The below section discusses how various digital technologies are impacting supply chain industry:

Artificial Intelligence (AI)

AI is intelligence demonstrated by machines, in contrast to the natural intelligence displayed by humans. The SCM World 2016 Future of Supply Chain Survey illustrated that the importance of artificial intelligence has grown rapidly, with 47 percent of supply chain leaders believing the technology is disruptive to global supply chain management strategies (World, 2016). According to experts supply chains have become so complex, and are affected by so many variables, that AI may be essential to help identify and predict problems and potential solutions. Supply chain planning and optimization, including demand forecasting, are among the key areas where AI is already beginning to be deployed.

Use Case 1: Chatbots in Procurement

AI based Chatbots can potentially provide several benefits to businesses, including reduced cost of transactions and sales cycle time in 'conversational interfaces'. According to Chyme (chymebot, n.d.), a bot development company, now salespersons can use chatbots in various scenarios to make themselves more productive. They can create new opportunities or update an opportunity in Salesforce for example. Or they can check the credit availability of a customer before closing a deal. They can create or update their sales forecast using chatbots instead of emails or spreadsheets. As AI matures, chatbots will probably help automate routine tasks and humans may be provided the skills to respond to more-complex queries. The potential challenge in the integration of chatbots for procurement, includes errors in chatbot integration that could increase because of the nature of the systems and the obvious lack of a traditional human touch affecting customer relationships.

Use Case 2: AI in Retail: Personalized Online Experiences and Self-Learning

According to a study, today only 2% of online shoppers make a purchase on their first visit to an e-commerce site. Ad retargeting has therefore become commonplace, a technique to recover the 98% of potential customers who do not purchase first time (Anand, 2017). With access to billions of data points on user behavior and real-time advertisement availability, retailers can use AI to dynamically identify specific customer segments in higher quantities to recommend more relevant products and services. Amazon's AI-driven product recommendations account for up to 35% of the company's revenue (Jacob, 2018).

Machine Learning

Machine Learning (ML) and Artificial Intelligence are not the same thing but not knowing the difference clearly could lead to confusion. AI is the demonstration of capability of a machine to imitate intelligent human behavior, whereas Machine learning is a subset of AI that include abstruse statistical techniques that enable machines to improve at task with experience (Yang, 2016). ML has the potential to form new patterns without human interference. ML algorithms compare the data with other constraints to make accurate predictions. Machine learning is revolutionizing supply chain management.

Use Case 1: Inventory Management

Many companies are now using machine learning to optimize business processes from customer service inquiries to plan next month's shelf supply based on satellite data (Walker, 2018). Supply chain and inventory management is moving towards smart automation. Walmart is testing warehouse drones to catalog and manage inventory, scan items, and check for misplaced items. According to Walmart, manually checking inventory is inefficient and can take few weeks for employees, but the same task can be completed in 24 hours using sophisticated drones that fly through the warehouse (D'innocenzio, 2016).

Use Case 2: Route Optimization

It often feels great when item ordered online is delivered the same day or in next 2 hours. But in background warehouse manager plans the most optimal routes for thousands of shipments in a day with hundreds of delivery man to various parts of the city. If we try to solve this problem ourselves, we might feel lost and confused. This happens in logistics industry too. This problem is known as Travelling Salesman Problem (TSP), a nightmare for organizations with a huge workforce. FarEye (FarEye, n.d.), a digital logistics company, has developed ML-based vehicle and real-time visibility platform. Its routing systems are backed by artificial intelligence and machine learning algorithms that can self-learn the 'correct' address just from delivery addresses, success and failures in the past. It allows personalization of deliveries by giving the flexibility to the customers to select the preferred time-slot and the expected time of arrival (ETA) precisely. Pretty interesting, right?

Augmented Reality

Augmented reality is the expansion of physical reality by adding layers of computer-generated information to the actual environment. One could say AR is reality modified by technology. One's perception of reality being manipulated. You may have heard of devices such as Google Glass or the more recent Microsoft Hololens. Both are products of augmented reality technology. International logistics company DHL is developing and implementing smart glasses in warehouses, creating their own augmented reality (DHL, 2014). AR has endless possibilities in the supply chain.

Use Case 1: Pick-and-Pack Services

Training new workers to navigate a large warehouse to find a product is one of the costliest parts of running a "pick and pack" services. With the help of AR glasses an imaginary line can be painted line on the warehouse floor to simplify the searching and training. During the peak holiday season, temporary workers need to be on-boarded quickly. New hires with constant feedback on their AR glasses can shorten their learning curve by knowing how they are doing and what can be improved. According to DHL report, field tests of these AR systems have proved they offer significant productivity improvements in warehousing operations and have reduced errors by as much as 40% (Samit, 2018).

Use Case 2: Last Mile Delivery

The growing use of e-commerce has led to a boom of last-mile delivery services, which is the final step in the supply chain and often the most expensive one. AR can save money by cutting the time spent on last-mile delivery nearly in half. According to a DHL report, drivers spend 40% to 60% of their day searching inside their own truck for the correct boxes to deliver next. Instead of having to remember how their truck was loaded that morning, augmented reality is used to identify, tag, sequence, and locate every parcel (Samit, 2018).

Internet of Things

Internet of thing is changing the world we live in. About a 15 years ago we probably would have one or may be at most two personal devices connected to internet. But today every person has about 6.6 devices connected to the internet it could be a personal phone, personal computer, work computer, personal tablet, gaming console, watches, media player, smart TV etc. Cisco has estimated that connected devices on the Internet will exceed 50 billion by 2020 (Afshar, 2017) . Today we live in world surrounded by sensors. These sensors are taking information from real physical objects that are in the world and uploading to the internet. In simple words the Internet of Things digitizes physical assets such as sensors, devices and machines. It connects people to things and things to things in real-time.

Use Case 1: Asset Tracking

Supply chain optimization, warehouse management automation and order fulfillment with help of real-time data can be enabled by IoT based asset management solution. For example, Real-time contingency delivery plan can be made to avoid any delays based on live traffic updates, could result in cost saving. Effective utilization of data in coordination with a command center could ensure 360-degree asset visibility across the entire organization.

Use Case 2: Forecasting and Inventory

IoT sensors can provide far more accurate inventories than humans can manage alone. For instance, Amazon is using WiFi robots to scan QR codes on its products to track and triage its orders. It would be wonderful to track inventory—including the supplies in stock for future manufacturing by a click of a button. No more missing deadline again. And moreover, all that data can be used to find trends to make manufacturing schedules even more efficient (Crawford, 2018). It's not an easy mission to make IoT systems function smoothly as a standalone solution or part of existing systems, there are still many technological challenges, including Security, Connectivity, Compatibility & Longevity, Standards and Intelligent Analysis & Actions (Banafa, 2017).

Virtual Reality

Virtual reality is fully immersive computer simulated environment that gives a user, feeling of being in that environment instead of when they are actually in. Virtual reality has been finding its way into supply chains, and those using the technology are reporting they are happy with the results. VR technology allows for supply chain managers to make more informed decisions than they otherwise would without the technology. With VR, managers can increase sales options and up-selling possibilities; offer a "walk-thru" experience prior to purchasing; visualize parts, quotes and pricing in three dimensions; merge various aspects of the supply chain; simplify and speed up in the order fulfillment cycle; grow revenue, profits and offer exceptional customer experience (ZDA, 2016).

Use Case 1: VR Shopping

Virtual Reality offers a futuristic way to engage with consumers. Consumers can download an app onto their phone and could enter the VR world of virtual retail store, with aisles and products they can engage with. This application of virtual reality offers a huge opportunity to take customer experience to the next level. For consumers this new way of interacting with brands is mind-blowing - they can experience the nature of a store and products virtually, from their own living room. VR turns experiences into data. When that data is tied to deep analytics and machine learning tools, a trip to the virtual store is harnessed into actionable data. VR now becomes yet another source of data that streams into the ever-growing pool of big data that is used for digital transformation (Benton, 2017).

Big Data

Big data is an evolving term that describes any voluminous amount of structured, semi structured and unstructured data that has the potential to be mined for information. Data which are not organized or can't be easily interpreted by a traditional database or data models are called Unstructured data such as Twitter tweets and social media posts. As per Forbes (Columbus, 2015), forward-thinking manufacturers are orchestrating 80% or more of their supplier network activity outside their four walls, using big data and cloud-based technologies to get beyond the constraints of legacy Enterprise Resource Planning (ERP) and Supply Chain Management (SCM) systems.

Use Case 1: Managing Risk in Delivery of Raw Materials

Any disruption in availability of raw material can affect the overall supply chain. For example, a proactive action by any company could be to engage big data analytics, map out all potential delays in delivery route, analyze weather statistics such as tornadoes, earthquakes, hurricanes, etc. Run predictive analytics to calculate the probabilities of delays. These analytics findings Companies can use to identify backup suppliers and develop contingency plans to make sure production isn't interrupted by natural disaster.

Use Case 2: Intelligent Procurement

Information is power and information flow is key in supply chain. Today big data offers more information than ever to businesses. With big data, organizations can make procurement decisions on more factors, enabling them to make better informed decisions that ultimately impact the bottom line. Purchasing decisions no longer must be made solely upon production requirements, but a combination of multiple inputs including: Planned production, Estimated customer orders, supplier capacity, Currency fluctuations, likelihood of any disruptive events, supplier's rate etc.

5G

5G short for 'fifth generation' is the next generation wireless technology that not only aims to significantly increase the speeds, expand coverage and responsiveness of wireless networks but also connect the world (and all the devices within it) in ways that was never imagined before. From logistics to smart-home security to self-driving cars, all the internet-connected devices in your life can talk to each other at lightning-fast speeds with reduced latency. It is expected to be so impactful that Qualcomm's CEO Stephen Mollenkopf has been quoted as saying "5G will have an impact similar to the introduction of electricity or the automobile, affecting entire economies and benefiting entire societies." Authors believe that 5G has such huge potential that it will not just have a direct impact on the supply chain industry but will also indirectly impact by unleashing the full potential of other technologies that already play a key role in the digital supply chain network.

Next section of this chapter, describes what we need to know about 5G, and how is it relevant for supply chain digital transformation. Authors have presented use cases to explain new possibilities within supply chain, which would be enabled by 5G.

5G AND ITS USE CASE CATEGORIES

Every new generation of wireless technology delivers faster speed and more functionalities for phones. *1G* brought the very first cell phones, *2G* let the text for the first time, *3G* brought internet in phones, *4G* delivered the speed that we enjoy today. But as more devices come online, and with the increased usage of data hungry applications, 4G networks have just about reached their limits. 5G can handle 1000 times more traffic than today's network and it will be up to 10x faster than 4G LTE with latency as low

Figure 2. 2G to 5G service additions
Source: CNN Money

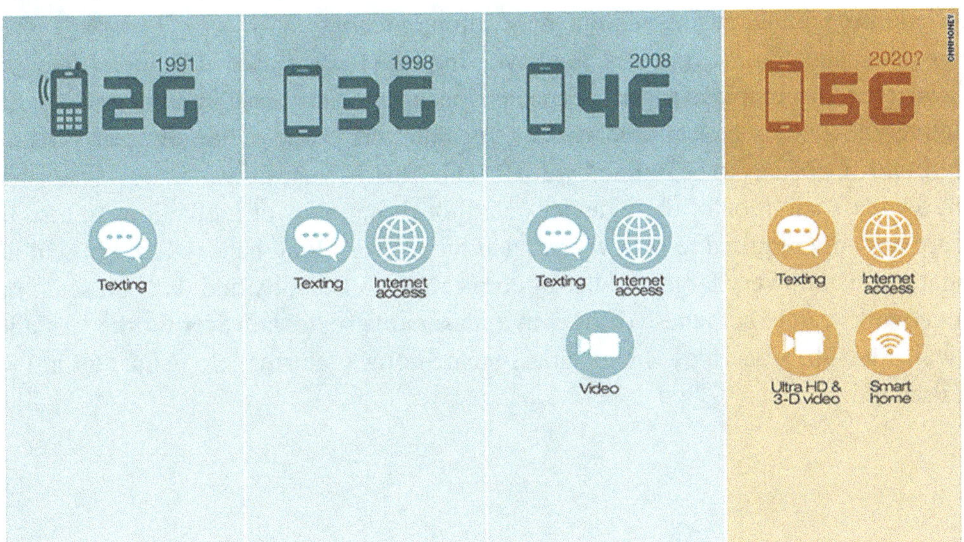

as 1 millisecond. Just imagine downloading an HD movie in under few seconds or opening websites in fractions of seconds. See Figure 2 below showing the service adds from 2G to 5G.

Until 4G, mobile operators had been focused on providing better services and experiences for mobile device users. However, 5G is not just about mobile phones, it is in-fact much more than that. 5G is being considered revolutionary as its realm is not just limited to the mobile world but impacts several other industries as well. As per Balázs Bertényi, chairman of 3GPP TSG RAN (Technical Specifications Group) “5G NR (New radio) Standalone systems not only dramatically increase the mobile broadband speeds and capacity, but also open the door for new industries beyond telecommunications that are looking to revolutionize their ecosystem through 5G.”

International Telecommunications Union (ITU), a specialized UN agency for information and communication technologies has divided 5G network services into three major categories namely eMBB, mMTC, URLLC. These categories will drive the innovation for the next-gen supply chain network:

1. Massive machine type communications (mMTC)
2. Ultra-reliable low latency communications (URLLC)
3. Enhanced mobile broadband (eMBB)

These categories will drive the innovation for the next-gen supply chain network.

Massive Machine Type Communications (mMTC)

Machine to Machine or M2M is a Machine talking to another Machine over a wired or wireless network in order to exchange information and possibly take actions without the need for any human intervention. Depending on the application, there are various network architectures that could be used for M2M communication including Cellular networks, WiFi, Bluetooth Low Energy, Zigbee, SIGFOX, and many more.

Wireless mobile networks are omnipresent and hence have huge advantage compared to these other network technologies. However, the high cost, short device battery life, and capacity limitations, associated with the existing wireless technologies like 4G, makes it less viable as a long-term solution. 5G is expected to change all of that and revolutionize modern industrial processes and applications including logistics, agriculture, manufacturing and business communications

Machine-to-machine communications, now evolving into the Internet of Things (IoT), is a vast opportunity for wireless communications. It is expected that a large number of internet devices that typically transmit relatively low volume of non-delay-sensitive data will come online. Business Insider predicts around 23 billion IoT devices to be online by 2019 (ITU, 2015).

However, for mass adoption of these devices, and for these kinds of predictions to turn into reality, the devices are not only required to be low cost, and have a very long battery life, but will also require a network that can handle very large number of connections efficiently and that can scale rapidly. The existing 4G networks can handle these devices at a reasonable scale, however for the vast adoption, 5G will be critical. Ehealth, wearables, smart cities, smart homes, efarms, elogistics, all are part of this category of use case.

Ultra-Reliable Low Latency Communications (URLLC)

URLLC enables wireless applications where high reliability and low latency are essential. Some applications have been delivered in the past by relatively expensive industry-specific or proprietary networks and IT systems; others are emerging applications, enabled by ubiquitous wireless connectivity, but with stringent requirements for safety or other operational reasons (ITU, 2015).

Driven by high dependability and extremely short network traversal time, URLLC, also referred to as "mission-critical" communications, will enable critical applications including autonomous vehicles, industrial and vehicular automation, remote medical surgery, and advanced AR and VR. 5G, by using techniques like Grant-free access to base stations, will enable it to meet the stringent latency and reliability requirements for URLLC.

Enhanced Mobile Broadband (eMBB)

Mobile broadband is a wireless technology that allows you to connect a mobile device such as your smartphone or tablet to a broadband internet connection wirelessly through a mobile phone network. It addresses the use cases for wireless access to multi-media content and services. The demand for mobile broadband has been increasing at a dramatic pace, leading the way for enhanced Mobile Broadband. This use case category has requirements for higher data rates and better coverage availability. For improved performance and seamless user experience, the enhanced Mobile Broadband will have new application areas and requirements than are available in existing Mobile Broadband applications. This usage category covers a range of use cases, including wide-area coverage and hotspot.

Hotspot is an area with very high user density, high data rate requirements, low mobility, and high traffic capacity. For example: at a sporting event with hundreds of thousands of spectators, there will be a requirement for very high traffic capacity to meet the needs of all the users, but those users will be static or moving slowly so the requirement for mobility will be low. Wide area coverage requires seamless coverage and medium to high mobility, with data rate requirement that are much slower compared to hotspot. An example of this is the passengers in a high-speed train using their mobile devices require a high degree of mobility to avoid dropped calls but the traffic capacity could be much lower than that of a hotspot.

Figure 3 depicts the 5G network services use scenario discussed in this section.

Fixed Wireless Access (FWA)

Apart from the three categories specified by ITU, another major category of 5G network services that is expected to benefit the connected society is Fixed Wireless Access (FWA). Today, fast broadband services are provided mostly through wired fiber connections to home or businesses. However, with 5G FWA all that could change or at least improve. 5G fixed wireless access aims to provide fast broadband speeds over the air. Compared with fiber-to-the-home (FTTH) and other wireline solutions, FWA offers a variety of benefits.

Benefits to Wireless ISP's includes significantly lower rollout costs, rapid service rollout and lower Operating expenses. This is because the bulk of the costs and most of the complexity involved in fixed access deployments are associated with the last mile: the portion of the network that reaches the user

Figure 3. 5G usage scenarios
Source: IMT Vision Framework and overall objectives of the future development of IMT for 2020 and beyond

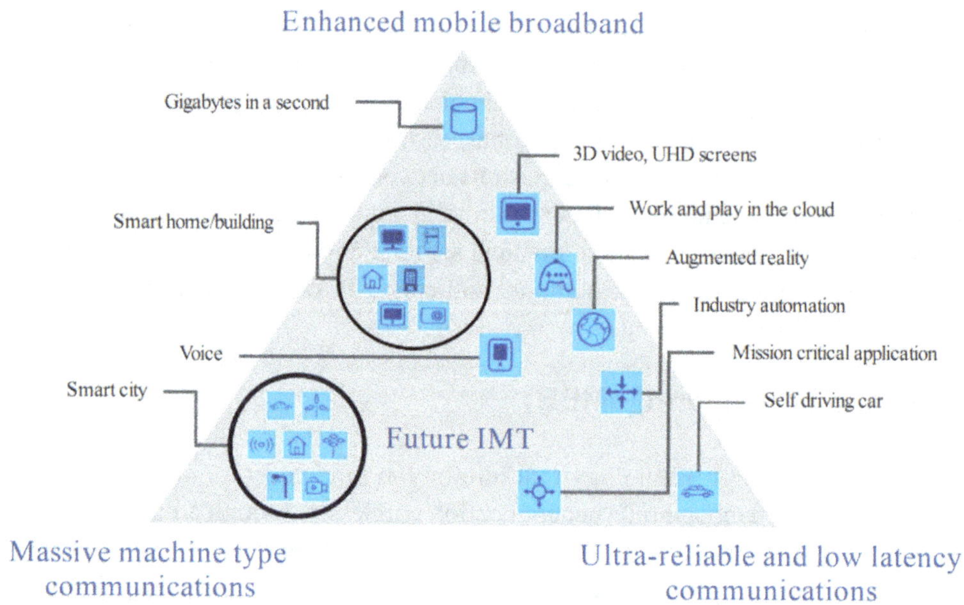

premises. To the consumer, the benefits are broadband connection when there was none, or the number of ISP choices available in any area and hence better service at possibly lower cost.

5G APPLICATIONS IN SUPPLY CHAIN

The use case categories described in the previous section of this capture opens plethora of applications. Below are some of the 5G applications that the authors believe would impact supply chain substantially:

IoT in Supply Chain

Supply chain and logistics involve a lot of moving parts. Keeping track of these items and getting them securely from origination to its destination is art. Many supply chain companies currently use QR code scanning or RFID to track these products but in a limited way.

QR codes are used to track names and prices of products, along with other data like serial numbers, part numbers, lots and dates. RFID can be used to track information such as order ID number, product bin location, order status, serial numbers for individual product components, and location logs. However, both QR codes and RFID can be easily copied making it less secure and open to misuse/thefts, etc. Moreover, they can be read only at a limited range, making it impossible to track them at longer distances away from their readers. This opens up possibilities of contentions when the product is damaged/lost/stolen etc.

Technology such as internet of things (IoT) can solve this problem and help in real time tracking and traceability of a product within a supply chain. By installing IoT sensors on each product, either on the inside or outside of packaging, it is possible to track items location easily and transparently. These sensors can give more information than just real time location. They can also provide real-time information if product is damaged during transit with help of temperature, pressure and other sensors. But IoT requires ubiquitous and low-cost internet connection throughout the supply chain. This gap can only be filled by 5G technology as described in the mMTC use case category of this chapter. 5G can truly speed up production, streamline complex logistical processes, reduce costs and maximize profits. This enables the supply chain to significantly improve customer value and achieve a sustainable competitive advantage.

Supply Chain Optimization Through Autonomous Driving and Communicating Vehicles

Trucks or delivery vehicles are one of the most important delivery mechanisms in supply chain. However, there are quite a few challenges in the trucking business that causes shipment delays, shipment losses and high cost of transportation. Some of those are:

1. One of the challenges is the shortage of drivers. Based on findings by trucking.org, they predict that there will be a shortage of 175000 truck drivers by 2024.
2. Next is the huge rate of truck accidents. According to 2017 report of NHTSA, an estimated 433,000 large trucks were involved in police-reported traffic crashes in 2015. Accidents are caused by driver error approximately 90% of the time
3. High fuel cost is another challenge. Apart from fuel efficient vehicles, implementation of vehicle platooning, which is where trucks drive close behind one another to utilize the road better and save time, fuel and emissions.

Autonomous or self-driving or driverless vehicle can solve these challenges. An autonomous vehicle is a vehicle that can drive itself without human control. They have GPS for guidance, sensors for environment sensing and for avoiding collision, and cameras for vision.

While sensors such as radar, and camera systems are essential, these sensors are limited by their line-of-sight (LOS) operation.

The high throughput and URLLC capabilities of 5G will enable autonomous vehicles to provide 360-degree non-LOS (NLOS) awareness, extending a vehicle's ability to detect farther down the road — even at blind intersections or in poor weather conditions. It would enable the vehicles to directly share their perception of the road, road conditions and surroundings, with each other and with road infrastructure in an efficient manner (Qualcomm, 2018). These capabilities are designed to allow the vehicles to build a real-world model of the surrounding environment by sharing high throughput sensor data with each other. In addition, vehicles can convey their intention and planned movements to each other using 5G, enabling better autonomous path planning with a higher level of predictability and determinism. The 5G capabilities can also allow autonomous vehicles to know their location more precisely and get more familiar with their surroundings by getting real-time local updates, such as 3D HD maps (Qualcomm, 2018). 5G can thus overcome the challenges and hence avoid shipment delays, shipment losses and high cost of transportation.

Smart Material Requirement Planning

For manufacturers, tracking components and raw materials for the final product to be integrated can be extremely valuable. While many organizations rely on barcode scanning to track work-in-progress assets, this method doesn't allow for quick access of a lost part or if the part was shipped to a wrong location or part gets stolen or there is a delay due to weather.

The Industrial IoT (IIoT) powered by 5G can provide access to real-time supply chain information by tracking materials, equipment, and products as they move through the supply chain. Effective reporting enables manufacturers to collect and feed delivery information into ERP, PLM and other systems. By connecting plants to suppliers, all the parties concerned with the supply chain can trace interdependencies, material flow and manufacturing cycle times. This data will help manufacturers predict issues, plan in advance and potentially reduces capital/operational expenditures (Darcherif, 2018). 5G also makes machine-to-machine connectivity a reality which could automate the entire process thus improving the manufacturing cycles.

Smart Sourcing of Raw Materials

Drones are being used to discover sources of raw materials necessary to manufacture finished goods. Because of their maneuverability and size, small drones can reach to places that might be difficult or even unsafe for human. Small or medium sized drones equipped with cameras can obtain high quality aerial views and, other geographical or physical characteristics of a region may be obtained through various sensors attached to the drones. There is a lot of valuable data that drone collects which could be transmitted and analyzed in real time and actions taken accordingly. However, the amount of data that could be generated could be extensive and requires a robust network. This can be made possible through the eMBB connectivity service that 5G will provide. 5G makes high data transfers at low latency possible and hence this could impact the sourcing of raw material in a meaningful way.

5G: KEY DIGITAL TECHNOLOGY ENABLER

As we have described, 5G is one of the key enablers of next generation Digital Transformation. In this section, we discuss how 5G could support other key technologies that enable Digital Transformation of the supply chain. The Figure 4 shows the key enablers leveraging 5G technology for the robust connectivity requirements.

5G and Big Data

With the advent of the new technologies like IoT, Social media platforms, fitness trackers, drones, smart homes and many more, vast amounts of data are being generated. As it has been discussed in the previous section, this vast amount of structured or unstructured data constitutes Big Data. This data needs to be processed and analyzed to make smart decisions. However, to perform these actions, the data must be securely transmitted to data centers which can perform the processing/analysis of the data.

Depending on the application, the transmission of data could be through wired or wireless connections. Wireless connections include wifi, Bluetooth, 3G/4G/5G mobile technologies, etc.

Previous mobile technologies like 3G/4G were predominantly focused on providing better mobile phone services, however 5G with its features of super-high speeds, low latency, high power efficiency, more bandwidth, network slicing, edge computing, was natively designed to cater to various categories

Figure 4. 5G as an enabler to other technologies

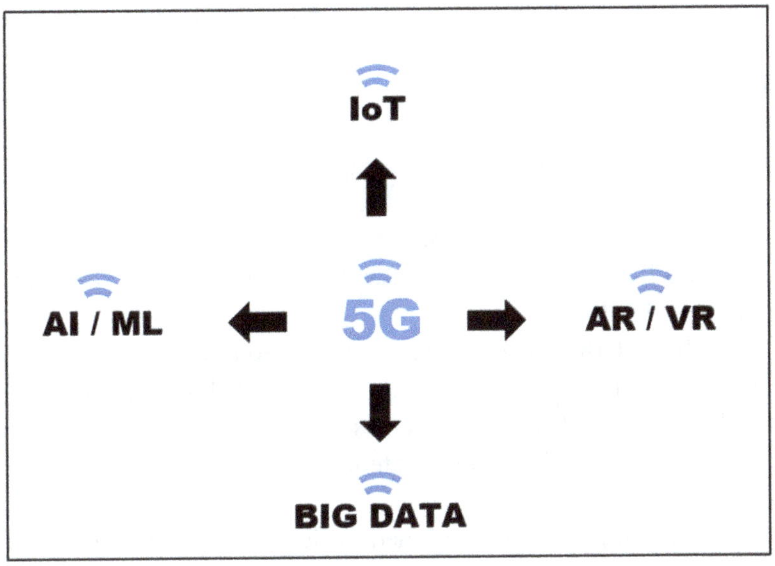

that are not just limited to mobile services. 5G is expected to be one of the key transmission technologies for Big Data.

Imagine several IoT based sensors (that rely on cellular technologies for transmission of data) in a smart city, monitoring everything from environment to vehicles to emergency services. These sensors continuously generate a lot of data and some of it is highly critical and time-sensitive in nature. 5G would be used to transmit all these data to the data centers. 5G can create slices for different types of data – emergency services can get a slice that could have the features of low latency, high speeds, and high bandwidth whereas environment monitoring gets another slice with no special treatment for transmission of data.

5G and AI / ML

As stated earlier, "AI involves machines that can perform tasks that are characteristic of human intelligence" and "Machine learning is simply a way of achieving AI."

Instead of writing thousands and millions of lines of software codes to accomplish a task, machine learning is a way of "training" an algorithm so that it can learn itself how. However, Training involves feeding large amounts of data to the algorithm and allowing the algorithm to improve over time. The data could generate from several mobile sources and the only transmission technology that can get those data to the data centers for processing by AI/ML technologies are 4G/5G. By using 5G and its unique features, the extent to where AI/ML can be applied has broadened substantially.

Consider the use case mentioned before. It often feels great when item ordered online is delivered same day or in next 2 hours. But how is that achieved? How does the warehouse manager plan most optimal routes for 1000s of shipment in a day with 100 delivery man to various parts of the city? This problem is known as Travelling Salesman Problem (TSP), a nightmare for organizations with a huge workforce. ML based vehicle and real-time visibility platforms have been developed that use mobile technologies for tracking purposes and for getting data from the field that helps the ML engine to learn more and provide optimizations that helps in solving the travelling salesman problem.

5G and AR / VR

From the section about AR/VR, we understand the capabilities of AR and VR technologies and how they could impact the digital supply chain. However, due to constraints in current mobile technologies, we haven't been able to fully utilize those capabilities just yet.

Constraints of providing low latency, high bandwidths, and faster speeds all at the same time can only be achieved with 5G technology.

As per Verizon (O'Malley, 2018) "Whether it's science, medicine, employee training, advertising or entertainment, the application areas for AR/VR are virtually limitless. But all these possibilities come with a logistical complication: an exponential increase in data demands. Only a 5G network will be able to provide the necessary bandwidth and low latency for AR/VR experiences to feel seamless and, ultimately, valuable."

An application of AR requiring 5G was mentioned earlier in the chapter. According to a DHL report, drivers spend about 40% to 60% of their day searching inside their own truck for the correct boxes to deliver at the last mile. Instead of trying to remember how their truck was loaded and where each box could be, AR headsets could be used to identify, tag, sequence, and locate every parcel within the truck. However, these AR headsets would heavily depend on the 5G networks to get all the required information about that specific parcel/s.

5G and IoT

Per Qualcomm Senior Vice President Raj Talluri (Talluri, 2017)– "Everyone already loves to talk about the IoT because we're just starting to see its potential, and that's exciting. But with 5G, we'll actually help realize the promise of a massively expanded IoT beyond what's possible with today's technologies. We'll be aware of and able to interact with our surroundings to new levels — even with "things" thousands of miles away — through very intelligent connected devices and sensors. These sensors will allow us to gather data continuously, to be proactive and, eventually, even allow our devices to act on our behalves. (Qualcomm, 2018)"

As described in 5G applications section, internet of things (IoT) can overcome the shortcomings of QR codes and RFID technologies and help in real time tracking and traceability of a product within a supply chain. By installing IoT sensors on each product, either on the inside or outside of packaging, it is possible to track items location easily and transparently. These sensors can give more information than just real time location. They can also provide real-time information if product is damaged during transit with help of temperature, pressure and other sensors. But IoT requires ubiquitous, low-power and low-cost internet connection throughout the supply chain. This gap can only be filled by 5G technology as described in the mMTC use case category of this chapter. 5G can truly speed up production, streamline complex logistical processes, reduce costs and maximize profits. This enables the supply chain to significantly improve customer value and achieve a sustainable competitive advantage.

FUTURE RESEARCH

The author predicts that more research dollars will be spent by organizations towards the development of 5G applications. Academia will also contribute in the development of 5G by introducing courses and building research programs around 5G. This will pave the way for several industry-wide use cases.

5G technology is in its early phase of adoption and its impact is not just limited to supply chain, it reaches far out into different verticals - Automotive, Constructions, healthcare, Manufacturing, and many more. Economists estimate the global economic impact of 5G in new goods and services will reach $12 trillion by 2035 as 5G moves mobile technology from connecting people to people and information, towards connecting people to everything (Rosenberg, 2018).

CONCLUSION

For supply chain transformation, organizations are harnessing technologies like AI, ML, Big Data, AR/VR, and IoT to digitize their supply chain. However, to realize the full potential of these technologies, a robust network that provides fast data speed, high bandwidth, low latency, enable low powered devices, and is highly available will be the key. 5G will be the network of future that empowers these technologies and provides a platform for billions of devices to come online. 5G will impact several industries – autos, healthcare, manufacturing, logistics emergency services, just to name a few. In fact, it is expected to be so impactful that Qualcomm's CEO Stephen Mollenkopf has been quoted as saying "5G will have an impact similar to the introduction of electricity or the automobile, affecting entire economies and benefiting entire societies."

REFERENCES

Afshar, V. (2017). *Cisco: Enterprises Are Leading The Internet of Things Innovation*. Retrieved from https://www.huffingtonpost.com/entry/cisco-enterprises-are-leading-the-internet-of-things_us_59a41fcee4b0a62d0987b0c6

AnandA. (2017, Nov 2). Retrieved from https://becominghuman.ai/machine-learning-and-retargeting-9ffb77d768c3

Banafa, A. (2017, March 14). *IEEE internet of things*. Retrieved from https://iot.ieee.org/newsletter/march-2017/three-major-challenges-facing-iot.html

Benton, D. (2017, Feb 21). *Retail, virtual reality and the supply chain*. Retrieved from https://www.supplychaindigital.com/scm/retail-virtual-reality-and-supply-chain

ChinaU. B. (n.d.). Retrieved from https://www.i-scoop.eu/industry-4-0/supply-chain-management-scm-logistics/

chymebot. (n.d.). Retrieved from http://chymebot.com/use-cases/

Columbus, L. (2015, July 13). *Ten Ways Big Data Is Revolutionizing Supply Chain Management*. Retrieved from https://www.forbes.com/sites/louiscolumbus/2015/07/13/ten-ways-big-data-is-revolutionizing-supply-chain-management/#38400f4e69f5

Crawford, M. (2018, Feb). *Six Supply Chain Trends That Will Impact Manufacturing in 2018*. Retrieved from https://www.gray.com/news/blog/2018/02/19/six-supply-chain-trends-that-will-impact-manufacturing-in-2018

d'Innocenzio. A. (2016, June 2). Retrieved from https://apnews.com/ee9b77dba1a5460a91fef2842ccb8955/wal-mart-testing-drones-warehouses-manage-inventory

D'innocenzioA. (2016, June 2). Retrieved from https://apnews.com/ee9b77dba1a5460a91fef2842ccb8955/wal-mart-testing-drones-warehouses-manage-inventory

Darcherif, A. (2018, April). Retrieved from The Industry 4.0 and IoT Ecosystem – Alexandre Darcherif – Medium: https://medium.com/@darchalex/the-industry-4-0-and-iot-ecosystem-e84935289191

DHL. (2014). Retrieved from http://www.dhl.com/content/dam/downloads/g0/about_us/logistics_insights/csi_augmented_reality_report_290414.pdf

FarEye. (n.d.). Retrieved from https://www.getfareye.com/blog/machine-learning-based-vehicle-routing-software

GoldmanD. (2018, Jan 29). Retrieved from https://money.cnn.com/2018/01/29/technology/what-is-5g/index.html

Goldman, D. (2018, Jan 29). *What is 5g*. Retrieved from https://money.cnn.com/2018/01/29/technology/what-is-5g/index.html

ITU. (2015, Sep). Retrieved from https://www.itu.int/dms_pubrec/itu-r/rec/m/R-REC-M.2083-0-201509-I!!PDF-E.pdf

JacobL. (2018, July 17). Retrieved from https://www.iqvis.com/blog/amazon-reorganized-ai-and-machine-learning/

JDA. (2016). SCDigest Supply Chain Digitization Benchmark Survey. *Supply Chain Digest*.

NextusC. G. (2016, April). Retrieved from https://www.supplychain247.com/article/the_state_of_digital_transformation_across_global_supply_chains

NexusC. G. (2017, July 12). Retrieved from https://www.supplychain247.com/paper/the_current_and_future_state_of_digital_supply_chain_transformation/gt_nexus

NGMN. (2018). *Next generation mobile network*. Retrieved from https://www.ngmn.org/about-us/vision-mission.html

O'Malley, J. (2018, June 27). *How 5G will improve augmented and virtual reality*. Retrieved from https://www.verizon.com/about/news/how-5g-will-improve-augmented-and-virtual-reality

Qualcomm. (2018, May). Retrieved from https://www.qualcomm.com/news/onq/2018/05/10/how-will-5g-unlock-potential-autonomous-driving

RosenbergD. (2018, Jan 18). Retrieved from https://www.weforum.org/agenda/2018/01/the-world-is-about-to-become-even-more-interconnected-here-s-how/

SamitJ. (2018, March 1). Retrieved from http://fortune.com/2018/03/01/5-ways-augmented-reality-is-disrupting-the-supply-chain/

Talluri, R. (2017, Jan 18). *How will 5G impact the Internet of Things*. Retrieved from https://www.rcrwireless.com/wireless/how-will-5g-impact-the-internet-of-things

Walker, J. (2018, Feb). *TechEmergence*. Retrieved from Inventory Management with Machine Learning – 3 Use Cases in Industry: https://www.techemergence.com/inventory-management-with-machine-learning/

World, S. (2016). *Artificial Intelligence and Future Supply Chains*. Retrieved from http://www.scmworld.com/artificial-intelligence-future-supply-chains/

Yang, L. (2016, Nov). *AI vs. Machine Learning vs. Deep Learning*. Retrieved from http://deeplearning.lipingyang.org/2016/11/

ZDA. (2016, Jan). *What Are Virtual Reality Supply Chains?* Retrieved from https://www.zdaya.com/2016/01/06/virtual-reality-supply-chain-recruiters/

KEY TERMS AND DEFINITIONS

5G: It is the fifth generation of cellular mobile communications. It succeeds the 4G, 3G, and 2G systems. 5G performance targets include high data rate, reduced latency, energy saving, cost reduction, higher system capacity and massive device connectivity.

Artificial Intelligence: AI is intelligence demonstrated by machines, in contrast to the natural intelligence displayed by humans.

Asset Tracking: Refers to the method of tracking physical assets, either by scanning barcode labels or RFID sticker attached to the assets.

Augmented Reality: Is the expansion of physical reality by adding layers of computer-generated information to the actual environment. AR is reality modified by technology.

Big Data: Is an evolving term that describes any voluminous amount of structured, semi-structured, and unstructured data that has the potential to be mined for information.

Big Data Analytics: Big data analytics is the often-complex process of analyzing voluminous amount of structured, semi structured and unstructured data that has the potential to be mined for information.

Digital Supply Chain Transformation: Application of digital capabilities to supply chain process, products to improve efficiency, enhance customer value, manage risk, and uncover new sources of monetization.

eMBB (Enhanced Mobile Broadband): New application areas and requirements in addition to existing Mobile Broadband applications for improved performance and an increasingly seamless user experience.

First Industrial Revolution: The transition into new manufacturing processes during mid 18th century to mid-19th century.

FTTH: Fiber to the home, also called fiber to the premises.

FWA (Fixed Wireless Access): It is the process of accessing a communicating network or internet on a fixed wireless network.

Industry 1.0: (mid-1800s) It was all about manual labor. Water-and steam-powered machines were used to help workers perform their job.

Industry 2.0: (early 1900s) Electricity became the prime source of power for industries. Mass production of goods using assembly lines became a commonplace.

Industry 3.0: (end 1900s) Inventions of computers and software lead to automation of tasks that were previously performed by humans.

Industry 4.0: (early 2000s) New industrial revolution that makes it possible to gather and analyze data across machines, enabling faster, more flexible, and more efficient processes to produce higher-quality goods at reduced costs. It includes internet of things, cloud computing, and cognitive computing.

International Telecommunications Union (ITU): Specialized agency of the United Nations that is responsible for issues that concern information and communication technologies.

Inventory Management: Inventory management is the management of flow of units into and out of an existing inventory.

ISP: Internet service provider, provider of internet services.

Last Mile Delivery: This term is used to describe delivery of the product to the final end user in home.

Machine Learning: Is a subset of AI that include abstruse statistical techniques that enable machines to improve at task with experience.

mMTC (Massive Machine Type Communications): Machine talking to another machine over a wired or wireless network in order to exchange information and possibly take actions without the need for any human intervention.

Pick and Pack: Pick and pack is a part of a complete supply chain management process, managing individual components of an order from master cartons (picked) and then placed into a box.

RFID: Radio-frequency identification uses electromagnetic fields to automatically identify and track tags attached to objects.

Route Optimization: It is the process of determining the most cost-efficient route. It sounds simple, but it could be complex process.

URLLC (Ultra-Reliable Low Latency Communications): URLLC, also referred to as "mission-critical" communications, will enable critical applications where high reliability and low latency are essential

Virtual Reality: Is fully immersive computer simulated environment that gives a user, feeling of being in that environment instead of when they are actually in.

Chapter 14
Supply Chain Processes Modelling for Digitalization:
A Scientific Classification and Practical Recommendation Model

Matthias Lederer
ISM International School of Management, Germany

Anna Quitt
ISM International School of Management, Germany

Remzi Avci
University of Erlangen-Nuremberg, Germany

Mario Büsch
ISM International School of Management, Germany

ABSTRACT

Process orientation is often seen as a central starting point for optimizing business performance. This is especially true for supply chain workflows because modeling, understood as specifying activities, data, resources, and control flows, is usually the first step in selecting and implementing digital approaches such as smart factories, virtual agents, and autonomous systems. Many different process notations are known (e.g., detailed vs. rough, flexible vs. standardized, etc.), and at the same time, fundamentally different SCM process types make various assumptions about suitable modeling (e.g., integration of value chain partners, standardization). This chapter presents an association model that suggests which notation fits best to which SCM type. The chapter discusses the benefits of specific notations for classical as well as modern challenges of SCM to help in the selection of notations. The resulting specifications serve as the basis for the holistic digitization of supply chains.

DOI: 10.4018/978-1-5225-7700-3.ch014

Copyright © 2019, IGI Global. Copying or distributing in print or electronic forms without written permission of IGI Global is prohibited.

INTRODUCTION

Nowadays, multiple fragmented (e.g., use of decision-making systems in individual steps such as supplier selection) or holistic (e.g., Efficient Consumer Response) digitization ideas for supply chains are discussed (Madjid, 2017). In most successful cases, data is used to implement better decisions and procedural improvements through digital information or virtually stored knowledge. In a first step, primarily routine tasks (e.g., interpreting invoices, ordering, desktop purchasing, tracking and tracing, etc.) were automated in supply chain. But with the ongoing megatrend of a digital world, even complex and extraordinary processes can be digitized (e.g., complex supplier negotiation using virtual agents, driverless transport systems in the warehouse, automatic goods receipt or exit control, neural networks for detecting critical points in a bill of material, etc.) (Brunet-Thornton and Martinez, 2018).

All these developments are accompanied by the digitization of processes. Modern business science and management practice stated for years that business challenges of SCM can be overcome by means of consistent and customer focused, i.e. value adding, process orientation (Page, 2016). Studies show that international markets, shorter lifecycles, and individual customer expectations can often only be handled with an internal enterprise configuration that thinks less in functions (e.g. sourcing department) than in workflows (e.g. production process) (Singh 2012; Aggarwal, 2004). With the availability of more sensors (e.g. from suppliers, within transportation medium, at the warehouse, at shipment) and advanced processing techniques (e.g., neural networks, generic algorithms, etc.), many approaches are being developed to digitize processes - SCM can greatly benefit from this (Nicoletti, 2016; Zhou and Chen, 2011). Supply chains (SC) in particular face the challenge of integrating several departments and coordinating multiple processes (Marchesini and Alcantara, 2016) and at the same time have to integrate data, methods and resources. Studies as well as individual case studies show clear evidences that positive effects within supply chain processes can only emerge when all required parties – internally as well as externally (e.g. suppliers, production, assembly, warehousing and sales) – are integrated into one fundamental process. Optimization, driven by individual departments or isolated target systems (e.g. focus on costs vs. customers), weaken digitalization initiatives for the entire supply chain (Vanathi and Swamynathan, 2016).

One of the essential prerequisites for digitization of supply chains is the ability to model underlying processes. This means that events, work steps, control flows and resources are described roughly or even specified in full detail. Resources include, for example, machines, people and parts as well as documents and information. Even in the classic BPM lifecycle, it is formulated that workflows are first modeled and then optimized (von Rosing, von Scheel and Scheer, 2014; Papajorgji 2013).

Two examples of the digitization of SCM processes will outline the need for modeling:

1. Picking errors should be avoided in logistics. As part of the automation a quality control, the process is initially modeled. This is the only way to analyze in which steps and for which resources digital techniques can be used to avoid order picking errors. For example, a new software might rely on the continuous measurement of weights (e.g., unloading, transport, and packaging) in the processes. A comparison with the integrated database automatically detects errors.
2. Industry 4.0 goes beyond the pure automation of known processes. Rather, it is about creating a smart factory that controls itself. For this, models are needed in all involved entities. This can be the product to be created (e.g., virtual model of the components), the necessary workflow (e.g., routes through the production lines), or background logistics (e.g., which events in processes indicate that parts need to be ordered).

These two fundamentally different examples of SCM digitization show that, the use of workflow software or holistic cloud / ERP systems requires to model relevant events (e.g., delivery arrives, product design faulty), activities (e.g., along the production line), participants (e.g., machines and people) as well as resources (e.g., data, documents and machines) in a model. The modelability may be implicitly (e.g., the procedures and business rules must be known to effectively use virtual agents) or explicitly given (e.g., the automation of transport logistics requires detailed plans of the routes and steps) (Bernardo, 2016).

However, the examples also show that the necessary models are fundamentally different. Some models are robust and durable (e.g., commodity warehousing), while others must be created on an ad-hoc basis and are executed immediately (e.g., a new product will be produced in a smart factory). The Business Process Management (BPM) discipline has developed different approaches how business processes can be modeled to support digitalization (Mishra and Sharma, 2014; Lederer, 2016). State of the art modeling techniques are for example BPMN, eEPCs or case-driven modeling (e.g. adaptive case management). Since every notation show different advantages and specifics (e.g. can be model-checked and transferred in software code) (Patig 2011; von Rosing, von Scheel and Scheer, 2014) and the different ideas for digitalization call for specific support by the underlying model, this paper will provide recommendations, which process modeling technique may support digitalization in different types of supply chain processes.

Therefore, the following research question will be answered in the context of this paper:

Which notations are most suitable for different supply chain process types to provide a model for digitalization?

In Chapter 2, a classification table is designed to assign the most appropriate modeling techniques to certain supply chain types. For this, the fundamental classification of Gattorna (2015) is used as one dimension to describe different supply chain designs. The process criteria of Lederer et al. (2017) serve as second dimension. They define which modeling techniques are suitable for which fundamental process properties. The combination of both dimensions will be presented as part of a Delphi study as documented by Lederer et al. (2019). In the discussion, the three modeling techniques most adequate for each supply chain design will be presented. Section 3 concludes this article with a summary and critical appraisal as well as implications.

MAPPING MODELLING TECHNIQUES TO SUPPLY CHAINS

The supply chain types as the first dimension (sub-section "supply chain types") come from the recognized publication of Gattorna (2015), who outlined in his studies and considerations that in business practice the existing supply chains can be grouped in five fundamental types. They are based on different customer buying behaviors and hence differ in their basic design, way of cooperation, flexibility, structure and goals (sub-section "Gattorna's supply chain types").

These essential process properties come from a study by Lederer et al. (2017). They evaluated, which state of the art modelling technique fits best to certain processes according to these properties (sub-section "Process build time techniques").

Existing Frameworks

Gattorna's Supply Chain Types

Gattorna defined the modern supply chain as "any combination of processes, functions, activities, relationships and pathways along which products, services, information and financial transactions flow in and between enterprises, in both directions, end-to-end" (Gattorna, 2015). He identified five prevailing consumer buying behaviors. Based on these, he defined five corresponding supply chain layouts also aligning business strategy, leadership and culture which will be used in this contribution to assess process modeling techniques (Gattorna, 2015):

(1) Customers of collaborative supply chains are interested in close integrated relationships with their suppliers fostering mutual gain. This type of supply chain is adequate for mature products and mostly predictable demand. The corporate incentive system is key, as it has to encourage teamwork and individual participation for maximum reliability and service culture towards the customer. (2) Lean supply chains are adequate for price-sensitive and transactional buying behavior. Surplus in general is not really appreciated, but routine and reliable products at lowest cost possible. Demand is predictable. Therefore, supply chain design focuses on continuously increasing efficiency of operations to process large quantities, raise standardization, and realize the maximum degree of economies of scale. (3) Agile supply chains primarily focus on speed, which customers expect in a structured and cost-efficient way. Demand is unpredictable and market conditions highly volatile. Therefore, customers are price sensitive, but aware that flexibility leads to a premium. (4) Campaign supply chains are mainly applied for capital construction projects, which require a tailor-made supply chain design due to its individual complexity. Customers require precision and controllability, think long-term and are risk-averse. It is relevant to supply on time, on demand, and on quality to meet the project budget. Solid planning and forecasting along the entire supply chain are hence critical methods that also require collaboration. (5) Fully flexible supply chains are relevant in case of unforeseen business disruptions as well as in emergency or humanitarian cases. All customers expect high responsiveness and speed from the supply chain, which needs to be activated instantaneously. Therefore, risk management for quick but resilient solutions is key.

Process Build Time Techniques

In their study, Lederer et al. (2017) present a collection of available modeling methods known in the BPM discipline. Among the 31 notations and methods, there are classical and well-known approaches such as BPMN or Case Management. Likewise, however, the list also includes rather unknown methods such as uBPMN and CCM, but their application appears very promising in very normative respectively flexible supply chains.

In addition to this classification, the authors follow the underlying idea in this article that these methods are particularly well or not well suited, if a process to be modeled has certain process characteristics. For this, the authors have created a state of the art list of process properties based on recognized publications. The characteristic values also come from current scientific contributions. This list of characteristics including their possible features is shown in Table 1.

Table 2 presents the evaluation table, which combines known state-of-the-art modeling techniques (columns) with fundamental process characteristics (rows). As a classification scheme, it shows which properties of processes can be satisfactorily supported by which technique. An entry in the table cells

Table 1. Process characteristics (PC), properties and scaling number (Lederer et al. 2017)

1	2	3	4	5
PC_1 Structuring				
Structured	structured with ad hoc exceptions	structured with predefined exceptions	loosely structured	unstructured
PC_2 Process Representation				
Activity oriented	Rule oriented	Artefact oriented	∅	∅
PC_3 Process Implementation				
Workflow engine	Rule engine	Program control flow	∅	∅
PC_4 Trend orientation				
Data-driven	Case-driven	Social-driven	∅	∅
PC_5 Process participants				
Person to person	Person to application	Application to application	∅	∅
PC_6 Knowledge intensity				
Knowledge-intensive	Automated/Repeatable	∅	∅	∅
PC_8 Interrelatedness				
Linked explicitly	Inferred link	∅	∅	∅
PC_9 Collaboration intensity				
Collaborative	Semi-collaborative	Non-collaborative	∅	∅
PC_11 Value repetition				
Ad hoc	Administrative	Collaborative	Production	∅
PC_16 Implementation				
Big bang	Step by step		∅	∅
PC_17 Process instantiation				
Automated	Semi-automated	Manual	∅	∅
PC_23 Process cycle time				
Long-running	Medium	Short running	∅	∅
PC_7, 10,12, 13, 14, 15, 18, 19, 20, 21, 22				
High	Medium	Low	∅	∅

indicates that the technique can be used when a process holds this value of the characteristic. For example: The cell 'P2_uBPMN/PC_6: Knowledge intensity' contains '2', i.e., 'Automated/Repeatable' (from Table 1). This means uBPMN is suitable for processes attributed with this property in the respective process characteristic.

The study results of Lederer et al. (2017) will be used as a list of possible modeling techniques for this article because it offers many advantages in answering the research question: (i) In contrast to other studies, well-known as well as rather unknown techniques are listed. This makes new scientific findings possible. (ii) The classification scheme can be used as a recommendation system. This has already been demonstrated in two field studies (Lederer et al., 2017; Lederer et al., 2018), but not yet for SCM. (iii)

Table 2. Domain-independent classification of modeling techniques (Lederer et al. 2017)

Characteristics \ Modeling techniques	P_1: S-BPM	P_2: uBPMN	P_3: BPMN Plus	P_4: Deontic BPMN	P_5: BPMN Gamification	P_6: Ad-hoc BPMN	P_7: BPMN light	P_8: AC-BPM	P_9: ArC-BPM	P_10: BPMN4RS	P_11: BPMNDiffViz	P_12: BPMN choreography diagram
PC_1 Structuring	1	1	3, 4, 5	4, 5	1 to5	4, 5	1, 2	1	1	1, 2, 3	1 to5	1
PC_2 Process Representation	3	1, 2, 3	1, 3	1, 2	1, 2	1	1	1	3	1, 3	1, 2	1
PC_3Process Implementation	3	1, 2, 3	1, 3	1, 2	1, 2, 3	1	1	1, 3	3	1	1, 2, 3	3
PC_4 Trend orientation	1, 3	1, 2	1, 2	2	2, 3	2	2	1	1	1, 2	1	1, 2
PC_5 Fixation	2, 3	2, 3	2, 3	2	1, 2	1, 2	1, 2	1, 2	1, 2	1, 2, 3	2, 3	2, 3
PC_6 Knowledge intensity	2	2	2	2	2	1	1	2	2	2	2	2
PC_7 Diversity of Information	2	2	1	2	2	1	2, 3	1, 2	1, 2	2	2	3
PC_8Interrelatedness	1	1	2	2	1, 2	2	1	1	1	1	1, 2	1
PC_9 Collaboration intensity	1	1, 2, 3	1, 2, 3	1, 2, 3	1, 2	1, 2, 3	1, 2, 3	1, 2, 3	1, 2, 3	1, 2, 3	1, 2, 3	1, 2, 3
PC_10 Value	1	1	1	1	1	1, 2	1	1	1	1	1	1
PC_11 Value repetition	4	4	4	4	4	1, 3	4	4	4	4	4	4
PC_12 Predictability	1	1	1	1	1, 2, 3	3	1, 2	1	1	1, 2	1	1
PC_13 Flexibility	3	3	1	1	1, 2, 3	1	2, 3	3	3	2, 3	3	3
PC_14 Model-ability	1	1	1, 2	2	1, 2, 3	3	1, 2	1	1	1, 2	1	1
PC_15 Complexity	3	2	2	3	1, 2, 3	1	2, 3	1, 2, 3	1, 2, 3	1, 2, 3	1, 2, 3	1, 2, 3
PC_16 Implementation	1, 2	1, 2	1, 2	1, 2	1, 2	1, 2	1, 2	1, 2	1, 2	1, 2	1, 2	1, 2
PC_17 Process instantiation	1	1, 2	1, 2	1, 2	1, 2	2, 3	1, 2, 3	1, 2	1, 2	1, 2	1	1, 2
PK_18 Robustness	1, 2, 3	1, 2	1, 2, 3	1, 2, 3	1, 2	3	1, 2, 3	1	1	1, 2	1	1
PC_19 Adaptability	1, 2, 3	1, 2, 3	1, 2, 3	1, 2, 3	2, 3	1, 2	2	1	1	2	1	1, 2
PC_20 Adaptivity	1, 2, 3	1, 2, 3	1, 2, 3	1, 2, 3	1, 2, 3	1, 2, 3	2, 3	1	1	1, 2	1	2, 3
PC_21 Selection	1, 2	1, 2, 3	1, 2, 3	1, 2, 3	2, 3	1, 2	2, 3	1, 2	1, 2	2	1, 2	2, 3
PC_22 IT needs	1	1	1	1	1	1	1	1	1	1	1	1
PC_23Process cycle time	1, 2, 3	1, 2, 3	1, 2, 3	1, 2, 3	1, 2, 3	1, 2, 3	1, 2, 3	1, 2, 3	1, 2, 3	1, 2, 3	1, 2, 3	1, 2, 3

The given list of modeling techniques is domain-independent and can therefore now be applied to the SCM domain in this contribution.

Methodology

In order to come to a recommendation as which modelling technique is suitable for which SCM type, the two dimensions described above need to be combined. The methodology represents the results from Lederer et al. (2019). Such an assignment of methods and process types is possible with different approaches and visualizations. In science and practice, among other things, Ishikawa diagrams and matrices are known as typical solutions. However, while the first ones have the disadvantage that they are not understandable in a large number of types and methods and do not allow multiple assignments (Best and Weth, 2009), matrices are characterized by a high degree of traceability for many entries. Furthermore, this contribution does not consider the interactions between properties and does not add any additional grouping within the dimensions. The assignment, therefore, follows the matrix approach of Greischel (2003), which represents the process properties and notations on the axes of a matrix.

In order to use the matrix as a classification and recommendation system, it has to be evaluated which of the methods described in Lederer et al. (2017) is suitable for which SCM type of Gattorna (2015). From the number of matches per notation, tendencies can be identified which modeling technique makes more sense and which one is less adequate. Although this contribution is not quantitative research, the number of true occurrences should be used as an indication.

The actual evaluation was logically based on a three-stage target activity grid method based on Best and Weth (2009) in the context of a scientific Delphi study (Kaplan and Norton, 2009): (i) The process properties of Lederer et al. (2017) were first applied line by line to the strategic dimensions of Gattorna (2015). (ii) This transformation, in turn, can be further developed to the feature expression of Lederer et al. (2017). (iii) The number of matches per SCM type gives a sequence of notations as to their suitability. Table 3 shows the resulting assignments. From 23 process properties, 16 strategic dimensions, 5 SCM types and a total of 69 characteristics of the process properties, 126,960 evaluation decisions are needed. In order to ensure objectivity despite the multitude of evaluations, two designated SCM experts with more than 35 years of SCM research and practical experience have made the assessments. After a separate evaluation, they explained deviations in a personal interview (Lederer et al. 2019).

RESULTS

The expert evaluation results in the following recommendation model (see Table 4). According to the generic model and based on the scaling, the notations described are the top three for each SCM type.

The advantages and limitations of using the recommended notations for the different SCM types are discussed as in Lederer et al. (2019) in the following sections.

Collaborative

As shown, in collaborative supply chains, customers are highly integrated into the value chain and their demand is hence predictable. These two central features are especially supported by the recommended process modeling notations:

Social BPM stands for a general trend in business processes to give more participation to teams and stakeholders. This is done, for example, by using tools for group decisions. Instead of prescribing the decisions with the help of business rules and regulations, the human competences are used by people

Table 3. Process characteristics (PC) properties (numbers) for the supply chain types (Lederer et al. 2019)

Lean	Collaborative	Agile	Campaign	Fully flexible
PC_1 Structuring				
1	2	2,3	3	3,4
PC_2 Process Representation				
1	2	2	2	3
PC_3Process Implementation				
3	1;	1	1,2	2
PC_4 Trend orientation				
1	3	3	2	2
PC_5 Process participants				
1	2,3	1,2	1,2	1
PC_6 Knowledge intensity				
2	1	1,2	1,2	1
PC_7 Diversity of Information				
3	1	2	1,2	1
PC_8 Interrelatedness				
1	1,2	1,2	1,2	2
PC_9 Collaboration intensity				
3	1	2	1,2	1
PC_10 Value				
1	1,2	2	1,2	3
PC_11 Value repetition				
1,2	1,2	1,2	1	1
PC_12 Predictability				
1	1,2	2,3	2	3
PC_13 Flexibility				
3	2	1	2	1
PC_14 Model-ability				
1	2	2	1,2	3
PC_15 Complexity				
3	2	1	1,2	1
PC_16 Implementation				
2	1	1	1	1
PC_17 Process instantiation				
1	2	2	1,2	3
PK_18 Robustness				
1	2	2,3	2,3	3
PC_19 Adaptability				
3	2	1	1,2	1

continued on following page

Table 3. Continued

Lean	Collaborative	Agile	Campaign	Fully flexible
PC_20 Adaptivity				
3	2	1,2	1,2	1
PC_21 Selection				
3	2	1	1,2	1
PC_22 IT needs				
1	2	1,2	2	2,3
PC_23 Process cycle time				
3	3	3	1,2,3	3

Table 4. Process modelling recommendations for the different SCM types (Lederer et al. 2019)

Rank	Modelling techniques	Number of true criteria occurrences
Collaborative		
1	Social BPM	25
2	BPMN Gamification	23
3	BPM 2.0	22
Agile		
1	Social BPM / Process Design Thinking	31
2	BPMN Gamification / BPM 2.0	28
3	Ad-hoc BPMN	26
Lean		
1	BPMN choreography diagram	28
2	Simulation-based BPMN / BPMN4CP	26
3	uBPMN	25
Campaign		
1	BPMN Gamification	39
2	Social BPM	38
3	Design Thinking	36
Fully flexible		
1	Collaborative BPM / Process Design Thinking	26
2	Ad-hoc BPMN/Adaptive Case/Mgt./ Collaborative Case Mgt.	24
3	Emergent Case Management	23

who work every day in the process. For SCM processes, the managers and operators involved in sourcing, production planning and distribution know best what the customer expects. Therefore, for example, in the approach of subject-oriented business process management (S-BPM) not end-to-end processes are defined by the management or process consultant, but rather the behavior of individual actors (e.g. the freight forwarder who plans first, then informs the customer in advance, then drives the tour and finally arrives at the customer). The complete recording of all behavior (e.g. the customer gets the preliminary information, prepares the warehouse and then receives the freight on the factory premises), gives a detailed picture of individual goals and their interdependence (so-called interaction diagram). Collaboration, which was perhaps previously given implicitly in the process, can thus be explicitly documented and even planned. The notation thus strengthens the desired collaboration by capturing dependencies based on the behavior of individual actors. This also serves the common understanding of value chains – an important prerequisite for success in this SCM type.

A similar way is BPM 2.0, which is the third-ranked recommendation of the model. The idea of this notation is that not only the behavior of individual actors is modeled, but involved persons can model the processes themselves. For example, Web 2.0 tools (e.g. processes as wiki entries) are made accessible to all parties involved in a workflow. Every actor (e.g. supplier, customer) can contribute ideas to the process. In SCM, physical storage, transport and handling play a central role in identifying process improvement. Therefore, people on-site might have the best ideas for optimization compared to a (possibly central) process documentation. Following the idea that the knowhow of the crowd produces the best results, this approach offers the opportunity to gain a high degree of integration while balancing all the requirements of the various roles. SCM is characterized by many conflicting objectives (e.g. customer demand for fast delivery versus cost reduction desire of the supplier through centralization of warehouses). The resolution of such conflicts significantly contributes to the success of a collaborative supply chain. BPM 2.0 contributes to integration in two ways: (i) Efficiency can be increased by allowing people to share ideas quickly and efficiently (e.g. in chat rooms/forums instead of modeling ideas in complex documents). (ii) Furthermore, the direct involvement of many people instead of focusing on a process modeler allows more ideas to be exchanged. Thereby, innovation is fostered that will perhaps resolve several conflicting goals.

BPM Gamification as an approach to process modeling and optimization can be used in addition to the two described methods. Persons or organizations involved in value creation processes are rewarded formally (e.g. monetary) or informally (e.g. levels of status) for meaningful contributions. Such contribution may be an improvement of the process model (including the activities, roles, documents, and IT systems) as described above. But it can also refer to affirming the desired behavior of the participants (e.g. more collaboration, more data sharing, and reduction of mistakes). Relevant for the use in the SCM will be to unite the different goals and partners in a uniform incentive system, so that the entire value added chain profits from gamification. This is especially true for SCM, since the consideration of only one process step or for only one participating organization would not lead to sustainable optimization in process orientation.

Agile

The recommended modeling approaches for agile SCM are very similar to those of the collaborative type. The essential distinction of the types lies in the fact that in agile processes, the collaboration needs to be realized on a very individual basis. For the methods to be used, on the one hand, this means that no great investment should require for the documentation and design of the processes. As in classical BPM, for example, extensive actual modeling with complex analyses are often necessary. This may not justify the expense for a one-time process, which runs only for one specific customer. On the other hand, the techniques must be capable of handling spontaneous and short-term exceptions. For SCM, this flexibility may results from customers demanding a short-term plan adjustment (e.g. different quantities or delivery times). Likewise, changing the required goods (e.g. quality, size, or special conditions such as cooling) can have a major impact on the process.

The fact that the recommended notations support collaboration in the process has already been discussed in the previous section. Therefore, the question should be answered to what extent the modeling approaches also support the described requirements for individuality and flexibility.

Design thinking in processes is a rather new method that helps to sustain the customer perspective in processes. In interdisciplinary teams, optimal processes are created through intensive discussions. Since this approach is usually organized in workshops, it is questionable whether it is suitable for very agile processes. After all, a Design Thinking Workshop generates effort for all organizations involved in SCM processes. Where Social BPM and BPM 2.0 provide a more cost-effective approach through IT support, Design Thinking may be more appropriate for creating templates. If basic decisions are documented in templates (e.g. in which cases the customer prefers which delivery conditions in general), detailed decisions for agile individual cases can then be defined as part of BPM 2.0 or Social BPM.

Ad-hoc BPMN describes a possibility, how – in processes documented with the extensive Business Process Model and Notation (BPMN) – also short term adjustments become possible. So-called light versions of the notation define a selection from the large set of possible model elements. This reduction in modeling scope could be made in the SCM, when the involved companies agree to such complexity reduction. By doing so, the effort of modeling can be reduced.

Lean

Lean supply chains can be observed in stable environments, where process optimizations are only possible through intensive and data-driven analysis (e.g. Six Sigma). Since the participants or at least the interfaces between them need to be defined in great detail, completely different modeling notations are to be expected in comparison to the previously discussed SCM types.

In fact, the model does not recommend collaborative or agile SCM methods. All recommended modeling methods have their central advantage in the combination of process scheduling with a detailed design of entities. This information density is used in SCM practice for incremental process improvements. While radical (large but high-risk) innovations are possible using the agile and collaborative methods (e.g. complete re-engineering in Design Thinking workshops), the recommendations for lean SCM rather support data-driven incremental improvements.

The BPMN choreography diagram, for example, is a further development of the established BPMN 2.0 standard, in which not only the professional but also the technical background of the process is documented. Similar to Social BPM, partners' interactions are modeled in the supply chain, but their internal states and requirements are not presented. Choreography diagrams do not replace the actual extensive process description (these contain all detailed activities), but instead enrich these models through communication channels. Therefore, they have the potential to support complex supply chains by displaying not only the control flows of the goods (activities) but also the flow of information (data, e.g. digital currencies in the future). Especially in times when genuine optimizations can still be achieved in established value chains only through high data integration, this approach is forward-looking. It lays the foundation for well-known ideas such as Vendor Managed Inventory, Predictive Production or Intelligent Forecasting.

If such a data-driven understanding of value chains exists, simulations become possible. For established processes, for example, new workflows, routings, storage strategies or even deliveries can be tested in the model before they are actually rolled out in practice. In lean process optimization (e.g. Loss Function, Six Sigma), simulation and observation data is often used extensively to balance between process alternatives. Due to the ongoing trend of globalization in value creation (e.g. global sourcing, outsourcing) simulations can also be used to simulate new partners in the supply chain in advance. In a nutshell, simulation-based BPMN offers a clever combination to link modeling processes with incremental innovation opportunities.

BPMN4CP is an extension of BPMN, which was originally developed for hospitals. However, the idea behind it also fits for modern lean supply chains. In essence, four major adjustments are made: (1) There is the possibility to model goals of different actors explicitly in one single diagram. Originally intended for the balance between doctors and the hospital's financial management, the approach can be transferred very well since a large number of partners are involved in a lean supply chain. Moreover, quality indicators are modeled in the control flow, which can be used directly for quantitative lean principles. (2) In addition to the control flow, there is a data and document view. It shows what data is available and what dependencies occur (e.g. generalization between documents such as contracts). The first advantage for SCM is that quality department can model quality data (e.g. scrap, on-time delivery, etc.) in the process right in the planning stage. As modern supply chains are sometimes often quite complex, the whole presentation helps to identify the source of poor quality more quickly in distributed networks. Completely new approaches such as deep learning in production or future-oriented new deliveries will be strengthened. (3) Activities in the control flow are divided into three types: diagnosis, therapy and support. In fact, there is a similar distinction in operational logistics. Decisions are made (e.g. for or against a supplier), material/data is processed (e.g. loaded/stored), and some activities are just enablers (e.g. maintenance). In this way, the complexity of a supply chain can be reduced visually. At the same time interesting new simulations and tests become possible. For example, it can be investigated which operative activity causes most errors. (4) Resources are bundled in BPMN4CP. This phenomenon is also known in SCM in the form of coupling (e.g. transport), packaging (e.g. paths), and commission (e.g. picking).

uBPMN, another recommended modeling notation, is also an extension of BPMN. It was originally intended for ubiquitous computing. However, it can, as BPMN4CP, be used optimally for supply chains, because systems that have to be permanently present (even in concurrency) can be explicitly modeled and connected.

In modern supply chains, IT systems are constantly collecting data (e.g. for tracking and tracing). These applications are mostly encapsulated as services (e.g. EDI interfaces) and should be permanently available. However, such concurrency issues cannot be represented in known SCM-specific modeling such as Value Stream Maps.

In summary, the recommendations all have the potential to contribute to the lean supply chain. They support the analytical approach of optimization, as it makes sense in this type. Although some notations were not primarily designed for SCM, their application could lead to new process insights.

Campaign

From process modeling point of view, Campaign supply chains have the central advantage that the actual modelling and design may create effort. For large and important projects, complex and unique SCM processes have to be created.

The recommendation of BPMN Gamification, which was transferred from the gaming scene to process domain, initially is surprising. After all, it has also been shown in the last sections that gamification can be used to persuade individuals to communicate their ideas for process optimizations (e.g. Design Thinking) or even to explicitly model them (e.g. BPM 2.0). Another considerable aspect of gamification is that people within the process can also be rewarded for services. Reward can either be offered for general process loyalty (e.g. adherence to the modelled control flow) or to special or excessive engagement (e.g. evaluation of more suppliers than required). The second reward style can convince in this SCM type: The Campaign supply chain lives from the motivation of the persons involved. While lean processes are more likely to manage the mass and number of process instants, in large projects all individuals must work together in a trusting manner. At the same time, champions must be sufficiently incentivized. Motivation is enhanced by this approach by meaningfully combination of BPMN activities to badges. For example, not only the identification of suitable suppliers, but also their selection and commissioning (i.e. several activities) are connected as a badge. If one actor of the process is particularly prominent, he/she can reach a higher level (measures progressively the success in the game) by points for successfully managing the bundle of activities. In this way, the motivation and commitment of individuals/individual organizations in major projects can be rewarded. This extension of BPMN provides a suitable approach. It would be conceivable, for example, to award the budget of a major project for this form of incentivization. The developers of this process modelling idea describe as a great advantage that assessment guidelines can be explicitly modelled. In evaluations, they also show the benefits of explicit rules in heterogeneous process teams. Especially in important and large projects (e.g. construction projects), policy decisions (e.g. local sourcing) cannot or should not be modelled directly in BPMN (e.g. due to compliance). Nevertheless, gamification can reward decisions and behaviour in line with the big goals of the entire supply chain. Especially in the political-social environment, which lives from individual heroes in a project, the notation can thus make a valuable contribution. However, it should be emphasized that gamification must be planned very well, because simple gamification approaches often fail in practice.

The benefits of Social BPM were already discussed above. The advantages and limits of this approach also apply to this type of SCM. Chances arise from the efficient goal and opinion alignment in heterogeneous groups involved in large-sized projects,

The described effort of Design Thinking Workshops can be worthwhile with this SCM type. Especially with heterogeneous process teams, but with one specific customer, this customer-centric process modelling can be used. An application can also make sense when rough processes are already in place for the large-scale project, but a more intensive focus on the customer is needed with radical innovations.

Fully Flexible

Fully flexible supply chains represent a type of process that faces many unforeseen exceptions. Often, basic process patterns must be quickly adapted.

It is, therefore, not surprising that the model of this article mainly offers notations and methods of case management. All sub classifications (e.g. Adaptive, Emergent, and Collaborative Case Management) have in common that processes exist as templates and not as detailed diagrams. In the traditional process management, processes are first modeled. Then they are explained to the people involved (human resources), rolled out in IT systems (IT as a resource) or equipped accordingly (machines as resources). These resources are used when the process is instantiated and executed. In short, this means that process execution is only possible after modeling.

For the particular type of SCM, however, it is crucial that not all features and exceptions can be modeled in advance. If people make mistakes (e.g. serious wrong order picking) or major errors (e.g. low quality of an important component), the process (e.g. packing and shipment) must be quickly adapted. This means that process steps, especially those where skilled workers with competences have to assess new situations, are redesigned during execution. The modeling and execution take place simultaneously. Case Management offers a convincing approach: Process instances are managed as a case. This means that for every new process instance (e.g. a delivery) there is a basic template for the case (e.g. in the steps of picking, packaging, route planning, and customer reception). If unforeseen events occur (e.g. packaging errors), the details within the basic steps (e.g. obtaining other packaging material) may be adjusted by experts.

This basic principle is shared by all sub-forms of case management. They combine good practices (templates) with the flexibility for major changes (exceptions). Thus, they support so-called knowledge workers, as experts can react flexibly to changes in a professional manner.

Adaptive Case Management focuses on the idea of reusing cases. Solved cases, that is those that have sensibly responded to exceptions with new process entities (e.g. changed actions, roles, and documents) are archived. If known exceptions occur, the known procedural solution can be used again as a template. This approach is particularly appropriate if the process contains both highly standardized (e.g. picking) and less standardized (e.g. supplier negotiation) steps.

Emergent Case Management tries to integrate approaches of BPM 2.0 into this approach. Web 2.0 tools are used. For example, if exceptions occur, skilled workers can contribute to the case in forums, wikis, chats, and other groupware tools (meaningful adjustments to the process model).

Collaborative Case Management supports when the activities with degrees of freedom need to be decided in a group. Applications are better known in the area of Product Lifecycle Management (PLM). Nevertheless, examples from the SCM are also conceivable. The template of the case may include, for example, the “selection of a suitable supplier”. However, if many and complicated criteria (such as those that are difficult to quantify) are taken into account, the team can include an additional process exception. For example, the team decides to organize a new tender. All process members decide as a team (group decision support system) about which suppliers to engage.

SUMMARY AND OUTLOOK

Process orientation in the company is an essential approach to meet modern business challenges. First, this applies to traditional SCM issues such as international competition, competitive pressure and integration within the value chain. Second, it also applies to the application of new technologies or in the overall context of digitalization - because the modeling of processes is considered as important first step for the digital transformation in SCM. At the same time, not all modeling notations are suitable for all different SCM processes. Rather, fundamental characteristics inherent in the various supply chains, such as the degree of flexibilization, standardization and customer-orientation, determine which notation SCM process models should be used.

This article is based on the approved and evaluated publications by Gattorna (2015) and Lederer et al. (2017). The first publication has described five major types of supply chain as stereotypes. The second study shows in an assignment model using process properties, in which situations, which modelling technique makes most sense. In a qualitative study, both results were combined within this contribution. In the results discussion, it emerges that SCM practitioners can benefit from the advantages and opportunities of various modern process notations. In each, the reasonable design alternatives differ greatly by SCM type.

Further research is needed to evaluate existing results in quantitative or case study-based investigations. Of course, the results are limited to the application fields of the studies used. For example, Gattorna (2015) as well as the resulting model of this contribution, right now, mainly focus on the customer and the buying behaviour. Therefore, there are no market-driven behaviour and neither product-driven or hybrid characteristics included. In addition, in practice, there are more hybrid SCM types appearing, which combine different stereotypes. The analysis of the appropriate notations is thus also dependent on the specifics of individual partners, opposites and situations. Furthermore, the described characteristics are generally valid - this shows the conceptually application in the discussion. Nevertheless, operational (e.g. notation requirements) as well as strategic (e.g. advancement of SCM) internal specifics are to be considered during productive use. Thanks to flexibility, the developed model can thus be used by SCM practitioners simply by adding their constraints to the given characteristics, classification or process types.

REFERENCES

Aggarwal, R. (2004). Making BPM Work. *DM Review*, *14*, 28–59.

Bernardo, N. (2016). *Lean and Digitize: An Integrated Approach to Process Improvement.* London: Routledge.

Best, E., & Weth, M. (2009). *Geschäftsprozesse optimieren.* Wiesbaden: Gabler. doi:10.1007/978-3-8349-9410-3

Brunet-Thornton, R., & Martinez, F. (2018). *Analyzing the Impacts of Industry 4.0 in Modern Business Environments.* Hershey, PA: IGI Global. doi:10.4018/978-1-5225-3468-6

Gattorna, J. (2015). *Dynamic Supply Chains: How to design, build and manage people-centric value networks.* London: Pearson Education Limited.

Greischel, P. (2003). *Balanced Scorecard.* Munich: Vahlen.

Kamalahmadi, M., & Mellat-Parast, M. (2016). Developing a resilient supply chain through supplier flexibility and reliability assessment. *International Journal of Production Research*, *54*(1), 302–321. doi:10.1080/00207543.2015.1088971

Kaplan, R. S., & Norton, D. P. (2009). Management mit System. *Harvard Business Manager Edition*, *2009*, 39–55.

Lederer, M. (2016). *Business Process Transparency Management.* Nuremberg: University of Erlangen-Nuremberg.

Lederer, M., Betz, & Schmidt, W. (2018). Digital Transformation, Smart Factories, and Virtual Design – Contributions of Subject Orientation. *Proceedings of the S-BPM ONE* '18. 10.1145/3178248.3178256

Lederer, M., Avci, R., & Schmidt, W. (2017). Should Process Management Add its Two Cents? A Classification Approach for the Selection of Process Management Build-Time Techniques for Software Development Purposes. In *Proceedings of the 43nd Euromicro Conference on Software Engineering and Advanced Applications*. IEEE. 10.1109/SEAA.2017.40

Lederer, M., Quitt, A., Büsch, M., & Remzi, A. (2019). (in press). One size fits all? An Analytical Approach how to make use of Process Methods for Different Fundamental Supply Chain Types. *International Journal of Supply Chain and Operations Resilience.*

Madjid, T. (2017). *Enterprise Information Systems and the Digitalization of Business Functions*. Hershey, PA: IGI Global.

Marchesini, M. P., & Alcantara, R. C. (2016). Logistics activities in supply chain business process. *International Journal of Logistics Management*, *27*(1), 6–30. doi:10.1108/IJLM-04-2014-0068

Mishra, P., & Sharma, R. K. (2014). A hybrid framework based on SIPOC and Six Sigma DMAIC for improving process dimensions in supply chain network. *International Journal of Quality & Reliability Management*, *31*(5), 522–546. doi:10.1108/IJQRM-06-2012-0089

Page, S. (2016). *The Power of Business Process Improvement*. New York: AMACOM.

Papajorgji, P. (2013). *Enterprise Business Modeling, Optimization Techniques, and Flexible Information Systems*. Hershey, PA: IGI Global. doi:10.4018/978-1-4666-3946-1

Patig, S. (2011). *BPM Software and Process Modelling Languages in Practice: Results from an empirical investigation*. BoD, Norderstedt.

Singh, P. K. (2012). Management of Business Processes Can Help an Organization Achieve Competitive Advantage. *International Management Review*, *8*, 19–26.

Vanathi, R., & Swamynathan, R. (2016). A Study on Influence of Supply Chain Strategies on Competitive Advantage of Textile Industry - An Integrated Model. *Journal Of Contemporary Research In Management*, *11*, 41–55.

von Rosing, M., von Scheel, H., & Scheer, A. W. (2014). *The Complete Business Process Handbook: Body of Knowledge from Process Modeling to BPM*. Burlington: Morgan Kaufmann.

Zhou, Z., & Chen, D. (2011). *Fundamentals of Digital Manufacturing Science*. Cham: Springer.

Chapter 15
Day in the Life of Supply Chain Analysts in a Digital World

Shiva R. Esturi
Micron Technology Inc, USA

Bo Liao
Western Digital Corporation, USA

ABSTRACT

This chapter discusses the role of supply chain analytics in managing digital supply chain, as well as the practical implementation approaches of supply chain analytics. The chapter first discusses a typical day in the life of supply chain analysts. It then discusses the categorization of supply chain analytics and some practical recommendations for the implementation of supply chain analytics. Finally, the chapter provides a case study illustrating some important considerations in supply chain design.

INTRODUCTION

Digital technology has been continuing to enable supply chains to be a competitive advantage. A decade ago, technologies that enabled supply chain to be faster and accurate included material requirements planning (MRP), enterprise resource planning (ERP), and in-memory computing for advanced planning and optimization systems. In the current era, technologies that are emerging include big data, machine learning techniques, social media, robotics and many more. Unlike before, there is an increased pace at which innovative technologies are being introduced. It is important than ever to identify specific technologies that provide competitive advantage.

Under the backdrop of fast-pacing technology advances, the role of supply chain analysts is also evolving. A decade ago, supply chain analysts are primarily responsible for creating supply chain plans from scratch on papers or in excel. In the past decade, along with the maturity of enterprise resource planning and advanced planning systems, their primary responsibility changed from creating the plan into analyzing the plan output from the advanced planning systems. In the future, most likely, the task of plan analysis will be replaced by Artificial Intelligence. Once we are there, the role of supply chain analysts will further shift into taking actions to tackle unexpected circumstances. One could imagine that

DOI: 10.4018/978-1-5225-7700-3.ch015

Copyright © 2019, IGI Global. Copying or distributing in print or electronic forms without written permission of IGI Global is prohibited.

a Supply Chain analyst receives alerts from Mobile Apps showing actions required to address certain urgent upstream supply issues.

Supply chain analytics in a digital world is more important than ever because of the volume and availability of data. In the past, supply chain analytics enabled efficient supply chain management by validating or replacing conventional wisdoms; but the value added to the business was limited by the availability of data and power of computer. In the digital world, a vast amount of supply chain data is produced and recorded daily, thanks to the big data infrastructure and cloud storage technologies. It is up to the capability of each company to either make efficient use of them or leave them untouched.

In this Chapter, we first discuss the four categories of supply chain analytics and their respective impact to the business. We then describe a typical day of supply chain analysts, and discuss how they may employ the concepts of supply chain analytics and optimization in daily life. Next, we discuss some critical factors of developing successful supply chain analytics teams. Specifically, we discuss the impact of decentralization for various supply chain analytics categories, and the implementation model of supply chain analytics teams. In the last section, we discuss a few practical considerations of enabling supply chain analytics and optimization in a medium-size or large-size company, using semi-conductor industry as a case study.

LITERATURE REVIEW

There is a vast literature discussing and evaluating the application of analytics in supply chain. We first review literature discussing the applications and performance of supply chain analytics, which are not necessarily placed in the context of digital technologies. Then we review literature that specifically discuss the application of data science and big data in supply chain design and management.

We first review the research evaluating applications of supply chain analytics. Trkman et al. (2010) conducted a systematic and structured analysis of the impact of business analytics on supply chain performance. Their research results show that the use of business analytics in critical process areas can affect supply chain's performance. Specifically, they show that the analytical capabilities indicators along could explain 66.7% of the variability in the performance of the companies in the sample studied. Chae et al. (2014) developed a theoretical framework for supply chain analytics and its impact on the performance of supply chain management. According to the paper, anecdotal evidence holds that the use of business analytics is positively associated with organizational performance, and the important question is whether the use of analytics for supply chain management is just hype or if it has a real effect in enabling performance improvement. The finding from Chae et al. (2014) indicates that the positive impact of analytics on supply chain performance could be real. They also identified relevant latent variables and indicators for empirical research on this topic. Sahey and Ranjan (2008) discussed the traditional and real-time business intelligence, and discussed the advantages of implementing real time business intelligence in supply chain solutions to support supply chain analytics. O'Dwyer and Renner (2011) discussed the promises of advanced analytics on supply chain management and presented several case studies. They stated that the focus of advanced analytics on supply chain will shift from the internal cross-functional sharing of data to greater coordination and shared understanding of the data flows across value chain partners. With this, individual silos within the supply chain will be torn down; instead, a single, broader supply chain will emerge.

There is also literature emerging studying the impact of big data analytics and data science in supply chain. Waller and Fawcett (2013) proposed the definition of data science in supply chain management as "the application of quantitative and qualitative methods from a variety of disciplines in combination with supply chain management theory to solve relevant supply chain management problems and predict outcomes, taking into account data quality and availability issues". The paper examined possible applications of data science, predictive analytics and big data in practice, and provided examples of research questions from these applications. Gunasekaran et al. (2017) studied the impact of big data and predictive analytics assimilation on supply chain and organizational performance. The paper conceptualized the assimilation of big data and predictive analytics as a three-stage process: acceptance, routinization, and assimilation. Their findings suggested that connectivity and information sharing under the mediation effect of top management commitment are positively related to the acceptance of big data and predictive analytics. Tan et al. (2015) proposed an analytic infrastructure for firms to assist firms to capture the potential of innovation afforded by data and to gain competitive advantage. They showed from case studies that the proposed data analytic approach enabled firms to utilize big data to gain competitive advantage by enhancing their supply chain innovation capabilities.

THE FOUR CATEGORIES OF SUPPLY CHAIN ANALYTICS

Supply chain analytics can be categorized as descriptive, predictive, prescriptive and cognitive analytics based on the complexity of the analytics and the business value it may provide.

To explain each of the categories, "descriptive analytics" is the type of analytics that provides answer to the simple question of "what has happened". For example, crutching historical demand data to arrive at average monthly demand quantity for a product is descriptive analytics. It is the type of analytics that is relatively less complex and provides less value to the business, compared to other three types of analytics. Rather than simply summarizing historical data, "predictive analytics" utilizes historical data to predict the future. In other words, it answers the question of "what will happen". The third category of analytics, "prescriptive analytics", goes beyond summarizing historical data and making future predictions. It optimizes for the solutions to tackle business problems. It answers the question of "what should we do about it". The final category of analytics, "cognitive analytics", is the category with highest complexity but also potentially bring the highest value to the business. "Cognitive analytics" is the type of analytics that learns from historical data and human decisions, with the objective of training the computer to mimic and replace human decisions and naturally interacting with people. Machine learning and artificial intelligence fall into this category of analytics. Figure 1 maps these four categories of supply chain analytics into various levels of analytics complexity and the value to the business.

As an example, consider the newsboy in the newsvendor problem. The newsboy gathering historical demand quantity and calculating the demand standard deviation is descriptive analytics. Him predicting forward-looking demand is predictive analytics. Knowing that the demand would be uncertain but may follow a distribution, him utilizing the newsvendor model to calculate how many newspapers to procure to maximize his expected profit, is prescriptive analytics. Alternatively, if he records his decision and outcome every day and train the computer to learn from the data and make decisions for the future, then he is implementing cognitive analytics.

Figure 1.

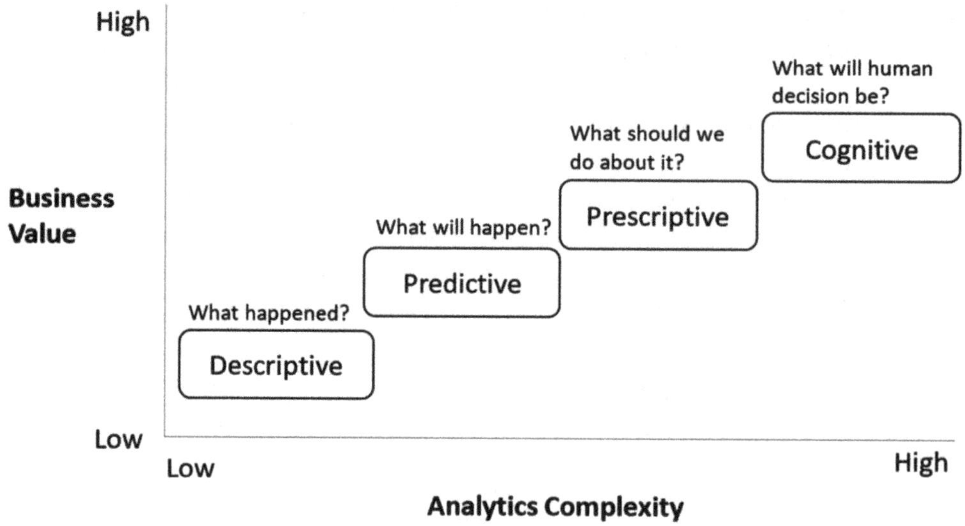

Below, we discuss the application and use cases for each of the analytics categories. Most of the mid-to-large sized companies are very sophisticated in utilizing the results from descriptive analytics. To enhance visualization power, business stakeholders commonly use charts, tables and dashboards to present data from different angles, as well as visually track the progress of key performance indicators for the business. To facilitate this, Tableau is a commonly used software that provides sophisticated descriptive analytics power. There are also several other business intelligence systems, reporting systems and cloud technologies that the companies may employ to extract, transform, load and describe the company's data.

A common use case of predictive analytics is statistical demand forecasting. For example, an Original Equipment Manufacturer (OEM) may implement statistical forecasting models to predict customer orders based on historical order data and its correlation with events. While it is sometimes possible to achieve acceptable forecasting accuracy by implementing simple out-of-box statistical forecasting models, the accuracy can usually be improved by incorporating some of the additional data that may have explained the demand pattern, such as product life cycle, product seasonality, promotions, price changes, market supply and demand balance, new product introductions, competitors' actions, inventory in distribution network, etc. Further, the outcome of the statistical forecasting models can be fine-tuned or adjusted by consensus and collaborative forecasting techniques. Companies are advised to establish a process that ensures both the statistical predictions and human collaborations are incorporated into the final numbers. For example, the initial demand forecast can be recommended by the statistical model, while the final numbers are enhanced through consensus among multiple departments such as marking, sales, operations and business units. Finally, these forecasting numbers may be collaboratively planned and replenished with key and strategic customers. Of course, the extent of statistical forecasting versus consensus and collaborative forecasting should vary by customers, products and markets. For example, strategic products sold to strategic customers may be more collaborative driven, whereas products that are established and has ample historical demand data may reply more on the statistical predictions.

There are ample use cases of prescriptive analytics. Consider a mid-sized manufacturing company. Below are examples of the problems that may be solved through prescriptive analytics and potentially save millions of dollars annually.

- What should be the inventory week-of-stock targets at each inventory stage in the supply chain?
- What is the optimal in-house versus outsourced manufacturing split?
- What is the optimal capacity buffer level to keep for each of the manufacturing equipment?
- Which product should be qualified to build at which factory?

Most of the prescriptive analytics involves tradeoff between multiple effects, and it is through optimization that finds the best solution. Taking the problems above, solving for the optimal inventory week-of-stock can be viewed as tradeoff between customer service level versus the cost of inventory holding (Manary and Willems 2008). Solving for the optimal in-house versus outsourced manufacturing split is a tradeoff between the cost premium of outsource manufacturing versus the idle cost of in-house facilities. Solving for the optimal capacity buffer level for manufacturing resources is weighing the depreciation cost of equipment against the missed demand opportunities due to capacity shortage. Solving for the best qualification structure between products and manufacturing sites is a tradeoff between manufacturing flexibility versus product qualification cost (Liao et al. 2017).

Cognitive analytics enables the computer to learn through historical data and business actions, with the purpose of compliment or minimize the need of human decision interventions for business process in the future. Cognitive analytics, if leveraged in an efficient way, can enable a company's supply chain to position products when and where its customers need them, even before requested by the customer. As a use case, one may analyze real-time point-of-sales information and leverage machine learning techniques to uncover the bullwhip effects over time; and ultimately provide instructions to manufacturing. This could potentially speed up the decision-making process in a manufacturing supply chain from weeks to days, due to a reduction in human decisions and interventions.

Cognitive analytics often leverages structured and unstructured data which are provided by the big data architecture. Big data architecture can also be leveraged to construct data lake for each functional areas of supply chain, such as planning, procurement, manufacturing, fulfillment, quality, etc. Efficient usage of the data lake and big data architecture will provide required information for analytics, and will help achieve quick wins in the respective functions. Furthermore, building bridges between these data lakes will enlarge the benefits by enabling cross-functional analytics and cross-functional decision making.

Day in the Life of Supply Chain Analytics and Optimization

Figure 2 shows a typical day of a supply chain analyst. He or she starts his day by reading a newspaper. Then, he stands in the line at Starbucks and grabs his morning coffee. He then goes hiking with his friends. When it gets close to the lunch time, he orders sushi in a Japanese restaurant for lunch. After lunch, he goes horseback riding and then do household chores afterwards. At dinner time, he enjoys a pizza dinner party with his or her friends. Then he goes to sleep and turns the lights off.

One may wonder how it can possibly be a typical day of a supply chain analyst. How can a person do these every day, and still get well-paid? Of course not. This is just a cartoon. However, taking a closer look at each of the activities described above, one could find the elements of supply chain analytics and

Figure 2.

optimization in each of them. Figure 3 shows the connections between these daily activities and the theories of supply chain analytics.

- Reading newspaper

Starting the day reading newspaper is related to the classic "newsboy problem" in supply chain analytics. In this problem, the newsboy faces uncertain demand and fixed unit price for newspaper, which is a perishable product. The newsboy needs to decide how many inventories to stock before the demand quantity is realized, knowing that unsold copies will be worthless at the end of the day. The optimal solution for the newsboy problem is to trade-off between the underage cost of stocking too less (in which case he would have unfulfilled demand) versus the overage cost of buying too many (in which case he will lose money on excess inventory) (see, for example, Cachon and Christian 2008 and Nahmias and Cheng 2009). See Porteus (1990) and Petruzzi and Dada (1999) for reviews of more applications and extensions of the newsvendor problems.

The same tradeoff needs to be weighed when a capacity planning team decides on how much equipment to procure for each manufacturing step in a supply chain, taking semiconductor manufacturing companies as an example. If the capacity is kept too high, the factory is going to incur idleness on equipment; on the other hand, if the capacity is kept too low, the factory will not have the capability to handle demand upsides. The optimal level of capacity to keep balances the incremental cost and benefits of having one additional equipment. Of course, the equipment buying decision is much more complicated than solving the newsvendor equation from traditional Operations Management textbooks. The newsvendor formula indicates the optimize solution is to stock the quantity such that the probability of satisfying demand equal to the underage cost over the sum of the underage and overage cost per unit. This is a simple equation which can be directly applied when there is only one type of unit to order in a single period. However, a capacity planning team in a medium to large-sized manufacturing company needs to decide on the number of machines to procure for hundreds of resources. Each of the resources are interconnected with each other through complicated manufacturing stages. Excess amount of equipment in one manufacturing stage can be a waste if the other manufacturing stages are not equipped with sufficient capacity. Advanced analytical models such as Monte-Carlo simulation and optimization is particularly useful to optimize for equipment-buying decision over hundreds of manufacturing steps. One may generate a large set of demand scenarios, simulate the WIP flow across manufacturing stages, calculate demand satisfaction and cost, and optimize for the equipment capacity over the expectation of these demand scenarios. Despite of the simulation requirement, the basic tradeoff studied here is the same as the tradeoff in the newsvendor model, which is the tradeoff between the incremental cost and benefit of having additional equipment.

- Getting coffee at Starbucks

Standing in a line to get coffee at Starbucks, one would estimate how long it will take for him to wait. Subconsciously, one could be applying Little's Law. Little's Law is a theorem by John Little which states that the long-term average number L of customers in a stationary system is equal to the long-term average effective arrival rate λ multiplied by the average time W that a customer spends in the system (Little and Graves 2008). Expressed algebraically, the law is $L = \lambda W$. In a stable system, the rate at which people enter Starbucks queue (called the arrival rate) is equal to the rate at which they exit it (called the exit rate). The estimation of wait time at Starbucks may go like this: suppose there are 20 people in the queue and one person is entering the queue every minute, then the average wait time a customer spends at Starbucks is 20 people divided by one person per minute, which is 20 minutes. Similarly, in a semiconductor supply chain, one can apply Little's Law to estimate the overall manufacturing cycle time and find opportunities to improve it. As an example, suppose the wafer start rate in a semiconductor fab (which is assumed to be a stationary system) is $\lambda = 1000$ wafers/day, and suppose the average work-in-progress (WIP) in the fab is $L = 45{,}000$ wafers. Then one can estimate the average time a wafer spends in the gab is $W = 45{,}000$ wafers /(1000 wafers/day) = 45 days.

By understanding and applying Little's Law, one can find opportunities to improve the manufacturing cycle time. Applying conventional wisdom solely, a supply chain analyst may tend to break the supply chain activities into smaller tasks, and then measure and continuously improve the process time of each task. While this approach will contribute to the reduction of manufacturing cycle time due to a reduction of process time, it is very common that the major opportunities for reducing cycle time lies in the reduction of queue time. It is clear from the Little's Law, that the wait time is longer at steps in which the average WIP is larger. By observing the manufacturing stages where WIP is most likely to accumulate, a supply chain analyst can focus on reducing the WIP at these stages, which will then reduce the overall cycle time. As another example, still taking a wafer fab to illustrate, the steps in a semiconductor assembly and test process could be 1) memory assembly → 2) transfer to a tray → 3) memory test → 4) transfer to a different packaging tray → 5) testing for customer applications → 6) shipping finished product. Applying the concept from Little's Law to reduce the overall cycle time, one can eliminate some of the steps by simplifying the manufacturing steps. For example, step 3)-5) may be combined into a single step. This way, the WIP accumulation between steps 3) through 5) is eliminated, which may reduce cycle time considerably, compared to simply reducing process time of a step specifically.

- Hiking with friends

Hiking with friends can be drawn parallels to the theory of constraints (Goldratt and Cox 2016). The objective of hiking with friends is for everyone to reach the mountain peak together in the shortest time possible. The hiking group would easily identify the slowest person in the group, which is the "constraint", and have him lead the line while everyone follows. Moreover, to move faster, the group may have the fastest person carry the backpack of the slowest person. By shuffling the burdens, someone else may eventually become the slowest person. The group can repeat the same exercise throughout the hiking journey to reach the peak in a shortest time possible.

The same concept as in hiking can be applied to a supply chain to achieve profitability and efficiency. The group of supply chain analysts needs to analyze the market and business scenario to understand whether the demand or the supply is constraining. Under the scenarios in which the demand is constraining, it is important for the supply chain analysts to ensure the supply does not exceed the demand significantly, as the extra supply will be salvaged. In a manufacturing company, supply chain analysts may move the supply downstream and offer short lead time for customers to create additional market. On the other hand, under the scenarios in which the supply is constrained, supply chain analysts need to ensure the most profitable demand is satisfied out of the constrained capacity. This can be achieved by putting brakes to supply replenishment. Once a target work-in-progress inventory level is reached, the supply chain will stop replenishment until the product is pulled by the customers. If the supply is more constrained, the inventory brakes will be held at more upstream stage of the supply chain, and build upon demand certainty to maximize demand satisfaction. See Noreen et al. (1995) for more applications and implications of the theory of constraints.

- Having Sushi for lunch

Imagine that someone visits a nice Japanese restaurant for Sushi, and the owner of the restaurant tells him "sorry, we ran out of rice and we will not be able to serve you sushi today"; what would be the customer's reaction? It is quite a waste for the restaurant to lose demand and customer goodwill by not carrying enough rice, which is a much smaller cost item compared to fish. Even worse, the fish could get stale and the restaurant would lose cost incurred stocking fish. It is unfortunate for the sushi restaurant to be in a situation like this.

Similarly, supply chain analysts need to plan the supply chain by anchoring around the expensive items. This requires placing sufficient stock on components with lower costs, and ensure the demand opportunities are not lost due to unavailability of the low-cost items. Taking the silicon memory business as an example, companies manufacturing silicon memory should avoid shortening demand due to under-stock of end-product packing materials. In summary, supply chain analysts need to consider all components of cost to serve demand, and, accordingly define heterogenous service level targets for diverse types of material in the supply chain.

- Doing horseback riding

Doing horseback riding can be made analogy the "bullwhip effect" in the supply chain. The whip in horseback riding oscillates stronger towards the tip than the portion closer to the handle. The similar behavior is commonly seen in the supply chain and is well-known as the "bullwhip effect" (Lee et al. 1997). Even small volatilities in the end-customer demand (i.e., point-of-sale) will amplify to the distribution center, compound to the manufacturer, and further amplify towards the upstream suppliers. Supply chain analysts are advised to understand various of factors contributing to the supply chain bullwhip effect, and tackle it effectively by leveraging statistical techniques and employing supply chain strategies such as implementing push-pull systems.

- Running household chores

A big part of running household chores is to replenish assorted items to the house. These include groceries, maintenance items, replacement items, etc. One would usually employ different replenishment strategy on different segments of items to decide the what and how many to buy. Aspects to consider when designing the replenishment strategy include:

- Perishables versus non-perishables
- High-cost versus low-cost
- Pictorial memory of current inventory levels
- Projected minimum or maximum inventory levels
- Family consumption patterns
- Expected events such as house parties

The same aspects are considered when a supply chain planner replenishments material and capacity for the supply chain. A supply chain planner in a medium-size to large-size company may handle up to hundreds of products. It is advised for supply chain planners to apply predictive and prescriptive analytics to predict future demand, segment products and customers to replenish the material and capacity in a way that maximizes the profit for the company. There is a vast of operations literature on inventory control models that can be applied in this context. See, for example, Nahmias and Cheng (2009) and Simchi-levi et al. (2008) for overviews of inventory control models.

- Having Pizza Party

When organizing a pizza party and deciding on how many pizzas of each kind to order, one is essentially solving a mathematical programming problem, which is, how many pizzas of each kind to order to provide maximal possible satisfaction for the whole party with minimum waste, while adhering to the dietary restrictions of each guests to come (such as vegetarian restrictions). It is one kind of mathematical programming problem with hierarchical objective layers. Similarly, when supply chain analysts decide on the quantity of each product to build in the supply chain, they are also solving a mathematical programming problem with hierarchical objective layers. With the primary objective of maximizing demand fulfillment, one should also consider the secondary objective of balancing the inventory with the capacity, and the third objective layer of minimizing the cost to the supply chain, while satisfying a series of constraints such as capacity and demand constraint, customer lead time constraint, etc.

- Going to sleep

Going to sleep is the time for "lights-off". In the field of supply chain analytics, "lights-off" refers to the automation of planning and manufacturing and planning. In the era of digital supply chain, a growing number of companies are employing automated guided vehicles (AGVs) with sophisticated routing algorithms on the manufacturing floor.

Critical Success Factors for Supply Chain Analytics Teams

Supply chain analytics teams may be centralized or decentralized. It is advised to weigh the advantages and disadvantages of both when deciding on the structure of the team. Centralized analytics teams is more

Figure 3.

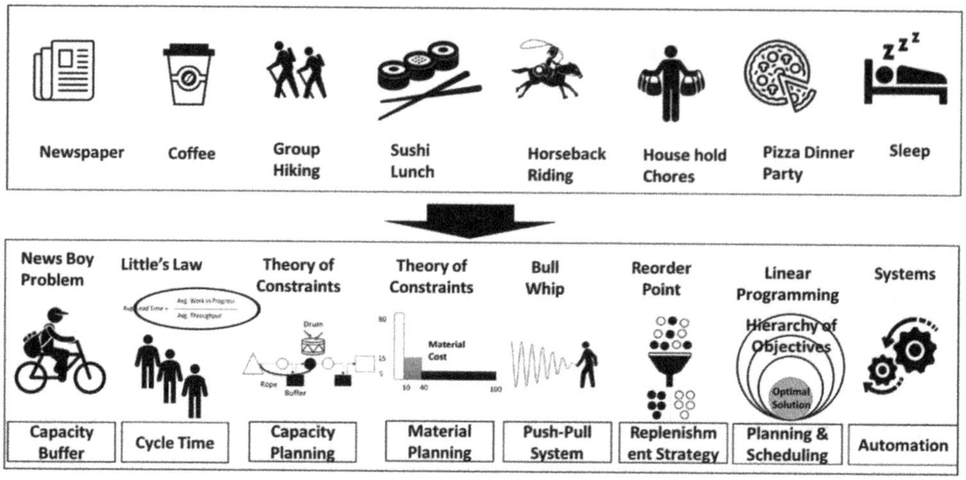

scalable, and creates more synergy across cross functional applications compared to the de-centralized analytics teams. However, decentralized analytics team could provide more agility and speed to react within each of the individual functions. In most of the cases, we would recommend creating centralized teams for descriptive analytics while keeping predictive and prescriptive analytics teams decentralized. This is because, descriptive analytics teams are often required to have considerable team sizes with data architecture, data engineering, and the skillsets of interacting with supply chain planning systems. Keeping the descriptive analytics centralized helps maintaining a sustainable and scalable team catering to the needs of each functions teams. On the other hand, predictive and prescriptive analytics teams are sometimes small teams with advanced analytics skillset and advanced degrees. They usually have the domain knowledge. Their expertise may play a dominant role in defining the right objectives for each of the analytics problems. Therefore, it is recommended to decentralize these analytics teams. However, even with the decentralized analytics teams, it is recommended to always have central governance of data architecture, analytical tool sets and systems.

For all kinds of analytics teams, it is important to understand and align the overall business objective cross-functionally while solving each of the analytics problems. Analytics carried out in solos with local objectives solely can be counter-impactful to the overall business. For example, if the analytics team under manufacturing optimizes solely on operating cost, whereas the analytics team under supply planning optimizes solely on service level, the decisions of both teams would be contradictory to each other and may counter the overall benefits of analytics. It is important to have an overall alignment on global business objectives while solving each of the analytical problems.

The implementation of supply chain analytics project usually requires the collaboration across multiple teams. It is advised that, for each analytical project, after the problem statement is defined and that the global objective is aligned, analytical project team be formed with an analytical expert, a functional expert and a system expert. The functional expert provides the business requirement and drives the data preparation and final user acceptance test. The analytics expert is responsible for developing the model, whereas the system expert is responsible for implementing the solution. See Figure 4 for a conceptual representation of the coordination relationship among the three experts. Throughout the project, all three experts need to collaborate closely to define the problem and design the solutions.

As an example, consider an analytical project of implementing statistical forecasting models in a manufacturing company. The analytics expert would be someone from the analytical team who tests multiple forecasting models and optimizes for parameters. The functional expert should provide the business requirement to the analytics expert—for example, which forecast granularity is required, or, is it weekly-level forecast at SKU level, monthly-level forecast at product-family level, or quarterly-level forecast at product-line level. The system expert needs to be able to either directly implement the solution inside the advanced planning system, or design an infrastructure to feed the forecast results into it.

The companies should also avoid the pitfalls of poorly-constructed supply chain analytics teams. One pitfall is having the infrastructure to develop the solution but having no infrastructure to sustain the solution. Even if the entire team is highly skilled in developing advanced analytics solutions, the efforts and time required to maintain the solution will accumulate, to the point where the team is stuck with handling past problems and not able to add additional value. To avoid this, it is important to either create a support functional team who is responsible for maintaining the analytical solutions, or develop data engineering capabilities within the team to automate the analytical solutions. Either way, the end goal is to embed the analytical solution into the supply chain system and the process footprint itself instead.

Supply Chain Design: A Case Study

In this section, we discuss some practical considerations of enabling supply chain analytics and optimization in a medium-size to large-size semiconductor company. Specifically, we discuss the centralization of supply chain analytics and the design of supply chain analytics objectives.

Supply chain optimization activities and projects may lead to sub-optimization if managed locally. In the example of sushi restaurant that we discussed in the "day in the life of supply chain analytics and optimization" section, it would harmfully impact the profitability of the restaurant if the supply of rice has been optimized in silos to minimize the cost of the rice, without considering the overall objective of the restaurant. The consequence of it could be loss sales for the restaurant due to lack of rice, while the stocks of fish goes perished.

Figure 4.

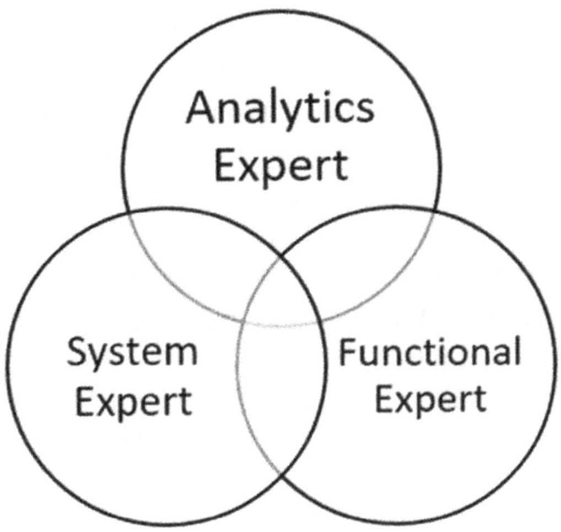

We advise that global supply chain optimization activities be carried out through a hierarchy of objective layers. To illustrate, in the above example in the sushi restaurant, it might be important for the restaurant to minimize the wastage of rice. Nevertheless, minimizing the excess of rice should not be the top priority of the restaurant. Instead, it could be an objective subordinate to the higher objective of serving customer demand in time. Towards the goal of achieving global optimization, it is critical for the business to define a hierarchy of objective layers. And once it is defined, the business needs to set guideline or policies for each objective that is subordinate to the higher objectives. For example, in the sushi restaurant example, the service level target for the inventory positioning of rice may need to set higher than the service level target for the inventory positioning of fish. These hierarchy of objective layers and corresponding supply chain guidelines and policies need to be established centrally through supply analytics and complemented by industry expertise, whenever applicable.

Next, we discuss the use case of centralized supply chain analytics and hierarchical objective design taking a typical vertically integrated semiconductor manufacturing company as example. Consider a typical vertically integrated semiconductor manufacturing company which owns fabrication plants and back-end manufacturing operations in-house. The fabrication plants, commonly called fabs, manufacture silicon wafers from raw wafers. The back-end manufacturing operations then convert the silicon wafers into semi-conductor chips. The semiconductor chips can then be used directly by end consumers, or used by other original equipment manufacturers (OEMs). Silicon fab operation is usually the most expensive operation in semi-conductor industries. It has long manufacturing lead times, typically in months, while the types of silicon wafers manufactured are under a hundred at any given time. In contrast, the back-end manufacturing operations is relatively inexpensive. It has much shorter manufacturing lead times, typically in weeks, but may produce thousands of different stock keeping units (SKUs).

Given the different attributes of cost, manufacturing lead time and product mix between fab operations and back-end manufacturing, the semiconductor manufacturing company needs to design different hierarchies of objectives when conducting supply chain optimization. The back-end manufacturing may be minimized for production cycle time, followed by the objective of maximizing agility, minimizing risk, and finally, minimizing the cost of production. On the other hand, the fab operations may be optimized for minimizing cost as the primary objective, and then optimized for maximum manufacturing throughput, followed by the objective of minimizing cycle time. The above objective layers, however, may change by products and business scenarios. For example, at the times of new product introduction, the time to market is critical for the business. Therefore, the optimization priority for both backend manufacturing and fab operations might be designed to minimize manufacturing cycle time, followed by the objectives of minimizing cost and maximizing agility.

Because the hierarchy of objectives for fab operations and backend manufacturing is different, the corresponding replenishment guidelines set for them also need to differ accordingly. For example, the business may deploy "push" replenishment strategy in fab operations to maximize for manufacturing throughput, whereas it makes more sense to deploy "push-pull" replenishment strategy (that is, deploying either push or pull strategy based on different business scenarios) in backend operations.

Table 1, 2, 3 and 4 show an example of hierarchy of objectives for backend manufacturing in a typical semi-conductor company. Table 1 includes a summary of three key objectives, ordered with descending priority. Table 2, 3 and 4 includes more details for each of the objectives, including the drivers for improvement and the key theories and concepts that may be applied when conducting corresponding analytics.

Table 1. Example objectives hierarchy of backend manufacturing in a semi-conductor company - summary

Priority	Objective	Focus	Key Performances Indices
1	Max Speed	Cycle time	Effective balance of Service Level and Inventory Turns • On time delivery to customer request date and to promise date • Supply chain inventory week of stock High service level for demand constraint scenario High inventory turns for supply constraint scenario
2	Max Agility	Risk Mitigation	Risk Index
3	Min Cost	Total cost	Total manufacturing and distribution cost

Table 2. Maximum speed

Priority	Cycle time components	Cycle time break down	Improvement drivers	Analytics
1.1	Overall Inventory WOS	Manufacturing & Distribution Lead Time | Build Ahead | Excess | Non Nettable | Service Level | Die Bank	▪ Design for product commonality (delay differentiation) ▪ Inventory buffer ▪ Capacity Buffer ▪ Low value material inventory buffer ▪ Replenishment Strategy (Push-Pull)	▪ Little's Law ▪ Multi Stage inventory & service level optimization ▪ News boy simulation ▪ Safety Stock ▪ Bull whip
1.2	Manufacturing & Distribution Lead Time	Theoretical Process Time | Que Time | Process Variability	▪ Reduce process variability, then reduce process time ▪ Simplify routings (eliminate steps) ▪ Scheduling ▪ Yield improvements	▪ Theory of constraints ▪ Little's Law ▪ Linear Programming ▪ Statistical tool kits
1.3	Work order performance	Theoretical Process Time | Que Time	▪ Minimize queue ▪ Minimize lot size	▪ Theory of constraints
1.4	Theoretical process time	Theoretical Process Time	▪ Simplify manufacturing process	▪ Factory Physics

Table 3. Maximum agility

Priority	Key drivers	Description	Analytics
2.1	Dual sourcing	Alternate suppliers and second tier suppliers at different geography for key components to mitigate risk of supply disruption	Simulation
2.2	Dual manufacturing sites	Alternate manufacturing sites at different geography to mitigate geo-political risks	Simulation

Table 4. Min cost

Priority	Key drivers	Description	Analytics
3.1	Inhouse vs outsource manufacturing split	Trade-off of un-used inhouse manufacturing cost and cost premium per unit for outsource manufacturing	Simulation
3.2	Capacity Buffer	Trade-off of incremental cost of each additional unit of capacity and margin potential of this additional unit of capacity	News boy simulation
3.3	Utilization vs inventory build ahead	Trade-off of cost of carrying inventory and cost of unused capacity	Simulation
3.4	Product and site qualification	Trade-off of cost of production qualification in additional site and upside flexibility to satisfy demand	Simulation Linear Programming
3.5	Minimize total manufacturing and distribution cost	Supply and Demand matching towards maximizing demand satisfaction, minimizing inventory and minimizing total manufacturing and distribution cost	Linear Programming

CONCLUSION

Supply chain analytics has become indispensable for supply chain management in a modern company. Through discussions of the life of supply chain analysts, we aim to provide the supply chain professionals an understanding of the interrelationship between analytics and supply chain management. Further, this chapter discusses some practical consideration in carrying out supply chain analytics successfully. More specifically, we discuss the four categories of supply chain analytics. It is vital for a supply chain practitioner to choose the right category of supply chain analytics based on the maturity and requirement of the company. We then discuss a few critical factors of the supply chain analytics teams, focusing on the centralization and decentralization of supply chain analytics and the implementation approach of supply chain analytics teams. Finally, we describe the hierarchical objectives design, taking a use case from semi-conductor company. The future research directions on this topic include empirical studies of the savings achieved by digital supply chain analytics, empirical studies of the correlation between the maturity of the supply chain analytics team versus the success achieved, and more in-depth case studies of supply chain analytics in a digital world.

REFERENCES

Cachon, G., & Terwiesch, C. (2008). *Matching supply with demand*. McGraw-Hill Publishing.

Chae, B., Olson, D., & Sheu, C. (2014). The impact of supply chain analytics on operational performance: A resource-based view. *International Journal of Production Research*, *52*(16), 4695–4710. doi:10.1080/00207543.2013.861616

Goldratt, E. M., & Cox, J. (2016). *The goal: A process of ongoing improvement*. Routledge. doi:10.4324/9781315270456

Gunasekaran, A., Papadopoulos, T., Dubey, R., Wamba, S. F., Childe, S. J., Hazen, B., & Akter, S. (2017). Big data and predictive analytics for supply chain and organizational performance. *Journal of Business Research*, *70*, 308–317. doi:10.1016/j.jbusres.2016.08.004

Lee, H. L., Padmanabhan, V., & Whang, S. (1997). Information distortion in a supply chain: The bullwhip effect. *Management Science*, *43*(4), 546–558. doi:10.1287/mnsc.43.4.546

Liao, B., Yano, C. A., & Esturi, S. (2017). Optimizing Site Qualification Across the Supply Network at Western Digital. *Interfaces*, *47*(4), 305–319. doi:10.1287/inte.2017.0898

Little, J. D., & Graves, S. C. (2008). Little's law. In *Building intuition* (pp. 81–100). Boston, MA: Springer. doi:10.1007/978-0-387-73699-0_5

Manary, M. P., & Willems, S. P. (2008). Setting safety-stock targets at Intel in the presence of forecast bias. *Interfaces*, *38*(2), 112–122. doi:10.1287/inte.1070.0339

Nahmias, S., & Cheng, Y. (2009). *Production and operations analysis* (Vol. 6). New York: McGraw-hill.

Noreen, E., Smith, D., & Mackey, J. T. (1995). *Theory of Constraints and Its Implications for Management Accounting: A Report on the Actual Implementation of The Theory of Constraints*. North River Press, Incorporated.

O'Dwyer, J., & Renner, R. (2011). The promise of advanced supply chain analytics. *Supply Chain Management Review*, *15*(1).

Petruzzi, N. C., & Dada, M. (1999). Pricing and the newsvendor problem: A review with extensions. *Operations Research*, *47*(2), 183–194. doi:10.1287/opre.47.2.183

Porteus, E. L. (1990). Stochastic inventory theory. Handbooks in Operations Research and Management Science, 2, 605-652.

Sahay, B. S., & Ranjan, J. (2008). Real time business intelligence in supply chain analytics. *Information Management & Computer Security*, *16*(1), 28–48. doi:10.1108/09685220810862733

Simchi-Levi, D., Kaminsky, P., Simchi-Levi, E., & Shankar, R. (2008). *Designing and managing the supply chain: concepts, strategies and case studies*. Tata McGraw-Hill Education.

Tan, K. H., Zhan, Y., Ji, G., Ye, F., & Chang, C. (2015). Harvesting big data to enhance supply chain innovation capabilities: An analytic infrastructure based on deduction graph. *International Journal of Production Economics*, *165*, 223–233. doi:10.1016/j.ijpe.2014.12.034

Trkman, P., McCormack, K., De Oliveira, M. P. V., & Ladeira, M. B. (2010). The impact of business analytics on supply chain performance. *Decision Support Systems*, *49*(3), 318–327. doi:10.1016/j.dss.2010.03.007

Compilation of References

Aberdeen Group. (2012). *Inventory Optimization – Impact of a Multi-Echelon Approach*. Boston: Aberdeen Group.

Accenture. (n.d.). Retrieved from https://www.accenture.com/us-en/insight-digital-procurement-process

Afshar, V. (2017). *Cisco: Enterprises Are Leading The Internet of Things Innovation*. Retrieved from https://www.huffingtonpost.com/entry/cisco-enterprises-are-leading-the-internet-of-things_us_59a41fcee4b0a62d0987b0c6

Ageshin, E. A. (2001). E-procurement at work: A case study. *Production and Inventory Management Journal*, *42*(1), 48–53.

Aggarwal, R. (2004). Making BPM Work. *DM Review*, *14*, 28–59.

Aiken & Keller. (2009). *The irrational side of change Management*. McKinsey & Company.

Akyuz, G., & Erkan, T. (2010). Supply chain performance measurement: A literature review. *International Journal of Production Research*, *48*(17), 5137–5155. doi:10.1080/00207540903089536

Alix Partners. (2017). *Homeward bound: nearshoring continues, labor becomes a limiting factor, and automation takes root*. Retrieved from https://emarketing.alixpartners.com/rs/emsimages/2017/pubs/EI/AP_Strategic_Manufacturing_Sourcing_Homeward_Bound_Jan_2017.pdf

Analytics, J. (2009). *White Paper: A Guide To Creating Dashboards People Love to Use*. Retrieved from: http://goo.gl/QGGHty

AnandA. (2017, Nov 2). Retrieved from https://becominghuman.ai/machine-learning-and-retargeting-9ffb77d768c3

Angeles, R., & Nath, R. (2007). Business-to-business e-procurement: Success factors and challenges to implementation. *Supply Chain Management*, *12*(2), 104–115. doi:10.1108/13598540710737299

APICS. (n.d.). *Rough-Cut capacity planning*. Retrieved from http://apicsforum.com/ebook/capacity_planning

Arkenberg, C. (2017). *Intelligent Logistics*. Retrieved from https://towardsdatascience.com/intelligent-logistics-e85de07c3570

ATKearney. (2015). Retrieved from https://www.atkearney.com/operations-performance-transformation/article?/a/digital-supply-chains-increasingly-critical-for-competitive-edge

Auramo, J., Kauremaa, J., & Tanskanen, K. (2005). Benefits of IT in supply chain management: An explorative study of progressive companies. *International Journal of Physical Distribution & Logistics Management*, *35*(2), 82–100.

Banafa, A. (2017, March 14). *IEEE internet of things*. Retrieved from https://iot.ieee.org/newsletter/march-2017/three-major-challenges-facing-iot.html

Bär, K., Herbert-Hansen, Z. N. L., & Khalid, W. (2018). Considering Industry 4.0 aspects in the supply chain for an SME. *Production Engineering*, 1–12.

Bell, C., Higgs, R., Vickers, S., Toncinich, S., & Haslett, T. (2003). *Using System modelling to understand the dynamics of supply chains*. Monash University. Working Paper 70/03.

Benton, D. (2017, Feb 21). *Retail, virtual reality and the supply chain*. Retrieved from https://www.supplychaindigital.com/scm/retail-virtual-reality-and-supply-chain

Bernard, M. (2012). *Key Performance Indicators (KPIs): The 75 Measures Every Manager Needs To Know*. FT Press. Retrieved from: http://goo.gl/v7r4hZ

Bernardo, N. (2016). *Lean and Digitize: An Integrated Approach to Process Improvement*. London: Routledge.

Best, E., & Weth, M. (2009). *Geschäftsprozesse optimieren*. Wiesbaden: Gabler. doi:10.1007/978-3-8349-9410-3

Bhatia, R. (2017). *Analytics India*. Retrieved from http://analyticsindiamag.com/inside-walmartlabs-indian-operations-fuelling-online-growth-global-retail-giant

Bienhaus, F., & Haddud, A. (2018). Procurement 4.0: Factors influencing the digitisation of procurement and supply chains. *Business Process Management Journal*, *24*(4), 965–984. doi:10.1108/BPMJ-06-2017-0139

Borri, F., & Boccaletti, G. (1995). From total quality management to total quality environmental management. *The TQM Magazine*, *7*(5), 38–42.

Brinch, M., Stentoft, J., Jensen, J. K., & Rajkumar, C. (2018). Practitioners understanding of big data and its applications in supply chain management. *International Journal of Logistics Management*. (accepted for publication)

Brown, A. S. (2003). *Modeling tough scheduling problems with project management software*. Paper presented at PMI® Global Congress 2003—North America, Baltimore, MD.

Brunet-Thornton, R., & Martinez, F. (2018). *Analyzing the Impacts of Industry 4.0 in Modern Business Environments*. Hershey, PA: IGI Global. doi:10.4018/978-1-5225-3468-6

Brusset, X. (2016). Does supply chain visibility enhance agility? *International Journal of Production Economics. Elsevier*, *171*, 46–59. doi:10.1016/j.ijpe.2015.10.005

Burgin, T. (1975). The Gamma Distribution and Inventory Control. *Operational Research Quarterly*, *26*(3), 507.

Büyüközkan, G., & Göçer, F. (2018). Digital Supply Chain: Literature review and a proposed framework for future research. *Computers in Industry*, *97*, 157–177. doi:10.1016/j.compind.2018.02.010

Cachon, G., & Terwiesch, C. (2008). *Matching supply with demand*. McGraw-Hill Publishing.

Camerinelli, E., & Cantu, A. (2006). Measuring the Value of the Supply Chain: A Framework. *Supply Chain Practice*, *8*(2), 40–59.

Campuzano Bolarín, F., Lisec, A., & Esteban, F. (2008). Inventory cost consequences of variability demand process with a multi-echelon supply chain. *Logistics & Sustainable Transport.*, *1*(3), 1–12.

Carter, C. R., & Rogers, D. S. (2008). A framework of sustainable supply chain management: Moving toward new theory. *International Journal of Physical Distribution & Logistics Management*, *38*(5), 360–387.

Casey, M., & Wong, P. (2017). Global supply chains are about to get better, thanks to blockchain. *Harvard Business Review*, 13.

Cassar, S., & Shinebourne, P. (2012). What does spirituality mean to you? An Interpretative Phenomenological Analysis of the experience of spirituality. *Existential Analysis, 23*(1), 133–149.

CDO Conclave. (2018, March). *10 amazing statistics about digital transformation.* CDO Conclave.

Chae, B., Olson, D., & Sheu, C. (2014). The impact of supply chain analytics on operational performance: A resource-based view. *International Journal of Production Research, 52*(16), 4695–4710. doi:10.1080/00207543.2013.861616

ChinaU. B. (n.d.). Retrieved from https://www.i-scoop.eu/industry-4-0/supply-chain-management-scm-logistics/

Christopher, M., Peck, H., & Towill, D. (2006). A Taxonomy for Selecting Global Supply Chain Strategies. *International Journal of Logistics Management, 17*(2), 277–287. doi:10.1108/09574090610689998

Christopher, M., Towill, D., Aitken, J., & Childerhouse, P. (2009). Value Chain Classification. *Journal of Manufacturing Technology Management, 20*(4), 460–474. doi:10.1108/17410380910953720

chymebot. (n.d.). Retrieved from http://chymebot.com/use-cases/

CMA. (2016). *Catman 2.0 - Driving Growth in a Shopper-Centric World.* Category Management Association.

Coleman, K. (2017). *Digital Transformation Strategy: A Matter of Survival.* Retrieved from http://www.projectmanagement.com

Columbus, L. (2015, July 13). *Ten Ways Big Data Is Revolutionizing Supply Chain Management.* Retrieved from https://www.forbes.com/sites/louiscolumbus/2015/07/13/ten-ways-big-data-is-revolutionizing-supply-chain-management/#38400f4e69f5

Corbin, J., & Strauss, A. (2008) Basics of Qualitative Research: Techniques and Procedures for Developing Grounded Theory (3rd ed.). SAGE Publications, Inc. doi:10.4135/9781452230153

Crawford, M. (2018, Feb). *Six Supply Chain Trends That Will Impact Manufacturing in 2018.* Retrieved from https://www.gray.com/news/blog/2018/02/19/six-supply-chain-trends-that-will-impact-manufacturing-in-2018

Cynthia, B., & Keith, L. S. (2011). Organizational Change Management: A Test of the Effectiveness of a Communication Plan. *Communication Research Reports, 28*(1), 62–73. doi:10.1080/08824096.2011.541364

d'Innocenzio. A. (2016, June 2). Retrieved from https://apnews.com/ee9b77dba1a5460a91fef2842ccb8955/wal-mart-testing-drones-warehouses-manage-inventory

D'innocenzioA. (2016, June 2). Retrieved from https://apnews.com/ee9b77dba1a5460a91fef2842ccb8955/wal-mart-testing-drones-warehouses-manage-inventory

Darcherif, A. (2018, April). Retrieved from The Industry 4.0 and IoT Ecosystem – Alexandre Darcherif – Medium: https://medium.com/@darchalex/the-industry-4-0-and-iot-ecosystem-e84935289191

Davenport, T. (2006, January). Competing on Analytics. *Harvard Business Review.*

Davila, A., Gupta, M., & Palmer, R. (2003). Moving procurement systems to the internet: The adoption and use of e-procurement technology models. *European Management Journal, 21*(1), 11–23. doi:10.1016/S0263-2373(02)00155-X

Davis, M. (2010). *Case Study for Supply Chain Leaders: Dell's Transformative Journey Through Supply Chain Segmentation.* Retrieved from https://www.gartner.com/doc/1468717/case-study-supply-chain-leaders

Deloitte. (2015). *Procurement talent management: Exceptional outcomes require exceptional people.* Retrieved from https://www2.deloitte.com/us/en/pages/operations/articles/procurement-talent-human-capital-management.html

Deloitte. (2017). *Disruptions in retail through digital transformation*. Retrieved from https://www2.deloitte.com/content/dam/Deloitte/in/Documents/CIP/in-cip-disruptions-in-retail-noexp.pdf

Deloitte. (2018). Retrieved from https://www2.deloitte.com/uk/en/pages/consumer-business/articles/retail-trends.html#

DHL. (2014). Retrieved from http://www.dhl.com/content/dam/downloads/g0/about_us/logistics_insights/csi_augmented_reality_report_290414.pdf

DHL. (2018). Retrieved from https://www.dpdhl.com/en/media-relations/press-releases/2018/95-per-cent-of-companies-yet-to-realize-full-benefits-of-digitalization-technologies-for-supply-chains.html

Dong, S., Xu, S. X., & Zhu, K. X. (2009). Research note—information technology in supply chains: The value of it-enabled resources under competition. *Information Systems Research*, *20*(1), 18–32.

Dudlicek, J. (2016, December). Shoppers in Need Are Friends Indeed. *Progressive Grocer*, p. 4.

Dundas. (n.d.). *Dashboards Demystified*. Retrieved from: http://goo.gl/OriOSu

Dykes, B. (2011). *Web Analytics Action Hero: Using Analysis to Gain Insight and Optimize Your Business*. Adobe Press. Retrieved from: http://goo.gl/OWZSKn

Eckerson, W. (2009). *Performance Management Strategies: How to Create and Deploy Effective Metrics*. TDWI Best Practices Report Q1 2009.

Enterprise Management Associates. (2012). *White Paper: Business Intelligence Platforms for Mid-size Organizations: Comparing Birst, MicroStrategy, Oracle and SAP BusinessObjects*. Retrieved from: http://goo.gl/lm2XRC

Eppen, G. D. (1979). Effects of centralization on expected costs in a multi-location newsboy problem. *Management Science*, *25*(5), 498–501. doi:10.1287/mnsc.25.5.498

Eruguz, A., Sahin, E., Jemai, Z., & Dallery, Y. (2016). A comprehensive survey of guaranteed-service models for multi-echelon inventory optimization. *International Journal of Production Economics*, *172*, 110–125. doi:10.1016/j.ijpe.2015.11.017

Famiyeh, S. (2018). Green supply chain management initiatives and operational competitive performance. *Benchmarking: An International Journal*, *25*(2), 607–631.

Farahani, P., Meier, C., & Wilke, J. (2017). Digital supply chain management agenda for the automotive supplier industry. In *Shaping the digital enterprise* (pp. 157–172). Cham: Springer. doi:10.1007/978-3-319-40967-2_8

Farasyn, I., Humair, S., Kahn, J., Neale, J., Rosen, O., Ruark, J., ... Willems, S. (2011). Inventory Optimization at Procter & Gamble: Achieving Real Benefits Through User Adoption of Inventory Tools. *Interfaces*, *41*(1), 66–78. doi:10.1287/inte.1100.0546

Farasyn, I., Perkoz, K., & Van de Velde, W. (2008). Spreadsheet Models for Inventory Target Setting at Procter & Gamble. *Interfaces*, *38*(4), 241–250. doi:10.1287/inte.1080.0345

FarEye. (n.d.). Retrieved from https://www.getfareye.com/blog/machine-learning-based-vehicle-routing-software

Fettke, P., Loos, P., & Zwicker, J. (2005). *Business Process Reference Models: Survey and Classification*. Third International Conference on Business Process Management (BPM), Nancy, France. Retrieved from: http://goo.gl/TQILgk

Fisher, M. L. (1997, March). What Is the Right Supply Chain for Your Product? *Harvard Business Review*, 105–116.

Forbes. (2012). *You Are In The Customer Experience Business, Whether You Know It Or Not*. Retrieved from https://www.forbes.com/sites/forrester/2012/08/28/you-are-in-the-customer-experience-business-whether-you-know-it-or-not/#7839e4025df8

Forbes. (2016). *Chipotle Lessons: Supply Chain Visibility and Higher Prices*. Retrieved from https://www.forbes.com/sites/kevinomarah/2015/12/16/chipotle-lessons-supply-chain-visibility-and-higher-prices/#24e6a5f2332b

Ford, M. W., & Greer, B. M. (2005). The Relationship between Management Control System Usage and Planned Change Achievement: An Exploratory Study. *Journal of Change Management*, *5*(1), 29–46. doi:10.1080/14697010500036031

Forrester Research, Inc. (2013). *Strategic PMOs Play a Vital Role in Driving Business Outcomes*. Author.

Fred, B. (2018). *A look into the future: The self-learning supply chain*. Retrieved from (http://www.supplychainquarterly.com/news/20180330-a-look-into-the-future-the-self-learning-supply-chain/)

Gattorna, J. (2006). *Living Supply Chains*. Harlow: Pearson.

Gattorna, J. (2015). *Dynamic Supply Chains: How to design, build and manage people-centric value networks*. London: Pearson Education Limited.

Geethan, K. A. V., Jose, S., Koshy, A., & Samuel, A. B. (2011). Methodology for Study of Characteristics and Time Reduction in Reverse Supply Chain Using System Dynamics. *International Conference on Sociality and Economics Development, 10*.

Glas, A. H., & Kleemann, F. C. (2016). The impact of industry 4.0 on procurement and supply management: A conceptual and qualitative analysis. *International Journal of Business and Management Invention*, *5*(6), 55–66.

Goldman, D. (2018, Jan 29). *What is 5g*. Retrieved from https://money.cnn.com/2018/01/29/technology/what-is-5g/index.html

GoldmanD. (2018, Jan 29). Retrieved from https://money.cnn.com/2018/01/29/technology/what-is-5g/index.html

Goldratt, E. M., & Cox, J. (2016). *The goal: A process of ongoing improvement*. Routledge. doi:10.4324/9781315270456

Govindan, K. (2017). Eco-efficiency based green supply chain management: Current status and opportunities. *European Journal of Operational Research, 10*, 57.

Govindan, K., Rajendran, S., Sarkis, J., & Murugesan, P. (2015). Multi criteria decision making approaches for green supplier evaluation and selection: A literature review. *Journal of Cleaner Production. Elsevier*, *98*, 66–83. doi:10.1016/j.jclepro.2013.06.046

Graves, S., & Willems, S. (2003). *Supply chain design: safety stock placement and supply chain configuration*. Academic Press.

Green, K. W. Jr. (2012). Green supply chain management practices: impact on performance. *Supply Chain Management: An International Journal*, *17*(3), 290–305.

Greer, B., & Ford, M. (2009). Managing Change In Supply Chains: A process Comparison. *Journal of Business Logistics*, *30*(2), 47–63. doi:10.1002/j.2158-1592.2009.tb00111.x

Greischel, P. (2003). *Balanced Scorecard*. Munich: Vahlen.

Guadalupe, R. T. (2011). Compras Inteligentes. *Expansion Magazine*. Retrieved from https://expansion.mx/expansion/2011/09/14/compras-inteligentes

Gunasekaran, A., Papadopoulos, T., Dubey, R., Wamba, S. F., Childe, S. J., Hazen, B., & Akter, S. (2017). Big data and predictive analytics for supply chain and organizational performance. *Journal of Business Research, 70*, 308–317. doi:10.1016/j.jbusres.2016.08.004

Handfield, R. (2002). Applying environmental criteria to supplier assessment: A study in the application of the Analytical Hierarchy Process. *European Journal of Operational Research, 141*(1), 70–87.

Harrison & O'Nell. (2017). *3 Changes Retailers Need to Make to Survive.* Retrieved from https://hbr.org/2017/11/3-changes-retailers-need-to-make-to-survive

Holland, L. (2003). Can the principle of the ecological footprint be applied to measure the environmental sustainability of business? *Corporate Social Responsibility and Environmental Management, 10*(4), 224–232.

Humair, S., & Willems, S. (2006). Optimizing Strategic Safety Stock Placement in Supply Chains with Clusters of Commonality. *Operations Research, 54*(4), 725–742. doi:10.1287/opre.1060.0313

IDC. (2016). *IDC FutureScape: Worldwide Digital Transformation 2017 Predictions.* IDC.

IDC. (2017). *IDC Forecasts Worldwide Spending on Digital Transformation Technologies to Reach $1.3 Trillion in 2018.* IDC.

INFORMS. (n.d.). *What is Analytics?* Retrieved from: http://goo.gl/odWhqS

Insider, B. (2018). *Amazon changes prices on its products about every 10 minutes.* Retrieved from https://www.businessinsider.com/amazon-price-changes-2018-8

Isern, J., Meaney, M., & Wilson, S. (2009). *Corporate Transformation under Pressure.* McKinsey & Company. Retrieved from http://www.mckinsey.com/insights/organization/corporate_transformation_under_pressure

ITU. (2015, Sep). Retrieved from https://www.itu.int/dms_pubrec/itu-r/rec/m/R-REC-M.2083-0-201509-I!!PDF-E.pdf

Ivanov, D., Tsipoulanidis, A., & Schönberger, J. (2018). Digital Supply Chain, Smart Operations and Industry 4.0. In Global Supply Chain and Operations Management (pp. 481-526). Springer.

Jackson, R. (2012). *Category Role - at the heart of category management for 20 years, but until now vague and even prejudiced?* Retrieved from http://www.shopperintelligence.com/wp-content/uploads/whitepapers/Category_Role.pdf

JacobL. (2018, July 17). Retrieved from https://www.iqvis.com/blog/amazon-reorganized-ai-and-machine-learning/

JDA Software Group, Inc. (2018). *Digital Supply Chain in Retail & Manufacturing: A State of the Industry Benchmark.* Retrieved from https://now.jda.com

JDA Voice of the customer. (2017). Retrieved from jda.com: https://jda.com/-/media/jda/knowledge-center/thought-leadership/voice-of-the-category-manager-executive-summary1.ashx

JDA. (2016). SCDigest Supply Chain Digitization Benchmark Survey. *Supply Chain Digest.*

JDA. (2017). *JDA Delivers Transformational Assortment Optimization.* Retrieved from https://jda.com/knowledge-center/press-release/jda-delivers-transformational-assortment-optimization-powered-by-dunnhumby

JDA. (2018). *Intelligent Manufacturing Survey.* Retrieved from https://jda.com/knowledge-center/collateral/2018-intelligent-manufacturing-survey-exec-summary

Johnston, D. (2012). *The Shift to Reshoring.* Retrieved from http://www.jda.com/realresultsmagazine/view-article.cfm?did=2867

Jordan, C. (2017). Curiosity, creativity and collaboration–creating a digitally integrated supply chain. *APPEA Journal*, *57*(2), 477–480.

Kamalahmadi, M., & Mellat-Parast, M. (2016). Developing a resilient supply chain through supplier flexibility and reliability assessment. *International Journal of Production Research*, *54*(1), 302–321. doi:10.1080/00207543.2015.1088971

Kaplan, R. S. (2010). *Conceptual Foundations of the Balanced Scorecard.* Harvard Business School Accounting & Management Unit Working Paper No. 10-074. Retrieved from: http://ssrn.com/abstract=1562586

Kaplan, R. S., & Norton, D. P. (2009). Management mit System. *Harvard Business Manager Edition*, *2009*, 39–55.

Karp, T. (2005). Unpacking the Mysteries of Change: Mental Modeling. *Journal of Change Management*, *5*(1), 87–97. doi:10.1080/14697010500057573

Kartz, J. (2011). *Creating High-Value Supply Chains.* Retrieved from http://www.industryweek.com/companies-amp-executives/creating-high-value-supply-chains

King, A. A., & Lenox, M. J. (2001). Does it really pay to be green? An empirical study of firm environmental and financial performance: An empirical study of firm environmental and financial performance. *Journal of Industrial Ecology*, *5*(1), 105–116.

Klosterhalfen, S., Minner, S., & Willems, S. (2014). Strategic Safety Stock Placement in Supply Networks with Static Dual Supply. *Manufacturing & Service Operations Management: M & SOM*, *16*(2), 204–219. doi:10.1287/msom.2013.0472

Kotter, J. P. (1996). *Leading Change.* Boston Harvard Business School Press.

KPMG, LLP. (2017). Transformation framework and select deliverable examples. New York, NY: Author.

Lafuente, R., & Sánchez, M. J. (2010). Defining and measuring environmental consciousness. *Revista Internacional de Sociologia*, *68*(3), 731–755. doi:10.3989/ris.2008.11.03

Larkin, M., & Thompson, A. (2012). Interpretative phenomenological analysis. In Qualitative research methods in mental health and psychotherapy: A guide for students and practitioners. John Wiley & Sons.

Lederer, M., Betz, & Schmidt, W. (2018). Digital Transformation, Smart Factories, and Virtual Design – Contributions of Subject Orientation. *Proceedings of the S-BPM ONE* '18. 10.1145/3178248.3178256

Lederer, M. (2016). *Business Process Transparency Management.* Nuremberg: University of Erlangen-Nuremberg.

Lederer, M., Avci, R., & Schmidt, W. (2017). Should Process Management Add its Two Cents? A Classification Approach for the Selection of Process Management Build-Time Techniques for Software Development Purposes. In *Proceedings of the 43nd Euromicro Conference on Software Engineering and Advanced Applications.* IEEE. 10.1109/SEAA.2017.40

Lederer, M., Quitt, A., Büsch, M., & Remzi, A. (2019). (in press). One size fits all? An Analytical Approach how to make use of Process Methods for Different Fundamental Supply Chain Types. *International Journal of Supply Chain and Operations Resilience.*

Lee, H. L., Padmanabhan, V., & Whang, S. (1997). Information distortion in a supply chain: The bullwhip effect. *Management Science*, *43*(4), 546–558. doi:10.1287/mnsc.43.4.546

Leonard & Coltea. (2013). *Most Change Initiatives Fail -- But They Don't Have To.* Retrieved from http://businessjournal.gallup.com

Levary, R. R. (2000). Better supply chains through information technology. *Industrial Management*, *42*(3), 24.

Liao, B., Yano, C. A., & Esturi, S. (2017). Optimizing Site Qualification Across the Supply Network at Western Digital. *Interfaces*, *47*(4), 305–319. doi:10.1287/inte.2017.0898

Little, J. D., & Graves, S. C. (2008). Little's law. In *Building intuition* (pp. 81–100). Boston, MA: Springer. doi:10.1007/978-0-387-73699-0_5

Lovell, A., Saw, R., & Stimson, J. (2005). Product Value-Density: Managing Diversity Through Supply Chain Segmentation. *International Journal of Logistics Management*, *16*(1), 142–158. doi:10.1108/09574090510617394

Mabert, V. A., & Schoenherr, T. (2001). An online RFQ system: A case study. *Practix*, *4*(2), 1–6.

Mackness, J. (1991). Top Management Commitment? In *Achieving Competitive Edge Getting Ahead Through Technology and People* (pp. 167–171). Springer. doi:10.1007/978-1-4471-1904-3_28

Madjid, T. (2017). *Enterprise Information Systems and the Digitalization of Business Functions*. Hershey, PA: IGI Global.

Manary, M. P., & Willems, S. P. (2008). Setting safety-stock targets at Intel in the presence of forecast bias. *Interfaces*, *38*(2), 112–122. doi:10.1287/inte.1070.0339

Mankins, M. (2014). *This Weekly Meeting Took Up 300,000 Hours a Year.* Retrieved from http://hbr.org

Marchesini, M. P., & Alcantara, R. C. (2016). Logistics activities in supply chain business process. *International Journal of Logistics Management*, *27*(1), 6–30. doi:10.1108/IJLM-04-2014-0068

Mason-Jones, R., Naylor, B., & Towill, D. (2000). Engineering the Leagile Supply Chain. *International Journal of Agile Management*, *2*(1), 54–61.

McAfee, A. (2012). Big data: The management revolution. *Harvard Business Review*, *90*(10), 60–68. PMID:23074865

McKinsey & Co. (2017). Retrieved from https://www.mckinsey.com/industries/consumer-packaged-goods/our-insights/driving-superior-value-through-digital-procurement

Mellins-Cohen, D. (2012). Segmentation: A How- To Guide. *High Beam Research*. Retrieved from http://www.highbeam.com/doc/1G1-289725005.html

Melnyk, S. A., Calantone, R. J., Luft, J., Stewart, D. M., Zsidisin, G. A., Hanson, J., & Burns, L. (2005). An empirical investigation of metrics alignment process. *International Journal of Productivity and Performance Management*, *54*(5/6), 312–324. doi:10.1108/17410400510604494

Melnyk, S., Stewart, D., & Swink, M. (2004). Metrics and performance measurement in operations management: Dealing with the metrics maze. *Journal of Operations Management*, *22*(3), 209–217. doi:10.1016/j.jom.2004.01.004

Minaya, E., Shumsky, T., & Trentmann, N. (2017). Retrieved from https://www.wsj.com/articles/executives-fear-trade-conflicts-could-dent-economic-growth-1529227800?mod=djemlogistics_h

Min, H., & Galle, W. P. (2001). Green purchasing practices of US firms. *International Journal of Operations & Production Management*, *21*(9), 1222–1238.

Mishra, P., & Sharma, R. K. (2014). A hybrid framework based on SIPOC and Six Sigma DMAIC for improving process dimensions in supply chain network. *International Journal of Quality & Reliability Management*, *31*(5), 522–546. doi:10.1108/IJQRM-06-2012-0089

Mulcahy, R. (2010). Business Intelligence Definitions and Solutions. *CIO Magazine*. Retrieved from: http://goo.gl/VA8Wzx

Mykytka, E., & Ramberg, J. (1984). On the Sensitivity of the EOQ to Errors in the Forecast of Demand. *IIE Transactions*, *16*(2), 144–151. doi:10.1080/07408178408974679

Nadler, D. A., & Tushman, M. (1989). Organizational Frame Bending: Principles for Managing Reorientation. *The Academy of Management Executive*, *3*(3), 194–204.

Nahmias, S., & Cheng, Y. (2009). *Production and operations analysis* (Vol. 6). New York: McGraw-hill.

Najmi, A., Gholamian, M., & Makui, A. (2013). Supply chain performance models: A literature review on approaches, techniques, and criteria. *Journal of Operations and Supply Chain Management*, *6*(2), 94–113. doi:10.12660/joscmv6n2p94-113

Nath, A. K., Saha, P., & Salehi-Sangari, E. (2008). Transforming Supply Chains in Digital Content Delivery: A Case Study in Apple. In *Research and Practical Issues of Enterprise Information Systems II* (pp. 1079–1089). Boston, MA: Springer. doi:10.1007/978-0-387-76312-5_32

Naylor, J., Naim, M., & Berry, D. (1999). Leagility: Integrating the Lean and Agile Manufacturing Paradigms in the Total Supply Chain. *International Journal of Production Economics*, *62*(1–2), 107–118. doi:10.1016/S0925-5273(98)00223-0

Neef, D. (2001). *E-Procurement: From strategy to implementation.* FT Press.

Netland, T. H., Alfnes, E., & Fauske, H. (2007). How mature is your supply chain? A supply chain maturity assessment test. EurOMA Conference, Ankara, Turkey.

Netland, T., & Alfnes, E. (2008). *A practical tool for supply chain improvement – experiences with the supply chain maturity assessment test (SCMAT).* EurOMA/POMS/JOMSA Conference, Tokyo, Japan.

NextusC. G. (2016, April). Retrieved from https://www.supplychain247.com/article/the_state_of_digital_transformation_across_global_supply_chains

NexusC. G. (2017, July 12). Retrieved from https://www.supplychain247.com/paper/the_current_and_future_state_of_digital_supply_chain_transformation/gt_nexus

NGMN. (2018). *Next generation mobile network.* Retrieved from https://www.ngmn.org/about-us/vision-mission.html

Nicoletti, B. (2018). The Future: Procurement 4.0. In *Agile Procurement* (pp. 189–230). Cham: Palgrave Macmillan. doi:10.1007/978-3-319-61085-6_8

Nielsen Marketing Research. (1992). *Category Management: Positioning Your Organization to Win.* NTC Business Books.

Nielsen. (2014). *Category management – common language between retailers and manufacturers.* Nielsen.

Noreen, E., Smith, D., & Mackey, J. T. (1995). *Theory of Constraints and Its Implications for Management Accounting: A Report on the Actual Implementation of The Theory of Constraints.* North River Press, Incorporated.

O'Malley, J. (2018, June 27). *How 5G will improve augmented and virtual reality.* Retrieved from https://www.verizon.com/about/news/how-5g-will-improve-augmented-and-virtual-reality

O'Dwyer, J., & Renner, R. (2011). The promise of advanced supply chain analytics. *Supply Chain Management Review*, *15*(1).

Otto, A., & Kotzab, H. (2003). Does supply chain management really pay? Six perspectives to measure the performance of managing a supply chain. *European Journal of Operational Research*, *144*(2), 306–320. doi:10.1016/S0377-2217(02)00396-X

Page, S. (2016). *The Power of Business Process Improvement.* New York: AMACOM.

Papajorgji, P. (2013). *Enterprise Business Modeling, Optimization Techniques, and Flexible Information Systems.* Hershey, PA: IGI Global. doi:10.4018/978-1-4666-3946-1

Patig, S. (2011). *BPM Software and Process Modelling Languages in Practice: Results from an empirical investigation.* BoD, Norderstedt.

Patterson, K. A., Grimm, C. M., & Corsi, T. M. (2003). Adopting new technologies for supply chain management. *Transportation Research Part E. Logistics and Transportation Review, 39*(2), 95–121. doi:10.1016/S1366-5545(02)00041-8

Petruzzi, N. C., & Dada, M. (1999). Pricing and the newsvendor problem: A review with extensions. *Operations Research, 47*(2), 183–194. doi:10.1287/opre.47.2.183

Pietkiewicz, I., & Smith, J. A. (2014). A practical guide to using interpretative phenomenological analysis in qualitative research psychology. *Psychological Journal, 20*(1), 7–14.

Pittman, P., Blackstone, J. H., & Atwater, J. B. (2016). *APICS Dictionary* (15th ed.). APICS.

Porter, M. (1996). What is Strategy. *Harvard Business Review.* PMID:10158475

Porter, M. E. (1996, November). What Is Strategy? *Harvard Business Review*, 4. PMID:10158475

Porter, M. E., & Heppelmann, J. E. (2014). How smart, connected products are transforming competition. *Harvard Business Review, 92*(11), 64–88.

Porteus, E. L. (1990). Stochastic inventory theory. Handbooks in Operations Research and Management Science, 2, 605-652.

Presutti, W. D. Jr. (2003). Supply management and e-procurement: Creating value added in the supply chain. *Industrial Marketing Management, 32*(3), 219–226. doi:10.1016/S0019-8501(02)00265-1

Project Management Institute, Inc. (2008). *A Guide to the Project Management Body of Knowledge* (4th ed.). PMBOK Guide.

Project Management Institute, Inc. (2013). *Proctor & Gamble upgrades nearly 20-year-old software and work processes.* Author.

Project Management Institute, Inc. (2017). *Embracing Benefits Realization Management – An Essential Element in Achieving Project Management and Business Success.* Author.

Project Management Institute, Inc. (2018a). *PMI's Pulse of the Profession – 10th Global Project Management Survey 2018.* Author.

Project Management Institute, Inc. (2018b). *Establishing benefits ownership and accountability – Benefits Realization Management.* Author.

Pruyt, E. (2013). *Small System Dynamics Models for Big Issues: Triple Jump towards Real – World Complexity.* Delft: TU Delft Library. Retrieved from http://goo.gl/ge98Wt

PwC. (2016). *Industry 4.0: How digitization makes the supply chain more efficient, agile, and customer-focused.* Retrieved from https://www.strategyand.pwc.com/media/file/Industry4.0.pdf

Qualcomm. (2018, May). Retrieved from https://www.qualcomm.com/news/onq/2018/05/10/how-will-5g-unlock-potential-autonomous-driving

Ramanan & Anil. (2011). *The Top Three Reasons Supply Chain Transformations Fail.* Wipro Consulting Services.

Rao, P., & Holt, D. (2005). Do green supply chains lead to competitiveness and economic performance? *International Journal of Operations & Production Management, 25*(9), 898–916.

Rogers, D. L. (2016). *The digital transformation playbook: Rethink your business for the digital age*. Columbia University Press. doi:10.7312/roge17544

Röglinger, M., Pöppelbuß, J., & Becker, J. (2012). Maturity Models in Business Process Management. *Business Process Management Journal*, *18*(2), 328–346. doi:10.1108/14637151211225225

Romanow, K. (2014). *Custom Research Inventory Optimization*. Retrieved from: http://www.consumergoods.com

Roscoe, S., & Baker, P. (2013). Supply chain segmentation in the sporting goods industry. *International Journal of Logistics Research and Applications*, *17*(2), 136–155. doi:10.1080/13675567.2013.837869

RosenbergD. (2018, Jan 18). Retrieved from https://www.weforum.org/agenda/2018/01/the-world-is-about-to-become-even-more-interconnected-here-s-how/

RuttenbergR. (2018). Retrieved from https://www.dunnhumby.com/re-inventing-category-management

Sabri, E. (2012). *Enduring Transformation: Performance measurement and governance make the difference*. Retrieved from https://www.apics.org/apics-for-individuals/apics-magazine-home/magazine-detail-page/2012/10/04/enduring-transformation

Sabri, E. (2012, September). Enduring Transformation. *APICS Magazine*, 45 – 47.

Sabri, E. (2013). Strategies for Supply Chain Transformation. *Supply & Demand Chain Executive Magazine*. Retrieved from http://www.sdcexec.com/article/11122122/companies-struggle-to-decide-when-and-where-to-begin-and-how-to-translate-their-vision-into-goals-goals-into-strategies-and-strategies-into-process-changes-and-projects

Sabri, E. (2013). *Strategies for Supply Chain Transformation: Supply& Demand Chain Executive Magazine*. Retrieved from http://www.sdcexec.com/article/11122122/companies-struggle-to-decide-when-and-where-to-begin-and-how-to-translate-their-vision-into-goals-goals-into-strategies-and-strategies-into-process-changes-and-projects

Sabri, E. (2015). *Optimization of Supply Chain Management in Contemporary Organizations: Mastering Change Management for Successful Supply Chain Transformation*. IGI Global.

Sabri, E. (2015). Supply Chain Segmentation - Concept and Best Practice Transformation Framework. In A. DeMarco (Ed.), *Optimization of Supply Chain Management in Contemporary Organizations* (pp. 87–116). Hershey, PA: IGI Global. doi:10.4018/978-1-4666-8228-3.ch004

Sabri, E., Gupta, A., & Beitler, M. (2006). *Purchase Order Management in B2B Environment: Best Practice & Technologies. J.* Ross Publishing.

Sabri, E., & Shaikh, S. (2010). *Lean & Agile Value Chain Management (LAVCM): A Guide to the Next Level of Improvement. J.* Ross Publishing.

Sabri, E., & Shaikh, S. (2010). *Lean & Agile Value Chain Management: A Guide to the Next Level of Improvement*. J. Ross Publishing.

Sahay, B. S., & Ranjan, J. (2008). Real time business intelligence in supply chain analytics. *Information Management & Computer Security*, *16*(1), 28–48. doi:10.1108/09685220810862733

Sahin, F., & Robinson, E. P. (2002). Flow coordination and information sharing in supply chains: Review, implications, and directions for future research. *Decision Sciences*, *33*(4), 505–536.

SamitJ. (2018, March 1). Retrieved from http://fortune.com/2018/03/01/5-ways-augmented-reality-is-disrupting-the-supply-chain/

Sellers, P. (n.d.). *The "tipping point" in Ford's turnaround.* Retrieved from http://www.forbes.com

Sen, S. (2009). Linking Green Supply Chain Management and Shareholder Value Creation. *IUP Journal of Supply Chain Management*, 6.

Silver, E., Pyke, D., & Peterson, R. (1998). *Inventory management and production planning and scheduling*. New York: Wiley.

Simchi-Levi, D., Clayton, A., & Raven, B. (2012). *When One Size Does Not Fit All.* Retrieved from http://sloanreview.mit.edu/article/when-one-size-does-not-fit-all/

Simchi-Levi, D., Kaminsky, P., Simchi-Levi, E., & Shankar, R. (2008). *Designing and managing the supply chain: concepts, strategies and case studies*. Tata McGraw-Hill Education.

Singh, P. K. (2012). Management of Business Processes Can Help an Organization Achieve Competitive Advantage. *International Management Review*, *8*, 19–26.

SolventureS.Rough Cut Capacity PlanningO. P. (n.d.). Retrieved from https://www.solventuregroup.com/content/rough-cut-capacity-planning/

Sony, M., & Mekoth, N. (2014). The dimensions of frontline employee adaptability in power sector: A grounded theory approach. *International Journal of Energy Sector*. Available at: http://www.emeraldinsight.com/doi/abs/10.1108/IJESM-03-2013-0008

Sony, M., Mekoth, N., & Therisa, K. K. (2018). Understanding nature of empathy through the lens of service encounter: A phenomenological study on FLE's. *International Journal of Productivity and Quality Management*, *23*(1), 55–73.

Srivastava, S. K. (2007). Green supply-chain management: A state-of-the-art literature review. *International Journal of Management Reviews*, *9*(1), 53–80.

Stefan, A., & Paul, L. (2008). Does it pay to be green? A systematic overview. *Academy of Management Journal*, *22*(4), 45–62.

Sun, H., Ren, Y., & Yeo, K. (2005). *Capability Maturity Model for Supply Chain Management. International Conference on Management Science and Applications*, Chengdu, China.

Supply Chain Council (SCC). (2014). Retrieved from: https://supply-chain.org/

Talluri, R. (2017, Jan 18). *How will 5G impact the Internet of Things*. Retrieved from https://www.rcrwireless.com/wireless/how-will-5g-impact-the-internet-of-things

Tan, K. H., Zhan, Y., Ji, G., Ye, F., & Chang, C. (2015). Harvesting big data to enhance supply chain innovation capabilities: An analytic infrastructure based on deduction graph. *International Journal of Production Economics*, *165*, 223–233. doi:10.1016/j.ijpe.2014.12.034

Thakkar, J., Kanda, A., & Deshmukh, S. (2009). Supply chain performance measurement framework for small and medium scale enterprises. Benchmarking. *International Journal (Toronto, Ont.)*, *16*(5), 702–723.

Thomas, K. (2012). Supply chain segmentation: 10 steps to greater profits. *Supply Chain Quarterly*. Retrieved from http://www.supplychainquarterly.com/topics/Strategy/201201segmentation

Thompson, M., Jones, G., & Lawson, A. (2000). *E-procurement: Purchasing in the Internet based economy.* Butler Group Report.

Tjahjono, B., Esplugues, C., Ares, E., & Pelaez, G. (2017). What does industry 4.0 mean to supply chain? *Procedia Manufacturing, 13*, 1175–1182. doi:10.1016/j.promfg.2017.09.191

Trkman, P., McCormack, K., De Oliveira, M. P. V., & Ladeira, M. B. (2010). The impact of business analytics on supply chain performance. *Decision Support Systems, 49*(3), 318–327. doi:10.1016/j.dss.2010.03.007

Turban, E., Outland, J., King, D., Lee, J. K., Liang, T. P., & Turban, D. C. (2018). Order Fulfillment Along the Supply Chain in e-Commerce. In *Electronic Commerce 2018* (pp. 501–534). Cham: Springer. doi:10.1007/978-3-319-58715-8_13

van Looy, A. (2013a). *BPMM Sample (N=69)*. Retrieved from: http://goo.gl/dbiVkQ

van Looy, A. (2013b). Which Business Process Maturity Model Best Fits Your Organization? *BPTrends*. Retrieved from: http://goo.gl/1yCkEA

van Looy, A. (2014). *Business Process Maturity: A Comparative Study on a Sample of Business Process Maturity Models*. Springer. doi:10.1007/978-3-319-04202-2

Van Weele, A. J. (2010). *Purchasing & supply chain management: analysis, strategy, planning and practice*. Cengage Learning EMEA.

Vanathi, R., & Swamynathan, R. (2016). A Study on Influence of Supply Chain Strategies on Competitive Advantage of Textile Industry - An Integrated Model. *Journal Of Contemporary Research In Management, 11*, 41–55.

von Rosing, M., von Scheel, H., & Scheer, A. W. (2014). *The Complete Business Process Handbook: Body of Knowledge from Process Modeling to BPM*. Burlington: Morgan Kaufmann.

Vujošević, M., Petrović, D., & Petrović, R. (1996). EOQ formula when inventory cost is fuzzy. *International Journal of Production Economics, 45*(1-3), 499–504. doi:10.1016/0925-5273(95)00149-2

Wade, G. (2016, December). The More You Know. *Progressive Grocer*, pp. 6-8.

Walker, J. (2018, Feb). *TechEmergence*. Retrieved from Inventory Management with Machine Learning – 3 Use Cases in Industry: https://www.techemergence.com/inventory-management-with-machine-learning/

Walton, S. V., Handfield, R. B., & Melnyk, S. A. (1998). The green supply chain: Integrating suppliers into environmental management processes. *Journal of Supply Chain Management, 34*(1), 2–11.

Wienberger, D. (2010). The Problem with the Data–Information–Knowledge–Wisdom Hierarchy. *HBR Blog Network*. Retrieved from: http://goo.gl/tDtQQD

Wilson, G. (2012). Designing and Building Great Dashboards - 6 Golden Rules to Successful Dashboard Design. *Geckoboard Blog*. Retrieved from: http://goo.gl/cJLCLK

Wiseman, C. (2018). *Scorecards for supply chain transformations. Unpublished work. KPMG*, LLP.

Woerner, B., & Aziz, L. (2007). *PMO leadership—a catalyst for accelerating growth within the information technology project management office*. Paper presented at PMI® Global Congress 2007—North America, Atlanta, GA.

World, S. (2016). *Artificial Intelligence and Future Supply Chains*. Retrieved from http://www.scmworld.com/artificial-intelligence-future-supply-chains/

Yang, L. (2016, Nov). *AI vs. Machine Learning vs. Deep Learning*. Retrieved from http://deeplearning.lipingyang.org/2016/11/

ZDA. (2016, Jan). *What Are Virtual Reality Supply Chains?* Retrieved from https://www.zdaya.com/2016/01/06/virtual-reality-supply-chain-recruiters/

Zelbst, P. J. (2010). Relationships among market orientation, JIT, TQM, and agility. *Industrial Management & Data Systems*, *110*(5), 637–658.

Zhou, Z., & Chen, D. (2011). *Fundamentals of Digital Manufacturing Science*. Cham: Springer.

Zhu, Q., & Sarkis, J. (2004). Relationships between operational practices and performance among early adopters of green supply chain management practices in Chinese manufacturing enterprises. *Journal of Operations Management*, *22*(3), 265–289.

Zhu, Q., & Sarkis, J. (2006). An inter-sectoral comparison of green supply chain management in China: drivers and practices. *Journal of Cleaner Production*, *14*(5), 472–486.

Zhu, Q., Sarkis, J., & Lai, K. (2008). Green supply chain management implications for "closing the loop". *Transportation Research Part E. Logistics and Transportation Review*, *44*(1), 1–18. doi:10.1016/j.tre.2006.06.003

Zincir, O., Ünal, A., & Erdal, M. (2017). Lean and Digital: A Case Study on Procurement and Supply Chain Professionals' Online Social Network. In Key Challenges and Opportunities in Web Entrepreneurship (pp. 79-102). IGI Global.

Zipkin, P. (2000). *Foundations of inventory management*. Boston: McGraw-Hill.

Index

E

F

G

H

I

K

L

M

O

P

R

S

T

U

V

W

Purchase Print, E-Book, or Print + E-Book

IGI Global books are available in three unique pricing formats:
Print Only, E-Book Only, or Print + E-Book. Shipping fees apply.

www.igi-global.com

Recommended Reference Books

ISBN: 978-1-5225-2016-0
© 2017; 375 pp.
List Price: $200

ISBN: 978-1-5225-0886-1
© 2017; 251 pp.
List Price: $160

ISBN: 978-1-5225-2075-7
© 2017; 2,266 pp.
List Price: $185

ISBN: 978-1-5225-1865-5
© 2017; 443 pp.
List Price: $200

ISBN: 978-1-5225-19614-4
© 2017; 365 pp.
List Price: $210

ISBN: 978-1-5225-1005-5
© 2015; 370 pp.
List Price: $205

Do you want to stay current on the latest research trends, product announcements, news and special offers?
Join IGI Global's mailing list today and start enjoying exclusive perks sent only to IGI Global members.
Add your name to the list at **www.igi-global.com/newsletters.**

Publisher of Peer-Reviewed, Timely, and Innovative Academic Research

IGI Global DISSEMINATOR OF KNOWLEDGE

www.igi-global.com Sign up at www.igi-global.com/newsletters facebook.com/igiglobal twitter.com/igiglobal linkedin.com/igiglobal

Ensure Quality Research is Introduced to the Academic Community

Become an IGI Global Reviewer for Authored Book Projects

The overall success of an authored book project is dependent on quality and timely reviews.

In this competitive age of scholarly publishing, constructive and timely feedback significantly expedites the turnaround time of manuscripts from submission to acceptance, allowing the publication and discovery of forward-thinking research at a much more expeditious rate. Several IGI Global authored book projects are currently seeking highly qualified experts in the field to fill vacancies on their respective editorial review boards:

Applications may be sent to:
development@igi-global.com

Applicants must have a doctorate (or an equivalent degree) as well as publishing and reviewing experience. Reviewers are asked to write reviews in a timely, collegial, and constructive manner. All reviewers will begin their role on an ad-hoc basis for a period of one year, and upon successful completion of this term can be considered for full editorial review board status, with the potential for a subsequent promotion to Associate Editor.

If you have a colleague that may be interested in this opportunity, we encourage you to share this information with them.

IGI Global
DISSEMINATOR OF KNOWLEDGE

www.igi-global.com

Celebrating 30 Years of Scholarly Knowledge Creation & Dissemination

CELEBRATING 30 years EST. 1988 Academic Publishing Excellence

InfoSci®-Books

A Collection of 4,000+ Reference Books Containing Over 87,000 Full-Text Chapters Focusing on Emerging Research

This database is a collection of over 4,000+ IGI Global single and multi-volume reference books, handbooks of research, and encyclopedias, encompassing groundbreaking research from prominent experts worldwide. These books are highly cited and currently recognized in prestigious indices such as: Web of Science™ and Scopus®.

Librarian Features:

- No Set-Up or Maintenance Fees
- Guarantee of No More Than A 5% Annual Price Increase
- COUNTER 4 Usage Reports
- Complimentary Archival Access
- Free MARC Records

Researcher Features:

- Unlimited Simultaneous Users
- No Embargo of Content
- Full Book Download
- Full-Text Search Engine
- No DRM

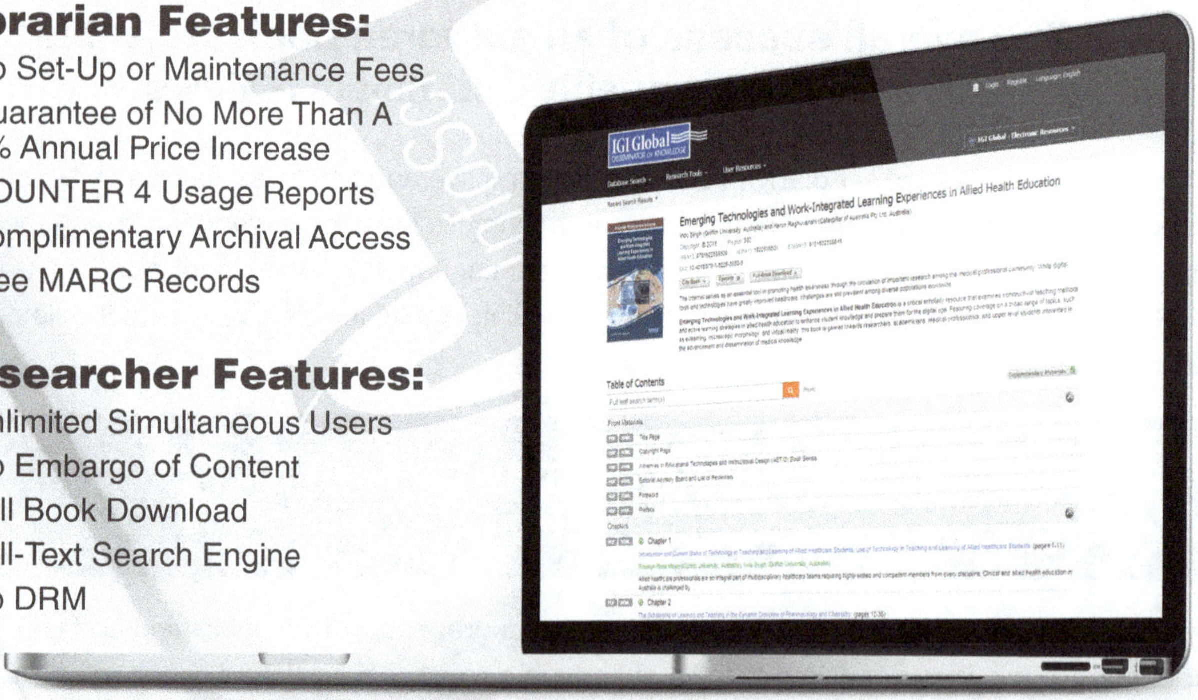

To Find Out More or To Purchase This Database:

www.igi-global.com/infosci-books

eresources@igi-global.com • Toll Free: 1-866-342-6657 ext. 100 • Phone: 717-533-8845 x100

IGI Global
DISSEMINATOR OF KNOWLEDGE
www.igi-global.com

IGI Global Proudly Partners with

eContent Pro International

Expert Copy Editing

eContent Pro International copy editors, with over 70 years of combined experience, will provide complete and comprehensive care for your document by resolving all issues with spelling, punctuation, grammar, terminology, jargon, semantics, syntax, consistency, flow, and more. In addition, they will format your document to the style you specify (APA, Chicago, etc.). All edits will be performed using Microsoft Word's Track Changes feature, which allows for fast and simple review and management of edits.

Additional Services

eContent Pro International also offers fast and affordable proofreading to enhance the readability of your document, professional translation in over 100 languages, and market localization services to help businesses and organizations localize their content and grow into new markets around the globe.

IGI Global Authors Save 25% on eContent Pro International's Services!

Scan the QR Code to Receive Your 25% Discount

The 25% discount is applied directly to your eContent Pro International shopping cart when placing an order through IGI Global's referral link. Use the QR code to access this referral link. eContent Pro International has the right to end or modify any promotion at any time.

Email: customerservice@econtentpro.com

econtentpro.com

Are You Ready to **Publish Your Research?**

IGI Global
DISSEMINATOR OF KNOWLEDGE

IGI Global offers book authorship and editorship opportunities across 11 subject areas, including business, healthcare, computer science, engineering, and more!

Benefits of Publishing with IGI Global:

- Free one-to-one editorial and promotional support.
- Expedited publishing timelines that can take your book from start to finish in less than one (1) year.
- Choose from a variety of formats including: Edited and Authored References, Handbooks of Research, Encyclopedias, and Research Insights.
- Utilize IGI Global's eEditorial Discovery® submission system in support of conducting the submission and blind-review process.
- IGI Global maintains a strict adherence to ethical practices due in part to our full membership to the Committee on Publication Ethics (COPE).
- Indexing potential in prestigious indices such as Scopus®, Web of Science™, PsycINFO®, and ERIC – Education Resources Information Center.
- Ability to connect your ORCID iD to your IGI Global publications.
- Earn royalties on your publication as well as receive complimentary copies and exclusive discounts.

Get Started Today by Contacting the Acquisitions Department at:

acquisition@igi-global.com

IGI Global
DISSEMINATOR OF KNOWLEDGE
www.igi-global.com

Available to Order Now

Order through www.igi-global.com with **Free Standard Shipping**.

The Premier Reference for Information Science & Information Technology

100% Original Content

Contains 705 new, peer-reviewed articles with color figures covering over 80 categories in 11 subject areas

Diverse Contributions

More than 1,100 experts from 74 unique countries contributed their specialized knowledge

Easy Navigation

Includes two tables of content and a comprehensive index in each volume for the user's convenience

Highly-Cited

Embraces a complete list of references and additional reading sections to allow for further research

Included in: InfoSci®-Books

Encyclopedia of Information Science and Technology Fourth Edition

A Comprehensive 10-Volume Set

Mehdi Khosrow-Pour, D.B.A. (Information Resources Management Association, USA)
ISBN: 978-1-5225-2255-3; © 2018; Pg: 8,104; Release Date: July 2017

For a limited time, receive the complimentary e-books for the First, Second, and Third editions with the purchase of the *Encyclopedia of Information Science and Technology, Fourth Edition* e-book.*

The **Encyclopedia of Information Science and Technology, Fourth Edition** is a 10-volume set which includes 705 original and previously unpublished research articles covering a full range of perspectives, applications, and techniques contributed by thousands of experts and researchers from around the globe. This authoritative encyclopedia is an all-encompassing, well-established reference source that is ideally designed to disseminate the most forward-thinking and diverse research findings. With critical perspectives on the impact of information science management and new technologies in modern settings, including but not limited to computer science, education, healthcare, government, engineering, business, and natural and physical sciences, it is a pivotal and relevant source of knowledge that will benefit every professional within the field of information science and technology and is an invaluable addition to every academic and corporate library.

Scan for Online Bookstore

Pricing Information

Hardcover: **$5,695** E-Book: **$5,695** Hardcover + E-Book: **$6,895**

Both E-Book Prices Include:

- *Encyclopedia of Information Science and Technology, First Edition E-Book*
- *Encyclopedia of Information Science and Technology, Second Edition E-Book*
- *Encyclopedia of Information Science and Technology, Third Edition E-Book*

*Purchase the Encyclopedia of Information Science and Technology, Fourth Edition e-book and receive the first, second, and third e-book editions for free. Offer is only valid with purchase of the fourth edition's e-book through the IGI Global Online Bookstore.

Recommend this Title to Your Institution's Library: www.igi-global.com/books

www.ingramcontent.com/pod-product-compliance
Lightning Source LLC
LaVergne TN
LVHW060304011026
849161LV00011B/2770